Mimic Fires

Mimic Fires

Accounts of Early Long Poems on Canada

D.M.R. BENTLEY

McGill-Queen's University Press
Kingston & Montreal • London • Buffalo

Legal deposit third quarter 1994
Bibliothèque nationale du Québec

Printed in Canada on acid-free paper

This book has been published with the help of a grant
from the Canadian Federation for the Humanities, using
funds provided by the Social Sciences and Humantiies
Research Council of Canada.

Canadian Cataloguing in Publication Data

Bentley, D.M.R.
    Mimic fires: accounts of early long poems on Canada
    Includes bibliographical references and index.
    ISBN 0–7735–1200–4
    1. Canadian poetry (English) – To 1867 – History and criticism.
    2. Canadian poetry (English) – 19th century – History and criticism. 3. Canada
    – In literature. I. Title.

PS8141.B46 1994   C811'.309'3271   C94 – 900224 – 0
PR9190.2.B46 1994

For Suzie

Contents

Preface

Early long poems on Canada have been a principal subject of my teaching and research for several years now. I first encountered them in the pages of the *Literary History of Canada,* which I read before starting an M.A. in Canadian Studies at Carleton University in 1974, and then in two anthologies that I used at Carleton and, later, at the University of Western Ontario: Michael Gnarowski's *Three Early Poems from Lower Canada* and David Sinclair's *Nineteenth-Century Narrative Poems.* My appreciation and understanding of the poems in and beyond these anthologies was deepened by the work of several other critics, scholars, and enthusiasts, not least Carl F. Klinck, Lawrence M. Lande, Desmond Pacey, R.E. Rashley, and Thomas B. Vincent. It was also sustained and encouraged by the writing and conversation of numerous colleagues and students at Western. What merit there is in this study thus devolves from a great many people, and I am profoundly grateful to all of them – as, of course, to the poets themselves – for the many pleasures and great satisfaction that I have derived from thinking, talking, and writing about early long poems on Canada.

Each of the chapters that make up this study contains an account of a single poem or, in the case of Thomas Moore, group of poems. Almost needless to say, there are many other poems that could have been included in the study if space and time had permitted. Several of these are already being researched and studied (some for the Canadian Poetry Press Series of Early Canadian Long Poems), and others will doubtless find their sympathetic proponents. By emphasizing the common concerns and sources of the poems, the accounts argue cumulatively for a continuity in writing about Canada in the eighteenth and nineteenth centuries – a continuity that could well be extended to the long poems of E.J. Pratt and other twentieth-century writers. Individually and in the aggregate, the accounts aim to inform and stimulate both specialized and general readers. To these ends they are preceded by a "General History" that seeks to place the poems in their geographical and social contexts and followed by a retrospective "Envoi" that offers some broad observations about the continuity of early long poems on Canada.

Work on the project from which this study developed began with a grant from the Academic Development Fund of the University of Western Ontario in 1986. A further grant from the Social Sciences and Humanities Research Council of Canada in 1990 made possible additional research, writing, and editing, as did assistance provided to students by the Ontario Work Study Bursary Program. This book has been published with the help of a grant from the Canadian Federation for Humanities, using funds provided by the Social Sciences and Humanities Research Council of Canada. I am deeply grateful to all these institutions for their support and encouragement.

To R.J. Shroyer, the Associate Editor of the Canadian Poetry Press Series and a continual source of the generous contention that stimulates and clarifies, I owe a special debt of gratitude. To Amanda St. Jean I owe special thanks for her careful work in entering, formatting, and proofreading the manuscript. I am also grateful to Gerard Stafleu and Eleanor Surridge for their computing expertise and assistance, and to Kerry Breeze and Harold Heft for their help in readying the manuscript for publication. In addition, I would like to thank the many talented people at McGill-Queen's University Press who contributed to the creation of this book, particularly Roger Martin, Joan McGilvray, and Karen E. Smythe.

As always, my greatest debt and warmest gratitude are to Susan Bentley, my dearest and most sensitive critic.

A NOTE ON CITATION, DATING, AND CHRONOLOGY

To reduce parenthetical clutter and to identify as precisely as possible the sources of quotations, page references have been given in roman type and line references in italics. Thus, "Anburey 1:90" refers to a volume and page in Thomas Anburey's *Travels* and *Malcolm's Katie 1: 35–47* refers to the given part and lines of Isabella Valancy Crawford's poem.

To assist the reader in establishing the temporal context of early long poems on Canada, the date(s) of publication of relevant works of non-fictional prose – most notably, the writings of explorers and travellers –

are supplied with initial citations. In the case of Jonathan Carver's *Travels through the Interior Parts of North America in the Years 1766, 1767, and 1768*, for example, "1778 f." indicates that it was first published in 1778 and thereafter reprinted.

In general, the poems selected for this study are examined in a chronological order based on the date of their first publication. The exceptions are Henry Kelsey's "Now Reader Read ..." which was not published until 1929; Joseph Howe's *Acadia*, which was not published until 1874; and John Strachan's "Verses ... 1802," which was not published until 1993. The first two of these are situated in the study by date of composition, and the third where Strachan's position in relation to surrounding and subsequent developments in Canadian culture seems to indicate.

Parts of this study have appeared in *Ariel* 21 (1990): 9–30, *Studies in Canadian Literature* 15.1 (1990): 21–61, and the Canadian Poetry Press Series of Editions of Early Canadian Long Poems.

I will send my fear before thee, and will destroy all the people to whom thou shalt come ... And I will send hornets before thee, which shall drive out the Hivite, the Canaanite, and the Hittite, from before thee ... By little and little I will drive them out from before thee, until thou be increased, and inherit the land. And I will set thy bounds from the Red Sea even unto the sea of the Philistines, and from the desert unto the desert unto the river ...

Exodus 23: 27–31

The wilderness and the solitary place shall be glad for them; and the desert shall rejoice, and blossom as the rose.

Isaiah 35:1

The honey-bee is not a native of our continent ... The Indians concur with us in the tradition that it was brought from Europe; but when, and by whom, we know not. The bees have generally extended themselves into the country, a little in advance of the white settlers. The Indians therefore call them the white man's fly, and consider their approach as indicating the approach of the settlements of the whites.

Thomas Jefferson, in *Notes on the State of Virginia* Query 6

It must be very gratifying to the Canadian born, or to him to whom Canada is Home, to know that the progress of literature has been co-equal with that of the settlement of the wilderness; and that if the latter has been made to bloom and blossom as the rose, the literature of Canada likewise blooms and blossoms beauteously ...

For ourselves, we have never doubted it. We were certain that the seed of Old England and of New England, which had been sown in Canada, could not be unproductive.

John Gibson, introduction to the New Series ... , *Literary Garland* 1.1 (1843)

It is a curious fact in natural history, that the wild bee has been in America the pioneer of the white man. Its first appearance on the Saskatchewan is within the memory of men still alive ...

The European flowers and weeds are usurping the place of the indigenous flora of North America.

Charles Mair, *Tecumseh*, Notes 10 and 11

A General History

Canadian poetry has a geographical basis because it is a record of life in Canada, and life in Canada has inevitably been shaped by the location and nature of the Canadian landscape. To the east of this water-enlaced land that stretches across the top of North America between the Atlantic, Pacific, and Arctic Oceans lie the sources of European civilization. To its west, in the Orient, lies one of the great mercantile and imperial goals of that civilization, and to its south, in the United States, one of western Europe's most powerful modern creations. By its position in space alone, Canada was destined to be a barrier between the West and the East, a place of contact between the "old" and the "new," an uneasy neighbour and partial alternative to the superpower to the south (Underhill 69). In Canada's northern and western hinterlands lie straits and bays and rivers named for the men who sought the northwest passage to the riches of the "far East." In the baselands of its east and south and west lie regions and cultures that have taken shape in the crucible of geography, and will continue to do so as long as people inhabit particular places and interact with different environments. "Exclusive of ... general characteristics" common to all parts of North America, wrote Crèvecoeur in 1782, "each province has its own [characteristics], founded on [its] government, climate, mode of husbandry, customs, and peculiarity of circumstances. Europeans submit insensibly to these great powers, and become, in the course of a few generations, not only [North] Americans in general, but ... provincials under some ... name ... The inhabitants of Canada, Massachuset, the middle provinces, the southern ones will be as different as their climates; their only points of unity will be those of religion and language" (61). Taking as its main points of unity the English language and the country now called Canada, this is a study of a selection of poems based on first-hand experience of Canada's physical and social landscapes. With two exceptions that mark the study's generic limits – Thomas Moore's lyrics and William Kirby's "Canadian Epic Poem" (*Annals* 85) – all the poems conform to W. MacNeile Dixon and H.J.C. Grierson's definition of the long poem as "neither epical in scope nor yet wholly lyrical in quality" (vii). All were written and most were published before the First World War.

On 2 May 1670, some twenty years before Henry Kelsey wrote the first poem in English about a part of Canada, the Hudson's Bay Company Charter was proclaimed by "CHARLES THE SECOND [b]y the grace of God King of England Scotland France and Ireland defender of the faith &c." (*Charters* 3). Legitimizing a scheme originating with two disaffected traders from New France, Radisson and Groseilliers, the Charter was designed to encourage the Hudson's Bay Company in its plans for "the discovery of a new Passage into the South Sea and for the finding some Trade for Furrs Mineralls and other considerable Commodityes"(3). As well as giving the Governor and "Company of Adventurers of England tradeing into Hudson's Bay" (4) exclusive commercial rights in the area that it christened "*Ruperts Land*," the Charter elevated "the said Governor and Company" to near baronial status as "the true and absolute Lordes and Proprietors of the same Territory" (11–12). In effect the creation of the HBC was the first outflanking of the French in Canada, and it brought from the north through Hudson Bay into the geographical core of the country as it now exists a small group of English speakers whose outlook was thoroughly mercantile and residually feudal. Kelsey's verse journal is the record of an attempt "through God's assistance to discover and bring to a Commerce" a part of the Canadian prairies, and it is signed "Sir your most obedient and faithfull Servant at Command" (5, 25; 2). Not until the end of the Georgian period (1714–1830) did mercantile and feudal assumptions cease to figure prominently in poetry written in and about Canada; much of Thomas Cary's *Abram's Plains* (1789) is given over to catalogues of extractable commodities (furs, trees, marine creatures) in Lower Canada, and the Colonel Thomas Talbot of Adam Hood Burwell's *Talbot Road* (1818) is nothing if not the neo-feudal lord of his settlement on the north shore of Lake Erie.

After the second and more successful outflanking of the French by the British on the Plains of Abraham in 1759, an increasing number of English speakers came to British North America. Some of these were simply on tours of duty with the armed forces or the civil service. Others merely wanted to make their fortune and then return home. But a few, like Cary (who arrived in ca. 1775 [Gauvin 123]), put down roots and took up permanent residence. As a result of the influx of Loyalists that followed the American War of Independence (1775–83) the number of English-speaking residents increased dramatically, both in Canada (which, after the Treaty of Paris in 1763, included the eastern valley of the Mississippi) and in Nova Scotia (which, by a 1749 Act of the British Parliament, comprised today's mainland Maritime provinces). By 1789 in Nova Scotia there was enough of a literate population to support a monthly magazine that expected to be graced increasingly with the "original productions" of "Native Genius" (John Howe in Daymond and Monkman 1:11–12), and in the same year in Lower Canada the Loyalist printer William Brown produced perhaps two hundred copies of Cary's *Abram's Plains* for sale by subscription and at outlets in both Quebec and Montreal (Bentley, intro. to *Abram's Plains* xxxix–xliii).

Although the term "Canadian Poetry" was not used with reference to a poem written in English in Canada until 1806 (Bentley, "An Early Specimen"), *Abram's Plains* contains all the ingredients of such a poem: descriptions of local scenery and people(s); a local pride grounded in an attachment to Lower Canada and an accreditation of its history; a communal consciousness founded on the sense of a common past and a shared future; and an educational component directed towards increasing local awareness, reinforcing communal values, and, hence, enhancing future prospects. (In *Poetry in Canada: the First Three Steps,* R.E. Rashley counts "pride and affection" for the local culture, a "consciousness of a past," and an "effort to reach back ... for what is worthy of preservation" among the enduring qualities of the "pioneer poets" [43]; and in "The Documentary Poem: a Canadian Genre" Dorothy Livesay offers "topical data ... held together by descriptive, lyrical, and didactic elements" as definitive of the "Canadian longer poem" [269; see also Kamboureli 3–46].) With *Abram's Plains* there begins for English writing in Canada a shift in perception that corresponds to the first of Clifford Geertz's "Four Phases of Nationalism": "the ... formative stage ... of confronting the dense assemblage of cultural, racial, local, and linguistic categories of self-definition and social loyalty ... with a simple, abstract, deliberately constructed, and almost painfully self-conscious concept of political ethnicity" (238–39). It is not fortuitous that in June 1790, a little over a year after the publication of *Abram's Plains,* the British Parliament enacted the Canadian Constitutional Act creating the Provinces Upper and Lower Canada, each with its own governor, council, and House of Representatives. Nova Scotia had boasted an elected assembly since 1758 and New Brunswick since 1785 (MacNutt 57–60, 101–02). Piece by piece the machinery that would eventually generate Canada's precarious nationhood – "one nation, eminently divisible" (Careless, "Limited Identities" 1) – was being put in place.

But even among colonials with a whiggish orientation towards natural rights, local representation, and social progress, a union on the scale of Canada was well-nigh unthinkable in the late Georgian and Regency periods (1760–1830; 1830–37). In *Canada* (1806) a young Tory, Cornwall Bayley, descries the extension of the British Empire westward from Quebec to Toronto (*452–53*) and envisages a glowing future for both the Canadas under British sovereignty. In *The Rising Village* (1825, 1834) another Tory, Oliver Goldsmith, envisages a common future for the mainland Maritime provinces but does so within strong statements of affection and admiration for Britain. Nevertheless the "imagined communities" (Anderson) of most colonial poets and politicians prior to the Victorian era were provincial or sub-provincial; Joseph Howe's *Acadia* (written 1830–34) focuses on Nova Scotia to the exclusion of New Brunswick, and the focus of Burwell's *Talbot Road* is on the pioneering past and prosperous future of only the southwestern corner of Upper Canada. Yet discernible in all of these poems – even (perhaps especially) in those whose concerns are narrowly local – are themes and patterns that, by the early nineteenth century, were radiating outwards to become the basis for transregional and transprovincial feelings of shared destiny. At the structural core of *Talbot Road* is the War of 1812, an event "of immense importance to the newly settled ... Upper Canada" (Careless, intro. to *The Defended Border* 1; and see John Webster Grant 68–69). "The effects of the war would stamp the Ontario community for generations to come," continues J.M.S. Careless; "the ... creation of heroes and legends out of the conflict reveals the impact that it made on the popular consciousness." And not just the "popular consciousness" of Ontario: Tecumseh is the hero of a poem by the Upper Canadian writer John Richardson (*Tecumseh* [1828]), but so, too, is he the hero of a poem by the Lower Canadian poet George Longmore (*Tecumthe* [1826]). Between its publication in London, England, in 1825 and Saint John, New Brunswick, in 1834, *The Rising Village* appeared in a Montreal periodical, a fact that attests to the pan-provincial appeal of its themes of pioneer heroism, agricultural improvement, and commercial success. In 1874 Howe's *Acadia*, which treats of similar themes, was published posthumously in Montreal by a printer – John Lovell – who also had offices in Toronto.

Tecumseh and *The Rising Village*: merely to juxtapose the two titles is to throw into relief one of the most constant themes and concerns in the long poems of the colonial period: Canada's Native peoples and their relations with the European settlers. In the War of 1812 (and earlier, in the War of Independence), several tribes had been Britain's invaluable allies against the Americans. Without Tecumseh and his Shawnee warriors, General Isaac Brock might not have been able to take Detroit in

1812, and there certainly would have been no British victory at Fort Meigs in 1813. At Moraviantown on the Thames River in October of the same year, "the British ... were ... quickly routed, [but] Tecumthe and his warriors continued" to fight "until their heroic chief fell ... and with him the spirit of his followers" (Longmore, *Tecumthe* 10). However with the cessation of hostilities in 1814 and the flood of British emigration that followed, the Native peoples became once again an inconvenience and an embarrassment. In Nova Scotia at the end of the eighteenth century the Micmacs and the Richibuctos had "defended with obstinacy a territory they held from nature" (T.C. Haliburton, *General Description* 47) and in the 1820s legal doubts surfaced about the Native peoples' rights in certain of the lands settled by Europeans (Bentley, "Concepts" 40–46). Were the Natives then friends or foes (Jaenan), noble or ignoble savages (Fairchild, Meek), independent children of Eden (Kidd), or ferocious animals from Hell (Goldsmith)? Was European civilization their curse or their saviour? Almost all the longer poems written in colonial Canada address and answer these and similar questions in one way or another, and few that treat directly of European emigration and settlement fail to deal at least obliquely with the issue of land ownership. As late as 1861 in *The Emigrant* and 1884 in *Malcolm's Katie,* Alexander McLachlan and Isabella Valancy Crawford send their pioneers into previously uninhabited areas to preclude anxieties and conflicts about matters of land "ownership and possession" (Monkman 133). Only the Archibald Lampman of *The Story of an Affinity* (written 1892–94) makes no mention whatever of Canada's Native peoples, and for an obvious reason: by the 1890s in central and eastern Canada, most Natives were out of sight and out of mind on such reserves as Caughnawaga (Kahnawake). Victorian paternalism had apparently triumphed.

If shared – or at least parallel – concerns were drawing the Canadas and the Maritimes together in the late eighteenth and early nineteenth centuries, regional and racial differences among their expanding European populations were at the same time pushing them apart. The period surrounding the War of 1812 was a time of Romantic nationalism in both the Old and the New Worlds. Between 1775 and 1825, dozens of new nations were born in Europe and the Americas. Byron's death in 1824 while serving the cause of Greek independence from the Ottoman Empire typifies the convergence of political and literary ideas of freedom and subjectivity in the years preceding and following the French Revolution. Facilitated, no doubt, by the medium of the French language, democratic and liberatory ideas found their way to a sympathetic audience of intellectuals in French Canada who did not hesitate to draw the obvious – and enduring – inference. In 1806 *Le Canadien* was founded in Montreal under the slogan "Nôtre langue, nos institutions et nos lois." In 1822 an attempt by British merchants and the colonial authorities to unify Upper and Lower Canada was defeated by Papineau's Canadien (or Patriote) Party and its supporters, including a number of anti-British MLAs of Irish origin (Monière 86–87). A prelude to the violence to come in the Rebellions of 1837–38 in both Upper and Lower Canada were the riotous charivaris in Montreal and elsewhere (Palmer 17–62) that Longmore addresses with nervous and reassuring good humour in *The Charivari* (1824). Before the "inner incompatibility of nation and empire" (Anderson 88–89) created Canada, the inner incompatibility of *nation* and empire threatened to preclude even the unification of the Canadas.

But if contraries are indeed the source of progress, as William Blake urges, then perhaps it was inevitable that the Rebellions of 1837–38 prompted the reconciliatory Durham Report of 1839 which, in turn, yielded the Act of Union between Lower and Upper Canada (henceforth Canada East and Canada West) in 1840. And inevitable also that the dialectical process did not end there, for as Careless in Blakean mood says of the united Canada in the 1850s: "its inhabitants could scarcely ignore the rise of conflict in this decade between English-speaking, Protestant Upper Canadian interests and French-speaking, Catholic Lower Canadians ... Still, the very sectional and sectarian problems of the union of the two Canadas led to proposals for altering it: for constitutional changes that might even bring in the other British Provinces as well. Hence the growing disunion between Canadas East and West itself fostered the trend to fresh ideas" ("The 1850s" 227). When Charles Sangster visited Quebec in 1853 during the excursion from Kingston that provided the basis for *The St. Lawrence and the Saguenay*, he saw the emblem of the urge to reconciliation and collectivity embodied in the Durham Report and the Act of Union: "the Monument to Wolfe and Montcalm" (in Bentley, appendix 123) that had been erected in 1828 at the suggestion of Lord Dalhousie. "WOLFE and MONTCALM! two nobler names ne'er graced / The page of history" (*604–05*), Sangster exclaims in his poem, but not before reminding his readers of Wolfe's defeat of the French and the "spoliation" by rebels and malcontents of the various monuments erected to his fame alone (*589–603*). Like the Irish poet Thomas Moore more than fifty years earlier and Susie Frances Harrison nearly forty years later, Sangster sees the French-Canadians primarily in stereotypical terms as adventurous voyageurs, contented habitants, and fetching damsels. Margaret Atwood has argued that "we are all emigrants to this place [Canada] even if we were born here ... and in the parts unknown to us we move in fear, exiles and invaders" (*Journals* 62). To judge by Sangster, Harrison, and many others, we are more obviously tourists whose vision – especially of the

French-Canadians and the Native peoples – can be clouded by stereotypes that conceal more than they reveal of the men and women behind
them.

Yet in many of the longer poems of nineteenth-century Canada the
central characters are in fact emigrants from the Old World or migrants
in the New. Indeed several works from the Victorian period (1837–
1901) – McLachlan's and Standish O'Grady's (1842) being the most
prominent examples – are entitled *The Emigrant,* and many others also
narrate a movement which is implicitly a "kind of satire" in its active
"rejection of an established order ... in favour of another to be established in a new land" (Scott and Smith xviii). McLachlan's socialistic
emigrants especially seek freedom from Britain's unjust social system
and the opportunity to create in Canada a more open and humane
community. Similarly the idealistic Max Gordon of *Malcolm's Katie*
leaves a settled society of which he at least partly disapproves to create
a better life for himself and his family in the open spaces of the West.
Yet the emigrants and migrants of McLachlan's and Crawford's poems,
like their real-life counterparts, also take with them both physically and
mentally much of the world that they have ostensibly left behind, and
they impose an order on their new environment that makes it resemble
as much as possible the lost homes of their hearts. In short they value
both their new, independent status and the old, established society,
making between the two a culture of compromise, a "middle ground"
(McInnis vii–viii), in which competing urges are barely reconciled and
always capable of creating conflict or threatening dissolution. This is
the "duality" in the "Canadian psyche" of which Atwood (*Journals* 62)
and W.L. Morton ("Relevance" 52–53) write, and it is imprinted, not
only on the Canadian landscape in the divisions of frontier and farm-
stead, wilderness and baseland, hinterland and metropolis, but also in
the geographies and politics of early Canadian poetry – in the baseland
orientation of J. Mackay's *Quebec Hill* (1797), for example, and in the
hinterland orientation of *The Huron Chief.*

Following the publication of his poem in 1830, Kidd was cudgelled
on the streets of Montreal for cheekily disagreeing with a scheme, proposed by the British consul in New York, that would have allowed American wheat being shipped down the St. Lawrence on its way to Britain
to be classified as Canadian and, hence, to take advantage of the preferential treatment extended to Canada under the Corn Laws (*The
Huron Chief 876 n.*). Sixteen years later the issue would not have arisen,
for "1846 saw the culmination of two long-maturing trends in British
imperial-economic thought. The ending of the Corn Laws [in that
year] spelled the doom of mercantilist control of imperial trade, and
the argument for refusing colonial self-government was fatally weak-

ened by removal of the principal reason for retaining colonial dependency" (McNaught 100). "Already the prospect [of a Canadian nation] is engaging the attention of thinking men," Alexander Morris told a Montreal audience in 1858, "and Canada and Acadia have begun to stretch out their hands to each other" (56). As well as thrusting Canada and the Maritimes towards independence and Confederation, the abolition of the Corn Laws in 1846 entailed closer economic ties with the United States (the Reciprocity Treaty of 1854–66) and provoked endless debates about Canada's destiny in a post-mercantile world. What Charles G.D. Roberts said in 1897 could have been said at any time during the previous half century or more: "the future presents to us three possible alternatives, – absorption by the United States, Independence, or a federal union with the rest of the British Empire" (*History* 439; and see Morris 47–48). This was the tense triangle in which discussions about Canada's future were conducted during the pre- and post-Confederation periods, and it cast its shadow on all aspects of the country's political, economic, and cultural life. In 1867 the British North America Act made Ontario, Quebec, New Brunswick, and Nova Scotia into a confederation capable of "daring and splendid expansion" to the north and west (Roberts, *History* 441), but drawn also by its needs and insecurities towards the south and east. During the same decades that Manitoba, Saskatchewan, Alberta, and British Columbia were added like gigantic dominoes to the Dominion, there were loud calls for a new Reciprocity Treaty with the United States and much flirting with the idea of an imperial federation with Great Britain. Eph Wheeler's pocket in Sara Jeanette Duncan's *The Imperialist* (1904) contains "twenty-five cents, an' a English sixpence, an a Yankee nickel" (11).

In 1883 Roberts, who two years earlier had described himself as a "Canadian Republican" (*Collected Letters* 29), moved from New Brunswick to Toronto to assume the editorship of the *Week*, the periodical that provided "the focus of the literary and cultural life of the young Dominion" (Pacey, *Creative Writing* 37). Three months later he resigned on account of the annexationist views of the *Week*'s British-born proprietor, Goldwin Smith, who would declare in 1891 "that the Americans may say with truth that if they do not annex Canada they are annexing Canadians ... They are annexing the very flower of the Canadian population ... since the men whom ... [Canada] has been at the expense of breeding leave it just as they arrive at manhood" (257–58). In 1897 Roberts followed his cousin Bliss Carman to New York, and thereafter divided his life among the United States, Britain, and Canada. In 1935 he was knighted for his contributions to Canadian and Commonwealth letters by King George V. Of the poets who elected to stay in Canada, few could ignore the lure of the literary markets to the south and east. With an eye on

American tourists escaping the pressures and complexities of the north-eastern cities to visit the picturesque and sublime scenery of Ontario and Quebec, Sangster had *The St. Lawrence and the Saguenay, and Other Poems* printed and registered for copyright purposes in New York State. By her own admission, Crawford "wrote largely for the American Press" (qtd. in Farmiloe v), but she published her one volume of poetry – *Old Spookses' Pass, Malcolm's Katie and Other Poems* – at her own expense in Toronto and sent the bulk of her review copies to England. Lampman's three volumes were printed in Ottawa, Boston, and Scotland, and, like *Malcolm's Katie*, his *The Story of an Affinity* is set in a landscape that could almost as easily be American as Canadian. Occupying the same psychic space as the spirit of Confederation (Heintzman) in late Victorian Canada were the wraith of imperialism and the incubus of continentalism (see Goldwin Smith 322 and 33). Waiting to be heard from again were other ghosts in the precarious homestead of the Canadian identity (Rotstein): French-Canadian nationality, Native (and Métis) rights, and regionalism. Thus Canadians entered the century that was supposed to belong to their country.

Until a few years ago the assertion was frequently heard that, after an awkward but promising infancy or adolescence in the post-Confederation period, Canadian poetry came of age in the late 1920s and 1930s with the arrival in Canada of high modernism. More recently the maturation of Canadian poetry has been linked to the arrival of low modernism in the sixties and, more recently still, to the arrival of postmodernism in the seventies and eighties. Perhaps such acts of historical revision and amnesia are inevitable in a country trying desperately to deny its colonial past, and present. Eighteenth, nineteenth, and early twentieth-century Canadian poetry, the arguments have run, does not sustain interest or reward study because it is colonial and derivative. Of course it is both of these things (as is later twentieth-century Canadian poetry), but does this make it unworthy of sympathetic attention and close analysis? In Canadian poetry, as in British architecture, "styles are ... *adopted* instead of *generated* ... *adapted* ... instead of *originated*" (Pugin 2). This is part of the character, if not the appeal, of Canadian poetry that should be taken into account, not used as grounds for derisive dismissal. Treated with "charity" (Davidson 137, 153) and "courtesy" (Steiner 147–78) rather than "condescension" (Thompson 12), early Canadian poetry has much to tell us, not merely about the past, but also about the present and the future – about where we came from, how we got here, and where we might be going. So I have found, at any rate, and I trust that my affection and respect for the poets who wrote early in this place will be evident in the pages to come. If I were to be allowed an overriding hope, it would be that this book, imperfect and limited as it is, will give readers an enlarged appreciation of Canadian poetry and the broader culture of which it is a part.

1 Henry Kelsey, "Now Reader Read ... "

The verse journal of Henry Kelsey (ca. 1667–1774) is the earliest first-hand account in English poetry of a part of what has become Canada. In the spring of 1691, probably on "a bend in the Saskatchewan River about twelve miles below [today's] The Pas, Manitoba" (Davies 309), Kelsey, then a young servant of the Hudson's Bay Company, planted a "Cross" at a place that he had earlier christened "deerings point" after Sir Edward Dering, the deputy governor of the HBC. Kelsey later used this event to conclude his brief verse journal about his "Journey" in 1690–91 from York Factory (now Churchill) on Hudson Bay to the Canadian plains:

> At deerings point after the frost
> I set up there a Certain Cross
> In token of my being there
> Cut out on it the date of year
> And Likewise for to veryfie the same
> added to it my master sir Edward deerings name
> So having not more to trouble you with all I am
> Sir your most obedient & faithfull Servant at Command
> HENRY KELSEY (*83–90*)

In these lines, and in the verse journal or epistle that they conclude, can be discerned the beginning of the complex relations among things, words, landscapes, writers, and audiences whose permutations and combinations constitute poetry on Canada.

In a critical climate freshened by deconstruction, feminism, post-structuralism, the new historicism, and post-colonial theory, Kelsey's "Certain Cross" at "deerings point" can hardly be seen other than as a monumental condenser of significances, determined and otherwise. A material and blatantly patriarchal emblem of Christianity inscribed with a date and a name that speak of the Eurocentric and residually feudal commercial enterprise in which he was engaged, Kelsey's "Cross" is freighted with sociological and textual implications. At once in and above the soil of Canada, it was not quite part of (yet not completely apart from) the terrain that it was intended, like the renaming of "deerings point," to claim for the HBC and Great Britain. An imperious palimpsest of indigenous materials and imported words – a Christian and commercial marker constructed of local wood and overwritten with information that would have been intelligible only to other Europeans – it was nevertheless a great deal closer spatially, temporally, and ontologically to the Canadian terrain than Kelsey's verse journal or, indeed, than Kelsey himself when he composed his retrospective poem either at York Factory in 1691, or, more likely, in 1693–94 when he was on leave in England (Davies 310). To the very extent that Kelsey's "Cross" and its inscriptions come close to being on and of Canada, they emphasize the huge gaps between the explorer, his verse journal, and the people, places, and things that they attempt to describe.

Nor apparently was Kelsey unaware of the gaps that yawned around him when he wrote his verse journal – the gap, on the one hand, between "*those* Indians & *their* Country (*23*; emphasis added) that he had scouted in 1690–91 and now wished to represent, and, on the other, between his own experiences in Canada and those of his armchair audience, whether narrowly construed as his HBC superiors or more broadly conceived as a tribunal of these and other contemporary and later readers. As the journal gets underway, Kelsey conveys his awareness, first of his audience's ignorance and likely incredulity, and then of his own inability – the inability of the written word – to convey his experiences in an entirety that would be convincing:

Now Reader Read for I am well assur'd
Thou dost not know the hardships I endur'd
In this same desert where Ever that I have been
Nor wilt thou me believe without that thou had seen
The Emynent Dangers that did often me attend
But still I lived in hopes that once it would amend
And makes me free from hunger & from Cold
Likewise many other things which I cannot here unfold ...

(*1–8*)

Unable either to achieve complete inclusiveness (which would be nothing less, of course, than the real presence of his experiences in the
poem) or to count on the next best thing, a "Reader" with shared or
similar experiences, Kelsey has no choice but to deal with absences and
unknowns. He must write in a commonplace "Book" (1) about what he
knows will be for his immediate audience the extraordinary and closed
book of the Canadian plains.

Seemingly sensing that the greatest danger he faced in transcribing
his Canadian experiences lay in the disbelief of his "Reader," Kelsey
attempts in the ensuing lines of his verse journal to generate a sympathy
for himself that might just forestall incredulity and, indeed, create an
imaginative empathy akin to shared experience:

> For many times I have often been oppresst
> With fears & Cares that I could not take my rest
> Because I was alone & no friend could find
> And once that in my travels I was left behind
> Which struck fear & terror into me
> But still I was resolved the same Country for to see
> Although through many dangers I did pass
> Hoped still to undergo them at the Last ...
>
> (9–16)

In the last lines of this passage especially, a literate reader will hear echoes of one of the most moving and memorable speeches in Shakespeare's *Othello*: the Moor's account in the first act of the play of how
Desdemona came to love him "for the dangers [he] had passed" and he
her "that she did pity them" (*1.3.167–68*). Among the similar places
and events mentioned by Othello and Kelsey are "desert[s]" and "hair-
breadth 'scapes"(*1.3.140, 136*). Such resemblances may be merely coincidental, and, of course, Othello's speech derives in part from an
explorer account that may also have been known to Kelsey, Sir Walter
Raleigh's *Discovery of the Large, Rich, and Beautiful Empyre of Guiana ...*
(1596). As the well-known examples of *The Strange and Dangerous Voyage
of Captain Thomas James* (1633) and "The Rime of the Ancient Mariner"
(Christy 1:clxxxix–cxciii) indicate, descriptions of hardships in remote
regions are commonplace both in travel writings and in the literature
that they inspired (Adams, especially 148–60). When Kelsey versified
his account of the "dangers" he endured in Canada in 1690–91, perhaps he had in mind the "ragged and tearing Rhymes" in which James
recounted the "dangers" that he had passed sixty years earlier in the
extension to Hudson Bay that bears his name (55–56). Yet the possibility should not be discounted that Kelsey partly modelled the opening

portion of his verse journal on Othello's speech to his Venetian "masters" (*19*) in the hope of appropriating something of its quality as an affective narrative, a "travels' history" from "boyish days" (*1.3.139, 132*) that succeeds so eminently well in eliciting feelings of empathy, belief, and trust from its audience.

Just why Kelsey needed to generate such feelings in his HBC superiors is unclear, but it is evident that, without them, he regarded his occupation as gone:

> Now Considering that it was my dismal fate
> for to repent I thought it now to late
> Trusting still unto my masters Consideration
> Hoping they will Except of this my small Relation
> Which here I have pend & still will Justifie
> Concerning of those Indians & their Country
> If this wont do farewell to all as I may say
> And for my living i'll seek some other way ...
>   (*17–24*)

Apprehending exclusion from probably the only community that mattered to him, and unable to corroborate his evidence through "those Indians" whose "Country" he was, in 1690, the first Englishman to see, Kelsey is almost as alone in his poetic attempt to make credible his effectively unique experiences in Canada as he was when he had "no friend" and was "left behind" on his travels. As much as the obvious tendency of any writer or speaker to describe personal experiences in the first person, Kelsey's consciousness of the singularity and aloneness of his own experience and resulting situation may account for the insistent, almost obsessive repetition of "I," "me," and "my" in the opening section of his verse journal. (Only two lines in the first twenty-four are without at least one of these words and three lines have two of them, making twenty-five uses of "I," "me," and "my" in all.) But a much more important point to be made about Kelsey's emphasis on his own trials and tribulations in the initial lines of his verse journal is that this emphasis is, in a classical sense, ethical or moral. It is an appeal on the basis of personal character that seems entirely appropriate, if not inevitable, in the circumstances. After all, and as Aristotle intimates in his discussions of ethical proof in the *Rhetoric*, "moral character ... constitutes the most effective" means of proof, particularly "if we have no evidence as to the fact itself" (17, 159). Not without reason did Kelsey characterize himself as a long-suffering, plain-speaking, modest, pious, and obedient "servant" of the HBC: he knew that his "Relation" was only as reliable as the relater. If his "masters" were to trust his tale they would first have to trust its teller.

It is to his "Journey" with "those Indians" from Hudson Bay to the Canadian plains in 1690 that Kelsey turns in the body of his verse journal:

> In sixteen hundred & ninety'th year
> I set forth as plainly may appear
> Through Gods assistance for to understand
> The natives language & to see their land
> And for my masters interest I did soon
> Sett from the house the twealth of June ...
>
> *(25–30)*

"As plainly may appear": the correspondence between this stylistic statement and the "plains ... of the Country" (79) traversed by Kelsey on his journey from "the house" (York Factory) to the western plains is probably fortuitous, but it nevertheless echoes forward to numerous attempts by later Canadian poets to find suitable forms for their hinterland journeys and terrains (Bentley, *Gay] Grey Moose* 43–75). But surely not fortuitous is the fact that Kelsey chose to write frankly, referentially, economically, and without ostentation – "plainly" – about an "individual experience" and "new things" (Trimpi 41) that, to be at all credible and creditable, had to be rendered with evident truthfulness and sincerity. As Wesley Trimpi has observed, the plain style, the classical *genus humile*, was "developed in the interest of the most efficient presentation of content as opposed to the cultivation of expression for its own sake" (42); its primary purpose, whether in the hands of Demetrius or Kelsey, is "to tell the truth" (107). James M. Whillans could almost be testifying to the ethical force of the plain style when he writes of Kelsey's verse journal: "outstanding in the human story is the stark courage with which Kelsey faced the ever-present dangers and difficulties on the long prairie trail in his search for peace among the tribes. The story is all the more effective because it is unadorned and modestly told" (18).

Trimpi's remark in *Ben Jonson's Poems: A Study in the Plain Style* that the "epistolary ... is the plainest of the plain styles" (60) helps to explain Kelsey's decision to cast his verse journal in the form of a letter ("Now Reader Read ... I am / Sir your most obedient & faithfull Servant at Command / HENRY KELSEY"). It also points towards Kelsey's possible model: the verse epistles of Jonson in *The Forest* and *Under-wood* (both of which were included in the *Works* of 1640–41), specifically the "Epistle to Master John Selden." Of almost exactly the same length as Kelsey's verse journal (eighty-six versus the explorer's ninety lines), Jonson's

"Epistle to ... Selden" is also written in relatively loose and unadorned decasyllabic couplets, and it foregoes the muse machinery that is foreign to the plain style. It thus begins abruptly, idiomatically, and, as it happens, with a description of its own stylistic premises that may have been all that Kelsey required to establish the tone and procedure of his own verse epistle:

> I know to whom I write: Here, I am sure,
> Though I am short, I cannot be obscure
> Lesse shall I for the art of dressing care,
> Truth, and the Graces best, when naked are.
>
> (*Complete Poetry* 144)

The resemblance between Kelsey's initial "Now Reader Read for I am well assur'd" and Jonson's later "So that my Reader is assur'd, I now / Meane what I speake" is perhaps too strong to be coincidental. And could there also be an echo of Jonson's closing "Farewell" to Selden in Kelsey's contemplated "farewell" to his "living" at the end of the opening section of his verse epistle? The evidence of indebtedness may not be conclusive, but it gains circumstantially with the recognition that the Selden of Jonson's "Epistle" is a character who might well have been appealing to Kelsey: a sedentary and humanistic scholar who is nevertheless an explorer, a man who has "all Countries seene ... Times, manners, customes! Innovations spide! / Sought out the Fountaines, Sources, Creekes, paths, wayes."

No doubt Jonson, the plain style, and other possible literary models (Warkentin 110–13) were almost as remote from Kelsey's mind as the Canadian plains themselves when he left York Factory on 12 June 1690. If he took any book with him at that time, it would have been the Bible, a text which, as Whillans observes, finds "more than an echo" (35) in Kelsey's verse journal (see especially 2 Cor. 11: 26–27). But on "the twealth of June" in "sixteen hundred & ninety'th year" when Kelsey set off "up the [Hayes] River ... with heavy heart" leaving behind him "all English part / To live amongst the Natives of this place / ... for one two years space" (*31–34*), he did take with him – as these very quotations indicate – another European and transportable means of ordering personal and communal life: the Gregorian calendar. As well as providing the framework for his measurements of linear time (*40, 52, 84, 86*), the calendar furnished Kelsey with a crude, chronological structure for the central and concluding sections of his narrative – a temporal container, as it were, that measures, shapes, and encapsulates the contents of these portions of his verse journal. Nor does the calendar constitute the only quantifying and delimiting element in Kelsey's work. Factually, the content of the later sections of the epistle is largely restricted by and to the commercial interests of the HBC – hence their emphasis, for example, on distances, portages, and tradeables ("six hundred miles southwest ... thirty three Carriages five lakes in all ... beavour in abundance but no Otter" [*44, 46, 78*], and so on). And formalistically, the content of the epistle is restricted by factors which, when expressed in the literary terminology of Kelsey's own day, do not seem very remote from these other quantifying and delimiting elements: the "measure" and "numbers" of the decasyllabic couplet. "Through its very appearance of artificiality," I.A. Richards remarks, "metre produces ... a 'frame' effect" (145), an effect that, in Kelsey's case, isolates and excludes, shapes and surrounds the contents of his verse journal just as certainly as do his chronological structure and commercial emphasis.

What this amounts to is that, however "plainly" displayed Kelsey may have wanted them to be, the "Indians & the ... Country" that he saw in 1690–91 are far from "naked" in his verse journal. On the contrary, they are dressed in the assumptions that Kelsey brought to his seeing and writing as a European, as a "Servant" of the HBC, and as a man with an urge to "Justifie" himself in verse. In Clifford Geertz's terms, Kelsey's various temporal-spatial, commercial-imperialist, and formal-rhetorical assumptions constitute a "thick description" (7–10), a series of interrelated frames or containers, schemes or grids that impose themselves in "layers" on both the "Indians" and the "Country" in his verse journal and, in doing so, draw them into the net of European culture. A striking instance of this layered assimilation and appropriation of the "Indians & their Country" occurs when Kelsey describes taking possession of the "natives ... land" for commercial and imperialistic purposes, and does so in a rhetoric of magnification that violates the tenets of the plain style in order to confer significance on the event and kudos on its perpetrator:

> The Inland Country of Good report hath been
> By Indians but by English yet not seen
> Therefore I on my Journey did not stay
> But making all the hast I could upon our way
> Gott on the borders of the stone Indian Country
> I took possession on the tenth Instant July
> And for my masters I speaking for them all
> This neck of land I deerings point did call ...
> (*35–42*)

Here as throughout Kelsey's verse journal (though not in his prose account of 1691–92), the "natives language" that he has set out to learn is silenced, and both the "Indians" themselves (the "'Assinae poets' [Assinipwatug] of the Hudson's Bay Company officers ... [of the] time" [Kenney 47 n.]) and "their Country" are commercially and poetically 'Englished,' the latter as the resonantly memorable "Inland Country of Good report," as the "stone Indian Country," and as "deerings point." It might be an exaggeration to say that only after "Wa-pas-kwa-yaw" (Whillans 55–56) has become known and iambically scannable as "deerings point" can it enter a regular decasyllabic couplet. Nevertheless, "This neck of land I deerings point did call" is notable, not only for the poeticizing flourish of its delayed verb (a device also evident earlier in the passage) but also for its unusual regularity and smoothness, qualities that set it off from its surroundings as a point of special importance both commercially and personally.

Although Kelsey carried with him on his inland "Journey" the means of judging his position in time, he did not, since he was on a business trip rather than an exploration as such, have in hand the technology for ascertaining his position in space. With no sextant or compass, he was thrown back on his own "Judgement" (*43*) for estimations of the distances that he travelled and the locations of significant points in the terrain. In effect instead of calculating his position as if in a Ptolemaic universe from "fixed" points in the heavens, he did so in a more typically post-Renaissance (Copernican) and imperialistic manner that is at once self- and other-centred. That Kelsey thus had two centres, one "there" and "English" (York Factory) and the other moving in and through the here and now, helps to explain his somewhat confusing use of locative adverbs and pronouns ("hence," "From," "that place," "this place") in his placement of "deerings point":

> Distance from hence by Judgement at the lest
> From the house six hundred miles southwest
> Through Rivers which run strong with falls
> thirty three Carriages five lakes in all
> The ground begins for to be dry with wood
> Poplo & birch with ash thats very good
> For the Natives of that place which knows
> No use of Better than their wooden Bows
> According to the use & custom of this place
> In September I brought those Natives to a peace ...
>
> (*61–72*)

Whatever spatial uncertainty and confusion there is here does not extend to Kelsey's consistent emphasis on the commercially important aspects of his southwesterly journey and the "deerings point" area. To judge what he is by what he sees – the length and difficulty of the trade route, the availability of various and useful woods, the presence of potential trading partners – Kelsey is *homo mercantile*: a man whose vision cannot but relate the periphery to the "centre" (Ray and Freeman 248–49), the here to the there and – at the scene of the poem's likely composition – the hinterland there to the metropolitan here. Yet this is also the beginning of first-hand knowledge of the local and indigenous in English poetry about Canada and, if it be granted that the relationships between centres and peripheries are still vexed in this country and its literature, a beginning with a certain, enduring cultural significance.

The "peace" to which Kelsey brought the Assiniboines in September 1690 turned out to be short-lived. "I had no sooner from those Natives turnd my back," he writes, than

> Some of the home Indians came upon their track
> And for old grudges & their minds to fill
> Came up with them Six tents of which they kill'd
> This ill news kept secrett was from me
> Nor none of those home Indians did I see
> Untill that they their murder all had done
> And the Chief acter was he thats called the Sun ...
>   (52–60)

Mercantile as Kelsey's interest in the "use and custom" of the "Natives" unquestionably was, and despite the opprobrium to which he here subjects "the Sun," there is nevertheless in this passage an urge to treat at least "the home Indians" – the Cree from the area of York Factory – as complex rather than simple characters, as people who are motivated by revenge ("old grudges") *and* boredom ("their minds to fill"), who have a social hierarchy and, in one instance, a name that Kelsey must have learned in order to translate. Kelsey's "home Indians" are not the admirable individuals with "narratable life histories" (Said 229) that are found, for example, in *The Huron Chief*, but neither are they the brutal and anonymous "savages" of such poems as *Quebec Hill* and *The Rising Village*. Violent, deceitful, and secretive they may be, but as actual and potential trading partners they are important enough to be a major presence in Kelsey's verse journal and, moreover, the subject of a lengthy "Account of ... [their] beliefs and Superstitions" at the conclusion of his prose journal of 1691–92 (19–24).

A hint of Kelsey's interest in the "beliefs and Superstitions" of the plains peoples appears at the end of the next portion of his verse journal, an account of the flora and fauna of the "deerings point" area and the region to the west:

> So far I have spoken concerning of the spoil
> And now will give account of that same Country soile
> Which hither part is very thick of wood
> Affords small nutts with little cherryes very good
> Thus it continues till you leave the woods behind
> And then you have beast of severall kind
> The one is a black a Buffillo great
> Another is an outgrown Bear which is good meat
> His skin to gett I have used all the ways I can
> He is mans food & he makes food of man
> His hide they would not me it preserve
> But said it was a god & they should Starve ...
>
> *(61–72)*

Once again the issue of naming becomes important as Kelsey struggles to convey what he has seen using a language in which there are either no nouns to describe a particular thing (trees that "Afford ... small nutts with little cherryes very good": perhaps chokeberries [Whillans 36]) or merely general nouns that require adjectival modification if the "beast[s]" of this "Country" are to be differentiated from similar creatures in other places. Thus the North American bison is described – for the first time in written English (Roe 315–16) – as a "Buffillo" (a word used previously by Kelsey with reference to the musk-ox [*28–29*]) that is "black" and "great," and the grizzly bear is "outgrown" to differentiate it from the smaller brown bears with which Kelsey himself and perhaps some of his readers would have been familiar. Of course, the very fact that the plants and animals of the Canadian plains can be represented in English indicates that the items in Kelsey's inventory of resources are not beyond control and assimilation.

A comparison between Kelsey's verse and prose journals indicates that the conventions and the restrictions of the decasyllabic couplet compounded his descriptive difficulties. In form and style the prose journals are relatively loose and, thus, a more accommodating vehicle for Kelsey's assimilative comparisons and differentiations: "this plain affords Nothing but short Round sticky grass and Buffillo and a great sort of Bear which is Bigger than any white Bear and is Neither White nor Black But silver hair'd like our English Rabbit the Buffillo Likewise is not like those to the Northward their Horns growing like an English Ox but Black and Short" (12–13). What once might have been called the transparency of these prose descriptions – that is, their success in generating mental images of the things to which they refer – contrasts strongly with the textuality of their verse counterparts. Particularly striking is the contrast between the prose just quoted and such rhetorically polished, even witty, lines like "The one is a black a Buffillo great" and "He is mans food & makes food of man," the former an example of adjectives straddling a noun for poetic effect (Pound 49) and the latter the most striking instance in the poem of chiasmus. Another notable textual effect is the poeticizing epithet and grammatical inversion of the fifth line: "Emynent Dangers that did often me attend." These and other violations of the plain style in the verse journal are probably inevitable given Kelsey's apparent urge, not merely to give a factual account of the resources of "The Inland Country" for the benefit of his HBC "masters," but also to write eloquently and memorably about a pathfinding expedition that he well knew to be his major claim to enduring fame. Surely it was for this second purpose that Kelsey placed his verse journal at the beginning of the commonplace "Book" that was given to him by "James Hubbud in the year of our Lord 1693" (1). Or, as James F. Kenney speculates: "perhaps [Kelsey's Book] was begun, when he was a young man, as a historical record of his achievements, with a preface in what he conceived to be the heroic manner" (39 n.).

Before returning his narrative to "deerings point" and marking the completion of his mercantile pilgrimage by setting up his "Certain Cross," Kelsey describes what may be the "Great Salt Plain" (C.N. Bell, qtd. in Davies 310) of Saskatchewan in a way that typifies most of the major concerns of his verse journal:

> This plain affords nothing but Beast & grass
> And over it in three days time we past
> getting unto the woods on the other side
> It being about forty sixe miles wide
> This wood is poplo ridges with small ponds of water
> there is beavour in abundance but no Otter
> with plains & ridges in the Country throughout ...
> (73–79)

It is tempting to see here what can frequently be found in much more recent poetry and painting from the prairie provinces: a minimalist and, in spots ("Beast ... grass"), nearly abstract style that is well suited to the great distances and perceived absences of the western plains. One line in particular – "And over it in three days time we past" – shows Kelsey at or near his modest best in the plain style, using a hint of trochaic lilt ("óver") and a rush of monosyllables to convey something of the feel of a long journey quickly and happily concluded. As prelusively and stylistically interesting as it may be, however, the sparseness of Kelsey's verse is in this instance primarily commercial in origin. Although in his prose journal of 1691 he describes a "grass [that] hath an Ear like our English Oats" (5) – and, hence, might be cultivatable (MacLaren, "Influence" 379–82) – in 1690 he apparently saw nothing of equivalent commercial potential until he reached the "Touchwood Hills country" (Bell, qtd. in Davies 310), where he found useful poplar trees and valuable beaver, but "no Otter." This economic emphasis is carried through to the conclusion of the verse journal in two passages that are closely linked and thickly layered by Kelsey's mercantile orientation and rhetoric. The first is a description of a band of "Natives" transformed into powerful trading partners by means of European weapons: "Their Enemies many whom they cannot rout / But now of late they hunt their enemies / And with our English guns do make them flie" (*80–83*). The second is Kelsey's resonant description of the erection of his "Certain Cross" at "deerings point" to assert the commercial and Christian presence of the HBC in the area. That Kelsey uses a loose form of chiasmus (*chiasma*: cross-shaped) to describe the "Natives" is rhetorical evidence that they, no less than "their Country," have come under the shadow of Britain's mercantile empire.

"Through God's assistance to discover and bring to a Commerce" (*Kelsey Papers* 5, 25): this was the impulse behind Kelsey's "Journey" to the "Inland Country" in 1690–91, and it brought with it and into his verse journal both an economic epistemology (the only things really *worth* seeing and recording were those connected with trade) and a mercantilist morality ("English guns" in exchange for local manpower and extractable goods). Kelsey was a peace-maker because peace was good for business. He was a "discover[er]," a marker, and a namer because in the pursuit of the Golden Fleece (Kenyon), be it "Bear," "beavour," or "Otter," raw materials had to be identified, market places established, and potential competition – in this case the Compagnie de Nouvelle France – discouraged. The very existence of his verse journal suggests that Kelsey conceived of himself as a minor hero of the commercial world in which he operated – a humble Argonaut whose dangerous exploits and archetypically circular journey on the peripheries of European civilization deserved to be chronicled and celebrated in an appropriately modest yet "signalizing" poetic form (Robson 41). "Now Reader Read ... " is the verse account of the staking of a claim; it is an early part of an Englishing of Canada that has been linguistic and cultural as well as commercial and demographic.

2 Thomas Cary,
Abram's Plains

Written primarily for the controlling élite of Lower Canada by a man whose "commitment" to the province was "unmistakable" (Gnarowski 13), *Abram's Plains: a Poem* (1789) contains generous amounts of the four ingredients essential to a distinctively Canadian poetry: local description, local pride, communal consciousness, and an educative, ethical purpose. A local pride grounded in a love of the Lower Canadian landscape and an appreciation of its historical resonances is evident even in the opening lines of the poem, where Cary uses the epic flourish of the delayed verb ("Grateful I sing") to initiate a celebration of the "pleasing views" now available at the scene of Wolfe's decisive victory and heroic death thirty years earlier. Later come celebrations, not merely of the province's landscape and history, but also of its seasonal variations (*499–503*), its healthy weather (*504–11*), and its sturdy inhabitants (*558–67*). There are even backhanded compliments for the chefs of Quebec and Montreal (*166–71*). Also abundantly evident in the poem, not least in its commemorative component and in its emphasis on the agricultural riches and commercial potential of Lower Canada, is a communal consciousness founded on the sense of a shared past and a common future. Where once was the tyranny of the French régime (*434–51*) and the discord of the Seven Years' War (*340–55*), there are now the "laws," "peace and ... plenty" (*444–48*) that will ensure prosperity to French and English alike. And especially near the end of *Abram's Plains* there is evident an educative and ethical emphasis that is calculated to secure communal standards and, in so doing, increase local pride, social cohesion, and future prospects. With his eye on the "soldier, statesman, and merchant" – the "great" and "rich" of Lower

Canada – Cary delivers a traditional moralist's warning against the "pride of pow'r" (*530–35*), and offers a version of James Thomson's "elegant Sufficiency" ("Spring" *1161*) – a life lived "Beneath ... mad ambition ... / Yet above want" (*572–79*) – as the moderating ideal by which his bourgeois audience should live. This is a blueprint for life in Lower Canada and, in concert with the local pride and communal awareness to which it is closely related, it reflects Cary's commitment to his adopted country and aligns *Abram's Plains* with an emerging English-Canadian identity.

The emphasis on local scenery, military history, and moral issues in *Abram's Plains* is in part a consequence of the poem's genre. Modelled to a great extent on Pope's *Windsor-Forest* (which, in turn, draws heavily on John Denham's seminal *Cooper's Hill*), *Abram's Plains* is a topographical poem, a poem in which (to quote Dr. Johnson's famous definition of "local poetry") "the fundamental subject is some particular landscape ... poetically described, with the addition of such embellishments as may be supplied by historical retrospection and incidental meditation" ("Denham" 77). In addition to the three elements mentioned by Johnson – "some particular landscape," "historical retrospection," and "incidental meditation" – *Abram's Plains* evinces two other characteristics of topographical poetry: a "controlling moral vision" and an "attempt to project ... stability into the future" (Foster 403, 402). As he contrasts the present tranquillity on the Plains of Abraham with the death and destruction that took place there in September 1759, Cary implicitly celebrates the merits of the *pax Britannica* and explicitly states his hope that "never more may hostile arms distain, / With human gore, the verdure of the plain!" (*340–41*). The contrast of "red against green, death against life" in these lines is indeed striking (Glickman 504). It is also consistent both with Cary's later characterization of his "muse" as a source of "peaceful parallels" (*454–69*) and with his repeated championship of life and fertility over death and sterility in the human and natural words (*372–403*, for example). In dying to achieve Quebec's freedom (for so Cary would have it), Wolfe is, if not quite a Christ-like figure in *Abram's Plains*, then certainly "the centre of a secular Passion scene" as he is in Benjamin West's *The Death of General Wolfe*, an influential "icon of the British Empire" that Cary may have seen either in the original (it was exhibited at the Royal Academy in London in 1771) or in the immensely popular engraving of William Woollett (Schama 25–38; Glickman 504). At the structural core of *Abram's Plains*, suffusing even the "landscape" of Cary's topographical poem, lies a Tory vision of the British Empire as a force for good, a progressive-conservative conviction that those fortunate enough to come into contact with British civilization will be elevated both morally and commercially. With its "fearless" birds, "grazing herds," and "learned dead" (presumably the classical and neo-classical writers and thinkers "who blest Mankind / With Arts, and Arms, and humaniz'd a World" [Thomson, "Winter" *432–35*]), the Plains of Abraham are in Cary's poem a metaphorical microcosm of a Lower Canada that for thirty years has enjoyed the benefits of British peace, order, good government, and mercantile economics. Not unlike Kelsey nearly a century earlier, Cary endorses peace at least in part because it provides the stability necessary for the civil and commercial development of his adopted home.

While the Plains of Abraham outside Quebec City provide the setting for the beginning and the end of Cary's poem, as well as for the iconic account of Wolfe's death at its centre, they are not the only unifying geographical entity in *Abram's Plains*. The other is the Great Lakes-St. Lawrence River system, which Cary follows, not upstream in the direction of exploration or settlement, but downstream from Lake Superior to the Gulf. Not fortuitously this is the direction of the mercantile flow of staples from the hinterland to the metropolitan centres of Montreal ("where centre all the forest's spoils" [*80*]) and Quebec City, and thence down the St. Lawrence estuary and, by extension, across the Atlantic to Britain. Cary's use of the St. Lawrence as a structuring device, as a thread along which to string the various descriptive, historical, and meditative components of *Abram's Plains*, places his work in the topographical sub-genre of the "river poem" (Aubin 224) and gives it further affinities with *Windsor-Forest*, as well as with poems written later in Canada or about Canada such as *Quebec Hill* and *The St. Lawrence and the Saguenay*. Perhaps the idea of following the Great Lakes-St. Lawrence River system from west to east came from Jonathan Carver, the controversial explorer and mercantilist whose *Travels through the Interior Parts of North America, in the Years 1766, 1767, and 1768* (1778 f.) provided Cary with the bulk of his information about the open trading area between Lower Canada and the territories of the HBC. As well as describing his journey in 1767–68 from the head of Lake Superior to the gulf of the St. Lawrence, Carver's *Travels* reveals that he well understood the mercantile potential of a waterway that could move even "virgin copper" with "cheapness and ease" from the interior through Quebec to "foreign markets" (138–40). Whatever its inspiration, the fact that the Great Lakes-St. Lawrence River system in *Abram's Plains* has both a structural function and a mercantile dimension indicates that in Cary's poem, as in Kelsey's, no easy distinctions can be drawn between the literary and commercial appropriation of Canada.

Working in concert with geographical and conceptual unities to hold together the diverse subject-matter of *Abram's Plains* is the poetic form of the poem. In the Georgian period, decasyllabic couplets were barely a matter of choice for minor poets bent on writing a longer poem in the Augustan tradition. But blank verse was a viable and attractive alternative, as Cary's weighing of the merits of the two forms in his preface to *Abram's Plains* confirms:

It may be said that the ... comparative merits [of Pope in *Windsor-Forest* and Thomson in *The Seasons*] ... cannot but with difficulty be ascertained, the one having wrote in blank verse the other in rime. It is true that Thomson has the advantage of not being fettered by rime, but to excel in blank verse ... requires a far more poetical fancy as well as greater strength of imagination than are requisite to please in rime, where correctness of numbers often passes on the generality of readers for every thing ...

Before I began this Poem I read Pope's Windsor-Forest and Dr. Goldsmith's Deserted Village, with the view of endeavouring, in some degree, to catch their manner of writing ...

(27–41)

Pope, Thomson, and Goldsmith: these are the neo-classical poets who were emulated by most of the authors of longer poems on Canada during the Georgian period. Bringing with it an aura of authority from such poems as *Windsor-Forest* and *An Essay on Man*, *The Deserted Village* and *The Traveller*, the decasyllabic couplet provided colonial poets such as Cary with the formal equivalent of the order, balance, and governance that they valued in their social world and physical landscape, and sought to reflect in their "descriptive poetry" (Cary, preface 7). Rational in its implications and rectangular in its shape, the decasyllabic couplet is a poetic analogue of the fenced field, the stone house, and other more-or-less symmetrical forms of European settlement. More than this, it is analogous to the "symmetry and convenience ... [of] the new buildings of London and Edinburgh" that one British visitor found conspicuously lacking in the old, French houses of Quebec City (Hollingsworth 201). In sum a topographical poem in decasyllabic couplets is to early Canadian poetry what a well-managed mixed farm centred on a house with a Palladian porch was to the landscape of the time: a manifestation in Lower Canada of British organization, power, and progress (Ruddel 222–23).

A part of Pope's work that was especially rich in lessons for Cary and later poets writing in Canada is the passage in *An Essay on Criticism* that rehearses several of the mimetic devices available to practitioners of the decasyllabic couplet. "The *Sound* must seem an *Eccho* to the *Sense*," asserts Pope before providing several illustrative examples:

Soft is the Strain when *Zephyr* gently blows,
And the *smooth Stream* in *smoother Numbers* flows;
But when loud Surges lash the sounding Shore,
The *hoarse, rough Verse* shou'd like the *Torrent* roar.
When *Ajax* strives, some Rocks' vast Weight to throw,
The Line too *labours*, and the Words move *slow*,
Not so, when swift *Camilla* scours the Plain,
Flies o'er th' unbending Corn, and skims along the Main.

(*365–73*)

Cary may have had these lines specifically in mind when he likened himself to an unbroken "steed" (an emblem, perhaps, of British liberty) near the beginning of *Abram's Plains*: "Courting fair health, I drive across the plain; / The balmy breeze of Zephyrus inhale, / Or bare my breast to the bleak northern gale" (*7–10*). (Apparently he also had in mind at least two other passages when writing these lines: *An Essay on Man 1:61–62* – "When the proud steed shall know why Man ... / ... drives him o'er the plains"; and Thomson's "Autumn," *60–61* – "the bleak North, / With Winter charg'd.") Mimetic lessons learned from *An Essay on Criticism* clearly lie behind many other lines in *Abram's Plains*, two examples of which will serve as illustrations:

Here sleepy *Saint Charles*, scarcely seen to flow
His mazy current solemn yields and slow;
Whilst, a strong contrast strikingly to form,
His stream *Montmorenci* sends down in storm ...
. . . .
Then noisy *Chaudiere*, thy foaming fall,
Midway arrested, forms a chrystal wall.

(*132–35, 514–15*)

This last couplet is particularly characteristic of Cary in its use of two devices – caesura and end-stopping – to reinforce a sense of stasis, in this case the stasis of a frozen waterfall. Earlier in the poem, after a lengthy account of a whale hunt that is loud with the alliteration of violent action (*228–43*), Cary uses the same devices, augmented by the long vowels of slowed movement, to add force to his descriptions of the harpoon's efficacy:

E'en while the waves he [the whale] lashes into storm,
A monstrous mass floats motionless his form.
The grampus, | of less bulk, | stays his swift course,
Arrested on his way by iron force.

The fierce sea-cow, I tho' cloth'd in stoutest mail,
Finds, I 'gainst man's arts, I his strength of small avail.
(*244–49*)

With a laconic finality that is disconcerting to readers today, two creatures that, like the whale, are now on the verge of extinction in the Gulf
of the St. Lawrence are "Arrested" and dispatched in a pair of halting,
end-stopped couplets.

A similar mimetic effect is evident near the beginning of *Abram's
Plains* when, with the help of Carver, Cary surveys Canada from the
Great Lakes to the Gulf. As is conventional in topographical poetry and
the parallel art of cartography (did he perhaps have in mind Carver's
"New Map of North America, from the Latest Discoveries, 1778"?), Cary
adopts the preternaturally elevated viewpoint that is necessary for the
registration of large geographical patterns. Looking down on a vast
expanse of territory with an eye for spatial form and exotic information,
he uses the resonantly Popean word "urns" (*19*) to describe the Great
Lakes, and allots to each a closed couplet reflective of its relatively
enclosed physical shape:

Thee, first of lakes [Superior]! as *Asia's Caspian* great,
Where congregated streams hold icy state.
Huron, distinguish'd by its thund'ring bay,
Where full-charg'd clouds heav'n's ord'nance ceaseless play.
Thee *Michigan*, where learned beavers lave,
And two great tribes divided hold thy wave.
Erie for serpents fam'd, whose noisome breath,
By man inhal'd, conveys the venom'd death.
(*21–28*)

Like entries in a trader's way-bill the Great Lakes are each given two
lines and a brief remark based on Carver who, for example, notes the
icy coldness even in summer of the water in "the Caspian of America"
(132) and has this to say about Lake Erie: "the most remarkable of the
species that infest [it] ... is the hissing snake ... When any thing
approaches ... it blows from its mouth with great force a subtile wind,
that is reported to be of a nauseous smell; and if drawn in with the
breath of the unwary traveller, will infallibly bring on a decline, that in
a few months must prove mortal" (167–68). Little wonder that history
has judged Carver an "accurate though somewhat gullible observer"
(Parker 54; Weld 2:167–68).

In marked contrast to the series of closed couplets describing the
Great Lakes in *Abram's Plains* is Cary's ensuing description of Niagara

Falls. Here the only triplet in the poem (*31–33*) and a line (*33*) lengthened to a hexameter (MacLaren, "Pastoral" 17) attempt to replicate the sight and sound of a natural phenomenon whose "stupendous" size and "amazing" noise (Carver 169–70) thus seem to be "stretching their container and almost bursting out of confinement" (Fussell 132):

> The streams thence rushing with tremendous roar,
> Down thy dread fall, *Niagara*, prone pour;
> Back foaming, in thick hoary mists, they bound, ⎫
> The thund'ring noise deafens the country round, ⎬
> Whilst echo, from her caves, redoubling sends the sound. ⎭
>
> (*29–33*)

Several of the techniques used by Cary to reflect the contours and commotion of the Falls – alliteration, trochaic substitution ("Dówn thy"), spondee ("próne póur"), and terminal verbs ("pour," "bound") – derive from descriptions of waterfalls in *The Seasons*, as do similar devices in the accounts of Niagara Falls in *Quebec Hill* and Cornwall Bayley's *Canada*. Unlike Bayley, however, Cary does not follow the precedent of Goldsmith in *The Traveller* and force the pronunciation of "*Niagara*" to conform to the scansion of iambic pentameter, but, on the contrary, places the word in an irregular line so as to allow for its North American pronunciation. Such respect for the local is consistent with the mimetic efforts that Cary lavishes on Niagara Falls, and both prepare the way for the compliment that follows when the sublimity of the Falls is compared to the "heavenly strains" of Handel's *Messiah* (*34–37*). The residents of Canada might be denied the "Hallelujah" chorus but they had access to one of nature's most sublime scenes.

Dedicated as he was to "exhibit[ing] ... picture[s] of the real scenes of nature" (preface *7–8*), Cary was more concerned to chronicle the development, of Canada's landscape and population under British rule. In doing this he relied conceptually and perceptually on the so-called "four stages theory" of social development which, as Ronald L. Meek has shown (230), was "a very common and a very important ingredient in Enlightenment thought in the field of the social sciences during the whole of the period from 1750 to 1800" (and, it may be added, continued to be common and important in Canadian poetry until at least the end of the Georgian period). According to this theory, which Meek traces to two independent progenitors – Adam Smith in Scotland and A.R.J. Turgot in France – all societies develop through four distinct phases, each defined by the mode of subsistence of its constituent members: (1) a savage stage based on hunting; (2) a barbaric (or pastoral) stage based on herding; (3) an agricultural stage based on farming; and

(4) a commercial stage based on trading. Of these four stages, the savage was held to be the "least civilized" (Meek 141–43) or the most "rough and rude" (Burwell, *Talbot Road 565*) and the commercial the most refined (Pye) or "polish'd" (Cary *418*). The great leap forward in what Henry James Pye (the poet laureate from 1790 to 1813) called *The Progress of Refinement* (1783) was held to occur with the advent of agriculture, when self-sufficiency begins to give way to the superfluity that, in conjunction with "property in lands," results in the creation of "civil society," commercial prosperity, and – in the words of Sir William Blackstone – the "leisure ... to cultivate the human mind, to invent useful arts, and to lay the foundations of science" (2:7–8). In efficient agriculture lay the seeds of advanced culture.

It surely cannot be counted a mere coincidence that in the same year (1789) in which a group of "anglophone merchants and a few prominent Canadiens initiated the formation of an Agricultural Society for the District of Quebec" (Ruddel 80), Cary has the Naiades of the St. Lawrence "chant, in cheerful carols ... [the] praise" of Ceres, the Roman goddess of tillage and corn, "Whose yellow harvests" not only "glad the shore" of the River (*45–46*) but also produce enough extra grain to "shower" on "craving realms" (*216–17*). Where there were once savage beasts and uncultivated tracts of forest (*47–48*), there are now domestic animals (*49, 408*) and productive farms. Where there was once a subsistence-level economy (Séguin; LeGoff; Ruddel 77–80), there is now – thanks to Loyalist farmers (*64–67*), improved (British) agriculture, and superabundant natural resources – "plenty redundant" (*251*): enough food both for "home supply" (*252*) and for profitable export. In the culinary sophistication evident in its urban centres (*93*) and the leisurely pastimes of its privileged inhabitants (*401–11*) lies the evidence that Lower Canada has reached the crucial agricultural stage of development and, indeed, has advanced towards the refinement that comes with commercial prosperity. Perhaps the most obvious evidence of this progress resides in the existence of *Abram's Plains* itself, "the offspring of a few leisure hours" which, Cary hopes, will "not be unpleasing to the lovers of polite learning" at "a time when literature seems to be emerging from the closet to illuminate our horizon" (preface *1–5*) – the horizon, that is, of a Lower Canada burgeoning physically and culturally under the genial sun of British civilization. What Mary Lu MacDonald writes of the Canadas between 1817 and 1850 applies equally to Lower Canada in 1789: "refinement of an intellectual as well as moral nature was considered ... to be of great social value, both to individuals and to nations" (*Literature* 250).

Whereas Kelsey depicts the "Natives" as people with individual names, complex emotions, and intriguing beliefs, Cary views them

through the post-Enlightenment lens of the four stages theory as stereotypical savages to be weaned from the nomadic life of hunting and
improved through contact with European civilization. "Europeans
resemble [God] more than any of the rest of his children," asserts Goldsmith in his *History of Man and Quadrapeds* (1774 f.), a much reprinted
application of the theory that very likely lies in the background of
Abram's Plains. Near the other end of the scale from Caucasians, the
"red or copper coulour[ed]" "natives of America" display primitive
"customs" similar to those of "savage nations in every country," the reason being that "a wild, independent, and precarious life, produces a
peculiar strain of virtues and vices: ... patience and hospitality, indo-
lence and rapacity, content and sincerity," "cruelty," stupidity, and
superstition (1:118–19). Even worse off because of their "rigorous climate" are the "uniformly dwarfish" "Esquimaux Indians" – Cary's
"dwarfish *Esquimaux*, with small pig's eyes" *(164)* – who are "treat[ed]
with the same scorn" by their "southern neighbours ... that a polished
nation would treat a savage one; and we may readily judge of the rudeness of those manners, which a native of Canada can think more barbarous than his own" (1:103–04, 107).

Significantly, it is with "incline[d] ... eyes" *(412)*, with the downward
and condescending gaze of one who occupies the racial and imperial
high ground, that Cary observes the Huron settlement at Lorette outside Quebec City:

> Here, of the copper-tribes, an half tam'd race,
> As villagers take up their resting place;
> Here fix'd, their houshold gods lay peaceful down,
> To learn the manners of the polish'd town.
>
> *(414–17)*

Agriculture is not mentioned in these lines, but earlier in the poem
Cary parallels the physical development of the Canadian terrain with
the moral development of the Native peoples:

> How blest the task, to tame the savage soil,
> And, from the waters, bid the woods recoil!
> But oh! a task of more exalted kind,
> To arts of peace, to tame the savage mind;
> The thirst of blood, in human breasts, to shame,
> To wrest, from barb'rous vice, fair virtue's name;
> Bid tomahawks to ploughshares yield the sway,
> And skalping-knives to pruning hooks give way;
> In *Circe's* glass bid moderation reign,
> And moral virtues humanize the plain!
>
> *(54–63)*

Not only in the Popean balance of most of its couplets, but also in its classical reference and its biblical allusion (Isaiah 2:4: "and they shall beat their swords into plowshares and their spears into pruning hooks ... neither shall they learn war anymore"), this passage exemplifies the neo-classical Christian humanism which for Cary is the apogee of civilization. Nor are the Native peoples the only fortunate recipients of such civilization in Lower Canada. Still to an extent the benighted victims of Roman Catholic superstition and irrationality (*362–97*), the French-Canadians have at least since the conquest been released into freedom and prosperity by British law and agriculture (*434–49*). Just as it was the duty of the conquerors of Lower Canada to ensure the exposure of the Native peoples and French-Canadians to civic virtues and Protestant reason, so it was incumbent upon the locals to accept with gratitude and grace the benefits of their new dispensation. "Grateful, ye peasants, own your mended state, / And bless, beneath a GEORGE, your better fate" (*450–51*). Thus ran the combined logic of British imperialism and the four stages theory, in actual or willed ignorance of the fact that the Hurons had practised agriculture for thousands of years in what is now Ontario and of the fact that under the terms of the Quebec Act (1774) the seigneurial land-tenure system was not abolished but retained and consolidated for the benefit of colonial entrepreneurs.

To give substance to his vision of a cultivated and prosperous Lower Canada, Cary repeatedly describes the agricultural landscapes and commercial activities of the province. At pains to refute Goldsmith's depiction of North America in *The Deserted Village* as a "dreary scene" of "matted woods" and "poisonous fields" infested with "rattling ... snake[s]," "crouching tigers," and "savage men" (*341–59*), he concedes the presence in Canada of "Thick-matted woods" and insects with "tumefying stings," but ignores the "tigers" (cougars), sanitizes the "copper-tribes," and, in a note based on Carver (517–18), maintains that in areas abounding in rattle snakes "nature good and wise" has furnished an antidote to their bite in the form of the "Rattle-snake plantain" (*116–27* and *127 n.*). The "task" of clearing land in Lower Canada is admittedly "hard" (*130*) but, once accomplished, the result is both commercially rewarding and aesthetically appealing. In a word, it is picturesque – like an eighteenth-century landscape painting in its harmonious combination of different colours, textures, and physical features. When he points to the "Order in Variety" of picturesque landscapes in *Windsor-Forest* (15), Pope hints at a balance in the external world between control (law) and freedom (liberty) that is implied by the landscape descriptions in *Abram's Plains*. Cary follows Pope in using the Here/There convention to order the variety of the Lower Canadian

landscape into left and right, foreground, middleground, and background:

> There, on thy banks, *Saint Charles*, rich meadows vie,
> In vivid green, to ease the dazzled eye.
> . . . .
> Here milch-kine lowing leave the grazing field,
> And glad to man their milky homage yield ...
> . . . .
> Next *Charlebourg*, blest in a bounteous soil,
> Where plenteous harvests pay the lab'ror's toil.
> Thy beauties, *Beauport*, open on mine eyes,
> There fertile fields and breezy lawns arise;
> Far as *Montmorenci*, thy pleasing stream,
> Romantic as a love-sick virgin's dream.
> Beyond the vales, still stretching on my view,
> Hills, behind hills, my aching eyes pursue.
> 'Till, in surrounding skies, I lose my way,
> Where the long landscape fading dies away.
>   (*398–99, 408–09, 418–27*)

If the picturesque aesthetic was tainted with "profound pessimism" following the enclosures in Britain (Bermingham 70), in Canada it was
attached to landscapes marked by agricultural success and potential. In
the foreground and middleground of Cary's word paintings are "rich
meadows," and "plenteous harvests"; in the background – in the reced-
ing space of the "long landscape" "Beyond the vales" – lie indefinite
areas for growth and expansion, mind-boggling visual and commercial
prospects (Hughes, "Goldsmith" 38–41). In *Abram's Plains*, as later in
Talbot Road and *The Rising Village*, the picturesque becomes, in the
words of John Galt, an aesthetic of "profitable beauty" (*Bogle Corbet* 3:3).
     Besides the extractive industries (fishing, whaling, logging, the fur
trade) the principal commercial activity that Cary cites as evidence of
Lower Canada's economic progress is shipbuilding. "Taking advantage
of the existence of supplies of Canadian white oak" and white pine –
Cary's "sturdy oak, [and] ... lofty mountain-pine" (*214*) – colonial merchants in Quebec began after the conquest to build "ships ... for use in
the timber trade," and in the period between 1760 and 1825 Quebec
City itself "became one of the most important shipbuilding centres in
British North America" (Ruddel 123). "On both sides" of the St.
Lawrence at Quebec "commerce a footing gains," observes Cary as he
proceeds to describe what must have been an exciting spectacle for residents of the City – the construction and launching of a large vessel:

Tall forests their high-waving branches bow,
And yield, submiss, to lay their honors low;
The plowing keel the builder artist lays,
Her ribs of oak the rising ship displays;
Now, grown mature, she glides with forward pace,
And eager rushes to the saint's embrace.
Then rising, Venus like, with gay parade,
Strait turns kept-mistress to the god of trade.

(*108–15*)

Like vassals giving homage to their sovereign, Canada's trees "bow" down to their imperial masters and yield up the raw materials that, in a manner analogous to Cary's own use of indigenous matter (Canadian content) within a master design (the topographical poem), the "builder artist" uses to construct a trading vessel. As the ship takes shape "she" is likened metaphorically to a maturing female and made the subject of a complex conceit. With "Her ribs of oak" she recalls the creation of Eve from a rib of the sleeping Adam (Canadian nature; and see the "Eden transplanted" [*294*] later in the poem). As she "rushes ... to the embrace" of the St. Lawrence shore, she resembles a nun, a "Sequester'd vestal" like those in Quebec's Hôpital Générale who, contrary to "great nature's law" and "th[e] Maker's will," shun "man's embrace" in favour of a "life confin'd" (*372–97*). And when, in maturity, she rises from the waves to become a "kept-mistress to the god of trade," she is explicitly compared with Venus, the classical goddess of love who is often depicted floating ashore on a huge shell. Almost needless to say Cary's substitution of the "god of trade" for Venus's legendary lover, Mars, the god of war, accords perfectly with the contrast at the heart of *Abram's Plains* between "Destructive war" (*52*) and prosperous peace. Both complex in itself and consistent with the poem as a whole, Cary's ship-building conceit may well have been intended as an allegory of the movement of Lower Canada from a state of pristine innocence (Adamic nature), through a stage of unsatisfying and unproductive sterility (the French régime), to a sexually and commercially gratifying maturity (British rule).

It is also possible that in Cary's depiction of the "builder artist" as a godlike creator of new (yet familiar) forms there is an element of flattery aimed at men such as James Black and Silas Pearson, the master shipbuilders of Quebec in the late eighteenth century (Ruddel 122). This would not be inconsistent with Cary's fulsome gestures towards the colonial élite elsewhere in the poem. The members of the Northwest Company in Montreal must have been delighted to hear their city called a "Great mart" and themselves "blest traders" (*80, 84*). The members of the military garrison at Quebec must have been equally pleased to be characterized as "British spirits, bold" (*99*) whose engineering feats rivalled those of God and Moses ("At their command floods back their billows heave" [*104*]). Nor would Lord Dorchester (Guy Carleton), a veteran of the Plains of Abraham, a hero of the defense of Quebec against the Americans in 1775–76 (*332–39, 516–25*), and the governor-in-chief of British North America from 1786 to 1796, have failed to be gratified by the panegyric that he receives near the end of *Abram's Plains*:

> There, stretching to the right, with oblique eye,
> The villa of fair *Dorchester* I spy;
> Where, from parade and crowds, she [the muse] chearful flies,
> The false, by royalty, taught to despise:
> There, tranquil, tastes the tender sweets of life
> That in the mother center and the wife:
> There simple treads the breeze-inviting plains,
> And all the glare of equipage disdains.
>
> (*484–91*)

A military hero, the supreme commander of Lower Canada, and an enthusiastic proponent of the province's commercial development (Creighton 102), Dorchester is the subject here of near iconic veneration. As Cary's couplets follow one another in almost perfect symmetry ("There ... Where ... There ... There") they become the poetic equivalent of a neo-classical colonnade, an architectural form that goes beyond the expression of rational order and balance to proclaim the presence of the powerful, the venerable, the sacred. Perhaps Cary, who in 1789 was a "clerk in a government office" (Gauvin 123), had hopes of entering Dorchester's retinue. Certainly this possibility is not belied by his subsequent career. In 1798–99 he was secretary to Dorchester's successor, Governor Robert Prescott, and, after failing to get elected to the House of Assembly in the riding of Quebec in 1800, he founded the *Quebec Mercury* (1805–1903), a newspaper in which he promoted the interests of "the conservative, English-speaking Quebec bourgeoisie, who sought to ensure the political and economic domination of the British in Lower Canada" (Gauvin 124). That there is a seamless connection between *Abram's Plains* and such views is a testament to a consistency that can be admired even by those who find Cary's political views repugnant.

From a literary-historical perspective, Cary is less remarkable for his relentless progressive conservatism or his unwavering British suprematism than for the fact that in 1789 he published a poem in English in

Lower Canada for an audience that was coming to think of this country as home. When he writes of "our horizon" in his preface Cary means the area bounded by the Atlantic Ocean to the east, the United States to the south, and the HBC territories to the north and east. When he writes in the body of *Abram's Plains* that "Our infant world asks but time's fos-t'ring hand, / Its faculties must by degrees expand" (*220–21*), he has in mind the future of what is now central Canada. Cary was an imperialist who believed that the transplanting of British traditions in Canada was for the good of all. He was a colonial who was convinced that the mercantile system of the British Empire would assure Canada's economic and social development. He was a Georgian neo-classicist whose poem contains a "typical eighteenth-century cluster of peace, prosperity, patriotism and plenty" (Cohen 7). But his patriotism was directed at least as much towards Lower Canada as to Great Britain, and therein lies his significance for the Canadian literary continuity.

In the final lines of *Abram's Plains*, Cary marries neo-classical diction and local content in a way that is as typical of the poem, as a whole, as it is representative of its author's English-Canadian identity. Echoing a phrase from *The Seasons* ("Winter comes at last, / And shuts the scene" ["Winter" *1032–33*]) and drawing inspiration from a passage in Carver ("In dark nights when there is much lightning ... [fire-flies] seem as if they wish either to imitate or assist the flashes" [492]), Cary seems to see in Canada's "shining fire-flies" a metaphor for his own small but bright colony on the St. Lawrence, as well as, perhaps, a metaphor for his own "mimic" yet distinctive poetic efforts:

> Now shade o'er shade steals gradual on the sight,
> Darkness shuts up the scene and all is night.
> Except, where darting cross the swampy marsh,
> From shining fire-flies lucid lightnings flash.
> When, from black sultry skies, long silver streams
> Send through the atmosphere their forked beams;
> With brighter glow then shoot the mimic fires,
> Each insect, *Caesar* like, to rival Jove aspires.
>
> (*580–87*)

3 J. Mackay,
Quebec Hill

For Canadian readers J. Mackay's *Quebec Hill; or, Canadian Scenery. A Poem. In Two Parts* is probably the most provocative and least likeable of the longer poems on Canada that were written during the Georgian period. Published in London in 1797 and reviewed quite widely in the British periodicals of the day (Bentley, intro. to *Quebec Hill* xxxv–vii), it was clearly directed towards readers at the centre of the Empire, perhaps with the aim of discouraging emigration to Lower Canada. Although Mackay begins by saying positive things about the "romantic scenery" of the province (preface *21–22; 1:22 n.*), he ends by affirming in no uncertain terms his preference for the "climate" and "manners" of Britain (*1:185–86*). In between he devotes a large amount of his poetic energy to illustrating the debilitating, brutalizing, and potentially fatal effects of a climate whose extremes of heat and cold he elevates to structural prominence through the division of his poem into the "Two Parts" of "Summer" and "Winter." Ironically *Quebec Hill* was not favourably received by British reviewers, but has remained of piquant interest to Canadian readers. Generously excerpted in Douglas Daymond and Leslie Monkman's *Literature in Canada*, it has recently been accorded a certain importance for its articulation of the "difficulty or impossibility" of finding in European "language and metrical forms" an "appropriate style" "to convey the very different North American experience" (Keith 26):

> Ye who, in stanzas, celebrate the Po,
> Or teach the Tyber in your strains to flow,
> How would you toil for numbers to proclaim
> The liquid grandeur of St. Lawrence' Stream?
> (1:49–52)

For this question, as well as for its wide-ranging, if mainly ascerbic, comments on the landscape and life of Lower Canada, *Quebec Hill* will continue to attract the attention of Canadian readers, especially those
interested in the relationship between Canadian subject-matter and
imported forms and styles.

Very little is known of J. Mackay beyond what can be gathered or
inferred from *Quebec Hill* and its preface. Apparently "the greater part
of the Poem was written in Canada, where ... [Mackay] spent a considerable portion of his time"(preface *8–9*), perhaps around 1793 when,
as he observes in a footnote *(1:156 n.)*, Jacob Mountain was appointed
"Bishop of Quebec, with a salary of £2000 per annum" (*Quebec Gazette*
[27 June 1793]). Mackay may have been James Mackay, "a young man
from Sutherland, son of Mackay of Kirtomy, a cadet of the noble house
of Reay" (William Wilfred Campbell 1:403). He may have been Lieutenant James Mackay(c.1738–1818), a veteran of the American Revolution
who was seriously wounded while fighting under Wolfe at Quebec. Or
he may have been Captain John Mackie (or Mackay), a ship's master
who sailed regularly between Britain and Quebec from 1792 onwards
(Bentley, intro. to *Quebec Hill* xii–iii). Some weight is lent to this last possibility by the focus in *Quebec Hill* on various marine and meteorological
phenomena, such as the origin of winds (*2:81–90*), and the freezing of
the ocean (*2:91–102*) that would have been of special interest to a
sailor. This is by no means conclusive evidence, however, and in the
absence of external information linking *Quebec Hill* to a particular J.
Mackay the background of the poem's author must remain uncertain.

Whomever he was J. Mackay seems to have found the programme for
his poem in a work which, directly or indirectly, lies behind several early
poems on Canada: J. Aikin's *Essay in the Application of Natural History to
Poetry* (1777). Arguing that "the grand and beautiful objects which
nature every where profusely throws around us, are the most obvious
store of new materials for the poet ... [and] the store which of all others
he has most sparingly touched," Aikin proceeds in his *Essay* to direct
would-be practitioners of "descriptive poetry" (Cary, preface *7*) to what
seems to him to be the greatest "store of new materials for the poet":
"countries where almost every object is new. Such, to the inhabitant of
a temperate climate, are the polar and tropical parts of the globe"
(4,101,140). Clearly this perception is to an extent implicit in the "Summer" and "Winter" portions of Thomson's *The Seasons*, both of which
are quoted frequently by Aikin and used heavily by Mackay; however it
is rendered almost diagrammatically explicit in Aikin's *Essay*, and in the
same broad antithesis that governs *Quebec Hill* – the antithesis between
the "burning ... Sun" of a tropical summer and the "dreary scenes" that
characterize winter in the "desolate regions" of the North (145,141).

When Mackay notes that "Some days in July and August are said to be as intensely hot [in Canada] as in the West Indies" (*1:160 n.*), it is as if he is drawing the Canadian summer towards one of the extremes which, in Aikin's view, will make it novel and "exotic" (148) to "the inhabitant of a temperate climate." Similarly, Mackay's repeated references to Siberia (*2:19, 84*) and Greenland (*2:90, 105*) could be taken as attempts to wed the Canadian winter to the other extreme said by Aikin to be "productive of novelty" in poetry. In any event both the "Summer" and the "Winter" parts of *Quebec Hill* are spiced with accounts of the "extremes of ardent heat and cold" (*2:188*) that can be assumed on the basis of Aikin's *Essay* to have generated in Mackay's British audience something of the astonishment – the pleasurable horror – associated with the sublime. In "Summer" there are "fiery cloud[s] that ... scorch ... the wind" (*1:353*) and "heats" so intense that they "affect strangers in an alarming manner" (*1:160 n.*). In "Winter" there is light so "bright" that it can impair the sight (*2:49-51* and *19 n.*) and wind so penetrating that it leaves "fields of ice ... like pendant charts" on the inside walls of houses (*2:127-32*). This is sensationalism, of course, but it is nonetheless grounded in fact – or, at least, in the observations of the Swedish natural historian Pehr (Peter) Kalm, whose *Travels into North America* (1770–71 f.) furnished Mackay with much information about Canada, including details of "north-east wind[s]" capable of "pierc[ing] ... walls of a moderate thickness, so that the whole wall on the inside of the house is covered with snow, or a thick hoar frost" (2:299).

Nor is the climatic structure and content of *Quebec Hill* the only aspect of the poem that appears to reflect Aikin's *Essay*. Towards the end of his discussion, Aikin expresses enthusiasm for the "infinite scope for new and striking description" that the "annual history" of the polar and tropical regions would afford "to the poet who should be able to draw ... from original sources!" (1148–49). More specifically, he refers to the "untameable fierceness of the beasts of prey" and the "exalted rage and venom of the numerous serpents" in such regions, singling out various exotic creatures, including the bear and the python for comment. In at least two lengthy passages in *Quebec Hill* (*1:65–80* and *2:73–80*), Mackay seems to have taken Aikin's advice and used "original sources" – possibly his own experience and certainly the chapter on North American fauna in Carver's *Travels* – to create of the Canadian wilderness what Aikin calls a "rich garden of Exotics" (146). In a lengthy passage in "Summer" there are three untameably fierce "beasts of prey" – "prowling wolves," "fiery tygers" (cougars), and "The surly bear," and two venomous snakes – the "rattling snake" and "the speckled adder." In a parallel passage in "Winter" there are once again the "wolf," the "bear," and "tygers," as well as a creature from Carver's *Travels* that is every bit as exotic as the python: the "caracajou" (or wolverine), which was supposed to kill elk and other species of deer by strangling them with its "circling tail" (*2:75–76*). Interestingly enough Carver's description of the carcajou's extraordinary method of despatching its prey incidently associates the creature with the extremes of temperature poetically valued by Aikin: "taking his station on some ... branches" of a tree, the wolverine waits until a deer, "driven by an extreme heat or cold, takes shelter under it; then he fastens upon [its] neck, and opening the jugular vein, soon brings his prey to the ground. This he is able to do by his long tail, with which he encircles the body of his adversary" (450). It may be the combination of Aikin and Carver that accounts for the presence in *Quebec Hill* of the "skylark" (*1:22*)and the "nightingale" (*1:274; 2:11–12* and *173*), two species not actually found in Lower Canada. Carver's list of the birds of North America contains "Larks" and "the Nightingale" (466) and Aikin remarks that "the plaintive character of the nightingale renders its introduction [into poetry] pleasing and proper," especially as a contrast to the lark, "whose character is always cheerful and sprightly" (22). To the British readers of *Quebec Hill,* Lower Canada must have seemed by its animal life at least a place at once exotic and familiar.

In the late eighteenth century the appropriate poetic form for the description of a particular landscape, be it as exotic as Lower Canada or as familiar as Tintern Abbey, was still the topographical or "local" poem. Within this broad category, with its threefold requirement of landscape description, "historical retrospection," and "incidental meditation," *Quebec Hill* belongs, as its title indicates, to the sub-genre of the "hill-poem" (Aubin 77–110, 298–314), the lineage of which runs back through such works as John Dyer's *Grongar Hill* and Thomson's *Spring* (where Hadley Park is described "from an eminence" [Aubin 85]) to the seminal *Cooper's Hill.* In addition to resembling Denham's poem in its verse form (decasyllabic couplets) and elevated perspective, *Quebec Hill* harkens back verbally to its primary topographical model at certain points – for instance, in its use of the word "aspiring" to describe the "heights" at Quebec (*1:2*; Denham *18*). Indeed, Mackay's desire to find "numbers to proclaim / The liquid grandeur of St. Lawrence' Stream" may well derive, not merely from the obvious source of Pope's *Essay on Criticism* ("And the *smooth Stream* in *smoother Numbers* flows"), but also from the famous passage in *Cooper's Hill* – "O could I flow like thee, and make thy stream / My great example, as it is my theme!"(77) – which John Hollander sees as the *locus classicus* of "the idea that lines of verse should move like flowing water" (151). In addition to being a focal point for Mackay's mimetic ambitions, the St. Lawrence serves as a structuring device in *Quebec Hill,* providing the thread upon which

Mackay strings the components of what in places becomes more of a "river-" than a "hill-poem." That Mackay follows the Great Lakes-St. Lawrence River system in an easterly direction from the hinterlands of the interior to the baselands of Lower Canada is consistent with the metropolitan orientation that predisposes him to favour "cultur'd" Britain over "wild" Canada (*2:205–12*). It also raises the possibility that Mackay had read *Abram's Plains* and conceived *Quebec Hill* as a response to Cary's very positive presentation of Lower Canada.

As if disputing Cary's assessment of the province's agricultural achievements, Mackay asserts in the first footnote to his poem that, while "the country around Quebec abounds in prospects in a high degree delightful to such as have a relish for romantic scenery," "the soil is, in general, poor, and unproductive of corn. Few parts of Canada are remarkable for their fertility in this respect; and it is the quantity, and not the quality, of their lands that enables the inhabitants of this country to export wheat and flour"(*2:22 n*). Subsequent footnotes (many of which, like this one, exist in a state of tension with more positive, or, at least, ambivalent, statements in the body of the poem) present various aspects of the Canadian environment that make it largely unsuitable for agriculture and commerce, and, hence, an unlikely venue for the development of an advanced civilization along the lines predicted by the four stages theory. As well as being "covered with forests and lakes," Upper Canada is "intersected with swamps" or "foetid fens," the source of "vapours" which, according to Kalm and the miasma theory of disease, were responsible for "fever and ague" (*2:287* and *n.*). As well as being cursed by intemperate winters, Lower Canada is dependent upon a river that is only partly and sporadically navigable (*2:146 n.; 2:141 n.*). In view of such formidable barriers to settlement and prosperity, it is scarcely surprising that, "of all the English who have chosen Canada as the seat of their endeavours to acquire opulence and independence, few have been successful" (*2:141 n.*). From time to time in *Quebec Hill,* Mackay does "praise the lovely country's brooks, its grove and moss-grown rocks" as he promises in his Horatian epigraph, but for the most part his tone is counter-pastoral and counter-bucolic. Lower Canada may boast quantities of "romantic scenery," but "Where cultur'd fields but narrow tracts display" and "commerce varies like the ether stream" (*2:207,143*) there is little reason to expect the emergence of the sort of refined and moderate Augustan civilization envisaged in *Abram's Plains.* Indeed does not the province's brutal and extreme climate alone dictate that society in Lower Canada will transcend only with great difficulty the primitive stages of its development?

In suspecting and implying as much Mackay merely echoes the environmental determinism of many of his sources and contemporaries, from Milton with his comments on the depressive effect of a "cold / Climate" on poetic inspiration (*Paradise Lost 9:44–45*) to Pye with his elaboration of the retarding effects of an "assailing climate" on the "expanding Mind" of a primitive civilization (*1:35,48*). "Those who expect to see 'A new Athens rising near the pole'" in Canada "will find themselves extremely disappointed," writes Arabella Fermor in *The History of Emily Montague*; "genius will never mount high, where the faculties of the mind are benumbed half the year. 'Tis sufficient employment for the most lively spirit here to contrive how to preserve an existence ... the cold really brings on a sort of stupefaction" (Brooke 103). To Mackay the long Canadian winters are debilitating both physically and morally. Once the cold descends, "drooping" craftsmen gather around fires to sustain the "vital heat" essential to life (*2:33–34*), and, though the cessation of labour during the winter months "procures for the man of reflection leisure to prosecute his studies," it drives less contemplative and rational types to the "scorching draughts" of alcohol that merely compound the stupefying effect of the weather or, worse, lead to gambling, amorousness, "riot and dissipation" (*2:145–54 and 141 n.*). Mackay does concede that the Canadian winter holds some "soothing charms" and "local pleasures" – "mental joys" for the studious, sleigh rides for the "wealthy," and, for the "wise man," the hopeful anticipation of spring, both temporal and eternal (*2:155–82*). But on the whole, he sees little to admire in a place whose climate and people are governed by the "extremes of ardent heat or cold" (*2:188*). Equating a temperate climate with a temperate intellectual and social life as had Montesquieu in his enormously influential *De l'Esprit des lois* (1748), Mackay cannot help but prefer England to Canada as a place to live, at least until the "chequer'd bliss" of this life gives way to the unalloyed bliss of the next (*2:217–30*).

Nowhere are the baleful effects of Canada's long winters more evident than in the country's earliest inhabitants. Since their migration in the distant past from Asia – a hypothesis endorsed by Carver (199) and implied by Mackay's phrase "yellow Indians" (*1:331*) – the Native peoples have been exposed for many generations to a climate in which, as Arabella Fermor says, it is "sufficient employment ... to contrive how to preserve an existence." Nomadic in their Asian origins and hunters in their mode of subsistence, the Natives of North America were in Mackay's eyes, as in the eyes of Carver and William Robertson (a formative influence in this regard on both men), a quintessential example of the savage stage of social development, with all its supposed characteristics. "The most frequent or the most powerful motive of the incessant hostilities among rude nations," writes Robertson, is "the passion of revenge, which rages with such violence in the breast of savages, that

earnestness to gratify it may be considered as the distinguishing characteristic of men in their uncivilized state ... The desire for revenge is com-
municated from breast to breast, and soon kindles into rage," which, in
turn, issues in war and cruelty (2:233 and 147–75). Or as Carver puts it
after paraphrasing and illustrating Robertson's arguments, a "diabolical lust of revenge ... is the predominant passion in the breast of every
individual of every tribe, and it gives the growing warriors an early pro-
pensity to that cruelty and thirst for blood, which is so necessary a qualification for such as would be skilled in their savage art of war" (340).
In Carver and Robertson, then, lie the source of Mackay's depiction of
Canada's Native peoples as vengeful and war-like hunters:

> Here, deep involv'd in woods, the Indians range
> In quest of prey, or panting for revenge;
> With fixt resolve, and nerves inur'd to toil,
> The roe to vanquish, or the foe to foil;
> With steady aim they hurl their darts from far,
> And bleeding victims own the pointed bar.
>
> (*1:81–86*)

Standing in for Carver's "diabolical lust" is Mackay's "involv'd in
woods," a phrase that recalls the activities of Milton's Satan both directly
through *Paradise Lost* ("Satan involv'd in rising Mist" [*9:75*]) and indirectly through Thomson's "Spring" ("all involv'd in Smoke, the latent
Foe" [129]). As people whom environmental circumstances have rendered systemically vicious, the Indians are objects of pity for Mackay, as
well as candidates for redemption through agriculture. "View the slope
of yonder hill," he writes with reference to the Hurons at Lorette:

> There, tam'd and staid, the Indian seeks repose,
> Nor still imagines all the world his foes;
> With art and care, he cultivates his lands,
> And gathers in their fruits with willing hands.
> Yet 'mong the few who shun the forest's gloom,
> And Europe's garb and languages assume,
> Still sloth and ignorance our pity claim,
> And fiery draughts debilitate their frame.
>
> (*1:225; 229–36*)

In a footnote to these lines Mackay observes that, although the Hurons
at Lorette "are now so far civilized as to cultivate their lands for subsistence; yet many of them still retain, not a little, of the indolent roving
disposition of their ancestors" (*1:229 n.*). More certain than Cary of the

depravity of the Natives, and more aware, too, of the mixed blessings of European culture, Mackay presents the Native peoples of Lower Canada as a half savage rather than a "half tam'd race" (*Abram's Plains 414*), a view entirely consistent with his overall pessimism about the state of civilization in "realms remote ... Hemm'd in by wilds, where savage nations stray" (*2:206–08*).

According to the four stages theory, neither written records nor permanent architectural structures were to be expected from cultures at the savage stage of development. "The *Indians* have ever been as ignorant of architecture and manual labour as of science and writing," observes Kalm, who deduces two consequences from this: an ignorance on the part of the Native peoples of the history of "this part of the globe before *Columbus* discovered it" and an absence for the European traveller of the "vestige[s] ... of antiquity" that make "journies through our old countries" a continual "pleasure" (2:276–77). Mackay agrees:

> No musty record can the curious trace,
> Engross'd by annals of the savage race:
> Involv'd in darkness their atchievements [sic] lay
> Till fam'd Columbus sought a western way.
>
> The Antiquarian here may search in vain
> For walls erected in Severus' reign;
> Or lofty tow'rs that their declension show,
> Or cities built some thousand years ago:
> For arts and antiques visit Eastern ground,
> Here, Nature simple and sublime is found:
> Alas! the human, sunk in folly, stays
> 'Mong the sublime, the physical displays.
>
> (*1:37–48*)

The absence of history and antiquity that Mackay perceives in Lower Canada is evident in *Quebec Hill* as a whole in a paucity of "historical retrospection." Where Cary notices the venerable fortifications of Quebec City (*451–69*) and even records in passing a Native myth (*148–50*), Mackay finds only the "deep-dug trenches" on the Plains of Abraham and the "stone" marking the site of Wolfe's death worthy of historical note – and then primarily as a pretext for a meditation on the devastating consequences of the pursuit of "Martial Fame" (*2:177–98*). Perceiving little grist for the mill of "historical retrospection" in Lower Canada, Mackay lards his topographical poem with landscape description and "incidental meditation" aimed, like the assertion of the absence of vis-

ible history, at dispossessing the landscapes and inhabitants of Lower
Canada of most of the claims to admiration that they might possess.

It is typical of Mackay's harsh perspective on Lower Canada in particular and human life in general that he observes a lack of picturesque
beauty on the Plains of Abraham ("no cultur'd field is seen, / No rural
hamlet variegates the scene" [*1:199–200*]), and uses the Plains instead
as a setting for the exercise of his favourite perceptual and rhetorical
gambit: the presentation of a deceptive appearance followed by the dis-
closure of an unpleasant reality. "Here oft the covey rests secure from
foes," he writes, quickly adding that the birds' security is merely a short-
lived dream because "A distant grove conceals the artful swain, / Who
... takes his deadly aim, / And pours his thunder on the trembling
game" (*1:201–06*). Elsewhere in the poem nature itself in the form of
Niagara Falls deceives, not merely birds, but also "fishes" and "savage
beasts," all of whom are dragged to their destruction in a cataract that
Mackay sees less as a source of sublime awe than as a reminder of the
grave danger that ensues when "control" and "thought" give way to
carelessness and passion (*1:93–122*). No wonder that in describing
"The rising mist [that] obscures the face of day" at the foot of Niagara
Falls (*1:105*) Mackay again alludes to Milton's Satan and, in his description as a whole, adds a moral dimension to his sources in Kalm (Bartram 79–94) and Thomson ("Summer" *590–606*). In *Quebec Hill*, as in
Abram's Plains, the landscapes of Canada are permeated with the topographical poet's "controlling moral vision" (Foster 403) – in Mackay's
case an almost obsessive and stereotypically Augustan vision that values
reason over passion and governance over freedom.

Given his temperamental preferences, it is entirely predictable that
the Lower Canadian landscapes most admired by Mackay are those that
reveal the highest degree of imposed order: the built environment of
Quebec City and the "verdant" (*1:147,268*) islands of Montreal and
Orleans. Mackay's attraction to the Île d'Orléans is particularly understandable in view of Kalm's description of it as "well cultivated ... [with]
nothing but fine houses of stone, large corn-fields, meadows, pastures,
woods of deciduous trees, and some churches built of stone" (2:332).
Here is an "Enchanting prospect," a "sweetly varied ... rural scene" of
"smiling plenty" that even the curmudgeonly Mackay is moved to
describe in picturesque terms – indeed, to praise so extravagantly that,
with its "purling streams," its "tuneful nightingale," and its "shady
grove" (*1:269–86*), it comes to resemble a paradisal garden, a *locus amoe-
nus* (Curtius 195–200; Rosenmeyer 179–205) or a "new Eden" (Glickman 509). Using the "Here/There" direction to reflect and emphasize
the "Order in Variety" that he admires, Mackay presents the Île d'Orléans as a site of both picturesque beauty and agricultural achievement:

Here, spreads the lawn, there, bends the golden grain;
Nigh each neat cot the well-stock'd garden lies;
And waving orchards, not unfruitful, rise.
Upon the stream quick beats the noisy mill,
And well-fed cattle gambol on the hill ...

(1:276–80)

This is the "profitable beauty" valued by Cary, Goldsmith, and others as evidence of their country's growth towards economic and social maturity. To Mackay, however, it is a deceptive picture created by the distance that lends enchantment and, as such, a prime candidate for the "deconstruct[ion]" that reveals its hidden reality (Glickman 509). When examined more closely the bright vision of the Île d'Orléans reveals itself to be "commix'd with shade" (*1:218*) like everything else this side of heaven:

Tho' gay the scene, with varied foliage shows,
And, view'd from far, in richer verdure glows:
More near, is seen, the harvest-choking tare,
And pointed thistles on each hand appear;
I see by orchards, crabs for apples borne,
And greedy locusts blast the springing corn.

(1:289–94)

Where distance had shown picturesque variety and agricultural plenty, proximity reveals ubiquitous blights whose biblical resonances – the "tares" of Matthew 13:24–30 and the "locusts" of Exodus 10:14–15 – confirm that there is no new Eden in Canada, but only another portion of a fallen world that must be endured, preferably in Britain.

While most of the "incidental meditation" in *Quebec Hill* has a derisive and moralistic thrust that is aimed at uncovering the pitfalls of life in general and especially life in Canada, the poem contains a number of speculative passages that reveal a scientific side to Mackay's personality, an interest in various northern phenomena of a perplexing or uncanny nature. One such phenomenon is the freezing of the ocean by the "northern winds" *(1:81)* in the North Atlantic near Greenland. Possibly taking as his points of departure Carver's speculation that the severe Canadian winters were caused by the "unit[ing]" of winds along the Great Lakes-St. Lawrence River system (77–79) and Thomas James's account of the "infinite Multiplication of Ice" in Hudson Bay (55–56), Mackay offers the following description of the action of the "northern winds" on the "mighty oceans":

Now link'd together, howling, they rush forth
To where, as yet, the agitated main
Disowns the bonds that Greenland's shores enchain:
A while, the ocean, mindful on defence,
With shifting billows blunts the cold intense:
Its surface thicken'd by the chill around,
More heavy, sinks into the depth profound;
And, as the billows from the wind recede,
Still warmer draughts the empty space pervade:
But when, in course, the waters all ascend,
And all confess the action of the wind,
More slow the surface from the blast recedes,
The cold the action of tide impedes,
The restless floods become a solid plain,
And frigid fetters bind the torpid main.

(*2:88–102*)

As verse, this passage confirms Mackay's suspicion that his "Poem might have been rendered ... more poetical, if less attention had been paid to veracity" (preface *15–17*); but it is largely accurate and, in terms of what was popularly known about hydrography in Mackay's day, fairly sophisticated ("Frost"). Almost despite himself, Mackay allows his didactic intent temporarily to disappear, albeit gradually to reassert itself in subsequent and horrified descriptions of the ability of the intense cold to "pervade each scene" of Canadian life and to freeze to death the "careless ... wand'rer" (*2:103–24*) as gruesomely as it does the famous "Swain" in Thomson's "Winter" (*276–321*). It is an index of the difference of temperament and purpose between Cary and Mackay that the earlier poet depicts a "trav'ller" deriding "Tales of Europeans lost in snow" as he "stalks secure o'er hills" on his snow-shoes (*560–63*) and the latter describes in forensic detail the reduction of his "wand'rer" to a "frozen corse, / That lies, perhaps, unheeded in the snow, / Till weeping thaws the hidden spot disclose."

Another northern phenomenon that evidently intrigued Mackay was the appearance of the mountains to the north shore of the St. Lawrence. As if in contradiction of the perspectival principle of minification (distant objects appear smaller), these mountains appear both larger and more distant when stripped of their frequent cloud-cover:

Unveil'd, the mountains show their lofty heads,
Which form a contrast to the humble meads:
Save, that, from far, the intervening space,
Th' unequal swellings of their sides deface;

That, richly cloth'd, in colours of the air,
Increas'd in size, and more remote appear.
(*1:319–24*)

Some of the most bizarre phenomena chronicled by Barry Lopez in *Arctic Dreams: Imagination and Desire in a Northern Landscape* are precisely of the sort described by Mackay in this passage: tricks or changes in the perception of distance that can occur in the North under certain atmospheric conditions. Writing in the empirical tradition that stems from Newton's *Opticks* and Locke's *Essay on Human Understanding*, Mackay knew that distances cause a perceived degradation in distinctness ("from far, the intervening space, / ... [the mountains'] sides deface"). He also knew that on a clear day the break-up of sunlight into prismatic colours ("colours of the air") by the surface of the mountains would make them seem greater in magnitude than he knew them to be ("increas'd in size"). Add to this his likely knowledge of refraction, which had been observed in northern latitudes to make distant objects seem closer on an overcast day or during fog and farther away ("more remote") on days that were sunny and clear (see James 89–90), and it is not difficult to understand the paradox that Mackay addresses: under certain conditions in Canada, mountains can defy the principles of perspective by appearing *both* bigger and farther away than they really are. In this instance, what has been "Unveil'd" is a source of wonderment rather than dismay, the basis for a thoughtful "scientific ... excursus" (Aubin 86) rather than the occasion for a moralistic excoriation.

To judge by reviews and excerpts in the periodicals of the day, one of the most popular books in Britain in the winter of 1796–97 when *Quebec Hill* made its appearance (Bentley, intro. xxxv–xxxvi) was Samuel Hearne's *A Journey from Prince of Wales's Fort, in Hudson's Bay, to the Northern Ocean* (1795). Perhaps Mackay wrote and published his poem in an attempt to capitalize on the popularity of Hearne's book, which, like *Quebec Hill*, offered Canada to its original British readers as an exotic "realm remote" inhabited by strange animals and war-like Natives. If so, however, he relied for his information about Canada, not on Hearne, but on Kalm and Carver, either or both of whom might have been in his mind when he wrote, near the beginning of *Quebec Hill*,

Oft have I heard Columbian climes pourtray'd,
And oft the dangers of the mazy shade,
In early youth, when, by the rural blaze,
The traveller told the tale of other days:
With him explor'd the wide-extending wood,
Or climb'd the hill, or cross'd the copious flood:

Now to these days faint memory refers,
As realiz'd th' ideal scene appears.
                    (*1:23–30*)

Was Mackay regaled with accounts of Canada by Kalm or Carver? The answer will probably never be known, but the evidence of *Quebec Hill* suggests that when he wrote the poem he had at his disposal more than a "faint memory" of their particular "tale[s] of other days." It suggests that he had their *Travels* close at hand when he composed his poem and, in many places, did little more than render those portions of their "tales" that suited his purposes into decasyllabic couplets whose form and diction owe large debts to Pope, Goldsmith, Milton, and Thomson. Nor is such a combination of "traveller[s]" and poets untypical in the longer poems about Canada from the eighteenth and nineteenth centuries; Cary's use of Carver and Pope is another example of this practice that has already encountered. If a typical compositional setting for *Quebec Hill, Abram's Plains,* and most of their successors in the Canadian continuity were to be envisaged, it would reveal the poet with some engaging travel accounts open to his left and some admired English poems open to his right. This is the primal scene, the site of the verbal intercourse which, in Cornwall Bayley's phrase, "Gives birth to song" on Canada (*Canada 34*; and see Bentley, "Isaac Weld").

4 Cornwall Bayley, *Canada*

On 26 July 1804 the *Quebec Gazette* reported the recent arrival at the port of Quebec of the *Jane*, a vessel carrying coals from Newcastle and a single passenger, one "C. Bayley Esqr." As James and Ruth Talman have long-since established, this passenger was Cornwall Bayley, a student until "Easter 1804" at Christ's College, Cambridge (Peile 11:351, qtd. in Talman 13), and the author of a "little volume" of verse, *Canada. A Descriptive Poem, Written at Quebec, 1805. With Satires – Imitations – and Sonnets,* which was printed in Quebec by John Neilson in late March or early April 1806 (Bentley, intro. to *Canada* xi, xli–xliii). In the advertisement to this volume, Bayley describes himself as "a Youth ... almost ... a School-boy" (*5, 6*). In fact when *Canada. A Descriptive Poem* was published, Bayley was twenty-two years of age and not long for this world. In October 1806 he returned to England, where he died in November 1807 of the tuberculosis that may have brought him to Canada in search of a healthier climate. "The air of Canada is reckoned the most salubrious and healthy of any in the world," observes Thomas Anburey (1:152), and as Bayley himself writes, echoing Thomson's "Winter" (*694–743*),

> with a keener air the biting North,
> Parent of health and pleasure rushes forth;
> His powers the frame invigorated speak,
> Brace every nerve and flush in every cheek!
> (*301–04*)

Bayley's movements between his arrival in Quebec in July 1804 and his return to England in October 1806 are impossible to follow with precision. From some of the miscellaneous poems in the *Canada* volume, it is evident that he spent part of his time at some remove from "the biting North" in New York and Philadelphia. Like (and perhaps because of) Thomas Moore, he may have found in the latter city a congenial group of friends in the circle surrounding Joseph Dennie, an ardently anti-democratic "ultra-conservative" (Eldridge 54) who, in Moore's words, combined a "love of literature ... [with] sound politics" (*Poetical Works* 122 n. 3). Certainly Bayley's political and religious beliefs – his hostility to Jeffersonian democracy, for example, and his hatred of free-thinkers and Atheists (the terms were almost synonymous at the time) such as Voltaire and "Columbia's serpent [Thomas] Paine" (*181f.*) – accord closely with those of both Moore and the Dennie circle. (Among the other members of the circle were Joseph Hopkinson, the author of "Hail Columbia," and Thomas Green Fessenden or "Christopher Caustic," the author of several satirical attacks on the principles and proponents of democracy.) On 31 August 1805 the literary periodical founded and edited by Dennie – the *Port Folio* – published Moore's "Lines Written on Leaving Philadelphia" ("Alone by the Schuylkill a wanderer rov'd, / And bright were its flowery banks to his eye" [*Poetical Works* 119]), a lyric loudly echoed in "Lines Written on the Banks of the Skullkill" ("Whilst a stranger I wander afar from the shores") in the miscellaneous section of the *Canada* volume. And between 15 February and 20 September 1806 the *Port Folio* played host to several groups of Bayley's poems, the first under a note stating that "they were all written before his 21st year, and many of them before his 16th." It is as intriguing to wonder whether Moore was Bayley's introduction to the Dennie circle as it is to speculate that the Irish poet pointed his young disciple towards the principal prose sources of *Canada:* Weld's *Travels* and Charlevoix's *Journal of a Voyage to North-America* (1744; trans. 1761 f.).

In concert with the autumnal setting of "Lines Written on the Banks of the Skullkill," the date attached by Bayley to the first group of his poems in the *Port Folio* – "Quebec, Dec. 24., 1805" – indicates that he returned from the United States to Lower Canada sometime in the fall or early winter of that year. The debts of Bayley's descriptions of the Great Lakes in *Canada* to Weld and other written sources such as Thomas Campbell's *The Pleasures of Hope* do not suggest that he travelled either to or from the United States in Moore's footsteps; more likely he used the popular and easier St. Lawrence-Lake Champlain-Hudson River route. In any case, his presence in Lower Canada during much of the winter of 1805–06 is confirmed by several other pieces of information. Between 23 December and 14 April he found in Cary's *Quebec Mer-*

cury a sympathetically conservative outlet for four poems whose subjects have echoes or equivalents in *Canada*. Two of these – an attack an Napoleon (23 December) and a celebration of Nelson's victory at Trafalgar (27 January) – were submitted to the newspaper from Quebec City. The other two – an elegy "Occasioned by the Death of Dr. R. Jones, of Montreal" (30 December) and a tribute to the women of Montreal entitled "The Montreal Nosegay" (21 April) – were submitted from Montreal. These differences of subject-matter and location are the consequence of Bayley's relationship with the daughter of the prominent Montreal doctor, poet, and man of letters, whose death in December 1805 called forth the first poem in English to be described as "Canadian poetry" (Bentley, "Specimen"). On 18 May 1806 Bayley married Helen Eliza Jones in Montreal, and she is beyond doubt the "MISS _____" to whom *Canada* is affectionately dedicated, as well as the person whose name is elided in the poem's concluding lines (*505–08*). A presentation copy of *Canada* in the Toronto Reference Library contains the following inscription in what must be Bayley's handwriting: "Miss Helen Eliza Jones from the author of this poem and of all her happiness and glory. Long may he reign over her!" The likelihood that Bayley moved to Montreal to be near Miss Jones shortly before or after placing *Canada* with his printer in Quebec on 14 March 1806 (Bentley, intro. xli–xlii) may account for the fact that "he had not an opportunity of correcting" the poem in proof (advertisement 7–8).

The Cambridge that Bayley attended with distinction for two years prior to coming to Canada (Talman; Axon, Appendix 2) was a university polarized by religious and scientific explanations of "the Mosaic deluge ... the method by which the earth had been created, and ... the significance and meaning of fossils, particularly those species now extinct" (Garland 54). This was a Cambridge under the "guidance of William Paley," whose *Natural Theology; or Evidences of the Existence and Attributes of the Deity Collected from the Appearances of Nature* (1802 f.) was an immensely influential contribution on the Christian side of the debate against the "skepticism of the French *philosophes*" and their disciples (Garland 68, 53). That Paley is explicitly mentioned in *Canada* (*95 n.*, 25), as are Voltaire, Shaftesbury, and other "Deistical writers" (*228 n.*), hints at the poem's continuation of Cambridge debates on Canadian soil and throws into relief the extent to which Bayley attempts through natural theology to reconcile religious "Revelation" with scientific "reason" (*95 n.*), particularly in his account of the origins and history of the flora, fauna, and Native peoples of North America.

The first hint of theological arguments to come in *Canada* appears in the "Plan of the Poem," where the title given to the section on Canada's flora and fauna – "The animal and vegitable productions of the Country" (7) – echoes the title of the equivalent chapter in a work by one of the principal heirs of the French Enlightenment in the United States: "Productions Mineral, Vegitable and Animal" in *Notes on the State of Virginia* (1785 f.) by Thomas Jefferson. Prominent among the "animal ... productions" of Canada in the body of the poem is the mammoth, a creature numbered among the animals of Virginia by Jefferson and believed by his critics to be the product of a credulous and atheistic imagination. "Mr. Jefferson ... has discovered another *Big-boned animal*," wrote one such critic in the *Port Folio* on 15 July 1805; "it is said to be larger than the universe, and to drink forty oceans at a swallow." Bayley's description of the mammoth is similar in tone, but resonant with echoes of the biblical Leviathan and Behemoth in Job 40:20,23 ("Behold, he drinketh up a river.") and *Paradise Lost 8:412–16, 470–72* ("Hugest of Living Creatures") that align it with the Christian account of creation:

> The Mammoth, hugest in the brutal train,
> Tow'r'd to the sky, and stalk'd across the plain,
> Drank the discolor'd river from it's bed,
> And shook the mountains at his every tread.
>
> (*51–54*)

This is a joke at Jefferson's expense, but it is softened by Bayley's acknowledgment through allusion that, according to the Bible, such elephant-like creatures as the mammoth and the behemoth did once exist. More than merely a set-piece "from the family of Aikin" (a phrase applied to an anonymous description of Canada's scenery and inhabitants in the *Port Folio* 5 [6 April 1805]: 102), Bayley's account of "The animal and vegitable productions of the Country" is a complex exercise in natural theology that puts the reader on the alert for evidence of a providential design in the appearances of nature.

In the lines surrounding his portrait of the mammoth Bayley presents the emergence of plants, animals, and, finally, the Native peoples in Canada in terms analogous to the biblical creation and its unhappy aftermath. In the beginning there was a "long and dreary night [of] ... / Chaos" where the St. Lawrence now flows (*37–42*). Then there were plants such as the "Cedar" and the "Maple" (*43–46*) and – on the "lengthen'd shore" that appeared after the subsidence of the Flood – animals such as the "Bear" and the "Elk" whose presence in both Asia and North America was construed by many Christian apologists as proof of the migration to the New World of animals originating in Noah's ark (*47–54*; Brerewood 97–98; Robertson 2:36). It may even be that Bayley's catalogue includes the mammoth – remains of which had recently been discovered in both Asia and North America – as further evidence of the view "so agreeable to reason, and so essential to Revelation " (*95 n.*) that "the two Continents [were] ... once united" and, hence, that the animals of Canada are the distant and environmentally unfortunate descendants of creatures put ashore on Mount Ararat. Very definitely the inhabitants of a cruel, post-lapsarian world are the vicious and destructive creatures that comprise most of the remainder of Bayley's Canadian bestiary: "The murd'rous Wolf that whelms his soul in blood ... / The Fox that lurks in ambush for his prey," and "The pilfering band of Squirrels dark'ning day" (59–62). Least attractive of all is the Rattle Snake – "the crested snake," "Sole suicide save man ... / Rattl[ing] her folds" – which comes trailing clouds of infamy from *Paradise Lost* ("Fold above fold ... [the serpent's] Head / Crested aloft" [*9:499–500*]) and supported by a note proclaiming its supposed suicidal tendencies: "The Rattle Snake has been known to bite *itself* when in danger" (*55–56* and *n.*). Only the nondescript "Otter" and the provident "Beaver" escape Bayley's opprobrium (*57–58, 60*), and perhaps he intended the parsimoniousness of the latter to be seen as a prudent response to a harsh environment and a fallen world.

Such were the "undisputed tyrants" of the "forest" (*64–65*) until the arrival of the ancestors of Canada's Native peoples – "savage hordes; / ... rushing from afar, / With brethren clans to wage eternal war!" (*66–68*). That these "clans" were migrants from Asia with demonic characteristics is indicated by the word "hordes," which refers specifically to "tribes of roving Tartars" (Bayley 24), and by the allusion to Satan's resolve to "wage by force or guile eternal War" in *Paradise Lost (1:121)*. That they were nomads at the lowest level of social development is further shown by their "light tents" and their indifference to "sex" (*66–67*), a quality attributed by the French naturalist Buffon to an innate lack of "sexual capacity" and by the more enlightened Jefferson to a diminution of sexual ardour through overexposure – to a blunting familiarity consequent on the fact that in nomadic societies "women very frequently attend ... the men in their parties of war and hunting" (58–60; and see Robertson 2:65 f.). As he attempts at various points in *Canada* to explain the origins and characteristics of the Native peoples in a manner consistent with both "reason" and "Revelation," Bayley relies heavily on what Bruce G. Trigger calls "degenerationism" or the "theory of degeneration" (*Natives* 51, 406): the theory that, as Noah's progeny "separate[d] and ... spread themselves ... over the whole earth" (Charlevoix 1:47) after the "*confusion of tongues*" described in Genesis 11 (Bayley 24), they became degenerate in proportion to the harshness of their environment and their distance in space and time from their origin. (The application of the same theory to the other passengers on the ark probably accounts for Bayley's dark view of many of Canada's animals.) As the lengthy note "on the subject of the origin of native Americans" that Bayley appended to *Canada* makes clear, the degeneration of people in inhospitable environments far removed from the cradle of civilization in Mesopotamia took place in all spheres, from "manners and customs" to language and religion: "Superstition would naturally creep into their religious ceremonies; the climate and local circumstances of the regions they colonized, would alter not only their manner of living, but even their bodily appearance – The loss of literature and education would corrupt their language – and the want of proper materials and opportunities would occasion that decay of arts and sciences which must finally terminate in barbarity" (24). Drawing upon a host of works both current and predictable (Carver 181–219; Robertson 2:238) and older and more obscure – including Edward Brerewood's *Enquiries Touching the Diversity of Languages and Religions, through the Chief Parts of the World* (1614) and Edward Stillingfleet's *Origines Sacrae; or, a Rational Account of the Grounds of Christian Faith ...* (1662) – Bayley uses the "theory of degeneration" as the cement, not just between "reason" and "Revelation," but also between the four stages theory and the biblical version of human history.

When Bayley focuses his attention on a representative "wild Indian" of his own day – a variant of the "poor Indian" of Pope's *Essay on Man* (*1:99–112*) – he sees a savage hunter-warrior who, while driven by the stereotypical passions of "Rage" (*81*) and a desire for "Revenge" (*79*), nevertheless displays certain physical, mental, and spiritual qualities that indicate the residual presence of his original, Mesopotamian culture:

> Mark yon wild Indian, leaning on his bow,
> Fatigue and labour streaming from his brow;
> Ev'n in his wild and undomestic state,
> In form superior and in reason great!
> Mark how the hand of Fashion or of Pride
> In barbarous custom decorates his side;
> Mark the snow-sandals that support his tread,
> The crown of Feathers waving o'er his head ...
> (*69–76*)

Since Bayley suggests elsewhere in *Canada* that while Native peoples have no written history and ancient architecture (*35–36, 454–55*, 24), they do possess the degenerate vestiges of ancient thought and biblical religion ("the phantoms of a purer creed / That worships Heav'n in *spirit* as in deed" [*109–110*]), it may also be that in describing the Indian's snow-shoes as "snow-*sandals*" and his headdress as a "*crown* of Feathers" he intended these things, and perhaps the Indian's "bow" as well, to be recognized as the distant descendants of items developed in the cradles of civilization and referred to in the Old Testament. When viewed sympathetically, as Bayley clearly intended, Canada's Native peoples evidently possess, not only admirable physical and mental qualities ("form superior and ... reason great"), but also certain "virtues" of character such as "Contempt of danger, and contempt of pain" (*87–88*) that bear the imprint of something "nobler" and immortal:

> Yes here are form'd the mouldings of a soul,
> Too great for ease, too lofty for controul;
> A soul, which ripen'd by refinement's hand,
> Had scatter'd wisdom thro' its native land;
> A soul, which Education might have given
> To earth an honor – and an heir to Heaven!"
>
> (*89–94*)

Bayley's "wild Indian" is "nobler" than he might first appear, but he is not a noble savage whose claim to admiration resides in his natural condition, his freedom from the taint of civilization. On the contrary, his admirable qualities are the residue of original civilization and would have been strengthened, not corrupted, by "refinement" and "Education."

Fortunately for the benighted Native peoples of Canada, Bayley suggests, the process of restoring them to a higher level of social development is already well underway. Thanks to the efforts and sufferings of "French Missionaries" (7) in Canada, the "endless bloodshed" and deliberate cruelty characteristic of "savage race[s]" has been replaced by Christian worship and "mutual love" (*125–132*). "The darted tomahawk" has yielded its tribute "to agriculture's throne" and "The war whoop's echoes and the slave's sad throes / Are hush'd in music, pleasure, and repose!" (*133–136*). But, while French colonization did to a great extent uncover the "Sun of Science" (or knowledge) that had been clouded over for the Native peoples by degeneration (*111–116*), the task is incomplete and continuing. With the British conquest came the institutions – British law, British freedom, the *pax Britannica* – that promise the full enlightenment and redemption of Canada's inhabitants, both Native and French. At the head of an army that brought peace with a sword, that "conquer[ed] but to save," Wolfe was the Christ-like harbinger of a new dispensation of "mercy" and "justice" for all in Lower Canada (*151–52*). Although a monument has yet to be built to his memory, Wolfe's spirit "still ... hovers o'er [Quebec's] walls" (*177–78*) and, as an allusion to Nelson's death in (and on) another

"Vict'ry" implies (*175*), over all Britain's military endeavours. It was Wolfe's guiding spirit that inspired the victorious resistance to the invasion of Canada in 1775–76 by treacherous and parricidal rebels, the serpentine and satanic American cousins of Voltaire, Robespierre, and their likes. It is Wolfe's example that "Albion's sons" (*180*) must emulate again if they are to defeat Napoleon and "stay the flood" that, in a vicious violation of God's promise to Noah in Genesis 9:9–17, "Strives to overwhelm the world" (*246*). To Britain has passed sole responsibility for beating back the deluge of darkness that, in the wake of the so-called Enlightenment, has engulfed vast portions of Europe and North America.

As should now be abundantly clear the "moral vision" that drives all the "historical meditation" and "incidental meditation" in *Canada* is as deeply Christian as it is conservative. Nowhere is this more obvious than in Bayley's perception of the French-Canadian culture whose "innocent manners" (7) and simple piety are pre-lapsarian to the extent that they derive from pre-revolutionary France and remain "guiltless" (*249*) of the crimes against God and man perpetrated in contemporary France and America. Agreeing with Anburey (1:66–67) and Weld (1:370–71, 415) that Lower Canada is free of religious animosity and "persecution" (*385–86*), Bayley is prompted by his pristine vision of Canadian culture to contradict the Irish traveller on at least two counts. Where Weld had seen occasional abuses of the seigneurial system by men of "rapacious disposition" (1:400–01), Bayley finds none (*387–396*); and where Weld had found much evidence that French-Canadians are given to "vanity," especially in the driving and decoration of their "carioles or sledges" (1:338–39, 392; 2:4,9), Bayley huffily disagrees: "His neat Calash (himself the artist) made, / For use and pleasure – not for vain parade" (*403–04*). Like Weld and numerous other Protestant writers such as Kalm and Cary, Bayley faults Roman Catholicism in Canada on two counts: "superstition" (*491*) – a belief in sacred images and like matters that runs contrary to reason; and "the vestal's solitary lot" (*484*) – the cloistered virtue of the nun that goes against nature and God by denying sexual pleasure and fertility (*496; Abram's Plains 373–96*). But while registering Weld's "tender sentiments" (Lambert 1:473) concerning one of the Ursulines at Trois Rivières who had come "to lament the rashness of that vow which had secluded her from ... participation ... [in] those innocent pleasures, which ... the beneficent Ruler of the universe meant ... his creatures should enjoy" (2:14; see *489–96*), Bayley emphasizes the charitable and artistic works of the nuns: their care of the sick and the poor at the Hôpital Général in Quebec (*479–82*) and their creation of "bark-work" curios for sale to tourists at Trois Rivières (Weld 2:16–17; *483–88*).

In Bayley's generous assessment there is neither grinding poverty nor excessive luxury in Lower Canada. Nor are there "brothels ... taverns" and gambling houses to cater to the Hogarthean vices found in England and Europe (*457–64*). The city of Quebec is a site of "order'd rest" whose principal building beside the General Hospital is the Seminary (*466–82*), and the surrounding countryside is populated by prosperous and independent farmers with faithful wives and large families (*397–412*). By Bayley's reckoning the chief sources of pleasure for these people are, in winter, "the genial smile / And frequent draught" of a fireside chat with friends (*327–28*) and, in summer, "the cheerful sunshine of the breast, / The active labour and the wanted rest, / The simple song – the pipe – the rural choir, / Charms that *once* bloom'd amidst the vales of *Loire!*" (*251–54*). What else could be expected in a remnant of Old France "afar from Atheist pride, / And bigot doctrines to deceit allied" (*379–80*)?

At the conservative heart of *Canada* is a scene in which a group of amicable habitants gathers in a domestic yet inclusive "circle" around "some healthful hoary-headed sire" – evidently a one-time voyageur – who feeds their "roving fancies" with tales of his travels and adventures in the *pays d'en haut* (*333–78*). Many of the details of the voyageur's reminiscence – his happy memory of "how the well-known song inspir'd the oar" (*343*), for example, and his characterization of Lake Erie as "wild" (*356*) – probably derive from Weld (2:52, 141–47, 155–61, 296–308), as does the story-telling scenerio, for as Weld observes of a typical French-Canadian, "he delights in talking to his friends and relatives of the excursions he has made to ... distant regions; and he glories in the perils which he has encountered" (2:9). But whereas Weld interprets all this as further evidence that "the spirit of the Canadian is excited by vanity" and, moreover, as a sign of a willingness to sacrifice "every social tie" to frontier wanderlust, Bayley offers a very different and more charitable reading of the French-Canadian character. After taking his "wonder wrapt" listeners in their imagination to Niagara Falls (which, ironically, Bayley insists on pronouncing "Níagára" on the authority of Goldsmith in *The Traveller 412*), the voyageur relives his "former thoughts of these stupendous falls" (*374*). In doing so he shows himself to be, at bottom, not vain or flighty but pious and humble:

He feels how grand – how infinite the tale,
Himself how little in Creation's scale;
And still too low his maker's works to raise,
Bids more expressive silence muse his praise!
(*375–78*)

The final line of this passage is taken almost verbatim from the final line of Thomson's "Hymn to the Seasons" ("Come then, expressive Silence, muse HIS Praise"), and – true to expectations generated by the equivalent descriptions of Cary, Mackay, and Moore – the remainder of Bayley's depiction of Niagara Falls combines elements of Weld's "Description of the River and Falls of Niagara" (2:108–35) and Thomson's description of a waterfall in "Winter" (*590–98*).

A rationale for the combinations of ideas and texts that are evident in the old voyageur's account of Niagara Falls is given earlier by Bayley in terms derived from the psychology of David Hartley, whose theory of the association of ideas constitutes an important stage on the journey from Locke's empirical epistemology to Coleridge's Romantic imagination. In essence Hartley's associationism, as expounded in his *Observations on Man* (1749 f.), is a systematic elaboration of Locke's conception of the human mind as a *tabula rasa* or "empty cabinet" (*Essay* 1:48) onto or into which impressions of the external world are conveyed by the senses, especially the sense of sight. Once stored in the memory, these discrete and simple "ideas of sensation" are connected together – associated – like links in a chain to form "complex and abstract" "ideas of reflection" (Priestley, *Hartley's Theory* xxxvii). Remembering Niagara Falls, an old voyageur thinks of God; thinking of an old voyageur – or Weld – reduced to silence by thoughts of God, Bayley remembers the conclusion of Thomson's "Hymn to the Seasons." Since Bayley was university educated, it is more than likely that he was acquainted with the *Observations on Man,* either in the original or in *Hartley's Theory of the Human Mind,* a popular digest with introductory essays by Joseph Priestley (a member until his death in February 1804 of the Dennie Circle). In any case Hartley's definition of the "imagination" or "fancy" in the following passage appears to have dictated the gist of the ensuing lines from *Canada:*

When ideas, and trains of ideas, occur, or are called up, in a vivid manner, and without regard to the order of former actual impressions and perceptions, this is said to be done by the power of *imagination* or *fancy.* (Priestley iii)

> Yet still the mind – imagination's cell –
> On scenes, which pall the senses, loves to dwell –
> Calls up reflection's ever-roving train –
> Links every thought in one successive chain,
> And as those thoughts in Fancy's realms we lose
> Gives birth to song, and consecrates the Muse!
>
> (*29–34*)

Elsewhere Hartley writes of the superiority of the "pleasures of the imagination," which "do not cloy [Bayley's word is 'pall'] very soon," over "sensible ones" such as those derived from "a beautiful scene" or "the beauties of nature in general," and, of course, he frequently resorts to the mechanistic metaphor of a "chain" with "connecting links" to describe the process of association (Priestley 255–57 and, for example, 22).

Bayley's belief that poetry is the product of the association of ideas is enacted at the outset of *Canada* in his description of the "view from Cape Diamond" (7). This phrase, like several other words and ideas from the opening lines of the poem – including Bayley's account of the sensory bewilderment and optical minification that occur when looking down at Quebec City and the St. Lawrence from a great height – derive from Weld's detailed descriptions of the views from Cape Diamond and elsewhere in his *Travels.* "Nature is here seen on the grandest scale," writes Weld; "the senses are almost bewildered in contemplating the vastness of the scene ... [I]f you stand but a few yards from the edge of the precipice, you may look down at once upon the river, the vessels upon which, if they sail up to the wharfs before the lower town, appear as if they were coming under your very feet" (1:354–56). Evidently Weld's description called up in Bayley's mind two somewhat similar texts: Edgar's putative account of the view from Dover Cliffs in *King Lear* ("How fearful / And dizzy 'tis to cast one's eyes so low! / The crows and choughs that wing the midway air / Show scarce so gross as beetles" [*3.6.11–24*]) and Johnson's comment on Edgar's speech to the effect that (to quote Bayley's footnote) "He who looks from a Precipice – finds himself assailed by one dreadful idea of irresistable destruction – but this overwhelming reflection is dissipated from the moment the faculties become collected – and the mind can diffuse it's attention to minute objects" (*1 n.*). Augmented by materials from *Paradise Lost* ("th' ascent of that steep savage Hill" [*4:172*]), the Bible ("and [they] led him unto the brow of the hill whereon the city was built, that they might cast him down headlong" [Luke 4:29]), Pope ("all reason's laws" [*Satires 5:117*]) and, no doubt, elsewhere, the passages from Weld, Shakespeare, and Johnson were linked by Bayley's mind "in one successive chain" – the opening lines of *Canada:*

> How steep th' ascent! how fearful from the brow
> Projecting thus, to mark the gulf below!
> Ev'n now the falt'ring strand appears to sink –
> My feet recoil with horror from the brink!
> One startling word might hurl the fleeting breath,
> Wafted in midway air, to realms of Death;

One more – one sudden glance – half snatch'd – would seem
Inevitable fate! – – Tis Fancy's dream –
And 'tis but for a moment! Reason's laws
Return, collected, from the transient pause;
A thousand charms the raptur'd soul employ,
And fear itself is overwhelm'd in joy.

(*1–12*)

The gift on display in the opening lines of *Canada* is primarily that of arranging words and ideas from elsewhere within decasyllabic couplets; however the passage just quoted also displays Bayley's skill at modulating the pace of his lines to reflect movements and pauses in the internal and external worlds: "One move – one sudden glance – half snatch'd – would seem / Inevitable fate ... Reason's laws / Return, I collected, I from the transient pause." This last line in particular shows that, like Mackay and Cary before him, Bayley has learned from Pope that "The *Sound* must seem an Echo to the *Sense*" and that a poetic utterance should "breathe, I or pause, I by fits" (*The Dunciad 2:362*) according to the demands of its subject-matter. It is an index of Bayley's mimetic skills and limitations that he uses the same "pause"/pause device twice more in *Canada*, once to describe a frozen waterfall ("The mountain torrents by the frost's control / Arrested pause, – " [*307–08*]) and once to describe the cessation of activity during winter ("Ev'n animation seems to pause!" [*315*]). Bayley's poetic repertoire is limited, but in places he does mange to convey a vivid sense of the shapes and sounds of Lower Canada, a further case in point being his use of repeated caesuras to mimic the contours of smoke issuing, as it were, reluctantly, from a chimney in winter: "Its vagrant smoke the cottage chimney hurls, I Shrinks from the cold, and, I as it issues, I curls" (*311–12*). The tension between centrifugal and centripetal verbs placed skilfully at the end and the beginning of a line ("hurls, / Shrinks") also contributes to the success of this vignette.

Bayley's carefully staged movement from a negative ("fearful") to a positive ("joy[ful]") response to the "view from Cape Diamond" in the opening lines of *Canada* may be explicable merely in terms of the combination of terror and pleasure associated with the sublime, or it may be a further reflection of Hartlean associationism that has extensive ramifications for the structure and content of the poem as a whole. One of Hartley's principal concerns in the *Observations on Man* is with the process by which the feelings of "pleasure and pain" that can accompany simple sensations of the natural world and other phenomena gradually give rise through accretive association to complex sensations of right and wrong, obligation and selfishness, God's goodness to man and – when things go badly awry – "superstition or atheism" (Priestley, *Hartley's Theory* 252, 325). For this chain of reflection to work properly – that is, to result in a "rational self interest" and, beyond that, in a love of God (Priestley 299) – there has to emerge a preference for the complex over the simple, the pleasurable over the painful. Hartley could almost be discussing the opening lines of *Canada* when he describes an early stage of the process at work in his analysis of "the pleasures arising from the contemplation of the beauties of the natural world": "if there be a precipice ... in one part of the scene, the nascent ideas of fear and horror magnify and enliven all the other ideas, and by degrees pass into pleasure, by suggesting the security from pain" (Priestley 252–53). Indeed when Hartley asserts that "grandeur," "novelty," and "uniformity and variety in conjunction" are the "principal sources of the pleasures of beauty" that lead from a contemplation of nature to a recognition of God's "bounty and benignity" (Priestley 252–53,323), he could be providing the programme for Bayley's entire prospect, which moves outwards from Cape Diamond to survey "All that Creation's rural sceptre yields," from "The bloom of vales" to "Alps on Alps" (*20–29*). It may even be that Hartley's extensive discussions of the "pleasures and pains of imagination, self-interest, sympathy, theosophy and the moral sense" (Priestley 250) provided Bayley with the idea of structuring *Canada* as a series of contrasts between the painfully negative and pleasingly positive trains of thought that are called to mind by a contemplation of Canada's physical and social landscapes (see, for example, *35–130, 131–88, 189–246*, and *247–412*). Certainly Bayley's pained catalogue of the follies and vices of Europe that he fondly thinks are absent from Canada and his "pleas'd" (*471*) surveys of the evidence of communal service, religious devotion, and artistic creativity that he sees in the country have precise equivalents in Hartley (Priestley 285–89). So, too, does his concluding conviction that "active virtue" (*494*) and physical beauty are combined in the "seraph forms" of such Canadian women as Helen Eliza Jones, who have it in their "power ... / To waken rapture or excite despair," to make life either "an endless feast" or "one continual waste" (*503–16*). Intent as he was on reconciling the natural with the supernatural, Bayley may have drawn special solace from Hartley's conviction that "beauty of ... person" in the "female sex" can "moderate, spiritualize, and improve" the "gross sensual [pleasures]" of sexual attraction, ultimately converting them, "in the virtuous," to the higher pleasures of "mutual love," pure "esteem," and "religious affection" (Priestley 269–70). In any event it seems clear that, either directly or indirectly, the *Observations on Man* influenced Bayley's conception of the mind's workings and the origin of poetry, as well as, possibly, the structure (and part of the content) of *Canada*.

In the final analysis it is not the heavenly beauty of "Canada's daughters" (*516*), nor even the pristine piety of the French-Canadian population, that allows Bayley in the concluding paragraphs of his poem to envisage a golden future for Canada; it is the fact that, since 1759, Canada has been the recipient of the best that the Old World has to offer in the form of British law, British refinement, and, above all, British "Freedom" (*420, 422, 432–33*). During ancient Roman times the enemy of "peace and science" (*418*), Britain is now Rome's enlightened successor – the bearer among "savage tribes" and "dreary scenes[s]" (*422–23*) of the peace and freedom long ago "exile[d]" (*433*) from Rome herself. As the paragons of British civilization in Canada, Bayley selects for the kind of praise that smacks of self-interest two members of the colonial élite: William Grant, an "aggressive member ... of the British bourgeoisie at Quebec" (David Roberts 274) whose "hand industrious" and "assiduous taste" were evident on his several properties in Lower Canada (280–82; and see Oliver 62); and Sir Alexander MacKenzie, a member of the Lower Canadian House of Assembly from 1804 to 1808, and earlier, of course, the "one exalted mind" that had explored "Millions of regions undescried by man; / Circling the globe from wide Atlantic's bound, / To where Pacific meets the joining round!" (*427–30*). As the geographical symbol of the British civilization represented by Grant, MacKenzie, and others like them, Bayley selects the St. Lawrence, the river that is to post-conquest Canada what the Loire was to pre-revolutionary France and the Tiber was to ancient Rome (*421*). But while the names of these rivers, like those of the Potomac and the Hudson (*190–91*), are almost synonymous with their respective cultures, the equivalent association between the St. Lawrence and British North America does not exist and must, therefore, be established. But how?

Bayley's solution to this problem is elegant and complex, and may show the operation again of a Hartlean "chain" of thoughts. Having allowed "reflection's ever-roving train" to connect imperial Britain and imperial Rome, Bayley sees the presence of "Freedom's *spirit*" (*433*) on the St. Lawrence as a sign of the commencement of a "golden reign" in North America, a reign that recalls the first Augustan age and, with it, the "tributary strain" of various poems composed by Horace in honour of Augustus (Octavian), the emperor responsible for the *pax Romana* and for temporarily returning Rome to constitutional rule after the military dictatorship of "[Julius] Caesar" (*413–36*). Three of Horace's "tributary" poems in particular – Ode 4.2 and Epode 9 (both of which repeat the phrase "Io, Triumphe!" ["Hail! God of Triumph!"] and Ode 4.15 (which credits Augustus with restoring fertility, peace, morality and the rule of law to Rome [Horace 90–91, 386–89, 344–47]) – seem to have combined with other materials in Bayley's "fancy" to produce the opening lines of his tribute to the St. Lawrence:

> Hail then, Majestic King of rivers, hail!
> Whether amid the placid-winding vale,
> Thy waters ripen nature's every bloom;
> Or, thro' the bosom of the forest's gloom,
> Their swelling currents with resistless tide,
> Break o'er the rocks, and lash their craggy side;
> Where ere thy waves reflect the face of day,
> Wide – rich – romantic – is thy regal sway!
>
> (437–44)

In these and the remaining lines of his paean to the beginning of a new "golden reign" in Canada, Bayley metaphorically likens the St. Lawrence to a British king at his coronation, the ceremony in which the future monarch is clothed or invested with various emblematic objects such as the orb and the sceptre. In Bayley's adaptation of the process of investiture to his "regal" river, the emblematic objects of the coronation ceremony are replaced by aspects of the Canadian landscape: the "placid-winding vale" of peace, the ripening waters of "fertility," and the "swelling currents" and mirror-like surfaces of a power that is as "resistless" as it is enlightened.

When the remainder of Bayley's tribute to the St. Lawrence is read in conjunction with its footnotes referring to Sorelle and Toronto under their new English names of William Henry and York, a further level emerges from this thickly layered portion of the poem. The two princes for whom these towns were named – William Henry, Duke of Gloucester and Edinburgh and Frederick, Duke of York and Albany – were respectively the son and brother of King George III, whose troubled reign (1760–1820) began shortly after the conquest of Quebec and thus coincided with the inauguration of Bayley's golden age in Canadian history. Viewed in this light, Bayley's highly selective catalogue of the "rivers – towns and villages" (7) of the St. Lawrence serves to identify the "Majestic King of rivers" with George III himself and to cast the various places mentioned in the catalogue as princes and peers rendering homage to their new monarch after his coronation:

> Thine is Chaudiere in wild impetuous force,
> And Montmorenci's more majestic course;
> Thine are the well-nam'd Cartier's bending woods,
> And Saguenay, himself a Prince of floods;
> Thine is Chamblee that still adorns her fort,

And neat Sorelle, the princely-favor'd port;
Here Kingston tow'rs o'er vast Ontario's sheet,
Here too Toronto, now an Empire's seat;
And here impending Albion's signal plays,
O'er the rude rock from whence my fancy strays!
                                    (*445–54*)

North, south, east, and west – for these are the directions in which Bayley's "fancy strays" – the "rivers – towns and villages" of Upper and Lower Canada pay tribute to a St. Lawrence dominated, finally, by the Union Jack that flies above Cape Diamond at the "high centre" (Anderson 25) of Britain's "Empire" in North America. In *The Death of General Wolfe* West aligns the general with the "might of the British Empire" by echoing his twisted body in the "billowing curve" of the flag that towers above him (Schama 34–35). As he pauses in his survey of Canada to gaze up at "Albion's signal," Bayley aligns himself with British imperialism and confirms the subordination to George III and the annexation to Great Britain of the region that some forty years earlier Wolfe had taken by force.

Although Bayley does stray far and wide in imagination at several points in *Canada,* the principal sites of his poem lie in and around Quebec's Upper Town and "Montrèal's mountain heighth" (*283*). And where better to "look *down on* and *over*" (MacLaren, "Pastoral" 16) the landscapes and inhabitants of Canada than from the elevated nodes of British power and wealth? Today the Citadel occupies the high ground in Quebec City and Westmount is still identified with anglophone wealth in Montreal. More than a trace remains of the patterns and assumptions that produced *Canada. A Descriptive Poem, Written at Quebec, 1805.*

5 John Strachan, "Verses ... 1802"

Between the publication of *Canada* in the spring of 1806 and his return to England in the fall of that year, Bayley paid a visit to a friend in Cornwall, Upper Canada. That friend was John Strachan, later the first bishop of Toronto and the great panjandrum of the Family Compact, who had emigrated from Scotland to Kingston, Upper Canada, in 1799. In 1806 Strachan was merely an Anglican deacon and a grammar school teacher, but his commitment to Canada was already strong and vitally evident in his educational programme. "He fervently held to the idea of an educated aristocracy," observes David Flint, and "not once did he lose sight of the fact that he was training the future leaders of the country" (7, 29). In 1807 Strachan solidified his commitment to Canada and his connection with the colonial establishment by marrying Ann Wood, a Cornwall woman who had recently been widowed by the death of James McGill's brother Andrew. "My wife has an annuity of three hundred [pounds] a year," Strachan informed a friend in Scotland; "she has a great share of beauty ... and as good an education as this county could afford, which by the way is not great" (*Documents* 26).

As he was leaving Upper Canada by boat on 22 June 1806, Bayley composed a poem thanking Strachan for his hospitality and wishing him happiness and success in his pastoral, educational, and amatory endeavours. "Still mayst thou keep thy Saviour's flock," wrote Bayley; "Still may thy dawn of learning break / On thy Canadian charge," and soon "May some Corinna ... be found / To cheer thy pensive hour" (Strachan, Papers). Bayley's allusion in these last lines is not merely to the poet who, by tradition, instructed Pindar in the art of poetic composition, but also to a poem that Strachan had inscribed in a copy of

Canada three days after Bayley's marriage to Helen Eliza Jones on 18 May 1806. A tribute to the "op'ning rose" of Bayley's genius, Strachan's poem concludes with the observation that to prevent the young poet's thoughts from "o'erleap[ing] / The bounds that Taste and Nature keep / A sweet Corinna guides [his] light / Like her who chasten'd Pindar's flight" (Bentley, intro. to *Canada* xlii). As he sailed down the St. Lawrence a month later, Bayley responded to Strachan's floral compliment with an appropriate combination of modesty and flattery:

> How vainly would my youthful muse,
> Her utmost flow'rs combine,
> And sing responsive to the strain
> That emanates from thine!
> (Strachan, Papers)

Almost certainly this flattering tribute was written in the afterglow of reading Strachan's "Poetry," a manuscript collection of his own poems that Strachan "began to copy ... July 29th 1802" (Papers). Perhaps it was owing to Bayley's encouragement that in February and March 1807 Strachan published two longer poems from his manuscript collection – "An Elegy" and "The Day" – in the *Port Folio*, the Philadelphia periodical in which several of Bayley's poems had appeared in 1806.

Probably because it deals specifically with Canada, the poem in Strachan's manuscript collection that provides the most revealing view of the conception of this country that he imparted to his pupils was not published in the *Port Folio*. Written and recited when Strachan was still living in Kingston and serving as tutor to the sons of Richard Cartwright, John Stuart, and other members of the local commercial and religious élite, "Verses ... 1802" offers an interpretation of Canada's past, present, and future that loses nothing in significance for being a creation of the man who was "by far the dominant personality in Upper Canadian life until his death in 1867" (Black 26). As well as leaving his mark on various religions and educational institutions that "remain with us still in some form today" (Black 27) – most notably, perhaps, Trinity College, Toronto – Strachan's schools at Kingston, Cornwall, and, later, York (Toronto) played a major part in shaping the minds of generations of influential Upper Canadians, including John Beverley Robinson, a future attorney general and chief justice who was a pupil both in Kingston and in Cornwall (Saunders 668). That "Verses ... 1802" was recited, not by Strachan himself, but by two of his pupils – "the first 66 lines" by James Cartwright and "the remainder" by Andrew Stuart (Strachan, Papers) – may be taken as an indication of the extent to which Strachan's ideas found their way into the minds and mouths of a powerful component of Canada's ruling class.

As befits the purpose for which it was intended – oral presentation on a formal occasion with an instructional component – "Verses ... 1802" is written in the decasyllabic couplets of rational authority and cast in the mould of a classical oration. Accordingly it divides into six parts: (1) an exordium (*1–66*) treating of the prehistoric migration of the Greeks to Ionia; (2) a narration (*67–104*) dealing with recent British and Canadian history; (3) a partition (*105–12*) introducing the argument that education is crucial to Canadian culture; and (4, 5, and 6), a confirmation (*113–20*), refutation (*121–42*), and conclusion, securing, defending, and restating the educational argument (Kennedy 92–95). Of Strachan's knowledge of the parts of a classical oration and their purposes as outlined, discussed, and practised by Cicero and his ancient and modern heirs there can be little, if any, doubt. In "A Dialogue," a frequently ascerbic treatment of contemporary intellectual life modelled on Thomas James Mathias's *Pursuits of Literature* (1794–97), he refers by name to Scotland's master-teachers of classical rhetoric, Hugh Blair ("the British Quintilian") and George Campbell (Kennedy 232–41). Blair's *Lectures* on *Rhetoric and Belles Letters* (1783) contains a detailed discussion of the parts of an oration, and Campbell, whose *Philosophy of Rhetoric* appeared in *1776*, was the professor of divinity and principal of Marischal College at Strachan's *alma mater*, the University of Aberdeen. "Of all [Campbell's] productions," writes Strachan in a footnote to "A Dialogue," "I prefer his *Philosophy of Rhetoric*, a book too much neglected" (Papers). Although Strachan attended King's rather than Marischal College at Aberdeen, he was a member of the "Marischal Disputing Society, a small group of keen debaters" (Flint 11) who, indubitably, made practical use of rhetorical strategies gleaned from Cicero, Quintilian, Blair, Campbell, and elsewhere.

According to Cicero, the purpose of an exordium is to "prepare ... the audience to receive the speech" by making "each listener *benevolus, attentus, docilis*, that is, well-disposed to the speaker, attentive, and receptive" (Kennedy 92–93). In these terms the opening lines of "Verses ... 1802" might at first glance seem unlikely to have succeeded. Drawing on *The History of Herodotus* and other sources Strachan presents his pupils and, presumably, their parents and friends with a brief and speculative account of the migration of the ancient Greeks to Ionia on the western coast of Asia Minor:

Ionia's fertile fields receiv'd the hosts
Of wand'ring heroes from the Grecian coasts;
Too num'rous grown to share their native plains,

They leave their weeping friends for new domains;
The Goddess Liberty in radiant charms
Points out the way and ev'ry bosom warms.
The sister arts in gorg'ous robes array'd
With solid science tend their vig'rous aid:
Inspir'd by these, the bulwarks quickly rise;
The lofty turrets seem to meet the skies;
The temples built of Parian marble blaze,
As placid lakes reflect the Solar rays;
The alters smoke beneath the sacred grove,
And poets chant the praise of mighty Jove.

(*1–14*)

The attention-getting aspect of these and the ensuing lines resides in the unstated but evident parallel between the migration of the ancient Greeks across the Aegean Sea and the migration of modern Britons across the Atlantic Ocean. The most obvious clue to this parallel is also the most affective part of the description: the reference to "weeping friends" left behind by those leaving for "new domains." "When you read this I am on the Atlantic," Strachan told his mentor, James Brown, in August 1799; "tho' I leave my country with the greatest indifference I leave my Friends with the most sincere regret" (*Documents* 13; and see Bentley, "Breaking" 97–101). Those among Strachan's audience who were also emigrants, either from Britain or from the United States, would have done more than perceive an experiential affinity between themselves and the Ionians; they would have been prepared to recognize further parallels between their own situation in Upper Canada and that of the Ionians in Asia Minor.

Throughout his exordium Strachan uses the example of the Ionian Greeks, not merely to add heroic resonance to the experiences of his audience (and thus to secure their good-will), but also to impress upon them the great potential and high destiny of their transplanted British culture. Despite (or, perhaps, because of) their abiding nostalgia for mainland Greece (*24*), the Ionians combined the "sister arts" with their "solid science" (knowledge) to produce fortified cities and splendid "temples" in their "new domain." On the basis of a "Strong Agriculture," they created an "Adventurous Commerce" which – to quote further from the portion of Pye's *Progress of Refinement* that Strachan repeatedly echoes in his exordium – "trust[ed] her swelling sail" to "the currents of the rising gale" and brought "The wealth of nations" to their thriving colony (*1:194–200*; see also *1:157 f.*). Or as Strachan puts it,

The verdant lawns the distant prospects cheer,
And Ceres' treasures crown the passing year;
The neighbouring mountains num'rous flocks sustain,
And dales re-echo to the singing swain.

. . . .

gilded ships unfurl their swelling sails
In quest of wealth, and court the rising gales.

(15–18, 21–22)

If such achievements and progress were possible for the ancient Greeks, Strachan implies, then why not also for Upper Canadians? Surely Canada, too, is blessed with the natural bounty and mercantile opportunities necessary for the development of "Strong Agriculture" and "Adventurous Commerce"?

Before addressing these questions directly, Strachan offers his audience details of two naval and military campaigns that they were obviously intended to see as parallel: the campaigns of the ancient Greeks against the Persians in the fifth century BC, and the campaigns of Britain against France and her allies in the late eighteenth century. Just as Darius, the king of Persia from 521 to 486 BC, was defeated at Marathon in 490 BC after attempting to punish the mainland Greeks for a revolt that began in Ionia, so Louis XV, the king of France from 1715 to 1773, was defeated at Abraham's Plains, Quiberon Bay, and elsewhere in a conflict – the Seven Years' War – which also had its beginnings in an overseas colony with the struggle in 1754 for control of the Ohio River valley. Just as Darius's son Xerxes took the torch from his father and, after initial victories on sea (Artemesium) and land (Thermopylae), went down to defeat in both arenas at Salamis and Plataea, so Louis XVI initiated the revival of French naval power and military ambition that led, after the early victories of Napoleon, to resounding British victories at Camperdown (1797) and the Battle of the Nile (1798). Strachan refers explicitly to both of these naval battles towards the end of his exordium, and ends this portion of his poem by extending his parallels between and among ancient and modern historical events and heroes. Thus Sir Ralph Abercrombie, who received a fatal wound at the Battle of the Nile, is likened both to General Wolfe and to Epaminondas, the Theban commander who was killed at the Battle of Mantinea (a decisive victory for the Thebans over the Spartans in 362 BC):

We gladly deck with palms of just renown
The heroes of the Nile and Camperdown;
We dropt a tear when Abercrombie fell
And, crown'd with victory, bade the world farewell

Like gallant Wolfe, forever dear to fame,
And the great hero of the Theban name.
(*61–66*)

A note to this passage ascribes its final couplet to Richard Cartwright
and quotes two earlier efforts by Strachan to connect Abercrombie,
Wolfe, and Epaminondas. At least one member of the original audience
of "Verses ... 1802" – Strachan's employer – was clearly aware of the resonances and continuities between classical and modern culture that the
poem was proposing in order to promote the ancient Greeks as an
example to Upper Canadians.

An exchange near the structural centre of Strachan's exordium anticipates the patriotic tone of its final lines and emphasizes two of the
most exemplary virtues of the ancient Greeks: their love of country and
their reverence for the past. Initiating the interaction is a speech on the
desirability of "patriot virtue" by "Neoclus' gallant son" Themistocles,
the Greek statesman and strategist responsible for the defeat of Xerxes'
navy at Salamis (*35–50*). Completing it is the response of Themistocles'
audience, a "youthful band" of young Greek men who "catch the sacred
fire" from the old man's emotional speech of "sweet remembrance" and
themselves "aspire" to perform "glorious deeds" like those of their
"fathers" and grandfathers at "Marathon," "Salamis" and "Thermopylae." Not only does this interaction provide the pretext for a call to "Britain's sons" in Upper Canada to emulate the Ionian Greeks by praising
Britain's glorious achievements and military heroes, but it is also a simulacrum of the instructive setting and inspirational purposes of "Verses
... 1802." Further evidence of the care taken by Strachan with the structure of his poem is furnished by the fact that the three ancient battles
mentioned by Themistocles in his speech-within-an-ovation are echoed by the three British victories – the Nile, Camperdown, and Abraham's Plains – mentioned at the conclusion of the exordium.

In the recapitulation of eighteenth-century military history that constitutes his narration, Strachan expands on the theme of "British
valour" in a manner calculated both to delight and, ultimately, to flatter
the adult members of his audience. Brief accounts of the Seven Years'
War (*67–74*) and the American War of Independence (or possibly the
Irish Rebellion of 1798–99 [*75–80*]) are followed by references to Britain's successive victories at Cape St. Vincent (1797), Camperdown, and
the Battle of the Nile over the fleets of "haughty Spain," the "Batavia[n]
Republic," and "the crafty Gauls" (*81–84*). As well as establishing the
steadfast consistency with which "Britain's sons" have defended their
country from its enemies, Strachan's chronicle of the military events of
the past fifty years places on view a pattern of historical repetition that

confirms the parallel articulated in his exordium and narration as a whole between ancient Greek and modern British history. The Greeks had the Persian Wars, the British have the French Wars; history repeats itself and, in so doing, continually calls forth the quality that Strachan seems most to admire: an unwavering and, if necessary, self-sacrificing loyalty to a country and its culture. It is because they have evinced this quality even at a great distance from Britain that the Loyalists in Strachan's audience are as worthy of public approbation as they are of government land grants:

> 'Twas yours, ye loyal bands, that dreadful day
> At risk of life your country to obey;
> To spurn the prudent road the dastard steers,
> A friend to either side as fortune veers.
> Nor have your merits passed without regard:
> Our grateful parent gives the just reward.
>
> (*85–90*)

"Patriot virtue" is not its own reward in Strachan's Tory vision of choices and consequences; it is part of the network of duties and obligations that defines British culture, honouring service and guaranteeing justice. As the seminal Tory thinker Lord Bolingbroke had written in *Letters on the Spirit of Patriotism:* "the service of our country is no chimerical, but a real duty ... To what higher station, to what greater glory can any mortal aspire, than to be, during the whole course of his life, the support of the good, the countroul of bad government, and the guardian of public liberty" (Saint John 27, 29; see also Mills 123).

In the passage that flows from his gracious bow to the Loyalists, Strachan reminds his Upper Canadian audience of their indebtedness to Britain for the Popean "peace" and "plenty" that now characterize their province:

> To her we owe that peace delights our plains,
> That joyous plenty through the hamlets reigns,
> That rising towns present a grateful view
> Where lately dismal wilds no op'ning knew;
> That gentle Spring assumes her annual toil
> And balmy roses in the garden smile;
> That flow'ry meads and infant buds appear –
> The hope and glory of the circling year ...
>
> (*91–99*)

Thanks to the benevolence of Britain (which apparently has even seasonal growth in its gift), Upper Canada has ceased to be a gloomy and depressing wilderness. It has been brightened and transformed by agriculture into a place of happiness, growth, and hope; indeed, with its "frugal bees [distilling] delicious fruits" and its "pleasant creams [filling] ... spacious goblets" (*99–100*), Upper Canada is a "land flowing with milk and honey," a "good land and large" like that to which Moses led the Israelites from Egypt (Exodus 11:5 and 33:2). Strachan closes his celebration of Upper Canada as a Loyalist Canaan with the first inkling in a long poem on Canada of the pioneer sublime:

> swains returning as the day declines
> Exult o'er prostrate oaks and burning pines,
> A pleasure greater than the conqu'ror knows,
> Whose doubtful triumph costs ten thousand woes.
> (*101–04*)

"When it is considered" that the "brilliant spectacle" of logs burning at night is one of the "first steps towards reducing a wilderness into fruitful country," Strachan would write in *A Visit to the Province of Upper Canada in 1819*, then "the scenery becomes powerfully interesting" (76).

From celebrating the patriotism of the Loyalists and the benevolence of Britain, Strachan turns in his partition (or exposition) to state the central argument of his oration. "Britain's precious gifts" will do nothing to inspire heroism or "amend the heart," he warns, if "mental pleasures" – "The chief delight of mortals here below – " cease to abound in Upper Canada,

> For when a fertile field no culture knows,
> The Sun his genial warmth in vain bestows;
> No gold[en] harvest glads the lazy swain,
> But weeds luxur'ant cover all the plain.
> (*105–12*)

Here Strachan turns from parallelism to the related mode of analogy: just as the gardens and fields of Upper Canada must be assiduously cultivated if they are to remain free of weeds, so, too, must be the minds of the province's young people. Implicit in this analogy are the points that Strachan urges in the remainder of his partition: "ignorance" and "vacancy of mind" are "cause" of "excess" and "vicious deeds" (*113–16*); it is the duty and obligation of Upper Canadians to obviate moral and social evil by promoting knowledge ("science") and education. If the physical and economic "prospects" of Upper Canada are to continue to brighten, its glowing achievements in the realm of agriculture must be repeated in the sphere of mental culture. "'Tis yours to change the scene," Strachan informs his audience; "bid Science rise / And cheer the prospects of these Northern skies; / Bid Science brighten each bewilder'd thought, / And speed the schemes with social pleasure fraught" (*117–21*). Education will do for the gloomy and "bewilder'd" mind what cultivation did for the "dismal" wilderness.

As Strachan proceeds in his confirmation to make his case for education in Upper Canada more persuasive and secure, he seems to be addressing Mackay's caustic observation in *Quebec Hill* that Canada is as deficient in ancient architecture as its inhabitants are in moral fibre. "The Antiquarian here may search in vain / For ... lofty tow'rs that their declension show, / Or cities built some thousand years ago," writes Mackay; "Here, Nature simple and sublime is found: / Alas! the human, sunk in folly, strays / 'Mong the sublime, the physical displays" (*1:41–48*). "What tho' no columns, busts, or crumbling fanes / Exalt the pensive soul to classic strains," asserts Strachan, "Here simple nature nobler thoughts inspires / And views of grandeur banish low desires" (*121–22, 127–28*). Nor is it entirely impossible that these couplets were written with Mackay in mind, for *Quebec Hill* was published in England two years before Strachan emigrated to Canada and, in addition to being widely (and, for the most part, poorly) reviewed in such journals as the *Analytical Review*, received a publication notice in the *Edinburgh Magazine* (see Bentley, intro. to *Quebec Hill* xxxvi–vii). A more likely explanation of the convergence of *Quebec Hill* and "Verses ... 1802" is that both Mackay and Strachan were responding to Kalm's remarks on the absence of "built towns ... high towers and pillars, and such like" in North America (*Travels* 2:276–77), as was Bayley when he, too (and in a manner and tone strikingly reminiscent of Strachan), noted the absence of "marble busts ... gothic towr's / ... [and] pillars glowing with Corinthian flowers" in Canada, but found instead an equitable and moral society in which "youthful science, and instructive proof" were in gratifying evidence (*455–56, 468*). If Bayley's echo of Strachan does not stem from knowledge of "Verses ... 1802," it certainly reveals a basis for the friendship between the two young poets. Since they were both members of the Church of England and both bent on extenuating the absence of ancient architecture in Canada, Strachan and Bayley must have been pleased by the consecration in 1804 of the Anglican Cathedral of the Holy Trinity in Quebec, a building modelled on St. Martin's-in-the-Fields in London and containing elements of the Coliseum and the Pantheon in Rome. "The improvements of Architecture, in every country, generally keep pace with the advancement of civilization and the progress of science ... from barbarism to refinement," proclaimed Alex-

ander Spark in the 17 August 1805 issue of Cary's *Quebec Mercury,* and
"several Edifices ... lately ... undertaken and executed" in Lower Canada
"indicate a degree of public spirit highly auspicious to the state of the
country, and ... seem to promise a rapid progress of colonial Improvement."

At the hortatory core of Strachan's confirmation is an eloquent
appeal to the audience to supplement the cultivation of "roses" and
wheat in Upper Canada with the cultivation of knowledge and education:

> Delay no more
> To plant instruction on Ontario's shore;
> Nor let your rising offspring wildly roam
> To seek the knowledge they should find at home –
> To change their patriot love for deadly hate
> And wish the int'rests of a forcign state
> Corrupt the noble feeling nature gave
> And find for filial love a speedy grave;
> For when they see no parent's tender cares
> They quickly learn to mock their distant fears.
>
> (*129–38*)

Appealing to parental feelings of affection and responsibility, Strachan's exhortation repeats some common arguments for the establishment of good secondary schools and colleges in British North America.
Such institutions, argues William Knox in his "Proposals for Promoting
Religion and Literature in Canada, Nova Scotia and New Brunswick"
(1786), "would diffuse Literature, Loyalty, and good Morals among the
Colonists: The want of them will be attended with ... bad Consequences
– either, Ignorance must prevail among the Inhabitants; or, they must
send their Children to Great Britain or Ireland for Education ... or, to
some College in the American States, where they will be sure to imbibe
Principles that are unfriendly to the British Constitution" (qtd. in Fingard 149). A recapitulation and expansion of the similar argument in
"Verses ... 1802" for an indigenous Upper Canadian educational system
can be found in *A Visit to the Province of Upper Canada in 1819,* where Strachan writes that "it is only by a well-instructed population that we can
expect to preserve our excellent constitution and our connexion with
the British Empire – or give that respectability to the Province which
arises from an intelligent Magistracy, and from having all public situa-
tions filled with men of information" (131). If the "pure patriotic
flame" (Strachan, *Documents* 29) was to be kept burning brightly in

Upper Canada, it had to be fuelled by education and fanned by knowledge.

In the January 1806 issue of the *Port Folio*, a reader on the "Banks of the St. Lawrence" – possibly Strachan – wonders whether the climate of Canada may cause him to write poetry that is cold and dreary. As already seen in relation to Mackay, similar views of the deleterious effects of northern climates on mental development and literary culture are expressed by Pye (*1:25–52*), Brooke (103) and Milton (*Paradise Lost 9:41–47*). Such fears are addressed indirectly in "Verses ... 1802" when, in his brief refutation, Strachan holds onto the hope that the "plant[-ing] of instruction on Ontario's shore" may one day yield fruit in great writers and scientists:

> At Kingston, bards may glow with Milton's fire,
> Or seek a calmer bliss from Dryden's lyre;
> A Bacon, too, may grace some future age,
> Or Newton reading nature's inmost page.
>
> (*139–42*)

Education can do more than create Arabella Fermor's "'new Athens'" on the shore of Lake Ontario; it can make Upper Canada the literary and scientific heir and equal of Great Britain.

The conclusion of "Verses ... 1802" is a rousing salute to knowledge as the source of all economic, social, moral, and behavioural good:

> Hail mighty Science! hail the fruitful cause
> Of Commerce, order, liberty, and laws;
> The passions gently move at thy control,
> And sweet compassion melts the rugged soul;
> All cares and wants before thy footsteps fly:
> Those teachest how to live and how to die.
>
> (*143–48*)

As the cause of "Commerce," Science is the source of progress and prosperity; as the source of "order, liberty, and laws" it is the agent of the British Constitution. By strengthening reason, it encourages self-control; by increasing sensitivity, it engenders fellow-feeling; by banishing worries and desires and teaching discipline and decorum, it preserves the *status quo*. In sum "Science" is a crucial component of a progressive-conservative culture: an absolute necessity if Upper Canada is to preserve its British character and continue to prosper.

The examination of Strachan's pupils that surrounded the recitation of his "Verses" in September 1802 indicates that the poem's climactic urgings on behalf of "instruction" and "Science" were part of a carefully orchestrated performance. "The order of the Examination," recorded Strachan, "was first, Poole England [who] read a speech on polite literature and recited part of Akenside's 'Ode on Science.' John McAuley then recited 'The Sword of Rennes' from Sterne's *Sentimental Journey.* Richard Cartwright read an eulogy on Mathematics which I had dictated." Further examinations (including one on the Newtonian science of "optics") followed as did other recitations (including one of "Sterne's apostrophe on slavery"), and there were speeches by James Cartwright on "Natural Philosophy" and Andrew Stuart on "Moral Philosophy" (Strachan, Papers). The examination concluded in "pleasant humour" with a comic rehearsal of the proceedings by (or at least read by) John Beverley Robinson. In view of Strachan's aggressive commitment to education in Ontario, it can scarcely be a cause of wonder that he went on to establish the Cornwall Grammar School, to enlarge the Home District Grammar School at York, and to assist decisively in the founding of Upper Canada College and no fewer than three universities (McGill, the University of King's College, and the University of Trinity College). Nor should it come as a surprise to learn that in later life Strachan was assisted in his endeavours to establish and expand educational institutions in Canada by his ex-pupils, the "sons of leading figures in government, business, and the professions" throughout Upper Canada, whom he had taught at Kingston, Cornwall, and York to be "British patriots ... Christian gentlemen" and "rulers of the next generation" (Craig 753). Apples rarely fall far from the tree.

6 Thomas Moore, Poems Relating to Canada

No nineteenth-century poet with first-hand experience of Canada had a greater impact on later Canadian writers than Thomas Moore. Adam Kidd dedicated *The Huron Chief* to Moore and Joseph Howe mentions him beside Robert Burns in the opening lines of *Acadia* (*36–38*). In *Bogle Corbet* John Galt recounts the local "tradition" that Moore's "Ballad Stanzas," the first of the Canadian pieces in "Poems Relating to America," was composed under a "small tree" on the north shore of Lake Ontario (3:4), and in 1853, during the touristic excursion that provided the basis for *The St. Lawrence and the Saguenay*, Charles Sangster made a pilgrimage to St. Anne's Rapids near Montreal because they had been "elevate[d] ... into classic ground" by Moore's famous "Canadian Boat Song" (in Bentley, appendix 125). A century later, A.J.M. Smith composed a deliciously bawdy vignette of the Irish poet in "Thomas Moore and his Sweet Annie." Echoes of the "Poems Relating to America" can be heard in works published in Canada throughout the nineteenth century, from Cornwall Bayley's "Lines written on the banks of the Skullkill" to Archibald Lampman's "Between the Rapids." Moore wrote only a handful of poems about Canada, and only one – "To the Lady Charlotte Rawdon. From the Banks of the St. Lawrence" – of any length, but these poems played an important part in shaping perceptions of the Canadian landscape and its inhabitants. The reasons for this are obvious: Moore was a writer of stature for his own and several later generations, and his poems were widely available in inexpensive and respectable editions. The shelves of almost any second-hand book store in Canada will testify to Moore's popularity in this country throughout the nineteenth century.

Yet Moore was only in Canada for a few months in the summer and fall of 1804. After travelling north through "the Genessee country" of New York to the shores of "Erie's stormy lake" in July of that year (*Letters* 1:76; *Poetical Works* 121), he crossed from Buffalo to Fort Erie, arriving on British North American soil on 21 July 1804. From Fort Erie he travelled "in a *waggon*" to Chippewa, a village within earshot of "Niagara's ... cataract" (*Letters* 1:75; *Poetical Works* 124), the eagerly anticipated goal of his journey. When he first visited the falls on 22 July, Moore's response was that of "any heart, born for sublimities" and prepared for North America's quintessentially sublime sight by his reading of various travellers' descriptions, most notably that of his compatriot Isaac Weld, which he regarded as the "most accurate" available (*Letters* 1:77). "Agitated by the terrific effects of the scene [at Niagara Falls] ... and receiv[ing] enough of its grandeur to set imagination on the wing," Moore "felt as if approaching the very residence of the Deity." After descending below the falls, his feelings of "pious enthusiasm" intensified to the degree that, as he recorded in his journal, "my whole heart and soul ascended towards the Divinity in a swell of devout admiration, which I never before experienced. Oh! bring the atheist here, and he cannot return an atheist!" (*Letters* 1:76–77). This is a rhapsodic but conventional response to a sublime spectacle that recalls Cary's description of Niagara Falls in *Abram's Plains* (*34–39*), but its literary origins lie in Weld's *Travels*, where a feeling of "reverential fear" in face of the "stupendous" sight and sound of the falls causes the "mind [to be] forcibly impressed with and awful idea of the power of that mighty Being who commanded the water to flow" (2:128–29). Susanna Moodie may also have had Weld at the back of her mind when she described Niagara Falls as a "wonderful symbol of the power and strength of the divine Architect of the universe" (*Life in the Clearings* 246), as, possibly, did Samuel Strickland when he asked "who can behold the mighty Niagara and say 'there is no God'?" (250).

Also very likely originating in Weld is Moore's conviction that Niagara Falls defies description and depiction. "It is impossible by pen or pencil to convey even a faint idea of their magnificence," he writes; "painting is lifeless; and the most burning words of poetry have all been lavished upon inferior and ordinary subjects. We must have new combinations of language to describe the Falls of Niagara" (*Letters* 1:77). Not only do these remarks seem to echo Weld's view that "no words can convey an adequate idea of the awful grandeur of the scene" (2:128), but they also bring to mind Mackay's question about "How ... [to find] numbers to proclaim / The liquid grandeur of St. Lawrence' Stream" (*I:52–53*). "Nor similes nor metaphors avail!," Susie Frances Harrison would later exclaim of "Niagara in Winter"; "All imagery vanishes, device / Dies ...

Before such awful majesty" (*Pine* 196). Perhaps feeling that words no more than pictures were dynamic enough to "convey ... [an] idea" of the "liquid grandeur" of Niagara Falls, Moore refers only briefly to them in "To the Lady Charlotte Rawdon," but does so in two lines – "See all ... [the] inland waters hurl'd / In one vast volume down Niagara's steep" (*26–27*) – that effectively deploy a terminal verb ("hurl'd") and emphatic alliteration ("vast volume") to mimic their percussive force. Later in the poem, when he imagines the appearance of the falls in winter, Moore exploits the arresting effect of an initial verb and an end-stopped line to mime the stasis of "Niagara's starry spray, / Frozen on the cliff ... / Like a giant's starting tears" (*116–18*). The simile in these lines is visually evocative, and may well lie behind Sangster's observation that the waterfalls at Trinity Rock on the Saguenay are "Like tears of Gladness o'er a giant's face" (*1200*).

Moore spent two weeks in the vicinity of Niagara Falls, initially enjoying the breathtaking scenery of the area and subsequently waiting impatiently for a boat to take him along Lake Ontario on the next leg of his journey to Nova Scotia and, thence, to England. (Interestingly enough, the commander of Fort George at this time was a "Colonel [Isaac] Brock" with whom the poet spent "many pleasant days," one of which included a "visit to the Tuscarora Indians" [*Epistles* 309 n.]) On his way from Niagara to Montreal, Moore apparently wrote the two lyrics that have had the most impact on Canadian poetry: "Ballad Stanzas" and "A Canadian Boat Song." The first, which Galt calls Moore's "Woodpecker poem" (*Bogle Corbet* 3:4), derives part of its inspiration from Weld, as a juxtaposition of its second stanza with the relevant passage in the *Travels* reveals:

> It was noon, and on flowers that languish'd around
>   In silence repos'd the voluptuous bee;
> Every leaf was at rest, and I heard not a sound
>   But the woodpecker tapping the hollow beech-tree.
>   (*Poetical Works* 124)

A few squirrels were the only wild animals which we met with in our journey through the woods, and the most solemn silence imaginable reigned throughout, except where a woodpecker was heard now and then tapping with its bill against a hollow tree.

                                                                              (2:320)

It is a measure of Moore's (and therefore Weld's) reach into nineteenth-century poetry about Canada that "Ballad Stanzas" provides the point of departure for both *The Huron Chief* and the chapter entitled

"The Log Cabin" in Alexander McLachlan's *The Emigrant.* The opening
stanza of the former, set on the shore of Lake Huron, describes a silence
broken by the "sound" of "birds that tapped the hollow tree" (4–5) and
the anapestic rhythm of the lyric that begins the latter, set on the shores
of Lake Ontario, clearly echoes the measure of "Ballad Stanzas." Like
Moore's poem, McLachlan's lyric treats of a cottage set deep in the
Canadian woods.

To judge by the works that it inspired, the appeal of "Ballad Stanzas"
for later writers lay in its presentation of the backwoods of Canada as a
paradisal realm of repose and virtue, qualities amply evident in its first
and last stanzas:

I knew by the smoke, that so gracefully curl'd
  Above the green elms, that a cottage was near,
And I said, "If there's peace to be found in the world,
  A heart that was humble might hope for it here!"
. . . .
"By the shade of yon sumach, whose red berry dips
  In the gush of the fountain, how sweet to recline,
And to know that I sigh'd upon innocent lips,
  Which had never been sigh'd on by any but mine!"
                                    (*Poetical Works* 124)

Completely ignoring the hardships and privations of life in the backwoods, Moore makes Upper Canada out to be a picturesque paradise of
rural retirement and innocent love. His emphasis on female purity
smacks of masculine insecurity and possessiveness, but it is entirely consistent with his Edenic vision of the backwoods, a vision that was bound
to appeal to later writers such as McLachlan who had made Canada
their home and wished others to do so too. Much the same can be said
of Weld's *Travels*, the enormous appeal and influence of which in nineteenth-century Canada may partly be explained by its outspoken preference for British North America rather than the United States,
especially as a destination for emigrants (1:411–27). That Moore shared
Weld's views of the relative merits of the two countries helps to explain
his idyllic presentation of the Canadian backwoods in "Ballad Stanzas."

The second of Moore's North American poems to exert a large influence on nineteenth-century Canadian writing also owes part of its inspiration to Weld. "A Canadian Boat Song Written on the River St.
Lawrence" has been credited with creating a "mythical image" of the
voyageur as a "pious, devout, singing" and somewhat primitive denizen
of the Canadian hinterland (Gross 78). But a more likely candidate for
this distinction is Weld's *Travels*. As well as calling attention to the sing-

ing of the French-Canadian oarsmen on the St. Lawrence ("they have
one favourite ... 'rowing duet,' which as they sing they mark time to,
with each stroke of the oar" [2:51]), Weld presents the French-Canadians generally and the voyageurs in particular as cheerful, religious, and
long-suffering characters whose flaws include superstition, vanity, and a
roving disposition that gives them an affinity with the Native peoples
(1:319–20, 338–39; 2:4, 8–9). Nevertheless, the role of "A Canadian
Boat Song" in promulgating a French-Canadian stereotype cannot be
doubted. After its appearance as sheet music in 1805 (Jordan 126) and
in *Epistles, Odes, and Other Poems* (1806), it was frequently reprinted and
often quoted. On 11 May 1807, for example, Cary reproduced it in the
Quebec Mercury as "The Rapids. A Canadian Boat Song" "arranged by T.
Moore, Esq." and in 1938 it is given to Moore himself to sing in Alan Sullivan's novel *The Fur Masters* (Gross 79). It was translated into French as
"La Chanson du Voyageur" (1826) by Dominique Mondelet (Gross 80)
and it gives its title to a chapter on "The Canadian Boat Song" as a genre
in William Kirby's *The Golden Dog* (1877). When he visited St. Anne's
Rapid in 1827, Basil Hall found "it ... difficult to say" how much of his
response to the scene was due to "the magic" of Moore's poem and how
much to what was actually there (1:199; see also George Henry 34).
When he visited the same scene in 1853, Sangster fancied "that many
tourists, approaching the Rapid ... humming the beautiful air to which
the words of the 'Boat Song' have been wedded" must have felt cheated
by the "mere ripple" that Moore had immortalized in the line "We'll
sing at St. Ann's our parting hymn" (124). "Notwithstanding this," he
adds, "the ground is sacred, one of the 'green spots upon memory's
waste' dedicate to Moore, and it will continue such, though the stream
were dried to-morrow, and nothing but the pebbles at the bottom
remained to mark the spot .... [W]ould that there were other like
[Moore] to fling their classic verse ... over the many Isles of Beauty and
nooks of fairy loveliness with which Canada is strewn" (in Bentley,
appendix 125–26). The fact that Sangster himself attempted to do precisely this in *The St. Lawrence and the Saguenay* suggest that Moore's
example exerted a motive influence on him, shaping his conception of
the Canadian poet's role in regard to the Canadian landscape.

   In a footnote to "A Canadian Boat Song," Moore cites as his source
for the poem's setting a passage in the "General History of the Fur
Trade" in Alexander Mackenzie's *Voyages*. "At the rapid of St. Ann [the
voyageurs] are obliged to take out part, if not the whole of their lading.
It is from this spot that the Canadians consider they take their departure, as it possesses the last church on the island [of Montreal], which
is dedicated to the tutelary saint of voyagers" (*Voyages* xxix). Another
obvious point of departure for the poem is Gray's "Elegy Written in a

Country Churchyard," the opening line of which – "The curfew tolls the knell of parting day" (117) – Moore echoes in his tone, diction, and time of day:

> Faintly as tolls the evening chime
> Our voices keep tune and our oars keep time.
> Soon as the woods on shore look dim,
> We'll sing at St. Ann's our parting hymn.
> Row, brothers, row, the stream runs fast,
> The Rapids are near and the daylight's past.
>   (*Poetical Works* 124–25)

A lengthy footnote giving details of the songs of the voyageurs on the St. Lawrence leaves little doubt that "A Canadian Boat Song" is based on a song heard by Moore and hence has some experiential basis. But the poem's sources in Mackenzie, Weld, and Gray also indicate that, like lesser poets writing about Canada before and after him, Moore generated "A Canadian Boat Song" by suiting the manner of an English poet to matter derived from his reading as well as his experience. In effect Moore has elevated a Canadian scene into "classic ground" by transforming prose accounts of it into verse that is "classic" because it has the hallmarks of the best English poetry.

The longest of Moore's poems on Canada – "To the Lady Charlotte Rawdon. From the Banks of the St. Lawrence" (*Poetical Works* 125–28) – consists of a brief narrative purporting to emanate from an "Indian Spirit" (*57–132*) surrounded by a frame devoted primarily to Moore's happy "recollections" (*177*) of times recently spent in England in the company of Lady Rawdon and her aristocratic circle. In its opening lines the poem quickly moves from the river of now to the river of then, replacing the amorphously "wooded" shores of the St. Lawrence with the historied banks of the "mazy" Trent in northeastern England where "Donington's old oaks, to every breeze, / Whisper the tale of by-gone centuries" (*3–6*). Because of its historical associations, the English landscape is more than vocal; it is "as sacred as the groves" in which "the pious Persian" hears "spirit-voice[s] ... sigh in every leaf" (*7–10*) and, in this way, not so very different from the Canadian landscape in whose "nightly breeze" (*55*) Moore will soon detect the murmur of the Indian Spirit. Before that occurs, however, Moore must toss some compliments in the direction of Lady Rawdon and rehearse for her his progress from Niagara Falls to the St. Lawrence. Never one to shy away from either flattery or false humility, he combines both in praising Lady Rawdon's singing of his "unpolish'd lays" in a voice so "tuneful" as to sound like "an answering spirit's tone" (*12–21*) – a contrived compliment which has at least the virtue of participating in the poem's overall concern with the spiritual. The Francis, earl of Moira, to whom *Epistles, Odes, and Other Poems* is dedicated, was Lady Rawdon's brother, a friend of the Prince of Wales, and a possible patron for Moore.

Less cloyingly connected to the central concerns of "To the Lady Charlotte Rawdon" is Moore's treatment of the Thousand Islands. As impressed as was Weld with the scenery of this area, he proclaims the "massy woods," flowered "islets," and "blooming glades" of Upper Canada a landscape "where the first sinful pair / For consolation might have weeping trod, / When banish'd from the garden of their God" (*33–36*). Perhaps taking his cue from this mythopoeic passage, John Howison writes in his *Sketches of Upper Canada* (1821) that the Thousand Islands reminded him of the "beautiful description of the Happy Islands in ... [Joseph Addison's] Vision of Mirzah," and made him think "that if the Thousand Islands lay in the East, some chaste imagination would propose, that they would be made an asylum for suffering humanity" (32). Not until Sangster drew upon Moore, Howison, and several others to celebrate the Thousand Islands as the Canadian home of "the Spirit of Beauty" were their natural attractions firmly wedded to a supernatural element (*The St. Lawrence and the Saguenay 64–93*). Yet Moore's conviction that Upper Canada's sublime and beautiful landscapes are among God's most "marvellous" creations – "miracles, which man, / Cag'd in the bounds of Europe's pigmy span, / Can scarcely dream of" (*37–40*) – contributed greatly to the province's appeal and mythos. If Adam and Eve might have come to Upper Canada for "consolation" in a fallen world, then so might others. One effect of this portion of "To the Lady Charlotte Rawdon" is thus to subtly reinforce the message of "Ballad Stanzas": those seeking what Moore calls in his preface to "Poems Relating to America" "the elysian Atlantis" – a "retreat" in "the western world ... from real or imaginary oppression" (*Poetical Works* 94) – had better go to Upper Canada rather than the United States.

After thus reinforcing his mythopoeic aggrandizement of Canada, Moore proceeds in "To the Lady Charlotte Rawdon" to emphasize an aspect of the country already mooted with the words "miracle" and "marvellous": the uncanniness of many of its natural phenomena. As "the last tints of the west decline, / And night falls dewy" on the pine-clad banks of the St. Lawrence, the time is ripe for heightened physical and spiritual vision, for the "Hesperian" effects whose origins in English poetry Geoffrey Hartman (138–46) traces to William Collins's "Ode to Evening." Indeed Collins's "Ode" is the likely model for this portion of Moore's poem both in its crepuscular setting and "hushed" tone and in its dual focus on the natural and the supernatural, on "the weak-eyed bat ... on leathern wing ... and elves / Who slept in flowers the day, / And many a nymph who wreathes her brows with sedge" (464–65). Predictably Moore relies heavily for his "Hesperian" observations on prose sources which he modifies in accordance with his spiritual concerns. A paragraph of Thomas Anburey's *Travels through the Interior Parts of America* (1789) in which the "luminous appearance" of "porpoises" swimming in the St. Lawrence is likened to "beautiful *fire*works in the water" (29) becomes the pretext for a comparison between a "gleaming porpoise" and a "watery" shooting "star" (*46–47*) that intimates a connection between the local and the cosmic, and makes space travellers of those who look on Canadian nature with imaginative eyes. By way of Jedidiah Morse's *American Geography* (1792 f.; see 1:221), a translucent lizard or "glass-snake ... / show[ing] the dim moonlight through his scaly form" transmogrifies the banks of the St. Lawrence into a scene of "enchantment," a magical realm in which there seem to be no barriers between the natural and the supernatural. What follows this careful process of induction is a midsummer night's "Fancy," a *jeu d'esprit*, modelled very likely on the exchanges among Puck, Oberon, and the Faeries in the opening scenes of Shakespeare's play, but with the replacement of Robin Goodfellow by the "Indian Spirit" whose narrative comprises the core of the poem.

Several aspects of the Indian Spirit's narrative will ring false to many readers today. By presuming to speak in the voice of an Indian Spirit (as earlier he had assumed the identity of a voyageur), Moore appropriates for his own literary purposes a voice of the Native peoples. By basing the Indian Spirit's narrative on passages in Carver, Mackenzie, and other European writers, he compounds his error and his culpability. By presenting the Indian Spirit as a cheerily peripatetic dove on the authority of Pierre de Charlevoix he puts himself beyond pity and beneath contempt. These are stinging, albeit uncharitably retroactive, criticisms, and they can be mitigated by a recognition that Moore does at least display some sensitivity to otherness by presenting the Indian Spirit's narrative in a poetic form – trochaic tetrameter – that is very different from the surrounding iambic pentameter and, moreover, that he introduces the narrative with a phrase – "words like these" – which characterize it as an approximation. Nor should it be ignored in Moore's defense that his depiction of the Indian Spirit refuses the prevalent stereotypes of the ignoble and noble savage, and that throughout "To the Lady Charlotte Rawdon" he evinces a marked preference for the "Indian names" of places in Canada, apparently agreeing with Weld that "Newark, Kingston, [and] York, are ... poor substitutes for the original names of ... Niagara, Cadaragui, [and] Toronto" (2:88). Moore may have been blind to his own linguistic participation in the imperial enterprise, but, as his trenchant remarks about slavery in "Poems Relating to America" confirm (*Poetical Works* 116–19), his racial sympathies lay with the abused and downtrodden. It was Moore, after all, who satirized Thomas Jefferson, then the President of the United States, as the "patriot, fresh from Freedom's councils come, / ... [Who] retires to lash his slaves at home; / Or woo, perhaps, some black Aspasia's charms, / And dream of freedom in his bondsmaid's arms" (116).

Whatever its political shortcoming's when viewed from today's perspective, the Indian Spirit's narrative is also a "visionary lay" (*133*) which, like Cary's elevated conspectus of the Great Lakes in *Abram's Plains* (*21–33*), permits the poet to depict places that he has visited only vicariously in the travel writings of others. More on the wings of Carver than a dove, Moore visits the northern Great Lakes, quoting in a footnote part of the traveller's description of Lake Superior ("the water ... was as pure and transparent as air, and my canoe seemed as if suspended in that element") which he adapts to his own purposes:

> Hither oft my flight I take
> Over Huron's lucid lake,
> Where the wave, as clear as dew,
> Sleeps beneath the light canoe,
> Which, reflected, floating there,
> Looks as if it hung in air.
> (*65–70*)

Here, as in Carver's original description (122–23), is another instance of the Canadian uncanny, and one that seems to have left an impression on at least two later poets: Kidd, who writes of the astonishingly "pellucid ... waters of the great *Lakes* in CANADA" in a footnote to *The Huron Chief* (876 n.), and William Kirby, who reckons the "waves" of Lake Superior so "transparent ... pure and limpid that they seem ... to bear / The bark canoe afloat in ... air" (*The U.E.* 10:180–82). Crawford also describes a "light canoe" suspended between earth and sky in the first of the interspersed songs in *Malcolm's Katie* (*1:137–45*), and she may well have drawn inspiration from Moore's Collinsian descriptions of various exotic animals and flowers, notably "a water-snake, / Wrapt within a web of leaves, / Which the water-lily weaves" (*78–80*) and a "flybird" encouraged to dream of a "heaven of flowers" by a "tangled wreath" of "golden-thread" – a water plant described by Carver (513–14) and woven into a "magic ... chaplet" by the playful and Puck-like Indian Spirit (*93–104*). It may even be that the "grey moose" in the manuscript of Howe's *Acadia* (Parks, intro. xxxi) is descended from Moore's "gray moose" (*107*), another species that enters the Indian

Spirit's narrative by way of Carver's *Travels* (*448*). As all of these examples and possibilities reveal, Moore's impact on later writing about Canada was greatest when he drew upon Carver and others to describe plants, animals, and landscapes that were actually to be found in Canadian territory. Noticeably without descendants in later poetry about Canada are Moore's more fanciful borrowings from his prose sources: the "glass-snake," for example, and – in the Indian Spirit's narrative – the "Wakon-Bird," a "species ... [of] bird ... of paradise" called, in "the ... [Indians'] language, the Bird of the Great Spirit" (Carver 472–73; *Poetical Works* 127 n.). To supplement reality with myth was one thing; to substitute myth for reality was another.

In the section of "To the Lady Charlotte Rawdon" that follows the Indian Spirit's narrative, Moore resumes the dialectic of observation and remembrance that shaped the first part of the poem. Moving in memory in the same direction as his boat – east along the St. Lawrence towards England – he draws heavily on Wordsworth ("Tintern Abbey," "Westminster Bridge") to rehearse for Lady Rawdon the process by which resemblance has triggered remembrance, transporting him once again from the "mingled maze / Of nature's beauties" in Canada to "Donington's green lawns ... breezy heights" and aristocratic culture (*145–54*). The poem concludes with a complete displacement of the Canadian present by glowing memories of the England to which Moore will soon be returning: "all that around me lies, / Stream, banks, and bowers have faded on my eyes!" (*181–82*).

Only one footnote graces the final section of "To the Lady Charlotte Rawdon" and it is of considerable significance. A quotation from *La Divina Commedia* that aligns Moore's boat on the St. Lawrence to the "mystic bark" (*139*) that Dante sees in the second canto of the *Purgatorio*, it has the effect of allegorizing the landscape in and around the poem, making Canada the Purgatory through which the poet is passing on his way to the Earthly Paradise of Donington and the Beatrice (or Matilda) of Lady Rawdon. From this Dantean context, it follows that the United States is the Inferno from which the poet has recently exited, an evaluation that certainly accords with Moore's very negative assessment of most of the Republic and its people in the "Poems Relating to America." "There ... is a close approximation to savage life" in the United States, he observes in his "Preface," a "youthful decay" which is as evident in the "violence" and "animosity" generated by the political system as in "the rude familiarity of the lower orders, and ... the unpolished state of society in general" (*Poetical Works* 94). Neither as "savage" as the democracy to the south nor as "polish'd" as the mature civilization to the east (*Poetical Works* 94), Canada occupies an intermediate position between America and England that corresponds, not just to Purgatory in the Dantean scheme, but also to the barbaric (or pastoral) and agricultural levels of social development as conceived by the four stages theory. It is no more fortuitous that the nomadic voyageurs on the St. Lawrence have "barbarous" accents (*Poetical Works* 124 n. 1) than it is that the most idyllic spot in Canada – the remote cottage in "Ballad Stanzas" – occurs in a rural and implicitly agricultural setting. In Canada there exists a mixed and middling society in which the boatsongs of the voyageurs are the folkpoems to be expected of a people at the pastoral stage of development, and the innocence of the backwoods reflects the virtue associated with agricultural societies.

The poems that follow "To the Lady Charlotte Rawdon" in "Poems Relating to America" are of comparatively little interest. "Impromptu after a visit to Mrs. _____, of Montreal" is a piece of chivalric frivolity in which Moore regrets not having been able to spend more time communing with a lady whose "eye had a glow, like the sun of her clime" (*Poetical Works* 129). "Written on Passing Deadman's Island in the Gulf of St. Lawrence, late in the Evening, September, 1804" is a version of the Flying Dutchman myth that is more a reflection of the poet's interest in the supernatural than a detailed response to the Canadian landscape, though it does refer, with an anapestic jauntiness that seems somewhat at odds with its macabre subject-matter, to

> a wreck on the dismal shore
> Of cold and pitiless Labrador;
> Where, under the moon, upon mounts of frost,
> Full many a mariner's bones are tost.
>
> (129)

A footnote to the poem refers blandly to the "delightful" scenery along the Gulf of St. Lawrence. Finally, "To the Boston Frigate on Leaving Halifax for England, October, 1804" contains a comparison between "chill Nova Scotia's unpromising strand" ("the bleak and rocky wilderness by which Halifax is surrounded") and "the beauty and fertility" of the province's interior (*Poetical Works* 130), but consists mainly of a general farewell to North America and a happy celebration of the island home to which the poet, Ulysses-like, will soon be returning.

The conclusion of "To the Boston Frigate" is the climax of the east-west movement of remembrance and return that shapes Moore's Canadian poems. "Each prosperous sigh of the west-springing wind / Takes me nearer the home where my heart is inshrin'd," he tells the ship's captain; "see! – the bent top-sails are ready to swell – / To the boat – I am with thee – Columbia, farewell!" (*Poetical Works* 131). When Weld left "this Continent" for Britain in January, 1797, he did so "without a

sigh, and without entertaining the slightest wish to revisit it" (2:376).
On account of a few people whom he "left with regret" (*Poetical Works*
130) – such cultured "elect of the land" as Joseph Dennie and his circle
in Philadelphia – Moore's feelings were a little more mixed, but there
seems little doubt that, on the whole, he shared Weld's relief in bidding
"farewell!" to North America.

An intriguing postscript to Moore's visit to Canada exists in the form
of a poem published in the *Quebec Mercury* on 3 November 1806. An
untitled tribute to the "girls" of Quebec that resembles "Impromptu" in
both matter and manner, "When the spires of Quebec first open'd to
view" is intriguing for two reasons. The first lies in its use of the name
"Annette" to typify the women of Quebec, for this reveals the emergence of a generic name for French-Canadian women a few years earlier than its masculine equivalent of Jean Baptiste (Francis Hall 65).
The two names derive, of course, from St. Anne and John the Baptist,
two saints whose names were in fact borne by many French-Canadians
and by several Catholic churches in French Canada, a case in point
being the "St. Ann's" of "A Canadian Boat Song." It is only remotely possible that George Longmore had Moore's poem in mind when he gave
the name Annette to the French-Canadian bride in *The Charivari*, but it
is probably safe to assume that "When the spires of Quebec first open'd
to view" played at least some part in promulgating a generic name that
shaped English perceptions of French-Canadians. In his views of the
"girls" of Quebec as in his perceptions of French-Canadian boatmen
and Upper Canadian landscapes, Moore reveals an eye for generaliza-
tion that can as easily flatten the individual into the stereotypical as it
can elevate the particular into the mythical.

The second intriguing feature of "When the spires of Quebec first
open'd to view" is that it is introduced by a note addressed to the owner
and editor of the *Quebec Mercury*, "Mr. [Thomas] Cary": "Sir – I am lately
arrived from England, and previous to my leaving that place, my friend,
Mr. Moore, gave me the following verses, which I request you will have
the goodness to insert in your paper, for the entertainment of his
friends." Were Moore's friends in Quebec merely the women flattered
in the poem and the government official who, according to the poet's
own account, "begged" "the master of the vessel" in which he was sailing
to Halifax to "defer sailing *one* day more, that ... [he] might join a party
at [the governor's] house the next day" (*Letters* 1:80)? Or did they
include Cary and Cornwall Bayley, an evident admirer and imitator of
Moore's work who had arrived in Quebec about a month before the
Irish poet? Did Moore see a copy of *Abram's Plains?* Did he show drafts
of his "Poems Relating to America" to Bayley? Did the three men discuss
the past and future of poetry in and about Canada? Did Cary acquaint

Moore with Carver's *Travels* and did Moore introduce Bayley to Weld's? It is tempting to say that the three poets *must* have encountered one another in a city as small as Quebec, but the historical record is silent on the matter and the literary historian must rest content with intriguing possibilities.

7 Adam Hood Burwell, *Talbot Road*

In the reminiscence of the old voyageur in *Canada* Bayley refers in passing to the region that, little more than a decade later, furnished the setting for the first surviving poem of length by a writer born in Canada: Adam Hood Burwell's *Talbot Road: a Poem*, published in two instalments in the *Niagara Spectator* in the summer of 1818. To Bayley the very subject that Burwell takes as his theme – the advance of European settlement on the shores of Lake Erie – is a source of delighted surprise:

> Now on wild Erie ... the scatter'd cot,
> But proves the former deserts of the spot;
> ... [and] the frequent fires that blaze, declare
> How cultivation even travels *there*!
>
> (*351–54*)

Behind these lines in *Canada* lie two passages that may also have been in Burwell's mind when he "Aw[o]ke [his] muse" (*1*) to celebrate Colonel Thomas Talbot's contribution to the "cultivation" of part of Lake Erie's north shore. The first of these is Weld's description of the violent storms that he encountered while travelling along the lake towards the "settlements ... now [in 1796] scattered" to its southeast (2:296–332). The second is Thomas Campbell's imaginative account in *The Pleasures of Hope* of the salutary effects of "Improvement" on what he, too, regarded as an extraordinarily "wild" part of the world:

> On Erie's banks, where tigers steal along,
> And the dread Indian chants a dismal song,

Where human fiends on midnight errands walk,
And bathe in brains the murderous tomahawk –
There shall the flocks on thymy pasture stray,
And shepherds dance at Summer's opening day,
Each wandering genius of the lonely glen
Shall start to view the glittering haunts of men,
And Silence watch, on woodland heights around,
The village curfew as it tolls profound.

(*1:325–34*)

When Burwell wrote and published *Talbot Road*, the day when "The Town, the Village shall be seen to rise" (*574*) on the north shore of Lake Erie still lay some distance in the future; however by 1818 the "glittering haunts of men" were abundantly evident along the Talbot Road – along, that is, the system of roads that eventually connected Port Talbot (the site of the Colonel's residence and the centre of his settlement) with Niagara to the east, Amherstberg to the west, and Westminster Township (near present-day London, Ontario) to the north. Surveyed mainly by the poet's brother, Mahlon Burwell, in 1809–11, the Talbot Road consisted in 1818 of "two great roads ... extend[ing] seventy or eighty miles" to serve "a land of promise to which emigrants, native Americans, and Canadians, [were] daily flocking in vast numbers" (Howison 168–69). Like the later and better-known settlement poems with which it invites comparison, Goldsmith's *The Rising Village* and McLachlan's *The Emigrant*, *Talbot Road* chronicles and celebrates the past achievements, present state, and future prospects of a pioneer community, in this case one that had taken root in a part of Canada which only a few years earlier had been regarded as particularly remote and inhospitable.

The fact that *Talbot Road* is carefully sited and dated at "*Southwold, / 28th May*, 1818" lends the poem a commemorative dimension reminiscent of *Abram's Plains*. It was fifteen years earlier, in May 1803, that Colonel Talbot took possession of his original land grant of five thousand acres in Middlesex County (Brunger 857). From 1817 onwards the anniversary of this event was celebrated on 17 May in Port Talbot (or, later, London), and for a time in the early twenties Burwell was secretary of the committee responsible for organizing the celebration. Was *Talbot Road* composed for the Talbot anniversary in 1818? Was the poem read aloud as part of the festivities, perhaps during or after a formal dinner, in Port Talbot? There is no external evidence to support these speculations, but some striking parallels between *Talbot Road* and the Talbot anniversary celebration described by Burwell in 1822 (see appendix to Williams ed. 89–90) suggest the suitability of the poem for the occasion.

Among the toasts drunk at the anniversary dinner in 1822 were several that have clear echoes in the themes of *Talbot Road* – a toast to Talbot himself, a toast to the Talbot anniversary (with the hope that it "may ... be celebrated every year with increasing festivity"), a toast to "Agriculture and Commerce," and a toast to the "Memory of General Brock." Between praising Talbot and looking optimistically towards the future of his settlement, *Talbot Road* similarly celebrates agriculture, "Commerce" (*563*), and the "patriot brave" (*401*) of the War of 1812, notably "Major General Sir Isaac Brock" (*374 n.*). If Burwell did key *Talbot Road* to the fifteenth anniversary of the Talbot settlement, then perhaps there is a contextual appropriateness to its seemingly sychophantic praise of Colonel Talbot.

Only in the extent and extravagance of its encomium to a powerful man does *Talbot Road* differ from other Canadian poems of the Georgian period. To the leading questions of "what master hand / ... projected, and ... plann'd" the Talbot settlement and who "Bade the wild woods their rudest forms resign, / And springing beauty o'er the desert shine?" (*11–14*), Burwell's muse replies emphatically and without hesitation:

'Twas TALBOT – he, with ardent, patriot mind,
The noble plan, philanthropic, design'd;
Began the same, upheld, and saw it close,
Tho' all the warring fates against him rose.
                    (*15–18*)

One possible referent for the last line here is the War of 1812, which, as chronicled later in the poem, dealt some severe blows to the Talbot settlement. But the line also intimates a knowledge on Burwell's part of the resistance to Talbot's "noble plan" and autocratic practices that had taken him between November 1817 and June 1818 to England to gain support from Lord Bathurst, the Colonial Secretary, for his practice of "personally selecting settlers and withholding their fees" until they had "completed their settlement duties" (Brunger 858–59). The fact that Burwell's poem was dedicated to Talbot "in [his] absence to England" raises the possibility that it was aimed, at least in part, at justifying Talbot's plans and practices to his detractors both in the settlement and in the province at large. This would further help to account for the encomiastic and propagandistic features of *Talbot Road*, as well as for Burwell's insistence on Talbot's "philanthrop[y]" and on the "freedom" and "Liberty" enjoyed by the inhabitants of his settlement (*16, 239, 141*).

By Burwell's account it was in about 1801, when Talbot began farming at Skitteewaabaa ("believed to be near the mouth of Kettle Creek on the North Shore of Lake Erie" [Brunger 857]), that he conceived his "noble plan" for a settlement in the area:

> On Erie's bank, first his lone cabin stood,
> Remote from man, amidst a tow'ring wood ...
>
> 'Twas here th' eventful scheme of Talbot Road,
> Great scheme! first from his mind spontaneous flow'd,
> Destin'd to bless, some not far distant time,
> The happiest country in the happiest clime.
>
> (*19–20, 23–26*)

As the expression "from his mind spontaneous flow'd" already suggests, Burwell's Talbot is the godlike and potent progenitor of a settlement that came into being as a result of his imaginative and physical penetration of a "fertile," "productive," and, inevitably, female nature whose woods he "pierc'd" in 1803 (*38, 77, 92*). At that time – and with a clear echo of Genesis 1:3–5 – he "brought to light" from "geographic night" "Bayham and Mallahide," "two fair towns" which had thereto lain in chaotic and unproductive darkness (*93–94*). As he interrogates himself about the "future state" of his property, Talbot articulates his "philanthropic" motives and clarifies his relation to Divine creativity. Nature, given to man for his use and benefit in Genesis 1:28, works "in vain" when it remains "untenanted" and "unappropriated," particularly when there are "thousands [who] want its 'vantages the while" (*97–100*; see also *39–46*). Appropriating for himself the "task" and "pleasure" of settling the north shore of Lake Erie, Talbot envisages his "work" as an act of transforming or reclothing an external world that both he and the narrator continue to view as female and, moreover, less attractive when naked and wild than when fully and elaborately dressed. "Earth shall resign the burden of her breast, / And wear a richer, variegated vest," asserts the prescient Talbot in a passage later echoed by the narrator: "Thro' nature's wilds the muse our steps hath led, / Where we've beheld her pristine form display'd, / And seen the changeful hand of time prepare, / A robe, more pleasing, for herself to wear" (*471–74*).

Carole Fabricant could be commenting on these and other passages in *Talbot Road* when she connects the eighteenth-century habit of viewing nature as "a maiden in need of sartorial assistance, as a goddess alternately being stripped bare and clothed in finery," with a desire to "redress" or "cancel out the ill effects of the Fall" by recreating a "Paradisial existence" in a corner of the post-lapsarian world (126–30). Not only was the ability to do this a sign of male power, observes Fabricant, but it also frequently involved a masculine fantasy of regaining an Eden as yet uncomplicated by woman – "a yearning to recapture that brief moment in human time when man had Paradise all to himself so that his mastery over the created world was absolute" (130). If there is an element of "masculine fantasy" in Burwell's depiction of Talbot, it is certainly continued and elaborated in the ensuing account of Talbot Road's first settler and second father, a "solitary man" who again deprives Nature of her virginity ("pierc[es] the woods"[*117*]) and demonstrates his "mastery" over her ("Then bow'd the forest to his frequent stroke" [*119*]). "Unaided and alone" (*113*), like Adam before the creation of Eve, this "solitary man" receives encouragement from some very Miltonic "Angels" who, after "breath[ing] celestial love" over his "labours," speak lines reminiscent of God's commands in Genesis 1:28 ("Be fruitful and multiply, and replenish the earth, and subdue it"):

> "Go on and prosper, for thine eyes shall see
> The steps of thousands, soon to follow thee;
> Go on and prosper, for the fostering hand
> Of heaven, shall plant this highly favor'd land."
> (*123–26*)

That the Angel's concluding words echo Gabriel's address to the Virgin Mary in Luke 1:28 ("Hail! thou that art highly favoured") is consistent with Burwell's view of Nature as *both* sacred *and* submissive, virginal *and* fertile. It is no more surprising that only perpetually youthful representations of fertility like the Roman goddess "Flora" (*68*) inhabit Burwell's pristine landscape than it is that in his list of the pioneers' chattels – "goods ... cattle ... wives, and little ones" (*148*) – actual women are, in Wanda Campbell's words, "sadly wedged between domestic animals and infants" (*"Bildungsgedicht"* 13).

Although Burwell draws heavily on Genesis in his account of the pioneering activities of the Talbot settlers, he also makes large levies on *Paradise Lost*, and for obvious reasons. Milton's epic is the quintessential English poem of transplantation and adaptation. As it opens, the fallen angels are faced with the task of assessing, exploring, and accommodating themselves to a new environment, as also, at its dramatic heart, are Adam and Eve. In Hell and in Chaos, Satan and his followers are enterprising strip miners, city builders, and road makers, occupations that had, if anything, closer parallels in pioneer experience than did Adam and Eve's encounter with the new and innocent world of Eden. This may account for the fact that in describing the conception and building of the Talbot settlement, Burwell draws almost as extensively on the first two books of *Paradise Lost* as he does on Milton's subsequent accounts of Eden in describing the pristine landscape and abundant natural resources of the north shore of Lake Erie. By relying on Milton's depiction of Satan and the fallen angels in his portrayal of Talbot and his "enterprising freemen" (*88*), Burwell allows some unintended ironies to cloud his attempt to present pioneer life in heroic terms. During his treatment of the War of 1812, however, he skilfully uses an allusion to *Paradise Lost* ("from succor far" [*9:643*]:"Succor far off" [*359*]) to parallel the remoteness of Eve and Upper Canada from much-needed support and, thus, to cast the United States in the role of Satan. Burwell may not always have been in full control of his echoes of *Paradise Lost*, but he clearly understood the value of Milton as a source of aggrandizing diction and resonating patterns.

So insistently does Burwell portray the north shore of Lake Erie as a terrestrial paradise, a "beauteous" "land ... created for delight" (*33, 85*) like the biblical Canaan and Milton's "Plantation for delight" (*Paradise Lost 9:419*), that *Talbot Road* resembles in places a tract encouraging emigration to the Talbot settlement. As Susanna Moodie observes in the introduction to *Roughing It in the Bush*, such tracts commonly depicted Upper Canada as a "highly-favoured region" blessed by a "salubrious climate ... fertile soil, commercial advantages, great water privileges ... proximity to the mother country, and ... almost total exemption from taxes," and they "prominently set forth all the *good* to be derived from a settlement in the Backwoods of Canada[,] while ... carefully conceal[ing] the toil and hardship to be endured in order to secure these advantages" (4–5). An ancestor of the tracts that Moodie had in mind is Strachan's *A Visit to the Province of Upper Canada in 1819* (1820), a work that enumerates the social and commercial superiority of Upper Canada over the United States as a destination for British emigrants (v–vi). To his credit, Burwell does not minimize the work involved in clearing a backwoods farm. Nor does he include low taxes and closeness to Britain among the advantages of the Talbot settlement. But he does depict the north shore of Lake Erie as a "highly favor'd" area and, moreover, does so as if addressing each of the other four categories mentioned by Moodie, as well as one mooted by Strachan:

(1) *Salubrious climate.* With his eye very likely on Kalm (2:361–62) and Weld (2:92), both of whom – like Mackay (*1:87–92*) – portray Upper Canada as "unhealthy" owing to the prevalence there of "intermittent fevers" (malaria), Strachan concedes that "the Province has, indeed, got a reputation for fevers and agues; but with much the same truth as it has for savageness and cold ... There are few countries, if any, on earth, more salubrious than Upper Canada" (*Visit* 183). As well as signalling his agreement with Strachan, Burwell's insistence that the "air" of Upper Canada is "Healthful" and his assertion that "Here health pre-

sides ... / And breathes the fragrance of eternal bloom" (*29, 49–50*) address the miasma theory of the origin of disease upon which Kalm's seminal perceptions were based. As Mackay states the theory: "the fever and ague, as well as other maladies, are ... prevalent in Upper Canada, a country ... covered with forests and lakes; and intersected with swamps, which in the summer season, emit vapours highly pernicious to the human constitution" (*1:87 n.*). When read in the light of the miasma theory, Burwell's emphasis on the amount of cleared land in the Talbot settlement is also a testament to the healthiness of the area, as is his emphasis on the abundance of moving water in the region (*34, 42–44, 55, 79*).

To the other criticism frequently levelled at the climate of Upper Canada – that it is too extreme for good health and successful agriculture – Burwell responds only obliquely and by omission: he makes no mention whatever of winter, characterizes "summer's breezes" as "Gentle and balmy" (*45*), and concedes that "Autumn's suns ... [are] scorching" (*259*), but usefully so (they dry fallen trees and, thus, make them easier to burn). Moreover, he repeatedly mentions "orchards" (*305, 611*), a near-emblem in Canada of the temperate climate and "friendly clime" (*551*) that are conducive to health, wealth, and happiness. It is as clear from Burwell as it is from Strachan that "the orchards, where [they were] hurt [in the severe winter of 1810] have been renewed ... and the climate is found, by emigrants, delightful" (*Visit* 48).

(2) *Fertile soil.* Burwell leaves no room for doubt that the land chosen by Talbot for his settlement is "by nature's bounty blest, / ... and its soil [is] the best" (*27–28*). Every viable farm and growing town on the Talbot Road is a testament to the "fruitful soil" (*551*) of the region, as are all the specific evidences of "Productive nature" (*77*) in the poem, from "flowery banks," "majestic hemlocks," and "tow'ring pines" to "fertile vales," "fruitful fields," "bleating flocks," and "well-stored gardens" (*38, 41, 507, 38, 90, 508, 613*). If a single emblem of the land's fertility were to be sought, it could be found in the "waving Cornfields" (*507*) that Burwell mentions at various points. In *Talbot Road,* as in *The Rising Village,* a "virgin crop ... of wheat" in a field "won from the wilds" (*463–64*) constitutes proof of the soil's ability to produce the crop that will enable a pioneer farm and an agricultural settlement to achieve, first a measure of self-sufficiency, and then the superabundance necessary for the achievement of commercial and social maturity.

(3) *Commercial advantages.* A decisive factor in the ability of a pioneer community to parlay agricultural production into commercial advantage was the presence of a mill to grind grain into flour. "To stimulate

settlement [in the area of his land grant, Talbot] ... acquired mill machinery in 1804 and two years later constructed a water-powered grist-mill which was of great value to the emerging settlement until its destruction by American troops in 1814" (Brunger 857). Three years after the Treaty of Ghent, Burwell calls attention to "Wellington mills, late built, on Catfish strand, / To answer agriculture's loud demand," and remarks – with a pun on "growing" that links agricultural fertility with social progress – that a "substantial" mill "should be found / Where a fine growing country spreads around" (*499–502*). Another commercial advantage possessed by the Talbot settlement – one implicit in the very title of Burwell's poem – was easy access to markets in Canada and the United States on enviable roads adjoining rivers such as the Catfish and the Otter (*191–210*) which, in turn, fed into the Great Lakes-St. Lawrence River system.

(4) *Great water privileges.* Since it is crucial to pioneer culture, not merely as an indispensable element of life and fertility, but also as a source of energy and as a means of communication, water figures prominently in *Talbot Road.* To portray the Talbot settlement as possessed of "great water privileges" by virtue of its proximity to the Great Lakes, Burwell had to contend with the perception of "wild Erie" as a lake made extremely "dangerous" by "sudden storms" and a lack of "place[s]" for [boats] to find ... shelter" (Carver 168). The source of this perception against whom Burwell conspicuously argues is Weld, who elaborates at length upon Carver, describing in detail the murderous storms on Lake Erie (2:154–62; 296–310) and asserting that "on its northern side there are but two places which afford shelter to vessels drawing more than seven feet ... namely, Long Point and Point Abineau [Albino]; and these only afford a partial shelter" (92:159–60). Burwell concedes that "western storms ... often vex the bosom" of Lake Erie (*444–45*), but he presents them as a challenge rather than a barrier to emigration (*180–82*), and he capitalizes upon Weld's description of the placid aftermath of a storm, when the fall foliage was "fancifully reflected in the unruffled surface of the ... lake" (2:297), to present "wild Erie" as more picturesque than dangerous:

> Uninterrupted roves the careless eye,
> Where hills and vales in gay perspective lie;
> Or where the lake its billowy surges pours,
> And round the beaten cliffs tremendous roars;
> Or, mirror-like, smooth and unruffled lies,
> And seems to mingle with the distant skies,
> Where oft the vessel glides with swelling sails,
> Or waits impatient for the fav'ring gales.
>   (*69–76*)

To Weld's assertion that there are only "two," "partial" shelters on the north shore of Lake Erie, Burwell replies that the "friendly tide" of "Otter Creek" near St. Thomas provides emigrants with both a safe harbour from the "rough lake" and a "broad highway" to the Talbot Road itself, "whence they transport with ease, / Provisions, furniture, or what they please" (*200–04*). With the implication that, thanks in part to "excellent water communication" (Strachan, *Visit* 40–42), the Talbot settlement is already entering the fourth stage of social development, Burwell observes that "e'en now" on Otter Creek "the Oar of fair Commerce plies, / And the first efforts of her Empire tries – / Ernest of future wealth" (*493–95*). When Burwell "summon[s] dark futurity to light" (*546*) and envisages the arrival in the Talbot settlement of "Commerce, the first of friends to human kind ... That tames the hardy savage, rough and rude, / And forms society for mutual good" (*563–66*), he sees a "barque, deep laden ... with wealth from India's distant shores" riding "safely on vast Erie's bosom" (*571–73*). With bigger vessels will come safe navigation on Lake Erie, and the full realization within the mercantile system of the British Empire of the "commercial advantages" provided by the "great water privileges" of the Talbot settlement.

(5) In *A Visit to the Province of Upper Canada in 1819* Strachan cites the absence of "danger from the Indians"(vi) as one of the advantages of Canada over the United States. Burwell makes a similar point by referring only briefly to "the hardy savage" and ignoring completely the presence of Native peoples in Upper Canada. Moreover, by describing the area developed by Talbot and his "thronging bands" (*159*) of emigrants as "desert[ed]" (*14*), he avoids "potential conflicts ... of ownership" (Monkman 133) and, like Goldsmith, McLachlan, and Crawford after him, alleviates any anxieties that the European residents of Upper Canada might have had about aboriginal rights in the lands they were settling. If a piece of land was "desert[ed]" then there could be no question under the prevailing Lockean view of property that ownership of it resided with the man who had mixed his labour with it. In *Talbot Road*, as in *The Rising Village*, the settlers' ownership of the land is reinforced by detailed descriptions of their "Herculean labours" (*271*).

The first task that settlers in Upper Canada had to undertake was the felling of large trees to prepare the land for cultivation and to provide the materials for a log house (Strachan, *Visit* 82–83). From the line with which he concludes his account of the preliminary work of the "woodman's ax" – "So evening clos'd, and so the morning broke" (*211, 226*) – it is apparent that Burwell regarded the felling of trees for the making of a farm and a house as roughly equivalent to the creation in Genesis 1 of order and plenitude from chaos and void. The reduction of "the stateliest forest trees" to "heaps on heaps ... [of] shivered timbers" is a sublime sight – "A scene of terror to the astonish'd eye" (*221–22*) – because it reveals the godlike power of man to transform the created world for his own purposes. Much less resonant and impressive is the first product of the settler's constructive skills:

> Then rose the cabin rude, of humblest form,
> To shield from rain, and guard against the storm;
> Logs pil'd on logs, 'till closing overhead –
> With ample sheets of bark of elms o'erspread,
> And rough-hewn planks, to make a homely floor,
> A paper window, and a blanket door.
> Such dwellings, first, the hardy settlers made –
> What could they more? – necessity forbade.
>   (*227–34*)

In these lines Burwell abandons for a moment the attempt to aggrandize the settlers that drives much of *Talbot Road,* and, instead, allows the realities of pioneer life to enter the poem and to dictate the movement of its Popean couplets. The caesuras that occur near the centre of each line but one of the passage mimic the additive process involved in building a log-cabin, and some well-placed extra stresses ("Lógs píl'd on logs ... And roúgh-héwn planks") give certain phrases an appropriate weight and unevenness. It is not unfair to describe Burwell's couplets throughout much of *Talbot Road* as wooden, but here it is as if one accrescent, "rectangular," and "interlock[ing]" form (Strachan, *Visit* 82) had found its appropriate reflection in another.

Very likely Burwell's lengthy account of the next stage of preparing land for cultivation – the incineration in the fall of "leafy brushwood" and "Dried ... fall'n timber" (*259–61*) – had a basis in his own observations of this activity in the Talbot settlement. Nevertheless, many details of his description of the "wide wasting conflagration" created by his typical Upper Canadian "Woodman" (*263–92*) derive from Weld's vivid account of a dangerous "conflagration" that he witnessed in Virginia in the spring of 1796 and attributes to "the negligence of people ... burning brush wood to clear lands" (1:160–61). Perhaps taking his cue from Weld's comment that a huge brush fire is a "sublime sight," Burwell concentrates on the aesthetic and psychological effects generated by "flaming log-heaps," concluding with their ability to conduct the awed mind towards the infinite:

> Now, through the shades of the autumnal night,
> The flaming log-heaps cast a glaring light;

In contrast deep – the clouds, of sable hue,
Spread their dense mantle o'er the ethereal blue;
Above is pitchy blackness – all below
Wide flashing fires – Around, far other show –
Majestic trees, whose yet unfaded bloom,
In pale reflection, gives a sylvan gloom –
A dubious maze, which leads th' uncertain sight
To the drear confines of eternal night,
As it might seem ...

(*279–89*)

It is not inconceivable that Strachan had this passage in mind when he
wrote of the "brilliant spectacle" of log-heaps burning at night in a new
settlement and observed that, when these fires are appreciated as "the
first steps towards reducing a wilderness into a fruitful country, the
scenery becomes powerfully interesting" (*Visit* 76). This is the pioneer
sublime that results eventually in "profitable beauty."

Before wending his way home to watch "the fire heaps" with his "wife
and sons," Burwell's "assiduous labourer" takes care "to trim the heaps,
and fire th' extinguish'd brands" (*289–98*), activities that define him as
the responsible (Canadian) counterpart of Weld's negligent Virginians.
In describing the labours of his typical "Woodman" as "Herculean,"
Burwell does more than flatter the strength of the pioneering farmer;
he connects him to the classical hero whose capacity to "drain ... swamps,
build ... cities ... [and] destroy ... wild animals and tyrants" caused him to be
viewed as the herald of civilization by the early Greeks (Galinsky 148–49).
Burwell's "Woodman" is in no sense a complex character, but with his
great physical strength, his patient commitment to making a farm, and
his patriarchal dedication to his family (after a "barn," an "orchard,"
and a "garden" on his own land will come "a farm for each deserving
son" [*304–10*]), he is the earliest exemplar in Canadian writing of the
settler as Herculean hero and, as such, the ancestor of such characters
as Max Gordon in *Malcolm's Katie* and Abe Spalding in Frederick Philip
Grove's *Fruits of the Earth* (Bentley, *The Gay] Grey Moose* 217–33).

Following naturally upon the settler's fire-lit discussion of his
"schemes for future happiness" with his "wife and sons" (*293–316*)
comes a lengthy *"Apostrophe to Hope and Anticipation"* (5) that can easily
escape attention because it seems merely to fulfil the requirement of
"incidental meditation" in a topographical poem and, moreover, relies
heavily both in spirit and diction on Campbell's *Pleasures of Hope*. Yet
Burwell's *"Apostrophe to Hope and Anticipation"* occupies the structural
centre of *Talbot Road* and contains a centrally important series of reflections on the varieties and uses of expectation in a pioneer culture, pro-

viding a spiritual framework for one of the principal motivating beliefs
of the emigrant and the pioneer – the belief that hard work and self-sacrifice in the present will be rewarded by ease and fulfilment in the
future. One key to the *"Apostrophe"* is the notion of "reward" (*278*) construed, not in the eschatological sense that the Christian elements of
the poem suggest, but in decidedly worldly and materialist terms. To
the settler's sons, the farms promised by their father are the "good
reward" that they "Resolve to merit, by attention true" (*315–16*). To the
poem's narrator, the "hopes of Talbot Road" rise and fall with its "prosperity" (*429–34*). In the *"Apostrophe"* itself, "Hope" and "Anticipation"
are elaborated largely in financial terms, the former as a "treasury"
whose "interest all our daily wants supplies" and the latter as a "daily stipend to the sons of hope" (*335–38*). The God who oversees these dis-
bursements is a thoughtful and thrifty banker who doles out "bounty
only as we need" while retaining the principal sum – the capital of
"Hope" and "Anticipation" – to protect his clients from the loanshark
of "Despair" and the prodigality that could reduce them to "bankrupts"
(*339–42*). In *Talbot Road,* as in the Protestant work ethic that under-
writes it, God and Mammon may not be identical, but they are in accord
enough to bolster the efforts and salve the consciences of the materially
ambitious Christians who constituted a goodly proportion of the
poem's original audience.

In the three verse paragraphs that follows his *"Apostrophe to Hope and
Anticipation,"* Burwell chronicles the "deadly blow [and] desolating
wound" (*362*) that were dealt to the Talbot settlement by the War of
1812. "Emigration ceas'd at once"; the clearing and cultivation of the
land came to a halt; there were fears of violence and anarchy, and eventually, in 1814, the reality of an attack by "a hostile band / That stript
the people, with unsparing hand, / Of food and clothing" while the
men of the settlement were away on "active duty, at the frontiers" (*361–
418*). But as the tone of Burwell's account of the Canadian resistance to
the American invasion indicates, the effects of the War of 1812 were not
entirely negative. The War gave the Talbot settlement a military hero in
the "dauntless spirit" (*374*) of Sir Isaac Brock and it generated the local
pride that enabled Burwell to refer to troops raised in Upper Canada as
a "patriotic band" of "woodland heroes" (*378–80*) and to think of
Upper Canada itself as "an infant country" (*351*). Unquestionably the
most positive aspect of the War of 1812, however, was its speedy and
happy conclusion. Peace is a precondition for prosperity in a mercantile system, and thus the "hopes of Talbot Road ... rose again" with the
cessation of "destructive war" and the resumption of "peaceful avoca-
tions" (*426–29*). "All join'd [the settlement's] fallen prosperity to rear"
(*433*); the "copious tide of Emigration" again flowed towards Talbot

Road (*435–36, 454*); and the road itself was extended "westward ... as originally 'twas designed" (*437–40*). Among the new settlers were many ex-soldiers – "men laborious *and brave*" (*460*; emphasis added) – who were encouraged for military purposes to locate themselves near the American border. The War of 1812 was over in 1814, but in 1818 its consequences for the culture and demography of Upper Canada had barely begun.

On the evidence of some obvious spatial, temporal, and verbal parallels, it appears that Burwell attempted to structure his poem symmetrically around the War of 1812. For example between the inception of the Talbot settlement and the "sound / Of war's dread trump" the earth "scarce ... r[a]n, / Its annual circuit twice around the sun" (*345–48*) and between the sounding of "the silver-throated trump of Peace" and the completion of settlement to the west of Port Talbot, "the seasons [again] twice ... roll ... around" (*419, 441*). Such symmetries may be partly a consequence of limited poetic resources, for Burwell is clearly a poet of few words who tends to repeat himself. Yet they are also the product of a geometric cast of mind, a formatively spatial way of thinking that Burwell shared, not only with his surveyor-brother, Mahlon, but also with many others who were responsible for the organization of Upper Canadian space in the nineteenth century. Like the Talbot settlement itself (and, later, the Huron Tract), *Talbot Road: a Poem* was shaped by a survey mentality, by a mind that delighted in straight lines, "proper angles" (*200*), and "cross-way[s]" (*450*), in geometrical designs, architectural plans, and comprehensive schemes. Nowhere is this more obvious than in the "*connected survey of Talbot Road, from its eastern to its western extremities*" with which Burwell follows yet another survey of sorts, "*a short recapitulation of the preceding parts of the Poem*" (5) that stresses the major steps in the development of both Talbot Road and *Talbot Road* from past to present (*471–86*). Inviting the reader to "see, as on a single sheet, / The Talbot Road unbroken and complete" (*485–86*), Burwell surveys as if from above the entire road system from Norfolk County in the east to Essex County in the west (*487–523*), using the most visually obvious aspect of decasyllabic couplets – their hypotactic arrangement in a column down the centre of a page – as an analogue for a small-scale survey (or map) of the region. Just as "Harwich and Raleigh range along the line" of the surveyor (*520*), so, too, do they "range along the line" of the poet. The numbers used by Mahlon and Adam Burwell were different, but both played a part in superimposing a rational, European order on the terrain of Upper Canada.

After a conventional assertion that *Talbot Road* is "a simple story plainly told, / For truth's sake" and an equally conventional petition to the reader to "excuse / The honest labours of [his] humble muse"

(*540–42*), Burwell devotes most of the remainder of the poem to the future of the Talbot settlement. Evidently aware that the commercial stage of social development could be a mixed blessing – that abundant wealth and leisure could produce "Luxury" and "Vice" (Pye *1:21–24*) as well as such things as "costly" architecture (*574–677*) and accomplished poetry (*643–52*) – Burwell envisages the Talbot settlement of the future as an ideal society in which morality and restraint operate to allow the benefits of "Commerce" to be enjoyed without its banes. Complementing a "Town" humming with "business" (*574–82*) is a "Village" whose "green" is the setting for various leisure activities, most prominently the creative and seductive rituals of courtship, which are carried out in "accents sweet as e'er from Petrarch fell" (*575–94*). A catalogue of communal and witty activities, from "The choral song ... [to] the satiric stroke" (*595–96*), suggests that the social graces will one day be practised with polish and refinement in the Talbot settlement. But will the sophisticated "youths and maidens" who practise them not be in danger of lapsing into moral turpitude? As if to forestall this question, Burwell immediately follows his description of courting couples and their frolicsome activities with a vignette of the village at the moment when it most resembles the biblical pillars of fire and cloud: "Now see the setting sun, / Follow'd by evening vapors, dense, and dun, / Impart his last rays to the village spire, / And paint the windows with the hues of fire" (*599–602*). To Christianity as a guiding presence in the lives of future inhabitants of the Talbot settlement, Burwell adds "science," the acquisition of knowledge, not for its own sake, but for moral purposes: "See science beaming with resplendent light / A guiding beacon to man's erring sight, / To set fair truth before the devious will, / That it may choose the good, and shun the ill" (*637–40*). With Christian morality and right reason to guide them, the "youths and maidens" on the green will assuredly pass unscathed through the hazards of courtship and marriage. "Transcendent in prosperity" as it will become, the Talbot settlement will also be a "Blest spot! sacred to pure, domestic joy, / Where love and duty find their sweet employ" (*604, 619–20*).

Given the strong preference for organized space that is apparent throughout Burwell's account of the settlement of the north shore of Lake Erie, it is not surprising that when he envisages the future of the Talbot settlement he sees no wilderness whatsoever, but only a thoroughly humanized landscape of "Town ... Village," and "A constant chain of cultivated farms" (*607*). Wild nature has either been tamed or domesticated. "Vast Erie's bosom" is now safe for large trading vessels and each prosperous farm a patchwork of geometric enclosures:

broad, waving fields of corn,
And meadows, breathing all the sweets of morn,
And orchards, bowing graceful to the breeze
That rustles thro' the foliage of the trees;
... well stor'd gardens, that, with care, produce,
Enough for fancy and enough for use.

(*609–14*)

As Wanda Campbell points out, "a garden that contains both the functional and the fanciful is a symbol of a settlement that has moved beyond the stage of harsh necessity into one of leisure sufficient to allow for cultivation of the finer arts" (*"Bildungsgedicht"* 17). Occupying the "high centre" (Anderson 25) of "every farm" in Burwell's vision of an advanced agricultural-commercial society is a "stately mansion" that "commands" all that it surveys (*615–16*), like the "great farm house ... With many windows looking everywhere; / So that no distant meadow might be hid" of Katie's prosperous father in *Malcolm's Katie* (*3:1–4*). As Carl Schaefer's "potent image" (Reid 183) of an *Ontario Farmhouse* (1934) confirms, such edifices ask to be looked up to as well as looked down from. They are both rural panopticons, seats of omniscience from which an Adamic, and even godlike, overseer "oft ... contemplates alone, / The little Eden that he calls his own" (*615–18*), and democratic castles, lordly but undifferentiated embodiments of financial independence and social respectability.

But perhaps the best gloss on the various types of houses found in *Talbot Road* and other nineteenth-century poems about pioneer life in Canada appears in a document issued in 1880 by the Department of Agriculture. "Houses may be described as in three classes," writes Robert Wallace in *Reports of Tenant Farmers' Delegates on the Dominion of Canada as a Field of Settlement.* "First, the little log hut or 'shanty,' simply made of axe-squared logs of wood, laid upon each other, and notched at the ends to keep them steady; roofed in the rudest style, and the seams daubed with clay, is warm and comfortable, and all that the simple woodsman wants; but as he improves in fortune this may give place to a more airy and stately edifice – a 'frame house' – constructed of uprights, covered on the outside with a double lining of boards ... and plastered within. The third style ... being more substantial and more costly, is only adopted by those who are well off. The walls are built of bricks ... [T]he roofs of frame and brick houses are covered with 'shingle'" (132; and see Rempel 9–22). With due allowance for regional variations – in *Acadia*, for example, the "seams" of the "Log House" are sealed with "moss and sea weed" (*388*) – Wallace's "three classes" explain the significance of houses as indices of agricultural prosperity in most early long poems on Canada. As Captain W. Moorsom wrote of Nova Scotia in 1830, "we still see ... an apt illustration of the progress of agriculture, dating within the last fifty years. A hut formed of rough logs, or long, straight trunks, placed one upon the other as they are cut from the forest, has now become the gable-end, or ... the 'washhouse,' to a neatly boarded cottage; a little farther on is seen a wooden frame house, of two or three stories ... full of windows ... and standing in a well-stocked garden" (174–75). A log cabin or "rude" shanty is "a harbinger of civilization rather than one of its manifestations" (Gowans 7), but boarded, framed, brick, and stone houses are manifestations of progress, prosperity, and even "refinement." The fact that Malcolm Graem's house has "stone walls" (*3:21*) testifies to the very considerable wealth and prestige of its owner. So, too, do the "walls snow-white" of Ranger John's "vast ... homestead" near Niagara Falls in *The U.E.* (*5:283, 288*).

The rationalization of external nature that is evident on the farms of the future Talbot settlement extends even – perhaps especially – to the parallel lines of trees that will flank the Talbot Road itself:

> On either side the road a stately row
> Of shady trees present a sylvan show,
> Whose tops, wide arching, o'er the center meet,
> And guard the passenger from the noon-day heat.
>
> (*621–24*)

Beneath these soldierly trees lies "nature's rich, green *velvet* spread / In grassy *carpets*, or ... tufted *bed*," inviting passers-by to a "softer walk" or "innocent delight" (*625–28*; emphasis added). The "changeful hand of time" – and man – has indeed prepared a robe "more pleasing" for Nature to wear. Thus is Upper Canada envisaged by her first native-born poet: completely domesticated and perpetually innocent, always the bridesmaid and always the bride, Eve before and after the Fall.

8 Oliver Goldsmith,
The Rising Village

It is probably no more than a coincidence that *Talbot Road* contains a line – "The Town, the Village shall be seen to rise" (*574*) – that could have provided the programme for *The Rising Village*. When Burwell's poem was published in the *Niagara Spectator* in the summer of 1818, Oliver Goldsmith (1794–1861) was in the process of returning to Nova Scotia after a year in England, where he would have stayed permanently if it had not been for the intervention of the Earl of Dalhousie, the lieutenant governor of Nova Scotia from 1816 to 1820 (and thereafter, until 1828, the governor-in-chief of British North America). Moreover, when Goldsmith wrote *The Rising Village* in Halifax between 1822 and its first publication in England in 1825, he did not need to consult an Upper Canadian settlement poem for inspiration. Closer to his heart and hand were the poems of his great uncle, particularly *The Deserted Village* and *The Traveller*, and a work by a fellow Nova Scotian, Thomas Chandler Haliburton, whose *General Description of Nova Scotia* was published in Halifax in 1823. "In my humble poem," wrote Goldsmith in his so-called *Autobiography*, "I endeavoured to describe the sufferings ... [that the 'poor Exiles' of *The Deserted Village*] experienced in a new and uncultivated country, the Difficulties they surmounted, the rise and progress of a Village, and the prospects which promised Happiness to its future possessors" (42–43). "The origin and growth of a modern Colony affords much matter of curious speculation," wrote Haliburton in *A General Description*; "to trace the difference between the state of man rising in the progress of years to civilization, and that of an enlightened people operating upon uncultivated nature, is at once an interesting and useful pursuit. What the sensations of these people were, when separated from their friends and homes by a thousand leagues of ocean, and first settled in the trackless forest of Nova Scotia, may be more easily conceived than described" (163).

The debts of the Nova Scotian Goldsmith to his Anglo-Irish namesake and his brilliant compatriot are numerous and obvious. Both *The Deserted Village* and *The Traveller* are mentioned explicitly in the dedication to *The Rising Village* (*3–13*) and echoed at various points in the poem (see Lynch, notes 44–57). Like *The Traveller, The Rising Village* is dedicated to an older brother named Henry; like *The Deserted Village*, it contains a critique of the luxury and vice that can attend commercial prosperity. In both diction and form *The Rising Village* sometimes bears the imprint of Milton, Pope, Thomson, Pye and others, but on the whole (and appropriately), it emulates the vocabulary and decasyllabic couplets of *The Deserted Village* and *The Traveller* (and, it may be added, *She Stoops to Conquer*) to describe the pioneering heroism and growing prosperity of those victims of the agricultural enclosures in Britain who had settled "at no great distance from the spot where 'Wild Oswego spreads her swamps around, / And Niagara stuns with thundering sound'" (dedication to *The Rising Village 12–13; The Traveller 411–12*). That Goldsmith was probably as unaware of *Abram's Plains, Quebec Hill*, and *Canada* as he was of *Talbot Road* need not hinder the recognition that *The Rising Village* exists within a colonial continuity of creative responses to the depiction of North America in *The Deserted Village* and *The Traveller.*

The fact that, unlike these two poems, *A General Description of Nova Scotia* is not mentioned either in *The Rising Village* or in Goldsmith's *Autobiography* does nothing to diminish its importance either as a seminal influence or as a source of local detail. In his depiction of the Native peoples of Nova Scotia as "wandering savages" who roamed "Acadia's woods and wilds" like "beasts of prey" (*44–46*) before the arrival of British settlers, Goldsmith almost certainly follows Haliburton, who, in turn, draws upon the four-stages historian William Robertson to describe the Micmacs and Richibuctos as "wandering tribes, who depend upon hunting and fishing for subsistence" and "nearly resemble ... animals" (*General Description* 46; and see Hollingsworth 68–69). In the vicinity of Halifax particularly, writes Haliburton, "these savages ... defended with obstinacy a territory they held from nature, and it was not until after very great losses, that the English drove them out of their former hunting grounds"(47). "Hideous yells announce the murderous band, / Whose bloody footsteps desolate the land," run the equivalent lines in *The Rising Village*, "And now, behold! [the settler's] bold aggressor's fly, / To seek their prey beneath some other sky; / Resign the haunts they can maintain no more" (*85–86,107–09*). Goldsmith was much less learned in the law than the future Judge Haliburton, but the two evidently shared an interest in the legal aspects of the settlers' colonization and retention of "territory ... held from nature" by the Native peoples of Nova Scotia. Indeed Goldsmith's suggestion that the British exiles were the first inhabitants of an empty wilderness (*53–66*), that the nomadic "savages" were the late arrivals in a landscape under cultivation (*73–100*), and that the European settlers, therefore, have rights in the land that Native peoples have unjustly violated demands to be read in a legal context which extends beyond Haliburton and Nova Scotia.

During a brief stint in his youth as a clerk in a Halifax lawyer's office Goldsmith read Blackstone's *Commentaries* and *Coke Upon Littleton* (the first volume of Sir Edward Coke's *Institutes*; *Autobiography* 34). In the former he would have encountered, not only the four stages theory, but also some highly enlightened and, for a colonist, quite unnerving reservations about the practise of "sending colonies" into "countries already peopled, and driving out or massacring ... innocent and defenceless natives" who had a "natural right" to the land they used and needed for subsistence (2:7). In the latter he would have encountered the precept – conspicuously violated when the Natives drive the settler from his "hut" to seek "refuge" in a "wood" made almost as dangerous by "savage beasts" – that "a man's house is his castle, *et domus sua cuique est tutissimum refugium* [and home is to everyone the safest refuge]" (162). Through his reading of Blackstone, Coke, and other legal reference works, Goldsmith would have been familiar with the common-law principle that possession is nine-tenths of the law, as well as with the argument of John Locke and many others that ownership of land devolves to a person who "hath mixed his labour with [it]" and, hence, "remove[d] [it] from the common state that nature hath placed it in" (*Two Treatises* 134). It is surely not fortuitous that Goldsmith emphasizes the "great deal of labour" involved in "clearing," cultivating, and "retaining possession" of the land in Nova Scotia (*72 n., 103*). Perhaps this Lockean point was aimed, with Goldsmith's other legalistic suggestions, at reassuring readers of *The Rising Village* that, despite claims to the contrary, the European inhabitants of Nova Scotia and similar colonies did have rights in the lands settled by their ancestors. Such assurances may have been especially necessary and welcome in 1825 and 1834 (when a second edition of *The Rising Village* was published in Saint John, New Brunswick) because of anxieties caused by the landmark American legal case of *Johnson v. McIntosh* in which Chief Justice John Marshall ruled that "the rights of Indians in the lands they traditionally occupied prior to European colonization both predated and survived the claims to sovereignty made by various European nations in the territories of the North American Continent" (*Guerin v. The Queen* 377–78).

A charge repeatedly levelled at Goldsmith is that he failed to pay sufficient attention to contemporary problems in Nova Scotia and, hence, produced a poem as lean on "the facts of colonial life" (Rashley 30) as it is rich in "vague benevolence" (Pacey, *Creative Writing* 12). To refute this charge, it is only necessary to juxtapose Goldsmith's patently satirical vignette of the "half-bred Doctor" of "doubtful skill" who "cures, by chance, or ends each human ill" (*217–18*) with Haliburton's remark that the "Medical Profession" in his province was plagued by "quacks and unqualified intruders" – "wretched pretenders" who preyed on the "fears and ignorance of the community," with "frequently serious consequences" (*General Description* 30–31). A paragraph in the dedication and several of the endnotes in the 1825 edition of *The Rising Village* attest to the close attention paid by Goldsmith to two other issues that were held to be crucial to Nova Scotia's social and commercial well-being: the establishment of province-wide schools and the improvement of agricultural production. No doubt the vignette of the ineffectual schoolmaster in *The Rising Village* (*229–50*) reflects Goldsmith's conviction that his own education at the Halifax Grammar School (ca. 1808–09) was blighted by the "witless instruction" of an emigrant Irish "Master" (*Autobiography* 35). Just as certainly, his praise for the Society for the Propagation of the Gospel in the 1825 edition of *The Rising Village* and his admission in the same place that his "remarks ... on ... schools are ... more applicable to a former period" (dedication *21–26*) reflect his awareness of the work done by the SPG since the war of 1812 to establish schools and train schoolmasters in Nova Scotia (see Fingard 134–58). It is a measure of Goldsmith's concern with contemporary issues in Nova Scotia and with the social relevance of *The Rising Village* that in 1834, when the province's educational system was even less of a source of worry than it had been in 1825, he deleted from the poem both his "remarks ... on ... schools" and his notes on the SPG. His satirical vignette of the village schoolmaster remained, however, for reasons that will shortly become apparent.

Also absent from the 1834 edition of *The Rising Village* are several glowing references to the earl of Dalhousie, including a lengthy note praising "his Lordship" for his role in establishing "Societies for the purpose of diffusing knowledge in agricultural pursuits, and of adopting an approved system of cultivation" ([Lynch ed.] 36). One reason for the deletion of these references is the fact that by 1834 Dalhousie had been removed from British North America and thus ceased to figure in either the "affairs of the country" (Gnarowski, notes to *The Rising Village* 44) or the destiny of the poet. Like Cary, Burwell, and other early writers, Goldsmith had much to gain from the goodwill of the colonial élite. (The dedication to the 1825 edition of *The Rising Village* also contains a flattering reference to Sir James Kempt, Dalhousie's successor in both Nova Scotia [1820–28] and Lower Canada [1828–30], as well as a preface by John Inglis, the newly consecrated bishop of Nova Scotia.) Another reason for the deletion of Dalhousie from the second edition of *The Rising Village* is that by 1834 the Agricultural Societies to which the earl had given his enthusiastic patronage prior to his departure from Nova Scotia had ceased to command attention and support. Their heyday had been the period from 1818 – two years after Dalhousie's arrival – to 1825, a year before the Nova Scotia House of Assembly terminated funding for the Central Agricultural Board, founded in 1819. During this period, and largely as a result of a series of letters in the *Acadian Recorder* by the Halifax merchant John Young ("Agricola"), thirty Agricultural Societies were established in various parts of Nova Scotia (MacLean 931). The "Founder ... Promoter" and "permanent President during his administration" of the Provincial Agricultural Society was, of course, Dalhousie, and the secretary and treasurer of the Annapolis Agricultural Society was none other than Henry Goldsmith (Young 195, 209, 213). That Young knew Oliver as well as Henry Goldsmith seems more than likely. In his business contacts with the Halifax Garrison (MacLean 932), Young may have dealt with the poet, who was employed in the commissariat – the supply division of the British Army – almost continuously between 1810 and his retirement in 1855. The two men had a common mentor in Dalhousie, to whom Young dedicated the *Letters of Agricola on the Principles of Vegetation and Tillage, Written for Nova Scotia* when they were published in book form in Halifax in 1822. It is even possible that Young wrote all or part of his son George Renny Young's laudatory review of *The Rising Village* in the 14 September 1825 issue of the *Novascotian* (see Bentley, "Goldsmith" 28 and 59 n. 23).

Whether he played a role in reviewing it or not, Young would have found much to admire in *The Rising Village* for the simple reason that he would have recognized many of his own ideas in the poem. As grounded in the four stages theory as he was familiar with the farming innovations of "Coke of Norfolk" (Thomas William Coke), Lord Townsend, Jethro Tull, and Robert Bakewell, Young preached agricultural improvement as the key to Nova Scotia's transcendence of the savage and barbaric (or pastoral) stages of its development to social maturity and commercial prosperity. Viewing the pastoral stage of Nova Scotia's development as the equivalent of the European "middle ages" – the period of barbarism between the agricultural civilization of the ancient Romans and the improved agricultural techniques of the Renaissance (136) – Young inveighed against "the belief that Nova

Scotia was destined for pasturage; and that all attempts to raise bread must be fruitless and unavailing" because of the province's poor soil, harsh climate, and primitive farming methods (123). As the heir to centuries of agricultural improvements in Europe and England, Nova Scotia was in a position to bypass quickly or entirely the "long" "childhood" of "error" and "superstition" which, in Goldsmith's parallel analysis, "delayed" Britain's progress from an "infant age" of "darkest ignorance" to the "splendour, science, power, and skill" of "manhood's prime" (*530–33, 551*). By encouraging tillage rather than pasturage in Nova Scotia, the Agricultural Societies promoted by Young and endorsed by Goldsmith would enable the province to become first self-sufficient in grain and other "common ... necessities of life" and then a net exporter of them (Haliburton, *General Description* 117). In so doing, they would assure Nova Scotia's economic and social progress. No wonder Young envisages "the rising spirit of improvement" as "'dovelike ... incumbent' over the rude and undigested mass of ... [Nova Scotia's] rural chaos" (154). No wonder Goldsmith ignores domestic animals (and, with them, the pastoral stage of development) and depicts instead the settler's "surprisingly" rapid (Rashley 28) and almost "alchemical" (Lynch, intro. xvi) transformation of a patch of forest into a field of "golden corn" (*72*). And no wonder the settler looks from his "humble cot" and "rising crops" towards "Heaven" with "future joys in every thought" (*114–20*). "To the gloomy shades" he has "introduce[d] culture in its dual senses of agriculture and the arts" (Sinclair viii). In a field of grain lies the seed of a prosperous and civilized world.

Although Goldsmith designates "[agri-]culture" "a nation's Noblest friend" (*517*), he does not explicitly argue with Blackstone and other four stages theorists that "tillage" initiates the development of "civil society" and its "long train of inseperable concomitants" – "states, government, laws, punishments ... the public exercise of religious duties ... and leisure ... to cultivate the human mind, to invent useful arts, and to lay the foundations of science" (2:7–8). Nevertheless he strongly implies such a progression in his account of the "new prospects" that gradually form a "neighbourhood" around the settler's farm (*121–30*) – the "tavern," a "useful" building because it provides the settlers with positive "social pleasures" (*131–64*); then the "village church," the most admirable manifestation of cohesive community spirit and meritorious simplicity in the poem (*165–96*); and, subsequently, the mixed and, increasingly, negative accretions of a "country store" (*197–216*), a doctor's office (*217–28*), and a "country school-house" (*229–50*). It is sometime after agriculture has brought these manifestations of "social life," both good and bad, to Nova Scotia that the settlers and their families are able to relax and enjoy the full range of leisure-time activities –

"sportive pleasures," "festive dances," "gambols and freaks" (*251–84*) – which indicates that their culture has transcended "rudeness" and achieved "refinement." But a mere rehearsal of Blackstone's description of the uses of leisure – "to cultivate the human mind, to invent useful arts, and to lay the foundations of science" – suggests that the "sports" of the settlers and their families, however "dear," "humble," and "guileless" (*281–82*), may not be the kinds of activities that will ensure Nova Scotia's continued ascent of the four-runged ladder of civilization. What will ensure this continued ascent are the activities of the SPG, the Agricultural Societies and – because the man renowned for his skill in tracing "the words 'Oliver Goldsmith'" in "large ... elegant letters" on the ice with his skates surely suffered from no excess of modesty (*Autobiography* 114) – the production of such accomplished poems as *The Rising Village*.

In its very existence *The Rising Village* does more than testify to the fact that, certain appearances to the contrary, the human mind was being productively cultivated in the wake of Nova Scotia's agrarian development. The poem also testifies to the truth of Young's contention that only a country shaped by cultivation can inspire the emotional and imaginative responses that are requisite for poetry and patriotism. Drawing on Addisonian aesthetics and Hartlean associationism in a manner reminiscent of Bayley, Burwell, and others, Young argues that, while a "tract" of "uniform forest" exhibits a "sameness of prospect" which is neither visually nor emotionally stimulating, "hills" "diversified" by a picturesque combination of natural and man-made shapes have the power both "to surprise and delight" and to "become associated in the imagination with ... memorable events of which they were the theatre." "The sight of such hills," he suggests, "gives rise to a train of ideas which carry us back to other times, and are allied to melancholy or pleasure" (see also Repton 113). "The wilderness is a term of cheerless import, and involves whatever is repugnant to the human heart, but [w]hen the lineaments of the country have become distinct and visible, it will win our affections, and fix and consolidate our patriotism." Quoting Sir Walter Scott's *Lay of the Last Minstrel* (5:173), Young maintains that "in Nova Scotia the emphatic and high-meaning words, 'This is my dear, my native land,' can never be uttered with the appropriate glow and enthusiasm, till we can fully and uninterruptedly survey its general aspect, with its hills and dales, its ravines and glens, its rocks and caves, its springs and rills, its uplands and meadows, now hidden under an uninteresting mantle of foliage" (403–04).

One of the few places in Nova Scotia that permits the uninterrupted view of the "extensive range of landscape" that Young sees as the source of imaginative stimulation and patriotic feeling is the Annapolis Valley, where, as he says in another Agricola letter, "some high points" allow a spectator "to descry [various] objects at a distance," including "the rich marshes below" (48). Not surprisingly it is to "some easy hill's ascending height, / Where all the landscape brightens with delight" (*447–48*) that Goldsmith first turns towards the end of *The Rising Village* to celebrate Nova Scotia as a "Dear lovely spot!" that "impart[s] / Joy, peace, and comfort to each native heart." (*447–48, 481, 484*). Earlier the lonely settler's spirits had sunk when, "looking round," he saw "His home amid a wilderness of trees" (*59–61*). Later his heart had leaped up at the sight of his "golden corn" growing "where the forest once its foliage spread" (*71–72*). Later still, the settler's eyes were delighted by the various "charms of rural life" that the "arts of [agri-]culture" have called into existence around him. Now the poet surveys the Annapolis Valley and sees "boundless prospects" that "Proclaim the country's industry and pride." As in *Abram's Plains*, the "Here / There" direction of the picturesque leads the reader's eye through a landscape of "profitable beauty" whose visual and commercial "prospects" seem nearly boundless:

> Here the broad marsh extends its open plain,
> Until its limits touch the distant main;
> There verdant meads along the upland spring,
> And grateful odours to the breezes fling;
> Here crops of grain in rich luxuriance rise,
> And wave their golden riches to the skies;
> There smiling orchards interrupt the scene,
> Or gardens bounded by some fence of green;
> The farmer's cottage, bosomed 'mong the trees,
> Whose spreading branches shelter from the breeze;
> The winding stream that turns the busy mill,
> Whose clacking echoes o'er the distant hill;
> The neat white church ...
>
> (*451–63*)

Because the landscape of Nova Scotia has been humanized by agrarian development, it has become lovable and loving ("grateful," "smiling," "bosomed"). Because it has been variegated and ordered by "the plastic hand of human application" (Young 50), it has become an inspiring source and fit subject for the neo-classical couplets that Goldsmith here marshalls with the help of commas and semicolons into a regular but varied sequence. As much as the "laboured verse" that, it transpires, adorns the "rude cut stones [and] painted tablets" beside the "white church" (*456–66*), Goldsmith's polished couplets reflect the idea that refinement in art is a concomitant of improvement in architecture.

Goldsmith's ensuing treatment of the pleasantly affective "charms" of post-agricultural Nova Scotia also takes the form of a highly ordered sequence of couplets:

> How sweet to wander round the wood-bound lake,
> Whose glassy stillness scarce the zephyrs wake;
> How sweet to hear the murmuring of the rill,
> As down it gurgles from the distant hill;
> The note of Whip-poor-Will how sweet to hear,
> When sadly slow it breaks upon the ear,
> And tells each night, to all the silent vale,
> The hopeless sorrows of its mournful tale.
>
> (*473–80*)

Very noticeable in these lines are techniques learned from *An Essay on Criticism*, particularly from Pope's examples of subjects requiring sibilance ("*Soft* is the strain when *Zephyr* gently blows, / And the *smooth Stream* in smoother numbers flows") and from his illustrations of the mimetic effectiveness of "long *Vowels* ("drags its slow length along"; "The line too *labours*, and the words move *slow*"). But to what purpose are these techniques directed, and why, of all possible birds, the Whip-poor-will? Not surely – to answer the second question first – because this particular bird suggests the "loneliness" of the settler, as Rashley suggests (48–49), but because, on the contrary, it represents a triumph over that loneliness. Now that their province has been humanized by agriculture, Nova Scotians can experience with pleasure the remnants of the "deep solitudes" and "wilderness of trees" that, fifty years earlier, had made their spirits sink. "Loneliness ... saddens solitude," as Bliss Carman would later say, but "sweet speech" – community – "makes it durable," even desirable (*Sappho* 27). Not only has "successful settlement " (Rashley 29) made possible a "delight[ed]" response to external nature (*477 n.*) but, as predicted by Young, intimated by the mere mention of Carman, and confirmed by the unusual (for Goldsmith) lyricism of the Whip-poor-will passage, it has made possible in Acadia the kind of bitter-sweet response to external nature that is commonly found in post-Romantic lyrics.

But why, of all birds, the Whip-poor-will? Goldsmith may have had in mind the Native legend, recounted by Kalm and others, "that these birds, which are restless and utter their plaintive note at night, are the souls of their ancestors who died in battle" (Lynch, notes to *The Rising Village* 56). If so, then perhaps the elegiac tone of the Whip-poor-will passage is Goldsmith's belated and oblique expression of regret at the treatment of the Native peoples in Nova Scotia. There are, however, two other likely sources for the Whip-poor-will passage and the note that accompanies it: "the Whip-poor-will (*Caprimulgus vociferus*) is a native of America. On a summer's evening the wild and mournful cadence of its note is heard at a great distance; and the traveller listens with delight to the repeated tale of its sorrows" (*477 n.*). The first is Haliburton, who lists the Whip-poor-will and gives its Latin name in his *General Description* (31) but does not accord special attention to the bird. The second is Weld, who observes in his *Travels* that, because the Whip-poor-will begins to make its "plaintive noise ... which is heard a great way off, about dusk, and continues it through the greater part of the night," "many have imagined the noise does not proceed from a bird, but from a frog, especially as it is heard in the neighbourhood of low grounds" (1:196–97). Weld's comments have the happy effect of suggesting that Goldsmith's lyric moment has a place in the continuum between the skylarks and nightingales of British Romantic (and pre-Romantic) poetry and one of their almost inevitable Canadian equivalents, the tuneful frogs of Charles G.D. Roberts and Archibald Lampman.

As decisive for social progress as agriculture was conceived to be by Young, Blackstone, Goldsmith, and many others, it was not, of course, the highest stage of development to which a society could aspire. That distinction belonged to the stage, necessarily and desirably both rural and urban, at which the advantages of agriculture were supplemented by those of commerce to produce a society that was advanced materially as well as morally. In *The Rising Village* the exemplar of the commercial stage of social development is inevitably Britain, the "chaste and splendid" motherland where "Cities and plains extending far and wide" embody "The merchant's glory and the farmer's pride," where "Majestic palaces" coexist in "peace and freedom" with "the shepherd's cot," and where "arts flourish, and fair science shine[s]" (*27–42*). To fault Goldsmith for not presenting a realistic image of Britain after the enclosures (Keith 27) is to miss the point that in *The Rising Village* a wealthy yet moral ("chaste") Britannia represents the ideally balanced agricultural and commercial stage of social development, toward which Acadia has in a few short years made gratifying strides. This surely is the thrust of the comparison that immediately follows Goldsmith's paean to Britannia: "Compar'd with scenes like these, how lone and drear / Did *once* Acadia's woods and wilds appear" (*43–44*; emphasis added).

No more than his great uncle and many others was Goldsmith unaware of the moral dangers that can come with material wealth. Quiet hints of these dangers can be heard in the "glory" of the "merchant" and the "pride" of the "farmer" in the description of Britannia just canvassed. Such hints become a little louder in Goldsmith's inventory of the items for sale in the "country store" which earns for its proprietor the title of "merchant" in the "Rising Village" (*197–216*). Among the items on the merchant's "spacious shelves" are at least a couple – "Shawls for young damsels" and "silks" – that suggest a drift towards "luxury" within a still innocuous commercial prosperity. But the phrase "all useful things," which caps the inventory of the store's contents, transforms the preceding couplets into a satirical catalogue in which the "silks," and even the "children's toys," appear blatantly incongruous, like (though for opposite reasons) the "Bibles" among the "Puffs, Powders, Patches … [and] Billets-doux" on Belinda's vanity in *The Rape of the Lock* (*1:138*): "Woolcards and stockings, hats for men and boys, / Mill-saws and fenders, silks, and children's toys; / All useful things" (*213–15*). In the first of the "Letters of Mephibosheth Stepsure," which succeeded The "Letters of Agricola" in the *Acadian Recorder* beginning in December 1821, Thomas McCulloch provides a description of a village store that parallels, and, in fact, may have inspired, Goldsmith's: "when a merchant lays in his goods, he naturally consults the taste of his customers. Accordingly, my neighbour's consisted chiefly of West India produce, gin, brandy, tobacco, and a few chests of tea. For the youngsters he provided an assortment of superfine broad cloths and fancy muslins, ready made boots, whips, spurs, and a great variety of gumflowers, and other articles which come under the general denomination of *notions*" (9). The desirable but by no means indispensable items in the stores of McCulloch and Goldsmith constitute tangible evidence of Nova Scotia's success within the mercantile economy of the British Empire. But they are also the sign of a capacity for self-indulgence that can rapidly go from bad to worse:

As life's gay scenes in quick succession rise,
To lure the heart and captivate the eyes;
Soon vice steals on, in thoughtless pleasure's train,
And spreads her miseries o'er the village plain.
Her baneful arts some happy home invade,
Some bashful lover, or some tender maid;
Until, at length, repressed by no control,
Thy sink, debase, and overwhelm the soul.
. . . .
Oh, Virtue! that thy powerful charms could bind
Each rising impulse of the erring mind.
                              (*287–94, 299–300*)

Unless Nova Scotians are morally vigilant, their rise to commercial prosperity will be accompanied by a rise in the forces that threaten society, not from without (as had the "savage tribes" and "savage beasts"), but from within – "thoughtless[ness]," disobedience, "heedless passions" (*297*), and the like.

The breeding ground for such anti-rational and anti-social forces in *The Rising Village* is the school house (Lynch, intro. xvii–xviii), a "log-built-shed" (*229*) that represents a backward step in the development of the community. As well as being ignorant, and thus unable to "guide ... aspiring mind[s]" through the "fields" of "art" and "science" (*233–34*), the village school-master fails to exercise moral authority over his pupils:

> No modest youths surround his awful chair,
> His frowns to deprecate, or smiles to share,
> But all the terrors of his lawful sway
> The proud despise, the fearless disobey;
> The rugged urchins spurn at all control ...
> (*241–45*)

"To break the natural ferocity of human nature, to subdue the passions, to impress the principles of religion and morality upon the heart, and to give habits of obedience and subordination to paternal as well as political authority" (*General Description*): these were the purposes of education as conceived by Tories like Haliburton and Goldsmith. In failing to modify fallen human nature in the direction of reason and obedience, the school-house in *The Rising Village* does nothing to prevent young Nova Scotians from succumbing to the vices that, according to Weld, characterize those rural areas of North America in which the work ethic has been eroded by easy circumstances or increased prosperity (1:206, 2:335–38). "It is to be lamented," says a farmer in Weld's *Travels* who has lost his son to the lure of quick money, "that dissipation is sooner introduced in new settlements than industry and economy" (2:336). In *The Rising Village*, the equivalent of Weld's account of a family blighted by the eclipse of "honesty industry, and ... humble virtues" is the interspersed love story of Flora and Albert.

Since the education of girls in Goldsmith's day was more often than not conducted in the home and confined to such "useful arts" as cooking and sewing, Flora is unlikely to have attended the village school-house. Certainly, a domestic education and a lack of exposure to the incompetent school-master would help to account for Flora's "gentle manners," "unstudied grace," and "purity," and for "the lovelier beauties of ... [a] mind" ruled sufficiently by reason to admit only "at length" that she reciprocates Albert's affection for her (*317–30*). In contrast, Albert is a predictable product of the village school-house – impetuous, passionate, and, in time, deceitful and treacherous in a manner linked through allusion to Shakespeare's Othello and Milton's Satan (*308, 313*; Wanda Campbell, *"Bildungsgedicht"* 26). When Albert abandons his "native plain" and bride-to-be on the eve of his wedding, Flora is catapulted into a "frenzy" that nearly results in her death "amid the snow" (*363, 385, 395*), a fate that would have made her fully parallel to the "Swain" who loses his way and dies in a snow-storm in Thomson's "Winter" (*276–321*). With the help of a kindly "peasant" and his "tender wife" (*403–05*), Flora physically survives her wintry ordeal; however, Albert's "unmanly arts" have left her with a "maddened brain" (*416–22*) from which she never quite recovers to be the source of fecundity implied by her name and, indeed, required by the Rising Village if it is to continue growing socially, culturally, and economically. (In describing Flora as a "frenzied" woman from whom "reason has fled" [*379–80*], Goldsmith may have had in mind Blackstone's remarks on "phrenzies" and "deprivations of reason" as impediments to marriage [1:438–39].) In *The Deserted Village*, "the land, by luxury betray'd," is explicitly likened to a "fair female" ("Flora was fair" [315] repeats *The Rising Village*), and the Anglo-Irish Goldsmith's poem also contains a "poor shivering female" who is undone both personally by a male "betrayer" and generally by the "baneful arts" that "pamper luxury" (*287–336*). The Nova Scotian Goldsmith would thus have had to read no further than *The Deserted Village* to see the threat posed to an entire society and its constituent individuals by the "vice [that] steals on, in thoughtless pleasure's train." Both individually, as a woman, and, allegorically, as Nova Scotia (Hughes, "Goldsmith" 34–35), Flora exemplifies the dangerous consequences of veering away from the values that built the province, and which, fortunately, are still very much evident in the "care," patience, striving, "kind solicitude," "friendly efforts," and mutual purpose of the "peasant" couple who nurse her back to what remains of her shattered life (*402–12*).

That a woman is the principal victim of an increasingly luxury- and pleasure-loving society in *The Rising Village* may simply be a result of Goldsmith's decision to combine romance and allegory in his cautionary tale. Both the victims of love and the personifications of countries are more likely to be gendered female than male. Nevertheless, it is possible that the ruination of a woman specifically in *The Rising Village* is a reflection of the view, expounded by some of the most important exponents of the four stages theory, that women were especially vulnerable to the "disorders" of advanced societies, including the "romantic and extravagant passions" attached by such societies to sexual love (Millar 88–89). With material luxury comes a moral laxness that is not only "inconsistent with good order, and with the general interest of society," argues John Millar in *The Origin of the Distinction of Ranks* (1771 f.), but also a sign of a retreat from refinement to rudeness that can leave women no better off than they were at the savage stage of social development. To Millar, the "bad consequences" for the "rank and dignity ... of women" that attend the "free intercourse of the sexes" in "luxurious nations" indicates that "there are ... limits beyond which it is impossible to push the real improvements arising from wealth and opulence" (101–02). More concerned to encourage than to dissuade "improvements," Goldsmith follows his excoriation of Albert for causing Flora's ruination with the assurance that such "tales of ... woe" rarely happen in Nova Scotia. "Here virtue's charms" circumscribe the "free intercourse of the sexes" and, more often than not, Acadia's "modest youths" and "fairest girls" pass virtuously through courtship to marital bliss and, ultimately, eternal life "on high [with] the spirits of the blest" (*427–40*).

In the paragraphs that follow the interpolated tale of Flora and Albert, Goldsmith oscillates between "Happy Acadia!" and "Happy Britannia!" (*485, 529*), and concludes with the wish that, as the worthy heir of British "laws ... liberty ... splendour, science, power, and skill" (*550– 51*), Nova Scotia will one day "rise, / To be the wonder of the Western skies" (*557–58*). Blind to the potential for conflict between the mother country and her colonial "sons" (*549*), Goldsmith saw no incompatibility between his local and imperial loyalties, and, like Cary, Strachan, and many others, predicated his progressive conservatism on the perpetuation of British culture in a land of economic opportunity. An admirer of both the ancient and the modern, a believer in both tradition and improvement (see Bentley, "Goldsmith" 30–31), Goldsmith envisaged the relationship of Britain and Nova Scotia, as a continuum stretching onwards and upwards until "empires rise and sink, on earth, no more" (*560*).

Perhaps because he was never as fully committed to British North America as Cary and Strachan, Goldsmith exhibits more than these writers the twin hallmarks of the uneasy colonial: an extreme veneration of Great Britain and a truculently defensive attitude to criticisms of life on the colonial periphery by visitors from the imperial centre. The former characteristic is abundantly clear in Goldsmith's depiction of Britain as the model of Acadian aspiration, and also in his praise of the motherland as "The first and brightest star of Europe's clime," "The home of fairest forms and gentlest hearts" and – with his eye a little belatedly on the Napoleonic Wars – "The land of heroes, generous, free, and brave, / The noblest conquerors of the field and wave" (*534– 45*). The latter – a prickly offshoot of local pride – is barely evident in the poem without a recognition that in his depiction of the first public building erected in the Rising Village, the tavern, Goldsmith is addressing several sarcastic comments by Weld on the tendency of the "lower and middling classes of people" in rural parts of North America to pester travellers with unwelcome questions (1:123–24, 135–36). "In a tavern," remarks Weld, "a stranger" or "traveller" is so beset by the "idle and impertinent curiosity ... [of] boorish fellows" that he "loses all patience with this disagreeable and prying disposition." Goldsmith concedes that pointless questions can "Exhaust [the] patience, and perplex [the] mind" of the "weary traveller" or "passing stranger," but he puts them in the mouth, not of the settlers, but of the keeper of the tavern (*133–40*), and then, in a manner reminiscent of Bayley's refutation of Weld's charge of vanity against the French-Canadians, he rises to the defense of the "hardy settler of the dreary waste" (*141–46*). Who can blame people "far removed from every busy throng, / And social pleasure" for seeking to "learn" from a passing "stranger ... whatever he can teach"?

> To this, must be ascribed in great degree,
> That ceaseless, idle curiosity
> Which over all the Western world prevails,
> And every breast, or more or less, assails;
> Till, by indulgence, so o'erpowering grown,
> It seeks to know all business but its own.
> (*147–52*)

With its repeated vowel, guttural, and plosive sounds, and its well-placed spondee (" to knów áll búsiness bút its own"), the final couplet in this passage suggests the poet's own indignation at the behaviour he is attempting to defend. The resulting tension reflects in miniature Goldsmith's divided attitude to Nova Scotia – his dismay at returning in 1818 to a colony whose past achievements and future prospects he would nevertheless celebrate with commitment and feeling in *The Rising Village*.

9 George Longmore, *The Charivari*

The publication in Montreal in April 1824 of George Longmore's *The Charivari; or Canadian Poetics: a Tale, after the Manner of Beppo* counts as one of many testaments to the literary vitality of the city that was by the 1820s the demographic and commercial capital of the Canadas. In the second decade of the nineteenth century, Montreal was home to several book dealers and printers, three English-language newspapers, and, at various times, four sophisticated periodicals, most notably Samuel Hull Wilcocke's *Scribbler* (1823–24) and David Chisholme's *Canadian Review and Literary and Historical Journal* (1824–26). Several of Burwell's poems were printed in these periodicals between 1821 and 1825 (see *The Poems;* Mary Lu MacDonald, "'New' Poems"), and in 1826 *The Rising Village*, first published in England in the previous year, appeared in the *Canadian Review*. Not until the 1920s would Montreal be a more vital centre for Canadian poetry in English.

As Mary Lu MacDonald has suggested, the extended title and contents of the *Canadian Review and Literary and Historical Journal* bespeak its alignment with the Literary and Historical Society of Quebec ("Notes" 32), the organization founded by Lord Dalhousie in 1824 to promote the knowledge and preservation of things "Historical ... and Canadian" (qtd. in Klinck, "Literary Activity in the Canadas" 128). (Charter members included the historians William Smith and François-Xavier Garneau; Isaac Weld was made an honourary member.) Chisholme's lengthy appreciation of *The Charivari* in the *Canadian Review* effectively aligns the poem with the aims of the Quebec Literary and Historical Society and, indeed, expands those aims to include the "domestic habits and social pastimes" (106) chronicled by Longmore.

"As far as can at this remote period of time be learned," writes Longmore in a brief but informative appendix on the charivari, the "custom ... had its commencement in the Provinces of Old France; and ... from thence ... was transplanted into Canada with the earliest settlers ... and has been kept up ever since ... It began from a respectful feeling, among the friends of any couple who entered a second time on the state of matrimony; and who took this method of testifying their regard for the parties, by assembling with horns, pots, pans, and other kitchen utensils, and serenading the new married pair ... With the increasing desire to render their amusements subservient for useful purposes, it has been employed to obtain money for charitable appropriations; and to those whose feelings did not beat responsive to this virtue, the Charivari has been obnoxious." Longmore's appendix concludes with the observation that "the chief features" of the contemporary charivari "are the ludicrousness of the masks and dresses which are assumed, whose diversity afford ample scope for the indulgence of whim, and the display of humour" (67).

By background and circumstances Longmore was well-qualified to give poetic expression to the charivari. Born into the family of a prominent doctor in Quebec in 1793, he was probably acquainted with the custom before leaving Lower Canada in his teens to attend military college in England. When he returned to Lower Canada as a lieutenant in the Royal Staff Corps in October 1819, he was stationed and resident in the Montreal area, where there were several large and well-publicized charivaris between 1821 and the poem's publication in the spring of 1824. The first of these, at Chambly in January 1821, was reported to the *Montreal Herald* in a manner that anticipates *The Charivari* in both tone and terminology. After visiting a newly married "widow and batchelor" armed only with "horses and cows' heads" (horns being, of course, a standard emblem of cuckoldry), their friends returned the next night with "two coffins," one graced with an inscription that so angered the bridegroom that he "fired a ball ... through the obnoxious allusion" and threatened to fire at two of the charivariers. "This circumstance closed the scene; for the bridegroom was apprehended, to the great consternation of his gentle partner, who swooned away in the disastrous commencement of the Honey-moon." A second charivari, at Terrebonne in February 1821, featured "an officer with an enormous head ... Midas, with an admirably accentuated pair of ass's ears," and some "Antlers" (*Montreal Herald* [24 February 1861]), costumes and props that are echoed in *The Charivari*, not least in the "pair of horns, which in their towering height / Surpass'd most antlers" (*1043–45*). The charivari at Terrebonne, however, did not degenerate into violence.

The same cannot be said of the two most notorious charivaris in the Montreal area in the early 1820s. The first of these also took place in February 1821, but in Montreal itself. Occasioned by the marriage of one "William Lunn ... of the Naval Department, to [a] Mrs. Margaret Hutchison," the widow of a prominent Montreal merchant, it lasted for three evenings of escalating violence (*Canadian Courant* [10 February 1821]; Talbot 2:299–304). Blows were exchanged between the charivariers and the constabulary; several people were arrested; and the door of the police "watch-house" was "reduced to splinters" by their liberators. "A special session of the magistrates was held, and a proclamation issued prohibiting a recurrance of the charivari and inviting all well-disposed persons to unite with the municipality in its suppression, if attempted." This proved to be of no avail, however, and matters might have gone from bad to worse "had not the bridegroom flung open a window [on the third evening] and capitulated by donating of £50 ... to the Female Benevolent Society." But this was mild by comparison with the charivari that raged for several days in Montreal in late May and early June 1823 after the bridegroom of one of the two couples involved angrily refused the demand for "a sum of money ... or an entertainment" (*Canadian Courant* [4 and 7 June 1823]; Mary Lu MacDonald, intro. 7–10; Palmer). Led by a man who styled himself "Captain Rock" after "the commander of one of the most cruel and blood-thirsty banditti that ever disgraced Ireland" (*Montreal Gazette* [7 June 1823]), this charivari culminated in the destruction of a house and the death of an innocent bystander. Amid fears of insurrection and calls for the invocation of the Riot Act, a grand jury specially convened in the summer of 1823 judged that, coupled with the deterrent effect of charges brought against "various individuals," the enforcement of existing laws would be sufficient to dissuade "others from engaging in such lawless proceedings in the future" (*Montreal Gazette* [13 September 1823]). As Mary Lu MacDonald very correctly observes, "it is against the background of English-Irish disputation, murder tribunals, and demands for law and order that [Longmore's] lighthearted tale of the charivari of Baptisto and Annette must be read ... To local readers [*The Charivari*] brought to mind ... horrors ... of the very recent past" (intro. 9–10). That these were, indeed, the associations of Longmore's original readers is corroborated by Chisholme's comment in his review of *The Charivari* that the poem contains a timely depiction of an "innocent" custom recently "snatched" from the "natives" of Lower Canada and exploited for the purposes of "riot and crime" by "strangers and foreigners" (*Canadian Review* 1 [July 1824], 187; qtd. in Mary Lu MacDonald, intro. 7).

To the very extent that it is a "lighthearted" treatment of an essentially "innocent" custom which the events of 1823 especially had transformed into a source of trepidation for many members of Montreal's middle and upper classes, *The Charivari* is a reassuring, restorative, and conservative work. Unlike some of the bridegrooms in 1821 and 1823 Baptisto endures the jokes, jeers, and ritual humiliation of the chari-variers with a "patience which avail[s] him / More than inflam'd resistance, or retort" (*1373–74*). By giving them "Full thirty gallons of old rum, at least" (*1368*) he not only secures their good "wishes" and "Humour" (*1370–72*) but also, as Tracy Ware observes, "demonstrates exemplary common sense" ("George Longmore" 214). The moral of the poem would not have been lost on the colonial establishment to which Longmore belonged by birth and profession: to prevent a recurrence or escalation of the violence surrounding charivaris in the early twenties, treat the custom as what it had previously been – a harmless excuse for "amusement" and largesse.

Nor was either Longmore or his audience blind to the possibility that radical social and political forces might turn the charivari to revolutionary purposes. Towards the end of the poem Longmore leaves Baptisto facing the charivariers in his nightshirt to digress at length on contemporary political affairs in England and Canada. References to "Independence" and "Reformation," to the British "Constitution" and the "decapitation" of Charles I climax in the denunciation of several prominent British radicals – including one, James Watson, who was charged with high treason after the Spa Field Riot of 1816, and another, "Orator" Hunt, who presided over the disastrous meeting of reformers in 1819 that became known as the Peterloo Massacre (*1062–1104*). Very fresh in the memory of Longmore's audience would have been the so-called Cato Street Conspiracy of 1820, the apparent attempt of a few extreme radicals to assassinate members of the British Cabinet and establish a provisional government in London. As the charivaris of the early twenties had revealed, violent "crowd[s]" and "mob[s]" were rarer in Canada than in England (*1062–63*), but by no means non existent. And in the obstinate refusal of a legislative assembly dominated by French-Canadians to grant the "supplies or ... finances" (*1116*) necessary to maintain the colonial government was there not a radical and republican urge to take control of Lower Canada away from the governor and his appointed councillors? In the vehement resistance of Louis-Joseph Papineau and his followers – Longmore's "'soi-disant' patriots" (*1127*) – to the union with Upper Canada that had been proposed by British merchants in 1822, was there not a reactionary and nationalistic urge to take Lower Canada along the road to self-determination? Were Montreal's increasingly violent charivaris not a sign at least of the potential for social unrest to be channelled towards rebellious ends? As Michael Cullen has pointed out, the enjambement that occurs between

Stanzas 127 and 128 of the poem, when Baptisto has woken to find the charivari below his bedroom window, creates a pause in which the possibility of rebellion is "activate[d]" (45):

> seizing an old pistol, [Baptisto] held the trigger
> Ready for bloodshed, – whilst his nerves now pump'd
> All his heart's courage, which swell'd somewhat bigger
>   As the shouts bellow'd louder, and hands thump'd
> And opening forth the shutter, there beheld
> A sight, as if the city had rebell'd
>
> Against his marriage ...
>
>   (*1011–17*)

As well as releasing, and then reigning in again, the nightmarish thought of rebellion, these lines show Baptisto on the brink of mimicing the behaviour of the bridegroom at Chambly. With his "evenness of temper," his lack of "petulance" (*1290–91*), his "mild and polite behaviour" (Wilcocke 169), and his sensible and placatory generosity, Bapisto provides a model of conduct for the "rich, the great" of Montreal who had more than once too often in the recent past resembled "Canute" in their "foolish" attempts to rebuff the potentially destructive and deadly energies of the charivari. As much as *Abram's Plains* thirty-five years earlier, *The Charivari* is a conservative's warning to the élite of Lower Canada to deal wisely and charitably with those less fortunate than themselves.

In an appreciative review of *The Charivari* in the *Scribbler,* Wilcocke remarks that "the originals of each portrait [in the wedding party] are to be found in Montreal" (168). Since Baptisto and Annette are by their names and characteristics French-Canadian, their "originals" may have been Jean-Baptiste Toussaint Pothier (1771–1845) and Anne-Françoise Bruyères. Not only does the date of their marriage – 10 January 1820 – accord with the wintry setting of *The Charivari,* but Pothier's age at the time of his marriage – forty-nine – corresponds closely to Baptisto's "fifty" (*354, 396*). Although little is known of Anne Françoise Bruyères, she was almost certainly in her twenties at the time of her marriage to an "old Batchelor" who could be described with little exaggeration as a "school-contemporary" of her father (*69, 402*). But in 1820 Anne-Françoise Bruyères's father, Ralph Henry, had been dead for six years. What, then, is to be made of the two stanzas describing her immediate family?

The wedding party met, and there was seated
  Annette's papa, and ma', – her sister, – her brother, –
The first was bred a surgeon, but he treated
  Cases of physic too, – or any other
Which added to his practice, – and had cheated
  (As it was said,) – Death of some later pother
In being before-hand with him, – and ending
His patient's pains – which is one way of mending, –

Altho' not the most pleasant, – then his son,
  His father's counterpart, was smiling Billy
Who, also, in the practice had begun
  And look'd a very Bolus, – rather silly
But quite good-natur'd, and more fond of fun
  Than Physic, – whilst, the sister like a lily
All white appear'd, – and Ma', whose orange gown
For twenty years, at least, – Had grac'd the town. –
                                        (*801–16*)

A possible key to these stanzas lies in Anne-Françoise Bruyères's extended family as it developed from her maternal grandparents, Captain William D. Dunbar and Thérèse-Josèphe Fleury Deschambault, and their two daughters. One of these daughters – Janet Dunbar ("ma'") – married and, with her four children (two boys and two girls), survived Ralph Henry Bruyères. The other daughter – Marie Josèphe Dunbar (1766–1812) – married and predeceased a prominent Montreal physician and surgeon called George Selby, leaving him with one child, a son named William ("Bill"), who followed his father into the medical profession and, indeed, practised with him in Montreal (Lefebvre; Lessard). Following the deaths in 1812 and 1814 of Marie-Josèphe Dunbar Selby and Ralph Henry Bruyères, the remaining members of the two families gravitated towards each other to the extent that they came to resemble a single family. Thus after Dr. William Selby married Marguerite Baby ("Ma'") in 1815, Anne Françoise Bruyères's sister Catherine Bruyères Kennelly (1797–1849) became a near-relative or parent ("proche parent" [Lefebvre 1594]) of the couple's five children, the first of whom – Jessie Selby (1818–92) – was the namesake of Anne-Françoise and Toussaint Pothier's only child, Jessy Louise (or Jessé Louise). Since it was the custom in French Canada for wedding parties to assemble at the home of the bride's father (Talbot 2:295), there is some likelihood that the "original" for the setting of the wedding party in *The Charivari* was the stone house of Anne-Françoise Bruyères's own "proche parent," Dr. George Selby ("papa"), at 153, Rue Saint-Paul in Montreal (Doige).

As well as making possible some plausible guesses at the "originals" of other "portrait[s]"in *The Charivari* (see Bentley, intro. xxiii–iv), the provisional identification of Longmore's wedding party serves at least two useful purposes. The first is to reinforce the poem's exemplary and reconciliatory nature by revealing the presence at its heart of a family group that is nothing if not a model of French-English interconnectedness and interdependence. By grace of circumstances and mixed blood, the Selbys and the Bruyères were members of an extended family that stood as proof of the ability of people of British and French extraction to live together in harmony in Lower Canada. A cacophonous charivari constitutes the climax of Longmore's poem, but nearer to its structural centre lie a wedding and a feast, two age-old symbols of reconciliation, harmony, and a new order. Before the arrival of the "parson" or "priest" (*875, 910*), the harmony of Annette and Baptisto's wedding is briefly disrupted by an angry and topical quarrel between Lawyer Shark and Sammy Grouse about the rights and wrongs of Lord Selkirk's dispute with the Northwest Company. And after the wedding has been performed the harmony of the proceedings is again threatened by "raillery's tongue" (*916*) and by the off-colour humour of Ireland's flamboyant representative among the wedding guests, a gold-clad Captain Casey who punningly asserts that "Baptisto has got in *a net*" (*920*). Perhaps drawing on Kalm by way of the principal prose source for *The Charivari,* John Lambert's *Travels through Canada, and the United States of North America, in the Years 1806, 1807, and 1808* (1810 f.; 1:289), Longmore makes Annette a model of the unperturbable good humour supposedly characteristic of French-Canadian women (*921–24*). Like Baptisto's "good sense," though in a different and, assuredly, less dangerous sphere (Captain Casey is no Captain Rock), Annette's "good nature" – her ability to take "all frolic in good part" – heals rather than opens wounds. *The Charivari* is "not a didactic allegory [where] every event has a one-to-one correspondence with an abstract idea" (Ware, "*The Charivari*"11), but it is a poem whose central events and characters embody many lessons for the racially mixed and sometimes rancorous society that inspired it.

The second purpose that is served by the provisional identification of the individuals portrayed in *The Charivari* is that of establishing the possible grounds and extent of the personal satire in the poem. This is particularly true in the case of the most fully drawn and complex of Longmore's caricatures, for while Baptisto is clearly a figure to be admired in his handling of the charivari, he is also the butt of numerous jokes which may rely for some of their effect on the reader's knowledge of

Toussaint Pothier and his position in Montreal society. For instance the humour of the following description of Baptisto's dandiacal obsession with the cut of his breeches ("small cloaths") clearly increases with the knowledge that Pothier was nicknamed "le beau Pothier à cause de son physique avantageux et de sa correction vestimentaire" (Massicotte, "Mutations" 271):

> his cloaths had fashion'd been of late,
> To the most novel cut, – the dandiest Schneider
> Was now consulted, and the very fate
> Of having his small cloaths, more tight or wider
> Than taste prescrib'd, engross'd his pride innate ...
> (273–77)

In a similar vein Longmore's depiction of Baptisto as "an Epicure, / [Who] lik[es] good living, such as soups, and sauces, / Ragouts and curries" (425–27), and whose "foibles" include "a slight excess in punch or wine" (217–18) gains in humorous effect with the knowledge that Pothier was a very "wealthy man" (Philippe Pothier 702) who lived extremely well ("vécût largement" [Massicotte, "Mutations" 271]) off the proceeds of his businesses and seigneuries. It is because he is probably based on a real person and cast in a universal mould that Baptisto has at once density and currency, the two qualities essential for a comic character to avoid the twin pitfalls of the merely topical and the overly general.

The provisional identification of Pothier as the "original" of Baptisto holds one other notable advantage: it allows the satire of *The Charivari* and the stance of its author to be placed with some precision in relation to Montreal society in the early 1820s. According to Edward Allen Talbot, who was himself married in Montreal in 1821 (*Montreal Herald* [19 May 1821]), the upper echelons of the city's society were divided into two "distinct classes: The FIRST ... composed of the civil and military officers, the most respectable professional men in Law, Physic, and Divinity, and the several members of the North West Company: – [and] The SECOND of merchants of large fortune" (2:283; and see Lambert 1:274–75). That Pothier had worked his way from the lower to the higher of these two classes principally on the basis of his wealth made him, in 1820, something of an *arriviste* in the group to which Longmore probably took for granted that he himself belonged by birth, if not rank. As Fernand Ouellet writes in what is likely to remain for a long time the finest assessment of Pothier's social position and political ideas, "Pothier nous apparaît comme un bourgeois devenu gentilhomme" (147). In the first two decades of the century when he was amassing his fortune in the fur trade, writes Ouellet, Pothier may well have identified himself "totalement avec la classe des capitalistes," but by the late twenties he "s'identifie complètement avec la noblesse" (147). From this it can be inferred that, at around the time of his courtship and marriage in 1820, Pothier was an assiduous (and, very likely, somewhat insecure) social climber – a prime target for social satire, as he hobnobbed with respectable professional men such as George Selby and members of the Northwest Company like Sammy Grouse (perhaps Alexander Henry) and, to impress his future bride, curtailed his "laughable queer habit ... / Of twitching constantly his prim perruque [wig]" (*279–80*).

Of the many poems to which Longmore might have turned as a model for *The Charivari*, few would have been as fitting as Byron's *Beppo: a Venetian Story*, which was first published anonymously in 1818. Not only does the subject-matter of *Beppo* – a pre-Lenten carnival of "fiddling, feasting, dancing, [and] masquing" (7) that ends with the amicable resolution of a marital triangle – contain many of the same features as a charivari, but its amused and chatty tone is exactly what Longmore needed for the gossipy but detached Old Bachelor who recounts the events surrounding the wedding of Baptisto and Annette. As "imperfect and inclined to err" as he is admirable and worthy of emulation (Longmore, *Tales* 294), Pothier/Baptisto is both a *bourgeois gentilhomme* and a Byronic hero, a "laughable" "foreigner" and a regency cavalier. Moreover, and precisely to the extent that it suits the subject-matter and tone of *Beppo*, the *ottava rima* stanza in which Byron cast his *Venetian Tale* (as well as the *Vision of Judgement* and, of course, *Don Juan*) is entirely appropriate to *The Charivari*. By imitating and, in places, merely borrowing the comical rhymes which give Byronic *ottava rima* much of its "quietly facetious" quality (Byron, qtd. in Fussell 146), Longmore ensures that his own poem will bring to the custom of the charivari a humour that is both appropriate and necessary. As Klinck aptly states, in *The Charivari* "Byron was ... happily naturalised in Montreal by a man who could impart the flavour of this ... English-French city" ("*The Charivari*" 36).

More than any other aspect of *The Charivari*, with the possible exception of its plethora of dashes and parentheses, the feature of the poem that is most likely to test the patience of a reader today is its numerous "long digressions" (*1225*) "*after the Manner of Beppo*" and *Don Juan*. Yet these digressions frequently contain material on such matters as British mobs and Canadian politics that, as already seen, are central rather than peripheral to the meaning of the poem. As Ware points out (quoting Leslie Marchand on the digressive technique of *Beppo* and *Don Juan*), the "meat" of these and similar poems does not so much lie in their stories as in their digressions ("*The Charivari*" 3). "If the Prose

Essayist carries us along with the truth in a direct and unbending course to his object," writes Longmore in his 1826 essay on Lord Byron, "the Poet ... lead[s] us through the beautiful labyrinths of intellectual grace, and brilliant scenery ... wafting us upon the wings of fancy through regions of his own bright creation, affords us on the way the most delightful amusement, and surrounds us with the most enchanting diversity and beauty" (*Tales* 292). This is an aesthetic of "variety" (*115*) and "wandering" (*1234*) that permits the poet considerable latitude of focus and pace as he leads the reader along "the paths of Poesy." As well as licensing the pattern of excursion (digression) and return that shapes *The Charivari* ("But to my tale" [*777*]), it is an aesthetic that grants the Old Bachelor a near-epistolary freedom to express his opinions on a variety of serious and amusing topics, some intimately and others tangentially related to his account of the smooth and bumpy course of Baptisto's love for Annette. Almost inevitably, there is a Byronic digression on the attributes of women that patriotically adds Canada's "daughters" to the list of those from other countries praised in *Don Juan* and elsewhere (*297–336*). Just as predictably, there is a digression on sexual love that wonders aloud, with numerous historical and mythological allusions, about the varieties, advantages, and shortcomings of that ubiquitous and central emotion (*129–76*). And, appropriately, there are also two digressions on Byron himself (*489–552; 1225–56*), each paying tribute to different facets of his genius, including his ability to sustain a long digression without becoming "Tiresome" (*1228*) and his talent for applying satire's lash, albeit in a cold-blooded manner not altogether to Longmore's liking (*Tales* 296).That Longmore was not uncritical in his admiration of Byron is further indicated by the fact that *The Charivari* contains digressions declaring the narrator's affection for his country and his family (*97–128; 737–76*), two subjects whose absence from the work of his cosmopolitan master Longmore notices with regret and apology in his essay on Lord Byron (*Tales* 295–96).

While Byron is the major poetic presence in *The Charivari*, he is by no means the only one. Behind Longmore's expression of local pride in his digression on Canada, for example, lies Sir Walter Scott (see *Tales* 13–18), and in his digression on maternal love there is something of the Wordsworth of the 'Intimations Ode'. With its explicit reference to Byron and its facetious rhyme of "maxim" and "tax him" borrowed from *Don Juan* (*3:1622–24*), the following stanza might seem free of further debts except, of course, to the sceptical seventeenth-century writer whose "maxim" it quotes:

'Tis Rochefoucault, who tells us in a maxim, –
  "There's something in th' adversity of friends
"Which does not quite displeases us;" Byron backs him,
  As I suppose, when he so oft extends
To all, his satire, – (though not fair to tax him,)
  But Man, – his mind so seldom rightly lends
To Heav'n, – 'twere hard to say and scan Earth's throng,
If Rochefoucault and he, are much in wrong.

                (537–44)

Yet arguably – and as Ware has intimated ("*The Charivari*" 3) – the most important literary presences here, especially in terms of Longmore's satirical norms and targets, are two writers whom the stanza does not name: Swift and Pope. Almost certainly, Longmore took La Rochefoucauld's famous "maxim," not from the original *Réflexions, ou sentences et maximes morales*, but from Swift's "Verses on the Death of Dr. Swift, DSPD," where it serves both as an epigraph ("In the adversity of our best friends, we find something that does not quite displease us") and as a point of departure ("As Rochfoucauld his maxims drew from nature, I believe 'em true" [485]). Pope's presence is more diffuse in the stanza, but, like Swift's, it is evident here and elsewhere in *The Charivari* in Longmore's inclination to look beyond "Man" to God, and to emphasize such markedly neo-classical values as balance, moderation, restraint, and right reason. In Ware's words, "a recognition of man's potentiality – the ability of the mind to adapt to heaven – combined with an awareness of man's actual imperfection" orients Longmore towards "the greatest satirists in [the] language" ("*The Charivari*" 3), particularly the Augustan satirists in whose values and techniques Byron's roots also lie. Loud local echoes of Swift, Pope, and – to merely mention one other important influence on Longmore's satire – the Samuel Butler of *Hudibras* may be relatively rare in *The Charivari,* but they are present in sufficient numbers to indicate Longmore's acquaintance and affinity with the Christian-humanist tradition that lay behind Byron and, for many of Canada's nineteenth-century poets, provided a conservative and religious counterbalance to Byron's scepticism and idiosyncrasy.

    If there is another writer who looms as large as Byron in the local debts and large patterns of *The Charivari,* it is Shakespeare. No doubt at least in part because of the fondness for amateur dramatics in British garrisons, allusions to *Hamlet, Othello, Macbeth, Romeo and Juliet, The Tempest, Much Ado About Nothing, The Comedy of Errors, A Midsummer Night's Dream, The Merry Wives of Windsor,* and even *Timon of Athens* dot *The Charivari* like raisins in a spotted dick. An epigraph from the opening scene of *Much Ado About Nothing* announces the poem's concern with the marriage and anxieties of an elderly "bachelor," and an echo of Puck's closing speech in *A Midsummer Night's Dream* brings down the curtain on Baptisto's charivari, pushing home the point that, thanks to the good sense of a decidedly unsupernatural "Prince of goodfellows" (*1379*), all is well that has ended well. As if to emphasize the potential for tragedy in what is happening, Longmore embeds clear allusions to *Othello* ("Chaos has come again" [*1200*]) and *Macbeth* ("'Give physic to the dogs'" [*1217*]) in the stanzas between the alarming onset of the charivari and its happy conclusion. In the poem as a whole, however, the allusions are more to Shakespeare's comedies than to his tragedies, and most frequently of all, to *A Midsummer Night's Dream*, a work not without its own component of charivari (Bristol 162–78). Indeed, so frequent and explicit are Longmore's allusions to this play that they ask *The Charivari* to be seen as a midwinter night's dream – an excursion into the carnivalesque realm between dusk and dawn where nightmares and disasters can occur but, in the event, do not because the poem's presiding goddess is "Thalia" (*4*), the muse of comedy, whose specialities are "gaiety, briskness ... pleasantry" (Tooke 187) – and, of course, happy endings.

Bound in with Shakespeare's dramatic works between the covers of *The Charivari* are at least a couple of the comedies of Ben Jonson. A second epigraph for the poem, and an early indication that "Poetry" itself will be one of its subjects (more of which in just a moment), comes from *Bartholomew Fair*, as, very likely, did the suggestion for the comparison of Baptisto with "a clown in England, at a fair" (*387*). From *The Alchemist* or *Volpone* (or both) perhaps came the inspiration for the likening of "Love ... [to] a true alchymist" (*396*) and – with contributions from other plays by Jonson and Shakespeare – the knowledge of the physiological theory of humours that Longmore uses at several points in the poem. The resonantly Jonsonian announcement that Baptisto's "temper [is] phlegmatic" (*211*) – i.e., that he is ruled by the cold and moist humour of phlegm – is of special interest because it classifies him as a cool character, a calm and sluggish personality, who is not likely to be excited to violence by the provocations of the charivari. Had Baptisto been governed by either yellow bile (and, hence, choleric: obstinate and quick to anger) or black bile (and, hence, splenetic: melancholy and peevish), he might well have acted angrily and ungenerously when confronted on his wedding night by:

> a hundred looks ... dealing
> Their jibes and ridicule in waggish mood
> And many other different modes, appealing

To the splenetic organs, which arouse
The bile, in every cause, which we espouse. –

(*1260–64*)

A "humorous" man in both a general and a specific way, Baptisto has
the lead role in a comedy of humours whose moral for Montreal's establishment in the 1820s was that more phlegm and less bile are needed in
face of "all ... curs'd promoters of the spleen" (*1344*), from "A lazy valet"
(*1338*) to a rambunctious charivari.

Since Longmore's literary models were selected from among the
front ranks of British writers past and present, it should occasion no surprise that he begins *The Charivari* with a lengthy and scathing attack on the
scribblers who have "sprung up" in "this [hemi]sphere" to insult the
classical muses with their "ballad-verse, " their "plodding ode[s]," and
their contemptible "sonnet[s]" (*1–48*). Quite likely inspired, at least in
part, by Lambert's observation that the writers in various Lower Canadian newspapers were constantly engaged in "scribbling warfare" with
"inky arms" (1:324), Longmore's satirical attack on an "inky," "motley,"
and unspecified group of local "scribblers" is largely carried out with
arms and ammunition seconded from Byron's *Hints from Horace* and
English Bards and Scotch Reviewers. Like Byron, Longmore has nothing
but contempt for the pedestrian and pretentious versifiers of his day
who

perchance
Within the murky confines of a garret,
  Invoke a muse of rueful countenance,
With palid cheek – grey eyes – and locks of carrot,
  More like fierce Hecate, than Thalia's glance,
Others, who Harpies – Furies – Fates, combine,
Thus cast a libel on the immortal Nine!

(*34–41*)

This is Apollo flaying Marsyas for artistic pretension, and it combines
ludicrous detail with classical allusion in a confident and insulting way
that echoes back, not just to Byron on Southey and parts of Wordsworth, but also to Pope on his literary dunces and their vulgar muses.
So vigorous and condescending is Longmore's attack that it occasioned
only a mild response from one of the "scribblers" whom he probably
had in mind. Alluding to the fact that in the advertisements for *The
Charivari* the author of the poem is given as "Launcelot Longstaff"
(*Montreal Gazette* [27 March 1824 f.]) – a pseudonym probably derived
from the *Salmagundi Papers* (Klinck, "Literary Activity" 131) by way of

Lambert's *Travels* (1:313) – Levi Adams declines in *Jean Baptiste: a Poetic Olio, in II Cantos* to "write a satire on these Errant Knights, / Yclept *old Bachelors*" (15). And little wonder: once flayed, twice shy.

Closely related to the literary satire in *The Charivari* is the question of how seriously to take the subtitle – *Canadian Poetics* – that graces all the advertisements and both title pages of the poem. Is the alternative title merely an arrow pointing to the satirical attack on the "motley group of bards" that begins the poem, or is it an invitation to view the climactic charivari as a literary phenomenon and the poem as a whole as a kind of exemplary treatise on Canadian poetry? Both Ware and Cullen incline towards the latter and larger view, seeing "the cacophonous charivari [as an] ... emblem of the state of Canadian poetry in 1824" (Ware, "*The Charivari*" 4) and as the energetic manifestation of a distinctively Canadian culture (Cullen 42–45). When taken together, and supplemented with the environmental determinism that was current in Longmore's day, the arguments of Ware and Cullen suggest a third way in which *The Charivari* and the transplanted custom of which it treats are at least analogous to a *Canadian Poetics*.

Within a few stanzas of his magisterial castigation of the "scribblers," and in the midst of his preliminary introduction of Baptisto and Annette, Longmore expresses his affection for his native land in a brief but significant description of the Canadian landscape:

> I like thee Canada; I like thy woods
>   When Summer's splendour shines on every tree;
> I like thy cataracts, and roaring floods
>   As if, old Chaos in Titanic glee,
> Had set the elements in tuneful moods
>   To rack their voices in rude revelry ...
>
>   (*97–102*)

With its emphasis on the turbulence and plangency of Canada's rivers and waterfalls, and its reference, perhaps by way of *Paradise Lost*, to the Hesiodic notion of Chaos as the antecedent of the gods (or, in Milton's case, "Nature" [*2:895*]), this stanza obviously foreshadows the "tuneful moods" and "rude revelry" of the charivariers who will make the street outside Baptisto's house "so echo with the strain" of their rough music that "You would have thought; Chaos had come again" (*1199–1200*). One implication of this parallel between the landscape of man and the custom of the charivari is that a resemblance between social behaviour and physical landscape is to be expected and even cherished. Crèvecoeur makes much this point when he writes that "the inhabitants of Canada, Massachuset" and other provinces in North America "will be as different as their landscape ... [I]t is with man as it is with the plants and animals that grow in the forests; they are entirely different from those that grow in the plains" (61, 66). From such deterministic assumptions (which, if anything, gained currency as a result of the Romantic movement), it is but a small step to crediting – or, as likely, endowing – poetry with characteristics resembling a particular landscape and its inhabitants. This correlation is, in fact, explicitly articulated by Scott in the influential introduction to the third canto of *Marmion*, where the northern poet explains his own "wild" and "unrestrain'd" poetics in terms of the wildness of his native landscape and its plant life (79). The suggestion, then, is that *The Charivari* is given the alternative title of *Canadian Poetics* partly because Longmore assumed a correlation, possibly even a consequential relationship, between landscape, social custom, and – given the operation of a mimetic aesthetic – poetic form. But Longmore does more than simply record, and, to a degree, simulate the cacophonous disorder found in the Canadian environment; he uses poetry to reflect and exemplify the bringing of discord and "Chaos" to order and harmony. His is an answerable style, a *Canadian Poetics*, because, in response to physical and social phenomena that both elicit affection and – from a conservative perspective – require restraint, *The Charivari* serves up local colour, colloquial vigour, and digressive waywardness aplenty but, always and finally, subordinates all three to established patterns of religious, social, and literary order.

A little over six months after the publication of *The Charivari* Longmore, his wife, and their two children left Montreal for England on the *Ottawa* (*Montreal Gazette* [20 November 1824]). Subsequent postings took him to Mauritius and the Cape Colony, where he died in 1867, never having returned to Canada (MacDonald, "Further Light"). A true product and servant of the second British Empire, Longmore nevertheless reveals in *The Charivari* and his other long poem set in Canada, *Tecumthe* (*Canadian Review* [December 1824] 396–432; *Tales* 74–177), the unmistakable hallmarks of a Canadian identity: local pride, consciousness of a common past, and the commitment to a shared future that issues in educative and ethical purpose. "Fair Canada – within whose snowy arms / My infant breath was nurtur'd," he wrote in *Tecumthe*, "[how] I lov'd to stray ... Where the swift Montmorenci pours its spray ... Or o'er the Diamond Cape ... And blythely sporting thence, o'er Abraham's Plain / ... o'er its flower-crown'd site – brave Wolfe's immortal fane" (*Tales* 85, 88). Longmore may not have read Cary or Strachan or Burwell, but in *Tecumthe* and *The Charivari* he wrote two poems that participate with *Abram's Plains*, "Verses ... 1802" and *Talbot Road* in the affection for Canada and its peoples that gave rise to "Canadian Poetry" during the Georgian period.

10 John Richardson,
Tecumseh

Tecumseh; or, the Warrior of the West: a Poem, in Four Cantos, with Notes was first published in London, England in late May or June 1828 (Daymond and Monkman, intro. xxvii). Dedicated "to Captain Barclay, and other officers Serving with the Right Division of the Army of Upper Canada, during the Late American War ... by Their Companion in Arms," it proclaims itself to be "by an English Officer" ([1828] iii). That "English Officer" was Lieutenant – later, Major – John Richardson (1796–1852), a veteran of the War of 1812, who went on to publish one more long poem (*Kensington Gardens in 1830*) and several works of fictional and non-fictional prose, including *Wacousta* (1832), *The Canadian Brothers* (1840), and the *War of 1812* (1842), a *Full and Detailed Narrative of the Operations of the Right Division, of the Canadian Army* in which, among much else, he recounts the circumstances surrounding the death of Tecumseh at the Battle of Moraviantown on the Thames River, near Chatham, on 5 October 1813. One of the notes to *Tecumseh* provides a description of the great Shawnee chief that is echoed in the poem itself and in the *War of 1812*: "during the latter part of his life, Tecumseh was generally distinguished by a large plume of ostrich feathers, the whiteness of which, contrasted with the darkness of his complexion, and the brilliancy of his black and piercing eye, gave a singularly wild and terrific expression to his features – it was evident that he could be terrible" ([1828] 116). Richardson's expressed intention in writing *Tecumseh* was "to rescue the name of a hero from oblivion," "to preserve the memory of one of the noblest and most gallant spirits that ever tenanted the breast of man" (v).

In a prospectus for *Tecumseh* printed in 1828 and 1829 in Upper and Lower Canada, Richardson further elaborates his intentions in the work, proclaiming himself "the Historian, the panegyrist of him who is now no more" and pronouncing his first venture into verse an "Epic Poem" (in Daymond and Monkman, appendix 183–84). He also claims as a special qualification his Canadian birth (at Queenston on the Niagara Peninsula) and emphasizes the particular appeal of his work to Canadians. Over two decades later, in 1842, he would make a similarly patriotic point in offering *Wacousta, The Canadian Brothers,* and *Tecumseh* as a "series of CANADIAN WORKS" (qtd. in Daymond and Monkman, intro. xi), with the poem selling for half of its original price of seven shillings in Britain and two dollars in Canada. This advertisement was published in Richardson's own periodical, the *New Era, or the Canadian Chronicle* (Brockville, Upper Canada) on 2 March 1842, some two months before a revised version of *Tecumseh* began to appear in instalments in the same place (1:i–xxi [22 July]; 1:xxii–xxxv, 2:i–xxvii [29 July]; 2:xxxviii–xli, 3:i–xxviii [12 August]; 3:xxix–xlii, and 4:i–xlv, and the notes to the poem [19 August]). Shorter by several stanzas than its predecessor of 1828, the version of *Tecumseh* published in the *New Era* contains many changes which, cumulatively, "serve to strengthen [Richardson's] epic design" (Wanda Campbell, *"Bildungsgedicht"* 34) and to substantiate his contention that Tecumseh was a man "whose memory there can be few Canadians unwilling to see transmitted to posterity" (Daymond and Monkman, appendix 184).

As the circumstances of its writing and publication indicate, *Tecumseh* participates in the surge of Canadian patriotism that followed the War of 1812, especially in Upper Canada. As well as leading to the creation of such unifying projects as the Welland Canal, the incipient nationalism of the 1820s and 1830s took two forms that are highly conspicuous in *Tecumseh*: anti-Americanism and consolidatory historicism. This was the period in which British soldier-settlers were strategically located in areas vulnerable to attack by American troops who, at their worst, are described as "hell-fiends" (*4:335*) in *Tecumseh*. It was also the period in which elaborate monuments were built to commemorate Canada's military heroes – a monument to Brock on Queenston Heights in 1824, a joint monument to Wolfe and Montcalm in Quebec City in 1827–28, and a monument to Wolfe on the Plains of Abraham in 1832 (see Bentley, "Monumentalités" 3–12). And, of course, its was the period in which Tecumseh was enshrined in several works of prose and poetry, including the two long poems by Richardson and Longmore (*Tecumthe* [1824]) that bear his name. "*Visible monuments*" and "*historical poems,*" observes Joseph Priestley in his *Lectures on History* (1788 f.), are the sanctioned means of "preserving traditions," and, of the two, historical poems are more effective because they are not fixed to a single place, not subject to physical decay, and not restricted to the commemoration of "only a *few events*, in a manner destitute of circumstances" (74, 76, 80). Priestley's view that historical poems are "a method of transmitting ... knowledge of important events with greater accuracy than by simple narration" (74) implies that such works as *Tecumseh* must be founded on an imaginative historicism that is at once true to the facts and complex in its treatment of them. Richardson would have had to go no further than the historical poems that lie in the background of *Tecumseh* – Scott's *Lady of the Lake*, for example, and Thomas Campbell's *Gertrude of Wyoming* – to recognize that for history to be enduringly memorable it needs to be vivified, not to say augmented, by the imagination.

An additional and easily overlooked source of Richardson's imaginative historicism is the work of Byron. There can be no question that *Don Juan* is the source of the stanza form of *Tecumseh* (*ottava rima*) and little doubt that Richardson erred once in choosing so playful a form for his "stirring subject" and again in adhering too strictly to the "form, with which Byron took such liberties" (Casselman xvii–xviii). Evidence for this lies in the many forced and repeated rhymes in *Tecumseh*, as well as in Richardson's quite frequent use of words, phrases, and even lines to fill the mould of his form. Nor can there be any question that part of Tecumseh's literary ancestry comprises the solitary, tormented, vengeful, and ethically equivocal heroes of such works as *The Giaour, The Corsair,* and *Manfred*. Indeed, it would be surprising if they did not, since the influence of Byron's flamboyant personality and works was at its height in England and Canada in the 1820s. Nevertheless Richardson's Tecumseh is markedly less sensual and libertarian than the typical Byronic hero, and the 1828 version of *Tecumseh* contains explicit challenges to Byron's religious scepticism and social irresponsibility. Two stanzas and notes that were excised in 1842 proclaim Richardson's belief in an after life of "human love, chastened by celestial refinement" (53–54, 125–26) and another stanza similarly expunged pays homage to Byron as "the soul of verse" but then proceeds to castigate him for "wast[ing] his giant mind in syren lays" and no "longer sing[ing] the deeds of other days" (96). Evidently, the Byron whom Richardson admired above all when he wrote *Tecumseh* was the Byron of *Mazeppa, Sardanapulus,* and the other historical poems and dramas in which "the deeds of other days" are shaped and vivified by a "lofty muse" ([1828] 96).

A sometimes uneasy tension between fact and embellishment is inevitable in any work of imaginative historicism, and *Tecumseh* is not the exception that proves the rule. The poem's opening words – "It is in truth" ("In truth" in the 1828 edition) – proclaim the authenticity of what is to come. "A mere work of imagination [*Tecumseh*] is not," asserts Richardson in his 1828 preface, but a poem whose principal interest lies in its "strict adherence to the wild poetry of [Tecumseh's] character ... Tecumseh, such as he is described, once existed; nor is there the slightest exaggeration in any of the high qualities and strong passions ascribed to him" (vi). To the suggestion that a female love theme would have "given a more general interest to the Poem" of the sort found in Chateaubriand's *Atala* and *Renée*, Richardson responds that "this would have been in violation of th[e] consistency he has been anxious to preserve," adding that, in any case, "the *sentiment* of love is almost wholly unknown among the Indian tribes, by whom the sex is held in the utmost inferiority and contempt" (vi–vii). Nevertheless the poem contains several characters and incidents that are "without historical warrant" (Riddell, *Richardson* 29, 30), including the introduction of a son called Uncas whose qualities give him less in common with the bland son sometimes attributed to the Shawnee chief (see Longmore, *Tales* 80–81) than with his namesake and probable inspiration in James Fenimore Cooper's *Last of the Mohicans* (1826). When Uncas is killed by the Americans shortly after his introduction and his untimely death, in turn, causes Tecumseh's aged father to die of a broken heart ([1842] 2:*226–32*), it becomes very clear that the purpose of his presence in the poem is to generate reader sympathy and passionate motivation for Tecumseh. More than merely an imaginary creation with a possible basis in historical fact, Uncas serves to condense and intensify the sense of personal harm by the Americans that Tecumseh apparently harboured, particularly after the Battle of Tippecanoe in November 1811, when his village was burned and many of his friends were killed by soldiers under the command of Governor (later General and President) William Henry Harrison. When Richardson proceeds with a poetic license rather than a "historical warrant" he does not so much abandon history as modify it "to give greater effect" (*Wacousta* 587) to the characters and events that he describes.

Probably the largest barrier that Richardson had to overcome in his attempt to memorialize Tecumseh as a "noble ... and gallant spirit" was his own perception of the Native peoples as ignoble savages. Almost as soon as he is introduced in *Tecumseh*, the Shawnee chief is depicted as a man driven by rage and a desire for revenge against the Americans – that is, by the two emotions that, according to the four stages theory, characterized all people in the savage state. As Weld puts it in the "brief Account of the Persons, Manners, Character, Qualifications, mental and corporeal of the Indians" upon which Richardson based much of *Tecumseh*, "no people are more sensible of an injury: a word in the slightest degree insulting will kindle a flame in their breasts, that can only be extinguished by the blood of the offending party; and they will traverse forests for hundreds of miles ... to gratify their revenge" (2:224, 264–65). "In his anger fiercely great," runs the equivalent passage in Richardson's poem, Tecumseh "Swore by the life-blood of each fallen foe ... to immolate / Fresh ranks, in vengeance for those hapless brave" ([1828] 20). With the deaths of his son and father, the "glowing furnace" ([1842] *2:223*) of Tecumseh's "fury" and "vengeful hate" for the Americans ([1828] 21) is heated to the point that he looks forward to the Battle of Moraviantown with "deathless ire" and "rage unpitying," relishing the thought of "each foe / Gasping, and writhing 'neath his vengeful blow" ([1842] *4:205–08*). Such thoughts are not verbalized by Tecumseh, however, for the reason that ignoble savages were believed to put a high premium on emotional restraint. "In their opinion," writes Weld, "no man can be a great warrior or a dignified character that openly betrays any extravagant emotions of surprise, of joy, of sorrow, or of fear, on any occasion whatsoever" (2:265). Thus it is that even on the death of his father and son, Tecumseh does not articulate his feelings, but, "firmly struggling with his secret woes, / Suppresse[s] the groan which half indignant rose" ([1842] *2:239–40*). After the destruction of his village and friends, Tecumseh stoically resolves to avenge them, "but [in] secret,"

> for no sound betrays
> The maddening, burning agony of soul
> Which o'er his brow and o'er each feature plays.
> Deeply he feels – but, feeling, can control
> The hell which on his quivering being preys ...
> ([1828] 21)

"Still red with recent slaughter," Tecumseh keeps "well the purpose of his soul," the passionate resolve to "deal ... vengeance" on the Americans "Like the fierce monsters of his native wood, / Till gorg'd with victims and with human blood" ([1828] 19). Probably realizing that these are descriptions of "a blood thirsty monster" (Wanda Campbell, *"Bildungsgedicht"* 86) rather than a "noble ... and gallant spirit," Richardson excised his account of Tecumseh's response to the destruction at Tippecanoe from the Canadian edition of the poem.

This excision goes some way towards distancing Tecumseh from the stereotype of the ignoble savage and justifying Klinck's description of him as a "noble savage" ("Early Creative Literature" 156). Also tipping the scales in the same direction is Richardson's suggestion that Tecumseh's rage for revenge was a response to American actions and, moreover, tempered by an abhorrence of the cruelty attributed to ignoble savages by Weld (2:276) and many others. By waging "stern War" (*2:22,35*) against both the Natives and the British, argues Tecumseh's father in the lengthy lament on the *ubi sunt* theme that opens Canto 2, the Americans have transformed Eden into a hell populated by "fiends" both white and brown. At Fort Michilimackinac in 1763, young men who had been content to play "innocuous" games like lacrosse were transformed into cannibals "who frantic tore / Each quivering limb, and quaff'd the reeking gore" (*2:79–80*). As if thinking of Alexander Henry's account of this massacre ("from ... bodies ... ripped open, the butchers were drinking the blood, scooped up ... and quaffed amid shouts of rage and victory" [80–81]), Tecumseh's father observes that the behavior of the "hellish fiends" at Michilimackinac was a "stain" on their race's reputation that "rolling ages could not wipe away:"

> It hung like a dark cloud above their fame,
> And blighted deeds of many a battle-day;
> Till now a Warrior – a Redeemer came,
> And shot through th[e] gloom a gladdening ray,
> And mercy render'd at Repentance' throne
> Bright offerings due, and faithful to atone.
>
> (*2:83–88*)

As a note to this passage makes clear, the final lines refer to the rejection of "cold, deliberate, [and] systematic cruelty" ([1828] 120) that Tecumseh demonstrated when he prevented the massacre of captured Americans at Fort Meigs, an act of "humanity ... [that was] long remembered and ... contributed to his reputation among whites" (Goltz 799). In his father's eyes, and, presumably, in Richardson's to some extent as well, Tecumseh was a messianic "Redeemer" who not only "atone[d]" for the previous sins of his people but also tempered their savagery with "Mercy" and, before the onset of further conflicts with and among encroaching Europeans, "briefly restore[d] pre-lapsarian" peace and innocence to the Native peoples (Daymond and Monkman, intro. xix). When "an aged fiend," a character descended from the same nightmarish vision of women as Lady Macbeth, butchers a young American officer to revenge the death of Uncas, Richardson simultaneously illustrates the re-emergence of savage cruelty in times of war and distances Tecumseh from it, for the act occurs when he is literally some distance away, "Near the pale ashes of his martyr'd boy / With folded arms and melancholy mood" (*2:362–63*). Whether based on the brutal murder of a "finely proportioned young" prisoner by an "aged ... [and]heartless [Indian] woman" recorded in the *War of 1812* (13–14) as William Renwick Riddell suggests (*Richardson* 31), or modelled on a similar incident involving an "Indian woman" and a Black slave in Weld's *Travels* (2:274–75), the murder of the young American officer is a further instance of Richardson's imaginative shaping of historical information for honorific purposes.

It is consistent with his highly sympathetic view of the Native peoples as essentially blameless victims of European aggression that Tecumseh's father defends his people from the charge of cruelty levelled by Weld and others:

> The white-man terms us cruel, while his blade
> Alone leaps thirsting for some victim's blood;
> He hunts the peaceful Indian from his glade,
> To seek for shelter in the pathless wood;
> Then talks of direst treason, when dismay'd
> He hears the war-cry where their homes once stood;
> Nor fails the wily hunter to abhor,
> Who differs from him but in forms of war!
>
> (*2:169–76*)

The truth of this statement, particularly (and, perhaps, exclusively) *vis-à-vis* the backwoodsmen who comprised a substantial proportion of the American army, becomes horribly apparent after the death of Tecumseh:

> Forth from a copse a hundred foemen spring,
> And pounce like vultures on the bleeding clay;
> Like famish'd blood-hounds to the corse they cling,
> And bear the fallen hero's scalp away:
> The very covering from his nerves they wring,
> And gash his form, and glut them o'er their prey,
> Wild hell-fiends all – and revelling at his death,
> With bursting shrieks and pestilential breath.
>
> (*4:329–36*)

In the 1828 version of the poem, these lines are followed by a stanza composed of dashes to represent either (or both) details too horrible to be described or (and) the outrage of the poem's speaker. "Many Kentucky Americans ... boast[ed] of having obtained a part of the warriors skin," notes Richardson; "they absolutely tore the skin from his bleeding form, and converted it into razor-straps!!!" (134). For Richardson, as for the "aged chief," the boundary between backwoodsmen and savages is tissue thin. So too is it for Weld, who remarks of the "back settlers" of Kentucky and elsewhere that they are "far greater savages than the Indians themselves." "It is nothing uncommon," he observes, "to see hung up in their chimney corners ... the scalps which they have themselves torn from the heads of the Indians whom they have shot; and ... I have read accounts of their having flayed the Indians, and employed their skins as they would have done those of a wild beast" (2:217–18).

Before leaving Weld, it is worth observing that his "brief Account ... of the Indians" is probably the principal source, not merely of Richardson's conception of the Natives' "Character," but also of the "aged Chief's" nostalgic descriptions of their dress, music, and dances. Perhaps Weld's "brief Account" had special resonance for Richardson because it was written at Malden near Amherstburg, where he "spent his boyhood" (Beasley 11), and contains descriptions of many sights and sounds that would have been familiar to him, including the music of the Indians on Bois Blanc Island (2:289–90), where he is supposed by Alexander Clark Casselman to have "acquired that close and accurate knowledge of Indian character and life that he afterwards so successfully used in his literary productions" (xv). First-hand knowledge of the Native peoples Richardson doubtless had, but when he came to describe their "deep-ton'd flute ... music," their cosmetic use of "vermilion dyes," and their "silver bands," "brilliant brooch[es]," and "moccasins attentive roll'd / And work'd ... With vari-colour'd quills of porcupine" (*2:102–20*), he turned to Weld (2:231–27), placing a positive construal on the traveller's comments that recalls Bayley, Burwell, and Goldsmith. As a juxtaposition of Weld's and Richardson's descriptions of a war dance reveals, the transformation of prose into poetry is sometimes accomplished in *Tecumseh* through the addition of tired clichés ("tranquil flood") and forced rhymes ("yell" / "dell"):

Of their grand dances, the war dance must undoubtedly ... be the one most worthy the attention of a stranger ... The chiefs and warriors who are about to join in this dance, dress and paint themselves as if actually out on a warlike expedition ... and join in a dance truly terrifying ... [L]eaping about in the most frantic manner ... they set up the war woop, and utter the most dreadful yells imaginable.   (2:292–94)

> The dance continues near [Lake Erie's] tranquil flood,
> But maidens mix not with the frantic brave;
> It is the war-dance, follow'd by the yell,
> Which awes the panther springing from his dell.
>   (*2:133–36*)

Despite Richardson's assertion that he was "utterly unprovided with notes on America" ([1828] 131) when he composed *Tecumseh* in

England in the twenties, he almost certainly had Weld's *Travels* beside him and might well have had its author in mind when he wrote of the "stranger" whose "softened gaze" fell on the "gay sons" of Lake Erie during the "peaceful days" before the War of 1812 (*2:121–24*).

If further evidence of Richardson's debt to Weld were to be sought, it could be found in the "old Chief's" observation that since the onset of the War the "birds of song [have] forego[ne] their wonted lay; / And naught is heard above the murmuring rill / But the wild plaining of the Whipperwill" (36), a statement glossed in the 1828 version of *Tecumseh* with the information that the "singularly wild and melancholy" "notes of this bird" are "to be heard only at night" "on the banks of Lake Erie and adjoining rivers" (121). "The heart naturally attuned to the enjoyment of solitude," continues the note, "may linger on those sweet banks, forming images of happiness ... until ... morning ... demonstrates ... that our fairest perceptions, and most exquisite sensations in life, are but the fleeting visions of a faithless dream" (121). This is clearly a post-Romantic elaboration of Weld's comment that "the whipperwill, or whip-poor-will ... is ... [so] called, from the plaintive noise that it makes ... through the greater part of the night ... frequently in the neighbourhood of low grounds" (1:196–97). But perhaps Weld's description of the Whip-poor-will was not the only one read by Richardson. In *The Rising Village*, it may be recalled, Goldsmith describes the bird's "note" as "wild and mournful" and, like the "aged Chief," associates its song with the "murm'ring of the rill" ([1825] *479–84* and *481 n.*). Whatever relationship there may be between *Tecumseh* and *The Rising Village* is complicated by the fact that when Richardson revised his poem in 1842 he changed the "old Chief's" "murmuring rill" to "rippling rill" and omitted the lengthy note describing the Whip-poor-will's song as "wild and melancholy." These similarities and differences may merely be permutations of stock diction generated by a single source, but they nevertheless raise the possibility that Richardson read *The Rising Village* either before 1828 (and allowed himself to echo closely Goldsmith's description of the Whip-poor-will) or before 1842 (and attempted to avoid echoing it). Whatever the case the many debts of *Tecumseh* to Weld's *Travels* are as unmistakable as they are typical of long poems about Canada written in the early decades of the nineteenth century.

If Richardson did read *The Rising Village* then he knew one more negative assessment of the Native peoples that his portrait of Tecumseh would have to contradict or radically modify. To achieve this end he not only revised *Tecumseh* in 1842, toning down the ignoble component of its treatment of the Native peoples, but also, in his initial conception of the poem, aligned Tecumseh with two highly positive and compatible character types: the epic hero and the military hero. A source for the latter lay in Richardson's personal experience of the military ethos, coupled with his first-hand knowledge of Tecumseh's conduct and appearance before and during the Battle of Moraviantown (*War of 1812* 124–26). For the latter, he seems to have drawn inspiration primarily from *Paradise Lost* and the classical translations of Pope (*Odyssey*), Dryden (*Aeneid*), and Cowper (*Iliad*), though Douglas Daymond and Leslie Monkman have also discerned the influence of *Paradise Regained* behind both the four-part structure of *Tecumseh* and Richardson's conception of the hero of his "Epic Poem" as a "Christ-like Redeemer" (xiv). No doubt *Don Juan* helped him to recognize epic conventions and devices.

As well as possessing the physical stature, the rhetorical skill, and the distinguished lineage typical of epic heroes, Tecumseh is surrounded by Richardson with the trappings of traditional epic. The poem begins *in medias res* on 10 September 1813 with the Battle of Put-in Bay off Amherstberg on Lake Erie (a defeat for the British under Barclay by a larger American fleet commanded by Commodore Oliver Perry). It then glances back to the events leading up to Tecumseh's involvement in the War of 1812, including the role played in his earlier life by his younger brother Tenskwatawa ("the Prophet" [*1:241*]), whose "millenarian religion" Tecumseh "transformed ... into a movement dedicated to retaining Indian land" (Goltz 796). Before the Battle of Moraviantown there is a list of the "Fierce tribes of Warriors" (*4:68*) who have assembled from far and wide to fight with the British, an epic device that recalls the catalogues of heroes in the second book of the *Iliad* and the seventh book of the *Aeneid* and serves to indicated the force of Tecumseh's leadership among the Native peoples. "Since our great Tecumtha has been killed," said the Ottawa chief Naywash in 1814, "we do not listen to one another, we do not rise together" (qtd. in Goltz 799). But perhaps the most striking epic device in *Tecumseh* is a Homeric simile that uses a syntactical structure reminiscent of *Paradise Lost* (*4:267 f.*) as the vehicle for a figure derived from Jefferson. It describes Tecumseh's resistance to American "encroachments on the borders of the Wabash [River]" in Ohio prior to the Battle of Tippecanoe ([1828] 115):

> Not the wild mammoth of Ohio's banks
> Dash'd fiercer splashing thro' the foaming flood,
> When his huge form press'd low the groaning ranks
> Of giant oaks which deck'd his native woods,
> Than rag'd Tecumseh through the deep phalanx
> Of deadliest enemies, soon bathed in blood,
> Whose quivering scalps, half-crimsoned in their gore,
> The dusky Warrior from the white-men bore.
>
> (*1:233–40*)

Almost certainly the inspiration for this simile came, in part, from the comparison between "the Monster [Joseph] Brant" and the "Mammoth" in Thomas Campbell's *Gertrude of Wyoming* (68), a poem regarded by Richardson as "beautiful and affecting" ([1828] 122). Not only does Richardson refer to Campbell's depiction of Brant in a note to *Tecumseh*, but he also follows the Scottish poet in using "the mammoth as an emblem of terror and destruction" and, moreover, glosses it with part of the same passage from *Notes on the State of Virginia* that appears in a note to *Gertrude of Wyoming* (90–91). Neither as original in conception nor as free from bathos as might be wished, the Tecumseh-mammoth simile nevertheless has a certain aptness, for, as reported by Jefferson, mammoths were creatures embedded in Delaware "tradition" that, with the exception of one "big bull," were destroyed by divine wrath in "ancient times." It seems more than likely that in the northerly progress of the surviving "big bull" – "he bounded over the Ohio, over the Wabash, the Illinois, and finally over the great lakes, where he is living at this day" ([1828] 116) – Richardson saw a mythical analogue for Tecumseh's movement northwards from the Ohio Valley to Upper Canada.

But perhaps the most epical aspect of the Tecumseh-mammoth simile is its emphasis on the sheer size and strength of the Shawnee chief. As Northrop Frye has pointed out in his discussion of mimetic modes in the *Anatomy of Criticism*, the heroes of traditional epic are invariably imposing in stature and divine in appearance, if not in fact (33–35). When first introduced in language and imagery that loudly echoes the initial description of Satan in *Paradise Lost* ("Say first" [*1:27 f.*]), Tecumseh is seen as if from below, a point of view that emphasizes his enormous size and power. Moreover, he is described as a "godlike ... spirit of the mountain" in the 1828 edition (14) and a "noble ... spirit of the forest" in the 1842 version:

> Say, who that moveless Warrior, who reclines,
> His noble form against the craggy steep;
> And, like some spirit of the forest, shines
> Pre-eminent above the silvery deep
> A monument of strength – while, o'er the lines
> Of his severe and war-worn features, creep
> Those burning thoughts which mark the soul of flame –
> Fever'd and restless in its thirst of fame?

$$(1:209–15)$$

Already present in this stanza is the association of Tecumseh with fire and light that appears throughout the poem, often in the form of references to lightning, furnaces, and comets (the last, like Richardson's comparisons of Tecumseh to a "panther" [*1:250; 2:136*], in possible allusion to that fact that his name was variously said "to mean shooting star or panther crouching in wait" [Goltz 795–96]). That Tecumseh's fiery qualities, like his inner torment and his revengeful disposition, link him with Milton's Satan does not necessarily mean that Richardson was the heir of Blake and Shelley in seeing Satan as the true hero of *Paradise Lost*. Nor do Tecumseh's Satanic associations mean that Richardson was one with Burwell in using material from the opening books of Milton's poem without sufficient attention to its origins and resonances. The disquieting admixture of negative and positive associations that surrounds Tecumseh is, rather, the consequence of Richardson's view of him as an ignoble savage with several redeeming qualities, most obviously his clement treatment of prisoners. The epical hero of *Tecumseh* commands admiration despite, not because of, the passionate and vengeful characteristics for which Richardson found an apt analogue in Milton's Satan.

Since *Tecumseh* is an epical celebration of arms and the man that was dedicated by an "English Officer" to his "Companion[s] in Arms," no special insight is required to perceive the military ethos at its core. To Richardson and his original readers, the war in which Tecumseh signalized himself was a hell of violence, cruelty, and ugliness. When "Captain Finnes ... and Lieutenant Garden ... were both killed by the same ball" at the Battle of Put-in Bay, "the blood of the one, and the brains of the other, were mingled together in one melancholy and undistinguishable mass"([1828] 113). When Tecumseh is killed, he "Lies pierc'd with wounds, and shapeless in his gore: / A lifeless loathsome mass" (*4:339–40*). War reduces people of all races and allegiances to a sickening pulp. Yet it can be humanizing as well as dehumanizing. Among the men "Serving with the Right Division of the Army of Upper Canada," there was a "bond of union" (*4:27*), a "sweet fellowship of thought and mind / Which flies the heartless circles of mankind" (*4:39–40;* and see *Wacousta* 16–17). There were also many examples of high dignity and courage on both sides of the conflict. At Put-in Bay the "gallant Barclay" is reduced to a "branchless trunk" (*1:113*) by a wound in his only arm. When the young American prisoner faces a horrible death under the hatchet of the "aged fiend," he is "not unmann'd" but "raise[s] his thoughts in confidence to Heaven, / And silent pray[s] his earthly sins forgiven" (*2:321–28*). It is within a military ethos that puts the highest value on such "personal intrepidity" ([1828] 115), no matter what the race or allegiance of its exemplar, that Richardson presents Tecumseh as a hero worthy to be remembered.

Nowhere does the Shawnee chief show himself worthier within this military ethos than in his speech urging the British commander on the Detroit front, General Henry Procter, to stand and fight the Americans rather than, as was his inclination, to retreat to safer ground. Despite Richardson's claim that "the language [Tecumseh] made use of to the General Officer ... was almost literally that ascribed to him in the poem" ([1828] 128), the speech that appears in *Tecumseh* differs radically from the version given in the *War of 1812* (119–20). As well as being, of necessity, graced with rhythm and rhyme, the closing words of Tecumseh's "Spartan" speech ([1828] 128) come trailing clouds of glory from the Moor's final speech in *Othello* ("then, must you speak ... Set you down this") and from Logan's famous speech to the Governor of Virginia as recorded by Jefferson and quoted by Thomas Campbell ("'there runs not a drop of my blood in the veins of any living creature ... Logan never felt fear. He will not turn on his heel to save his life" [93–94]):

> "But since the blood runs coldly thro' thy veins,
> And love of life belies the Warrior's creed,
> Go – flee – and leave to hostile swords these plains,
> Then tell thy Father of the glorious deed:
> Yet say, that well one native Chief maintains
> The faith he pledged, and on this spot will bleed –
> For, by the Spirit of our mighty sphere,
> Tecumseh moves not while a foe is near."
>
> (*3:201–08*)

A horror of cowardice and a refusal to retreat: these are the salient characteristics, the "'Warrior's creed,'" by which Richardson's Tecumseh lives and dies. Together with an imagined loyalty to the King ("thy Father," George III), they are the "glowing and brilliant qualities" that, to Loyalist eyes, elevated Tecumseh to within hailing distance of Brock as a hero of the War of 1812.

Richardson's complex construction of Tecumseh as an ignoble savage and as a military-cum-epic hero is perhaps most apparent in the stanzas describing his death. "Drunk with human gore" and "towering" above the field of battle "like some dark ... fiend," Tecumseh spots the commander of the Kentucky Riflemen, Colonel Richard Johnson, and "with loud yells that devils might appal" wounds him with a "ball from his rifle" (*4:297–304; War of 1812* 124). As he rushes forward with "vengeful blade" to kill Johnson, Tecumseh enacts a pattern of hand-to-hand-combat between opposing leaders that is as typical of classical epics as the Homeric simile in which his action is expressed. Derivative though it is of *Paradise Lost 1: 612–15,* the simile effectively mirrors the speed and violence of Tecumseh's descent on the wounded Johnson:

> Like the quick bolt which follows on the flash
> Which rends the mountain oak in fearful twain,
> So sprang the Warrior with impetuous dash,
> Upon the Christian writhing in his pain.
>
> *(4:313–16)*

Tecumseh's revenge is not complete, however, for Johnson "dr[aws] a pistol from his belt, and sh[oots] him dead" (*War of 1812* 124):

> The baffled Chieftain tottered, sank and fell –
> Rage in his heart, and vengeance in his glance;
> His features ghastly pale – his breast was hell –
> One bound he made to seize his fallen lance,
> But quick the death-shades o'er his vision swell,
> His arm drops nerveless – straining to advance –
> One look of hatred, and the last he gave,
> Then sank and slumbered with the fallen brave.
>
> *(4:321–25)*

A miniature of Richardson's complex portrait of Tecumseh as an ignoble savage turned hero, this stanza contains a narrative movement which suggests that only in death did the "Chieftain" transcend his violent passions and demonic nature to achieve the peace and honour traditionally accorded to the "fallen" – in 1828, "glorious" (105) – "brave." As if purged of "rage," "hatred," and his desire for "vengeance," Tecumseh at last joins the heroes of the British military tradition who, in the words of Collins's well-known "Ode, Written in the Beginning of the Year 1746," "sink to rest / By all their country's wishes blest!" (437).

That Tecumseh thus became in death one of the "glorious" or "fallen brave" makes all the more despicable the "indignities" perpetrated upon his body by "Kentuckian Americans" ([1828] 124). A gross violation of civilized, Christian values, the flaying of Tecumseh's body for souvenirs was also an "Insult ... [to] the memory of the brave" (*4:350*) that, to compound the offence, denied him the ceremonial burial and monumental tomb usually accorded to great military heroes. Such is the enormity and nature of their crime that the desecrators of Tecumseh's body are subjected to three stanzas of cursing at the conclusion of the poem, including the hope that "they who left" his body a "loathsome mass" will "e'er howl, and creep / And creep as vile through life as cruel in that hour" (*4:342–43*). In keeping with Richardson's overall concern with the preservation of Tecumseh's memory, the poem concludes by calling down the curse of recollection on the despoilers of the chieftain's body: "May remembrance" of their "infernal" and "inhuman" deeds "Like adder stings recoil upon each heart, / And blast the promise which their creeds impart" (*4:347–52*); may some family member "Recall *his* deeds" – the deeds of the Tecumseh who "spar'd their blood in many a battle dire" – and send them "conscience-stricken" to the grave (*4:353–60*). As a remembering forward of those very deeds, *Tecumseh* is thus both a monument and a scourge, a perpetual testament of "That Chieftain's worth" and a punitive record of his despoilers' "shame" (*4:360*). It is, as it were, a medallion struck in his honour, with his "wild ... terrific" and yet merciful features on one side and, on the other, scenes of the gallantry and savagery of the conflicts in which he fought and died.

11 Adam Kidd,
The Huron Chief

Adam Kidd has long enjoyed a limited but tenacious reputation as the most colourful and controversial poet of pre-Confederation Canada. For many years Kidd's remark in his preface to *The Huron Chief, and Other Poems* (Montreal [1830]) that he had fallen "from the cloud-capped brows of a dangerous Mountain" (*39–40*) was taken literally (Baker 157), and a fondness for Native women was assumed to be the reason for his failure to reap the benefit of a "long round of professional studies" for the Church of England priesthood (preface *37–38;* Klinck, "Adam Kidd" 497; Edwards, "Adam Kidd" 375). More recently the story of the public thrashing received by Kidd in consequence of a denigrating reference in *The Huron Chief* to James Buchanan, the British consul in New York (*876 n.*), has restored a reputation for hazardous flamboyancy that had been briefly tarnished by Carl F. Klinck's discovery that Kidd's fall from a "dangerous Mountain" was metaphorical – an allusion to his having fallen afoul of the superintendent of his divinity studies, the Venerable Archdeacon George Jehoshaphat Mountain (the son of Jacob Mountain, the first Anglican Bishop of Quebec). As evident in these stories about Kidd as in *The Huron Chief* itself is the truth that through his attitudes and activities he placed himself in opposition to the high centres of secular and ecclesiastical authority in Lower Canada and the United States. In addition to inveighing against the Anglican Mountains and the British consul, Kidd championed the Native peoples' way of life and condemned the missionary activities of European "Creeds-men" (1251). Both anti-establishment and pro-Native, Kidd is the colonial antecedent of the numerous Canadian poets of the

present century who have rejected the culture of the high centre in
favour of living and writing on the margins.

Born in ca.1802 in Northern Ireland (the more Protestant, open, and
liberal part of the island), Kidd may have come to North America as
early as 1818, perhaps spending some time in the United States before
moving to Lower Canada and becoming a candidate for the Church of
England priesthood (Edwards, "Adam Kidd" 375). The 22 February
1822 issue of the *Quebec Gazette* contains a poem signed "A.K." at "St.
Paul Street, Feb. 2d.," and several other pieces appear in Quebec and
Montreal newspapers between 1822 and 1825 (some under his pseudonym of "Slievegallin," a mountain near his birthplace). Apparently in
1828–29 and 1830–31, perhaps having already fallen afoul of the
"M***T**N, / Who nothing loves, but what's his own, / Or some *thing*
else that wears a gown" (*514–16*), Kidd travelled extensively in the
United States and Upper Canada, gathering material for *The Huron
Chief, and Other Poems* and for a projected volume of "*Tales and Traditions*
of the Indians" (preface *49*). This second volume was never published
because early in July 1831 Kidd was dead, virtually unmourned and
scarcely missed – except in such newspapers as the *Canadian Freeman*
(21 July 1831) and *Le Canadien* (6 July 1831) whose sympathies were
Irish or radical or both.

A little over two years before Kidd's death, another Montreal newspaper of the same stripe, the *Irish Vindicator* (2 June 1829 f.), began publishing advertisements for *The Huron Chief, and Other Poems* that describe
the volume as containing "[about] 200 Octavo Pages, printed in the
neatest manner, and on good paper, with THREE ELEGANT ENGRAV-
INGS, illustrative of American Scenery and Indian Character. The
Poems will appear in boards and be delivered to Subscribers only at
FIVE SHILLINGS" (11 September 1829). Several months earlier, on 30
December 1828, an appetite-whetting excerpt from the volume had
appeared in the *Quebec Mercury*. Later a spate of letters in the *Irish Vindicator* (23 and 5 February 1830), the *Brockville Gazette and General Adver-
tiser* (12 March 1830), and the *Montreal Gazette* (7 June 1830) indicate
that Kidd started selling subscriptions to *The Huron Chief, and Other
Poems* as early as the fall of 1828 and that the book was not published
until mid-February 1830. When it finally did appear from "The Office
of the [Montreal] Herald and New Gazette," *The Huron Chief, and Other
Poems* contained only one engraving, a frontispiece depicting the chief
of the title poem over the caption "I'm the Chieftain of this mountain."
Even in the contrast between the lower case "mountain" of the Huron
chief and the upper case "Mountain" and "M***T**N" of Kidd's subsequent outbursts can be seen his preferences for the Native and natural
over the artificial and imposing.

Also absent from the volume, though listed in its table of contents, is a poem entitled "To the Rev. Polyphemous" that was almost certainly a libelous attack on Archdeacon Mountain. In its place are three innocuous poems subsumed by a note stating "on consideration, it has been thought proper to substitute these ... in place of the address to POLYPHEMUS, which, perhaps, was too satirical for a publication of this nature." Beside this note in the copy of *The Huron Chief, and Other Poems* signed "John Strachan, 1830" (in the Baldwin Room of the Toronto Reference Library), Strachan has written: "thus depriving the volume of what with posterity, would have given it some value." Less playful than Strachan was a "Churchman" (*510*) who may also have been among the "fifteen hundred" mostly "respectable" subscribers claimed by Kidd for *The Huron Chief, and Other Poems* (preface *47–48*; Montreal Gazette [7 June 1830]). Referring to the portion of *The Huron Chief* in which the narrator proclaims his love for an Indian woman named Kemana (*469–666*), Job Deacon, a fellow divinity student of Kidd's in Quebec and later an Anglican priest at Adolphustown in Upper Canada, wrote "perverted taste to be first attracted to a Squaw!" (Baldwin Room, Toronto Reference Library). Adjacent to a subsequent reference to the "pain" caused by "A *Mountain* Demon" (*793–800*), Deacon wrote: "it was thine own foolish wayward inclination and not 'a Mountain Demon,' that has blighted thy prospects. *Justice to the illustrious dead,* whom thy heartless calumny cannot reach [presumably Jacob Mountain (1749–1825)] ... The living [presumably Archdeacon Mountain (1789–1863)] is able, if inclined to justify his own conduct; but I apprehend is too conscious of his integrity, and too exalted in mind, to condescend to notice your base scurrility contained in this inharmonious doggerel." These were not the only criticisms levelled at *The Huron Chief* by its original readers. In a letter to the *Montreal Gazette* (7 June 1830), "Q" accuses Kidd of a multitude of literary sins, including "pure nonsense," repeated rhymes (nine instances of "minute" / "in it"), and excessive borrowings from Thomas Moore, the poet to whom *The Huron Chief, and Other Poems* is dedicated as "THE MOST POPULAR, MOST POWERFUL, AND MOST PATRIOTIC POET OF THE NINETEENTH CENTURY, WHOSE MAGIC NUMBERS HAVE VIBRATED TO THE HEARTS OF NATIONS."

A juxtaposition of the most Weldean lines from Moore's "Ballad Stanzas" with the opening stanza of *The Huron Chief* does not contradict Q's assertion that, as "honestly" intimated by his dedication, Kidd owes a "'pretty considerable' debt in the way of *borrowing* from Tom Moore":

It was noon, and on flowers that languish'd around
In silence repos'd the voluptuous bee;

Every leaf was at rest, and I heard not a sound
  But the woodpecker tapping the hollow beech-tree.
                    (*Poetical Works* 124)

On Huron's banks, one summer-day,
When all things bloomed with beauty gay,
I wandered undisturbed and free,
  Nor heard a sound, save wood-doves cooing,
Or birds that tapped the hollow tree,
  Where owlets sat, their play-mates wooing,
And harmony had filled the throng
Of pleasure, as I moved along.
                    (*1–8*)

Indebted as it is to Moore and, behind him, Weld, the opening stanza
of *The Huron Chief* is rich in meanings that emerge in light of the poem
as a whole and Kidd's sympathy for Native culture. In a note to *Gertrude
of Wyoming*, a poem echoed elsewhere in *The Huron Chief*, Campbell
states that in the "figurative language" of "the American Indians" "the
dove is ... as elsewhere, an emblem of meekness." Moreover, in the body
of his poem Campbell uses a further instance of the "metaphorical
manner" of the Native peoples – a "hollow peace-tree" – as a symbol of
peace betrayed (*Poetical Works* 80, 79, 50). In so doing, he draws upon
another work known to Kidd, albeit indirectly: Cadwallader Colden's
History of the Five Indian Nations of Canada (1727 f.), where, to quote a
footnote to *The Huron Chief*, Colden states that "the Five Nations always
express peace by the metaphor of the tree" (*427 n.*, and see *History of
the Five Nations* 1:51). It is no small irony that Kidd's source for the quotations from Colden in *The Huron Chief*, as for much of his knowledge
of Native culture, seems to have been *Sketches of the History, Manners and
Customs of the North American Indians* (1825) by James Buchanan, the
British consul in New York whom he attacks in a footnote. Kidd also
drew information and inspiration from such sources as Mackenzie's *Voyages*, Henry's *Travels and Adventures*, Jefferson's *Notes on the State of Virginia*, and William Tudor's *Letters on the Eastern States* (1820 f.), but his
principal prose source was the work of the man whom he called "impu-
dent" for his suggestion that the St. Lawrence be opened as a free-trade
route for American grain destined for Great Britain (see Bentley, notes
to *The Huron Chief* 91–92).
    While a reader familiar with Campbell and Colden, or aware of the
owl's call as a sign of foreboding (*1434*), might hear the ominous note
struck in the opening lines of *The Huron Chief*, the enraptured narrator
of the poem persists for several stanzas in his belief that he is moving

through "A splendid world of fairy bliss" such as might have been frequented by "Eden's daughters" (*35, 14*). Identified as deceptive by con-
ditional phrasing ("*Seemed* wrought in nature's richest hue, / As *if* to tell
me" [*19–20*; emphasis added]), the narrator's illusions are shattered
when his reverie is suddenly interrupted by the sorrowful song of a
Native woman. "Happy and blest were the days of my childhood ...
When ... love's purest essence had deeply inspired me," she sings,

> But the hand of the white man has brought desolation –
>> Our wigwams are plundered, our homes are no more, –
> And MORANKA, the glory and pride of the Nation,
>> Died bravely defending the Indian's shore.
>
> (*65–68*)

A footnote to these lines quotes the Moravian missionary John Heckewelder by way of Buchanan's *Sketches* (18) to the effect that "complaints which the Indians make of the ingratitude and injustice of the
Whites" are "long and dismal," and expressed with "the eloquence of
nature, aided by an energetic and comprehensive language, which our
polished idioms cannot imitate" (*65 n.*). As sensitive as Heckewelder is
to the otherness of Native language and speech, Kidd recalls the Moore
of "To the Lady Charlotte Rawdon" in casting the song of Moranka's
widow in a poetic form ($abab_4$) which differs sharply from that of
poem's narrator ($aabcbcdd_4$). Indeed, the phrase with which Moore
introduces the narrative of the Indian Spirit in his poem – "words like
these" – has a clear echo in Kidd's introduction of the song of Moranka's widow: "I heard soft words of sorrow swelling, / Like these" (*38–
39*).

Yet "how does one *represent* other cultures" (Said 325)? Kidd's answer
was to cast the sorrowing widow's song in a form reminiscent of poems
in Moore's *Irish Melodies* ("Oh! Breathe not his Name") and Byron's
Hebrew Melodies ("The Destruction of Sennacherib"), two works that
treat of cultures other than those of the Anglo-Scottish élite of Upper
and Lower Canada. Not only were Moore and Byron associated with the
remote and exotic in Kidd's day, but the latter especially was ranged on
the side of liberty against authority by his death in the Greek War of
Independence and by the refusal of the Anglican Church to bury his
remains in Westminster Abbey, a decision defended by the ecclesiastical
Mountains (Edwards 375) and reviled by Kidd in a "Monody on the
Shade of Lord Byron" (*The Huron Chief, and Other Poems* 137). Not fortuitously Kidd's vitriolic attack on "M***T**N" in *The Huron Chief* makes
reference to "the Churchman's" – that is, the Anglican's – "rant ... /
Against the great, immortal BYRON!" (*510–13*). The sympathy for people

of another culture that is signalled by the shift in voice and form in the song of Moranka's widow is confirmed and deepened by the narrator's subsequent and startling proclamation: "Nor shall my heart here now deny it – / I saw, I loved the lonely one, / Because she loved her Hero gone!" (*78–80*). An adamant statement of spontaneous affection for someone of another race and culture, this is clearly an explosive moment in the poem and a prelude to the later declaration of sexual attraction to a Native woman ("who will blame me when I tell, / I loved KEMANA over well!" [*475–76*]) that so disgusted Job Deacon. In both instances, it should be observed, Kidd employs literary allusions in a highly subversive manner: "I saw, I loved, the lonely one" echoes Julius Caesar's "I came, I saw, I conquered" to replace the rhetoric of imperialistic domination with the language of affection for a victim of imperialism; and "I loved KEMANA over well" associates the narrator with Othello, another outsider who "loved not wisely but too well" (*4.2.344*).

After his avowal of love for Moranka's widow, Kidd's narrator experiences a momentary conflict between a strong desire to "share" her "sorrow" and a stronger realization that it would be "madness" to intrude on her "solitude" and "destroy" her mourning ritual (*121–28*). No sooner has he "resolved [his] steps to take, / Along the windings of the lake" (*129–30*) than his progress is interrupted once again, this time by "SKENANDOW" (*190*), the Huron chief himself. Now the very presence in the poem of a Huron bearing the name of the "distinguished Oneida Chief" (*142 n.*) who died in 1816, approximately two years before Kidd's probable arrival in North America, injects a disconcerting element of indeterminacy into the proceedings. Can it be that the student who, according to the preface, "travel[led] through the immense forests of America" and fell from "the cloud-capped brows of a dangerous Mountain" (*16–17, 39–40*) is someone other than the itinerant narrator who encounters "the Chieftain of this mountain" (*141*) on the shores of Lake Huron and who, nevertheless, rails twice in the poem proper against the "*Mountain* demon" (*796*)? As well as frustrating the reader's expectation of a straightforward continuity or discontinuity between the author and the narrator of *The Huron Chief*, the presence of Skenandow, Tecumseh, and other chiefs in the poem pushes its historical context towards undecidability. Is it set towards the end of the War of 1812, when Tecumseh (who survives the action of *The Huron Chief*) was, of course, killed; or is it set in the 1820s when Archdeacon Mountain was in the ascendency in Lower Canada? That such questions are not amenable to the "either … or" solutions of ordinary common-sense but, on the contrary, force the reader towards an acceptance of the possibility of "both … and" – the poem's narrator is both the poet and a *persona*, the poem's context is both the past and the present – may be taken as further evidence of Kidd's attempt to subvert the assumptions of his original readers. *The Huron Chief* is a medley of personal experience and historical events that contests rational taxonomies and unifying structures with a libertarian proliferation of contexts, forms, and points of view. Whereas *Abram's Plains*, *The Rising Village* and other poems of the Georgian period affirm and reflect the presence of a European order in Canada, Kidd's thoroughly post-Romantic poem confronts that order with the aesthetic and intellectual alternatives against which he wishes it to be judged and found dangerously wanting.

It is as consistent with the libertarian tendencies of Kidd's narrator (*97–104*) as with his sympathy for the Native peoples that after Skenandow offers "to guide [his] wand'ring feet" on a "way" that is "not the white man's" (*139–40*) he affirms the freedom of his "affections" (*169–76*) and begins to speak in the same form – the long ballad stanza – used by the chief. Within a few moments of this symbolic and symbiotic realignment with a "way" – a form and culture – perceived in the wake of Romanticism as primitive but dignified, simple but noble, the poem is once more interrupted. This time the disruption of linear progression takes the form of a "plaintive" and, again, balladic lament by a young "SIOUX" warrior (*233*) for his beloved "TA-POO-KA" whom he believes "Is dead! – forever gone!" (*220*). Later in the poem Kidd reveals his sympathy for Native culture by noting that "the *Tana Arboria*, or tree frog, [is] called by the Indians *Atheiky*" (*927; Mackenzie cix*); here he does so by observing that the "word [TA-POO-KA] requires a slow accent" if it is to be pronounced in the Native manner (*238 n.*). It is given to Skenandow to explain that Ta-poo-ka and the Sioux warrior are star-crossed lovers. Rather than marry an "aged Chief" selected by her father, she chose to take her own life by plunging "within the foaming surge of Lake Huron" (*239–300*). "There, ever since," says Skenandow, "the spirit-bride ... In her canoe, is seen to glide, / Across the curling water's brim" (*301–04*). In the present century, this tale and its cognates as found, for example, in Moore's "Lake of the Dismal Swamp," Sangster's "Tapooka" (a clear derivative of *The Huron Chief*), and Alan Sullivan's *The White Canoe and Other Verse* have been recognized as *ersatz* Indian legends that were disseminated through the works of Henry Rowe Schoolcraft (*Narrative* 330), James Athearn Jones (2:207–22) and, in Kidd's case, Buchanan's *Sketches* (179–80). (Schoolcraft's enormously influential version of the tale appears under the title "Constancy of an Indian Girl.") To Kidd, however, these materials must have seemed authentic; in a subsequent note, he states that "the Indians compared everything that was beautiful" to "the unfortunate TA-POO-KA ... She was the idol of the Nation – every young heart worshipped her" (*821 n.*). Whereas Richardson follows Weld in asserting that "the *sentiment* of love is almost wholly unknown among the Indian tribes, by whom the sex is held in the utmost inferiority and contempt" ([1828] vi–vii), Kidd treats Ta-poo-ka and her bereft lover Alkwanwaugh as a Huron and Sioux Romeo and Juliet whose love is as intense and enduring as it is "Pure [and] gen'rous" (*237*). The Native peoples of *The Huron Chief* are stereotypical noble savages, but at least this means that, in contrast to the anonymous and animalistic "tribes" of *The Rising Village*, they are named and sympathetic characters with "narratable life histories" (Said 229).

After Skenandow's emotional yet reticent telling of the tale of Ta-poo-ka and Alkenwaugh, the narrator's eyes fill with "admiration" for the "holy man" and, in resonantly Rousseauian fashion, he declares "That Europe's pomp [he'd] quick resign, / To dwell within [the] groves of pine" "where nature's child delights to stray" (*313–14, 319–20, 333*). Alluding to Goldsmith's remarks on the positive lessons to be learned from extending hospitality to strangers (*Traveller* 21–22), Kidd transfers the decasyllabic couplets of rational and social order from the cultivated landscapes where they are usually found to an unspoiled wilderness in which "every prospect rising to the view, / Half tells the joys our happier fathers knew, / Before the plans of art had come between, / And made of beauty's shades a barren scene" (*329–32*). "Oh, happy home!," he exclaims, "where nought but nature's plan / Is felt, and practised, by contented man; / No shifting system here we ever trace, / But all things have their own, their proper place" (*333–36*). Following this celebration of natural over civilized order, the narrator accepts Skenandow's invitation to "share / The Indian wigwam for the night" (*353–54)* and the two set off towards a Huron village. There the narrator finds a "circle" of "joy" and "beauty" (*541–42, 1062*) that is the Rousseauian counterpart, not only of the expanding circle of European settlement in *The Rising Village* (and, later, in *The U.E.* [*6:35–36*] and *Malcolm's Katie [1:110]*), but also of the "long *round* of professional studies" to which Kidd was subjected in Quebec (preface *37–38*; emphasis added). It is in the village, during a dance in which the Huron youths experience "joy's excess" and exhibit "all the sweet charms of playfulness" (*466*), that the narrator's love for Kemana is awakened.

As well as being a transgression of the imperialistic ethos, this love enables the narrator – now very obviously Kidd – to forget the "woes" of his recent past (*486*) and to remember instead his "boyhood's days" in Ireland, where, "Ere thought, or reason, took command, / [He] strayed with heart as light as feather" "o'er SLIEVEGALLIN'S mantled braes" (*493–96*). In an ensuing meditation on time itself, he regrets the rational and progressivist tendency to evaluate times past in relation to a supposedly "wiser" present, a present that "disapproves" of hours "gone by"

"Till every moment of the past, / Seems fool, or madman, to the *last*"
(501–08). Instead of this evaluative and dismissive approach to time,
Kidd advocates a child-like enjoyment of the present, a carefree concentration of the here and now that consists for him of Skenandow, his
happy "clan" *(529)*, and, above all, Kemana. But the narrator's escape
from his sorrowful past and his complete immersion in his happy
present comes abruptly to an end when Skenandow delivers a lengthy
and elegiac speech on his own vanished youth and impending death.
"'I am an aged hemlock,' said [the] distinguished Oneida Chief
[Skenandou], 'the winds of one hundred and twenty years have whis-
tled through my branches'" (*142 n.; Buchanan* 178). "Now, as the oak
upon the hill, / Whose aged branches feel decay ... all my vigour wastes
away" (589–92), says his namesake in *The Huron Chief*, with a simple
acceptance of his mortality that moves the narrator to conceive of the
Huron village as a "type" of Eden, "that pure sanctu'ry, / Where, first
repenting, man ... talk[ed] in prayer alone with God" *(633–40)*. Bowing again towards Rousseau, Kidd adds that "It was a pure, a holy sight
... To see devotion's fervent soul, / By Nature's God alone directed ...
To a sunny sphere of bliss, / Possessing joys unknown in this" *(641–49)*.
So ends what the narrator calls his "life's first happy day" *(655)*.

In Skenandow's concluding statement that his "life will gladly meet
its close" "with this remnant of [his] tribe" lies an ominous acknowledgment of the dark past and darker future of his people. A lengthy footnote to this statement draws on various sources, including
Bartholomew de Las Casas' *The Spanish Colonie* (1552; trans. 1583), to
discuss the nature and extent of the suffering and destruction visited on
the Native peoples of the New World by European disease, avarice, big-
otry, and cruelty *(613 n.)*. After the narrator has said his fond farewells
to Kemana and her clan, he is treated by Alkwanwaugh to "the tale / Of
days, that live but in tradition – / And all the joys that cheered the vale,
/ Where dwells the remnant of the Nation" *(667–70)*. Although somewhat vague and garbled, most notably by a chronological confusion of
Eustache Atsistari (ca.1602–42), the Huron warrior who mounted a successful attack against the Iroquois in 1641, and Shastaretsi (16?–1685),
the head chief of the Hurons at Sillery and Notre-Dame de Foy outside
Quebec in 1676 *(673 n.)*, Alkwanwaugh's tale and the footnote that
accompanies it testify to the nature and extent of Kidd's researches into
Huron history. "In all my inquiries respecting [Atsistari]," he writes, "I
received the most honourable, and the most interesting accounts, and
particularly from OUI-A-RA-LIH-TO, the oldest Chief of the village of
Lorette ... During my visit to this old Chief – May, 1829 – he willingly furnished me with an account of the distinguished warriors, and the traditions of different tribes, which are still fresh in his memory, and are

handed from father to son, with the same precision, interest, and admiration, that the Tales and exploits of Ossian and his heroes are circulated in their original purity, to this day, among the Irish" (*673 n.*). The parallel made explicit here between the oral histories of the Hurons and the Irish is already implicit in the epigraph of *The Huron Chief*, a slightly modified quotation from "Croma: a Poem," one of James Macpherson's spuriously Ossianic fragments (2:160): "Where are our Chiefs of old? Where our Heroes of mighty name? / The fields of their battles are silent – scarce their mossy tombs remain!" It seems more than likely that a history of political and cultural repression was one of the links that connected the Hurons and the Irish in Kidd's mind.

The climax of Alkwanwaugh's account of Native history is his recitation of the famous speech of John Logan, the Mingo chief, to Lord Dunmore, the Governor of Virginia, in 1774. A rendition in ballad stanzas of the transcription of Logan's speech in Jefferson's *Notes on the State of Virginia* (and Campbell's *Gertrude of Wyoming*), Alkwanwaugh's recitation carries forward the theme of the Natives' generous hospitality to Europeans and their stoical attitude to death. It also narrows the focus of the poem to the sufferings of Native peoples at the hands of treacherous and supposedly Christian Americans, for as a footnote explains "LOGAN was a ... friend of the whites, until, his wives and little children ... were basely murdered in the spring of 1774, by [the Maryland frontiersman] Colonel [Michael] Cresap and his Christian followers, whom he had long befriended" (*736 n.*). Consistent with this new concentration on events south of the border is the fact that shortly after the recitation of Logan's speech Alkanwaugh and the narrator pass from Lake Huron to Lake Erie along the St. Clair River, where a song sung by a passing hunter named "KEKAPOO" in anticipation of rejoining his wife ends forebodingly with a prayer to the "Spirit of the great and free" to "Protect us from the white man's laws" (*841–42*). A subsequent footnote confirms that Kidd regarded the United States as a more hostile environment than Canada for the Native peoples: "the Indians belonging to Great Britain have an utter dislike to the ... Americans ... Nor am I surprised at this feeling – for there is scarce a day but brings them some cruel accounts of the destruction and massacre of their brethren in the United States – and, even at this moment, in Georgia, the poor Indian is hunted from his home, and barbarously murdered" (*1256 n.*).

With their geographical proximity to the United States making disaster almost inevitable, Alkwanwaugh and the narrator enter a "lovely bay" (*869*) on Lake Erie where they are greeted by yet another song, this one sung by "A voice as soft – divinely sweet / As summer winds o'er rose buds playing" (*879–80*). To the deeply suspicious narrator, this "enchanting" song brings dark thoughts of "Syren spells to lure away /

The heart to some unthought of danger" (*887–88*). But as the laws of romance and tragedy of course decree, this song is sung by Alkwan-waugh's lost lover Ta-poo-ka who, it transpires, was rescued from drowning in Lake Huron by "three kind *Chippewas*" and thereafter raised "as his daughter" by "OU-KA-KEE, the good, the kind – / A noble Chief of noble mind" (*992, 1118, 1091–92*). As heavy with sentiment as it is laden with foreboding, this episode contains some of the best-achieved writing in *The Huron Chief.* Appropriately cast in the Venus and Adonis stanza, Ta-poo-ka's song begins with a stanza worthy of Moore and not a little indebted to him:

> Here now, beneath this lonely shade,
>> Far, far from home, I sit reposing,
> And listen to the wild cascade,
>> While evening's curtain round is closing,
> And every bird, with spirit gay,
> Sings, sweetly sings its vesper lay.
>
> (*909–14*)

"Far, far from home ... Sings, sweetly sings": effective precisely to the extent that they are affective, these symmetrical structures deepen the elegiac mood of the song both by slowing its pace and by reinforcing the contrast between Ta-poo-ka's sadness and the happiness around her. In the margin beside the similarly well-modulated lines describing the meeting of Ta-poo-ka and Alkwanwaugh – "A look – a pause – and then a start, / Quick as the impulse of the heart" (*955–56*) – the less than sympathetic Job Deacon was moved to write "certainly finely conceived and well expressed."

As he records with delight the life of Ou-ka-kee's village, the preparations for the marriage of Ta-poo-ka and Alkwanwaugh, and the arrival of Skenandow on the morning of the wedding, the narrator several times reiterates his earlier comparisons of the Huron camp with Eden and Heaven. The Natives' "world of peace – a world of love" is "A type of all that dwells above" (*1241–42*), he observes at one point, and at another he remarks that "The scene – the place – the happy hour" remind him "much of MILTON'S bower: / Where first the parent of mankind / Conducted Eve – with beauty blushing, / And feelings pure, and unconfined, / As yon pellucid stream" (*1044–48*). No sooner is the "wedding over," however, than thoughts of the "Sectarian" rivalries and "crimes" of European "*Creeds-men*" (*1242–58*) darken the narrator's mind and, like the reference to "MILTON'S bower," indicate that the note of *The Huron Chief* must soon turn tragic. With nightfall, the satanic attack duly comes with a "foul incursion" of "white," probably American

and certainly "Christian foe-men" who set fire to Ou-ka-kee's "peaceful
forest home" (*1294, 1347, 1357, 1338*) and cause the deaths of numerous people, including Alkwanwaugh (by violence) and Ta-poo-ka (of
heartbreak). Nor are the parallels with *Paradise Lost* confined to the
destruction of an Edenic world and an Edenic love. As even the trinitar-
ian resonances of the "three kind Chippewas" intimates, the closing
portions of *The Huron Chief* consistently align the Native peoples with
the unfallen angels and the "Christian foe-men" with Satan's hellish
cohorts. The battle in the forest beside Lake Erie thus becomes a type
of Milton's War in Heaven; Tecumseh – the "Napoleon of the West"
(*1317 n.*; and see George Henry 129) who arrives in time to "Decide the
horrors of the fight" (*1322*) in favour of the Natives – becomes a type of
Christ; and "the Christian foe-men three" (*1357*) who are captured at
the close of the battle become a demonic version of the Trinity – a type,
perhaps, of Milton's unholy trinity of Satan, Sin, and Death. Abdiel-like
in his role as the one just European on the scene, the narrator speaks a
radical Romantic's version of the truth when, as darkness shrouds the
"day's unholy crime" against humanity, he explicitly associates "Missionary evil" with "hell – / And all the crimes with it connected" (*1363,
1374*).

After the flames from the Ou-ka-kee's village have spread to the
nearby forest, ensuring that the "beasts no longer can recline" (*1327*)
in what once was a peaceable kingdom, the narrator speaks one of the
most metaphorically rich stanzas in *The Huron Chief*:

> And from the cloud-capped mountain high,
>   Where now the fearless eagle sleeps,
> The stream sends forth a broken sigh,
>   While tumbling down the rugged steeps –
> And from the hollow, blasted pine,
>   Where heaven's light'ning played along,
> And wild grapes close their tendrels twine,
>   Comes forth the screech-owl's boding song.
>   (*1427–34*)

The allusion here to *Paradise Lost* ("Earth felt the wound, and Nature
from her seat / Sighing through all her Works gave signs of woe, / That
all was lost" [*9:782–84*]) places the preceding events in the context of
the Fall, while the surrounding metaphors speak of European usurpa-
tion, treachery, and destruction. The "mountain" that was once the
sacred precinct of Skenandow is now surmounted by the predatory
emblem of the United States. The stream that was once associated with
the purity and freedom of life in the wilderness is now a sad emblem of

an irreparable fall. The tree that was once "hollow" is now "blasted": a
metaphor of an insincere peace violated by powerful destructive forces.
Foreshadowing death and destruction yet to come are the "tendrels" of
"wild grape" and the "screech-owl's boding song" – the former, the
plant that will "guard the holy shrine" of Skenandow at the close to the
poem, and the latter, the demonic fulfillment of the seemingly playful
and harmonious "wooing" of the "owlets" that occupied the "hollow
tree" in the poem's opening stanza.

The tragic denouement of the final lines of *The Huron Chief* is precipitated by "the Christian white men, three" whom the Hurons have "Fast
pinioned to [a] bas-wood tree" to await their punishment for "crimes"
which, in the narrator's view, "should not be forgiven" (*1459–62*).
Although the "youthful heroes" among the Hurons are in favour of exe-
cuting the "cold – unfeeling Christian whites," the older chiefs argue
persuasively for their release on the grounds that "They might repent"
and, in addition, that "Perhaps [their] wives and children mourn"
(*1483, 1492, 1538, 1580*). After tipping the balance towards clemency
by combining his immense powers of "persuasion" (*1548*) with the merciful approach to prisoners of war that he displayed at Fort Meigs,
Tecumseh leaves it to an equally eloquent and forgiving Skenandow to
release the three prisoners on the condition that they no more "roam,
/ To rob the Indian of his home" (*1593–94*). As well as containing an
informative catalogue of Native tokens of peace – "WAMPUM ... the tree ...
the chain ... And the hatchet" (*1564–68*), the speech that Skenandow delivers
to the prisoners while releasing them suggests that his act is a reconsecra-
tion of the tree especially as an emblem of peace rather than destruction, liberty rather than bondage. But, of course, this merely sets the
scene for another gross act of betrayal, for once "TECUMSEH and his
heroes" have departed, "the *three*, / The captive *three*, of Christian feeling!" return with a "direful band" to ambush the remaining Natives as
they "seek their home" and kill Skenandow (*1611–50*). That the chief
manages to kill two of the three but is himself killed by the third suggests, like the survival of one representative of evil in a gothic tale (or
movie), that there will be no end to the treachery and destructiveness
of Europeans in North America.

The final stanza of *The Huron Chief* presents the death of Skenandow
with Ossianic pathos:

SKENANDOW fell! – and calmly sleeps
   By ERIE's darkling groves of pine,
Where gently now the wild grape creeps,
   As if to guard the holy shrine –
Nor shall his name be e'er forgot –

But future bards, in songs of grief,
Will sadly tell of that lone spot,
Where rests the noble HURON CHIEF!
                    (*1651–58*)

Part of the inspiration for this stanza can be found in "Conlanth and
Cuthona," the penultimate piece in *The Poems of Ossian*: "The chief of
Mora dies. The vision grows dim on my mind. I behold the chiefs no
more! But, O ye bards of future times, remember the fall of Conlath
with tears. He fell before his day" (3:338). Building on the parallel
between Celtic and Native "chiefs," Kidd has brought forward the
mood, the tone, and some of the diction of this passage and combined
them with names and plants indigenous to North America, most notably the vine which, nearly a century later, F.O. Call would use as an
emblem of the poetic forms appropriate to the Canadian wilderness in
Acanthus and Wild Grape.

When he wrote the final stanza of *The Huron Chief*, Kidd may also have
had in mind William Tudor's statement in his *Letters on the Eastern States*
that "the history of [the Native peoples], long after they shall have
become extinct, will be interesting to our posterity, and furnish subjects
for poetry and romance" (292). Certainly, the elegiac tone of *The Huron
Chief* extends beyond particular individuals to entire tribes. "From the
days of the American Revolution until this very hour," Kidd writes in his
preface, "the poor Indians have been so cruelly treated, and driven
from their homes and hunting-grounds, by the boasted freemen of the
United States, that the MOHICANS, the NARAGANSETTS, the DELA-
WARES, and others, once powerful Tribes, have now become totally
extinct – while the remaining Nations are daily dwindling away, and in
a few years hence will scarcely leave a memorial to perpetuate their
names, as the once mighty rulers of the vast American regions" (*23–30*).
"It is worthy of remark," runs a note based on the charter of the
Boeothick Institution in the 13 November 1827 issue of the *Royal
Gazette*, "that the BOETHIC, or Red Indians, once a numerous and a
powerful tribe inhabiting the western shores of Newfoundland, and the
coasts of Labrador, are almost extinct" (and, in fact, became so on 6
June 1829 with the death of Shanawdithit, or Nancy, the last of the
Beothuks [*1370 n.*]). It is ironical, but entirely understandable, that
one of the first fully sympathetic treatments of the Native peoples in
pre-Confederation poetry was written, like *The Last of the Mohicans*, at
the time when their extinction seemed both inevitable and imminent.
A cynic might observe that the Native peoples entered Canadian poetry
as wholly admirable characters only when they had ceased to be a
threat.

Was Kidd's Skenandow based on a particular Huron chief? In addition to Oui-a-ra-lih-to, "the oldest Chief of the village of Lorette," whom Kidd claims to have visited in May 1829, there are several likely candidates. By implication, J.M. Lemoine in *Picturesque Quebec: a Sequel to Quebec Past and Present* (482) identifies Kidd's hero with François-Xavier Picard Tahourenché (1810–1883), a secondary chief of the Lorette Hurons between 1840 and 1870, when he was named grand chief (Tehariolina 83–84). A more likely possibility, if only because he is mentioned in Kidd's preface as one of the chiefs who will "shortly ... translate" *The Huron Chief* "into their respective tongues" (*55–58*), must be Nicholas Vincent Tsaouenhohi (1769–1844) – Kidd's "SAWENNOW-ANE" – the grand chief of the Hurons at Jeune Lorette from 1811 to his death in 1844 (Tehariolina 82; Sioui). The fact that Tsaouenhohi spoke both English and French (and wrote the latter) agrees with Kidd's observation that "SAWENNOWANE, and other Chiefs ... speak and write several languages." The resemblance between the frontispiece to *The Huron Chief* and a famous engraving of "Nicholas Vincent Isawanhonhi" by Hullmandel after a painting by Edward Chatfield strengthens the connection between Skenandow and "Sawennowane" (see Bentley, intro. xxiv–xxvii). An explanation of the medal worn by "the Chieftain of this mountain" in *The Huron Chief* is provided by the caption to Hullmandel's engraving, which states that the "Principal Christian Chief and Captain of the Huron Indians Established at La Jeune Lorette near Quebec [is] Habited in the Costume of his Country as when Presented to his Majesty George IV on 7 April 1825, with Three Other Chiefs of his Nation by Generals Brock and Carpenter. The Chief Bears in his Hand the Wampum or Collar on which is Marked the Tomahawk Given by his Late Majesty George III. The Gold Medal on his Neck was the Gift of his Majesty on this Presentation" (National Archives of Canada C–38948; see also Bentley, intro. xxv). Accounts of the departure and presentation of Tsaouenhohi and his fellow Huron chiefs appear in the *Quebec Mercury* on 16 November 1824 and 31 May 1825.

Despite the similarities between Skenandow and "Sawennowane" the hero of *The Huron Chief* is very likely a compound of several chiefs who were known to Kidd in life and print. Of these, one more deserves special mention because the report of his death in the 6 April 1829 issue of the *Quebec Gazette* accords so closely with Kidd's theme of personal and racial extinction that it cannot help but seem a source of inspiration, if not for the poem, then for the poet's visit to Lorette a month later:

DIED,

On friday the 20th ult. at Indian Lorette, near the city, *Wen-wha-dahronhé* or Gabriel Vincent [Owawandaronhey], the third chief of the Hurons residing at that village: he was the only remaining Indian of the village who had descended in a direct line, without intermixture of blood, from the original tribe inhabiting the borders of Lake Huron: he was also one who retained most of the habits, and the only one who reared his family in the use of the language, of his fore-fathers, the younger inhabitants of the village now speaking the French language only and not understanding their own. After a successful and arduous chase on snow shoes of three elks, on the South side of the river, he was attacked by a pleurisy, and passing three days in the woods unassisted, disease had taken firm hold of him, so that a few days' sickness carried him off at 57, yet in the prime of life.

12 Joseph Howe, *Acadia*

Acadia was first published in 1874 in the posthumous *Poems and Essays* of Joseph Howe (1804–73), but, as M.G. Parks has established, it was written in the early 1830s (Parks, intro. xi–xii). At that time Howe was making trips to various parts of the Maritimes, including, in September 1833, Lochaber Lake in eastern Nova Scotia (*819–52*), which he found greatly changed since his previous visit in June 1830. "You may remember that I was in love with the sylvan appearance of the Lochaber or College Lake when in this country last," he told his wife Susan in a letter of September 1833; "then the ancient woods were scarcely broken upon on either margin, and the whole scene was as beautifully wild as it had been a thousand years before. Now every lot has been taken up – clearings are making and log houses are building in every direction – and in a few years more there will scarcely be a tree to be seen" (qtd. in Parks, intro. xii). Howe's nostalgia for the pre-settlement state of Lochaber Lake does more than establish that "most, if not all, of *Acadia*" was written between 8 July 1832, when he began the poem with some lines that he considered "full of truth" if "not perhaps worthy of the subject," and his dismay a little over a year later at what was well on the way to becoming "a flourishing farming district" (Parks, intro. xi–xii). It also suggests a certain ambivalence on Howe's part to the progress that he celebrates at several points in *Acadia*.

Howe's celebration of both agricultural development and unspoiled wilderness in *Acadia* finds echoes in his political views and personal life in the early thirties. By family background a Loyalist, an imperialist, and a patrician, he was also a patriotic Nova Scotian with democratic ideas towards which he was increasingly leaning at this time. By 1834–36, in fact, the balance of his political views had tipped from the mild Toryism that he had espoused earlier to the moderate reform principles that would lead him in subsequent decades to advocate responsible government, first in the *Novascotian* (which he had acquired from his Loyalist father in 1828) and then in the political arena, where his stance as a "conservative reformer" gave him common ground with both Whigs and Tories (Beck 370). Yet Howe's willingness to entertain differing points of view has led to charges that his political dealings were inconsistent (Beck 367–70) and that *Acadia* "exhibits a lack of unified sensibility" (Gingell-Beckmann 18). Something of the same capacity for being both conservative and liberal is evident in Howe's personal life. Devoted to his wife Susan, with whom he had ten children between 1829 and 1848, he was also rumoured to have "fathered numerous illegitimate children" and was notorious for his ribald humour both on and off the floor of the Nova Scotia House of Assembly (Beck 363, 370). Perhaps the traditional and unconventional strains of Howe's personality, like his conservative and reformist tendencies, can be partly attributed to the fact that he was a late Georgian who experienced both the liberating warmth of Romanticism and the retarding chill of colonial Victorianism.

A topographical poem written entirely in decasyllabic couplets, *Acadia* is formalistically conservative and refined, yet it contains several covertly licentious passages in which Nova Scotia seems to furnish the pretext for Howe to describe the female body: "Now to the eye its glowing charms [are] revealed," runs part of the description of Lochaber Lake; "Now, like a bashful Beauty, half concealed / Beneath the robe of spotless green, she wears / The rich profusion of a thousand years" (*833–36*). In this and other passages to be examined shortly, there is a confusion of tenor and vehicle that imparts an element of voyeuristic eroticism to the thoroughly conventional depiction of Nature as female and, in doing so, raises questions about the psycho-sexual motivation of several parts of *Acadia*, not least the extraordinarily graphic description of the violent massacre of a settler family by vengeful Micmacs. If *Wacousta* is early Canadian literature's "most extensive peep-show," as Dennis Duffy has suggested, then perhaps *Acadia* is its most compressed one, for here, too, "characters are forever being peered at by others," most prominently by the narrator (52). Perhaps both *Wacousta* and *Acadia* need to be understood as products of an age that demanded and relished the covert and distanced depiction of sex and violence. Perhaps part of Howe's reason for writing *Acadia* was to express ideas and attitudes similar to those that earned him opprobrium elsewhere. Perhaps the second part of *Acadia* lacks integration, not merely because, by the mid-thirties, he was being drawn increasingly into the journalistic and political arenas, but also because of some uncertainty on his part about the poem's subject and purpose.

In the skilfully rhetorical opening lines of *Acadia*, however, these seem quite clear. The subject of the poem is Howe's native and beloved Nova Scotia, and its purpose is to express and inspire patriotic feelings. "Where does the Sun its richest radiance shed? / Where are the choicest gifts of Nature spread?" To these and the other questions with which *Acadia* gets under way, Howe offers a reply that is as unabashedly subjective and sentimental as it is derivative of the opening lines of James Montgomery's *The West Indies*, which also belabour the commonplace point that "man, in every varying clime / Deems his own land ... the spot of earth supremely blest, / A dearer, sweeter spot than all the rest" (qtd. in Parks, notes 42). The one place in which every "flower," "hill," and stream will have special resonance for *Acadia*'s readers is their "native land," the "blest spot"

> Where rest the honor'd ashes of our Sires,
> Where burn, undimm'd, our bright domestic fires,
> Where we first heard a Mother's silvery tone,
> And felt her lips, enraptured, meet our own,
> Where we first climb'd a doting Father's knee
> And cheer'd his spirit with our childish glee.
>   (*11–16*)

Generalized and derivative though they are, these lines convey an unmistakable sense that the group whose patriotic feelings are being prompted and defined by one of its own consists of native-born Nova Scotians. Later in the poem Howe articulates with great sympathy the feelings of older emigrants to Nova Scotia, but at the outset his stated aim is to earn Acadia's approbation by kindling the fire of patriotism in her native sons:

> In ev'ry prayer I breathe to Heaven's high throne
> My Country's welfare blends – and could my hand
> Bestow one flower't on my native land,
> Could I but light one Beacon fire, to guide
> The steps of those who yet may be her pride,
> Could I but wake one never-dying strain
> Which Patriot hearts might echo back again,
> I'd ask no meed – no wreath of glory crave
> If her approving smile my own Acadia gave.
>   (*56–64*)

Envisaged as an outgrowth of filial love directed towards a beloved woman, Howe's love for Acadia has oedipal overtones that answer to Melanie Klein's model of artistic creativity whereby the irretrievably lost body of the mother becomes a "beautiful" land to be recovered vicariously in a work of art (334). Some support for such a psychoanalytical reading of *Acadia* is given by the prominence in the poem of family units that are destroyed, threatened, or diminished, and by the poem's concluding contention that even in exile "Acadia's sons" are sustained by "dreams" of the "lovely forms" of their motherland (*1019–30*).

Whatever his unconscious motives (if any) for writing *Acadia*, Howe had thought carefully about the origins and value of the "amor patriae" that he sought to inculcate in his fellow Nova Scotians. "The abstract or cosmopolitan idea of Knowledge, is that it is of no country," he told the Halifax Mechanics' Institute on 5 November 1834, "but the all wise Being, who divided the earth into continents, peninsulas, and islands ... evidently intended that there should be a local knowledge and a local love binding his creatures to particular spots of earth, and interesting them peculiarly for the prosperity, improvement and happiness of those places. The love of country, therefore, though distinguished from ... universal love, boasts an origin as divine, and serves purposes scarcely less admirable ... Is that feeling alive in our breasts? Is it abroad in this country? Has Nova-Scotia received the power to attach her children to her bosom, and make them prouder and fonder of her bleak hills and sylvan vallies, than even of the fairer and more cultivated lands from which their parents came?" (*Address* 4–5). In the belief that, though his "audience [is] composed of all countries" in the United Kingdom, "their children are already natives of Nova-Scotia," Howe proceeds to give "direction" to the "feelings of patriotism" – the "filial reverence and care" – that these children must feel for "the little Province where they drew their earliest breath" (5). "I wish to build up Agriculture, Commerce and Manufactures, upon the surest of all foundations – the mental and moral cultivation of the people," Howe says in summary; "if knowledge is power, let us get knowledge. If our position presents difficulties, let us study to overcome them; and if we can only surpass others, by a higher measure of patriotism, sagacity, and endurance, than they possess, let us never cease to hope and labour until that standard is attained" (19). Very obviously, Howe's purpose in writing *Acadia* was to encourage the patriotic feelings that would provide the basis for economic and cultural progress in Nova Scotia.

To substantiate his claims on behalf of patriotism in his *Address ... Before the Halifax Mechanics' Institute* Howe cites numerous cities and states from Athens to England whose "growth and prosperity" have depended less upon "their territorial extent, or their natural situation and advantages ... [than] upon the discipline, knowledge and self devotion of their inhabitants" (12). Cued by Montgomery, and, no doubt, by some of the poems upon which *The West Indies* is itself based (most notably, Thomson's "Winter" and Goldsmith's *The Traveller*), Howe adopts a slightly different strategy in *Acadia*, aligning Nova Scotia with places as superficially likely and unlikely to generate patriotic feelings as Canaan and Lapland (*17–30*). Adding Byron (*The Two Foscari*) and Samuel Rogers (*Italy*) to the list of his poetic sources, Howe also treats exile from "the scenes that [have] blest ... childish hours" as a potentially fatal disease, a home-sickness that, at the very least, causes psychological anguish. Having thus associated physical well-being with proximity to a beloved homeland, particularly one with a healthy climate like Nova Scotia (*65–80*), Howe concludes his statement of *Acadia*'s high theme by linking patriotism with holiness, heroism, and great poetry: in addition to issuing in "sacred thoughts and ... daring deeds" such as those of Nelson at Trafalgar, patriotic feeling inspired the "patriotic strains" of Burns, the "seraphic lyre" of Moore, and the "rude wreath" which, with becoming modesty, Howe hopes to "Twine ... around [his] Country's brow" (*31–42*). Far from being the last refuge of the scoundrel that it was for Johnson, patriotism is for Howe the source of great achievements and high aspirations.

Making up the "rude wreath" that Howe offers Acadia are the usual components of topographical poetry: a "particular landscape ... poetically described ... historical retrospection and incidental meditation." On the precedent of *The Seasons*, Howe begins with a description of the Acadian landscape in the spring, when a renewal of "life and beauty" in the natural world generates a corresponding resurgence of "hope and gladness" in the human spirit (*91–94*). A fresh page in the Book of Nature where "Man reads in glowing lines his Maker's love" (*96*), spring in Nova Scotia is also a time when Howe's fancies turn quickly from the sacred to the sensual. Goldsmith had discreetly sexualized Flora by likening her to the "May-flower," a plant "indigenous to the wilds of America [or 'Acadia'; see (1834) *316 n.*]" that possesses "white [leaves] ..., faintly tinged with red, and ... a delightful fragrance" ([1825] *318 n.*). Howe treats the same flower as a "modest" but arousing girl, a floral Eve or a sexy Lucy:

> The Mayflower buds in simple beauty bring
> Home to the heart the first glad thoughts of Spring;
> A herald more attractive never bore
> Tidings to man of pleasure yet in store;

Gently reposing on its mossy bed,
In modest loveliness it rears its head,
And yields its fragrance to the wanton air
That lifts its leaves to rest and revel there.
Long may we greet its charms at early morn;
Long may its buds Acadia's wilds adorn;
Long may its tints, so delicately rare,
Rival the bloom her lovely daughters wear.

(*99–110*)

By turns risqué and chivalric these lines do more than posit a parallel between the mayflower and the "daughters" of Nova Scotia: they treat each in terms of the other to affirm the affinities between and among plants, people, and their native landscape. Most of the trees and flowers in the ensuing catalogues of Nova Scotia's plant life are less anthropomorphized than the mayflower, but several continue the suggestion that the Acadian environment is productive of a curiously innocent yet seductive "Beauty" (*138, 154*).

A summary comment that the beautiful plants of Nova Scotia were "the bright robe that Nature round her cast, / Ere the soft impress of Improvement's hand, / By science guided, had adorned the land" (*156–58*) prepares the way for the "historical retrospection" that constitutes most of the remainder of *Acadia*. Looking back to the time before Nova Scotia's "wild beauties were by [agri-]culture graced" (*159*), Howe first sees the Micmacs as "dusky Savage[s]" whom he treats in a manner consistent with his liberal-conservativism. Both a skilful hunter who "stray'd" through the wilderness uttering "death notes" and "bedew[-ing] the flowers" with "blood" and the "Lord of all the loveliness his eye survey'd" who "bow[s]" to "God ... but stoop[s] to none beside" (*161–66, 172*), Howe's representative Micmac is by turns the ignoble savage of the four stages theory and the noble savage of post-Rousseauian Romanticism. No more fortuitously than in *The Rising Village*, the Native peoples are introduced in conjunction with the animals that they hunt in *Acadia*, for as the author who provided prose sources for both poems wrote: the "savages" are as "much at home ... [in] the forest" as the "wild animals" whom they "nearly resemble" (T.C. Haliburton, *General Description* 46, 52). Inhabiting the "ancient groves" of Nova Scotia with the "fearless" caribou and "the gay Moose" (which with notoriously "jocund gambol springs, / Cropping the foliage Nature round him flings" [*173–76*]), the Micmac is animalistic by association and mode of subsistence. "Mark his agile figure, as he leaps / From crag to crag, and still his footing keeps, / For fast before him flies the desp'rate deer ...

His hardy limbs are equal to the race" (*187–92*). Yet Howe also shows "the forest's dusky child" living an idyllic life that is passionately in tune with the natural world. As he stands over a "fallen tenant of the wild" – the deer that he has just slain – he gazes over the surrounding terrain with a "glow of pride" that is both justified and ominous, for the sense of ownership that he "proudly feels" for the "beauties" of Acadia is likened to that of the "am'rous Othello" for "The budding beauties of Venetia's maid" (*199–218*). Neither callous nor sentimental about the fact that the "dusky Savage" is doomed, like the deer, to become a "fallen tenant" of Nova Scotia, Howe views the Micmacs with pity and fear as the admirable yet flawed victims of a tragic destiny and a superior culture.

In the chapter "Of Property in General" in his *Epitome of the Laws of Nova Scotia*, a four-volume compilation printed by Howe in 1832–33, Beamish Murdoch includes a discussion of the "right of European nations to dispossess the aboriginal inhabitants of America, of the territories of the new world" that could well have been in Howe's mind when he wrote *Acadia*. Confining his remarks to "these Northern regions" where Britain and France took possession, not of "agricultural and comparatively civilized countries," but of "an uncultivated soil ... filled with wild animals and hunters almost as wild," Murdoch argues that "it might with almost as much justice be said that the land belonged to the bears and wild cats, the moose or the cariboo, that ranged over it in quest of food, as to the thin and scattered tribes of men, who were alternately destroying each other or attacking the beasts of the forest ... I do not think that they themselves had any idea of property (of an exclusive nature) in the soil, before their intercourse with Europeans" (2:56–57). More inclined than Murdoch (let alone Goldsmith) to credit the Micmacs with an "idea of property," Howe nevertheless depicts them as nomadic hunter-warriors whose relationship with the land over which they "stray" and "ramble" (*161, 222*) is usufructuary rather than "exclusive" (see *Poems* 89–90; Hollingsworth 68–69; and Moorsom 109–13). The "sylvan city" to which the hunter returns is a "Camp," a temporary dwelling typical of a culture at the savage or most "rude" stage of social development (*227–28*). As such, it recalls the dwellings of the wandering tribes of the Old Testament who – and here Howe's Romantic primitivism surfaces again – lived closer to the Edenic state than do the more permanent and accomplished societies of the post-agricultural period (*229–38*).

The repetition of the word "rude" in Howe's description of "The simple homes of Nature's sons" (*238*) leaves little doubt that, though enviable in many ways, the Micmacs existed at the lowest of the four stages of social development:

> Some slender poles, with tops together bound,
> And butts inserted firmly in the ground,
> Form the rude frames – o'er which are closely laid
> Birch bark and fir boughs, forming grateful shade,
> And shelter from the storm, and sunny ray
> Of summer noon, or winter's darker day.
> A narrow opening, on the leeward side,
> O'er which a skin is negligently tied,
> Forms the rude entrance to the Indian's home –
> Befitting portal for so proud a dome.
>
> (*239–48*)

Very likely the four stages theory came to Howe through a variety of channels, including Haliburton's thoroughly Robertsonian *General History of Nova Scotia* (1823) and *Historical and Statistical Account of Nova Scotia* (1829; see Parks, notes 39). That one such channel was the *Travels* of Isaac Weld is indicated by the parallels between Howe's description of a Native "Camp" and Weld's: "the skeletons of their huts consist of slender poles, and on them [birch] bark is fastened with strips of the tough rind of some young tree: this, if sound, proves a very effectual defence against the weather. The huts are built in various forms: some of them have walls on every side, doors, and also a chimney in the middle of the roof ... Many of the Indian nations have no permanent place of residence, but move from one spot to another, and in the hunting season they all have moveable encampments, which last are in general very rude" (2:239–40). The fact that Howe would have seen Micmac "Camp[s]" with his own eyes helps to explain why some of the details of their culture that he subsequently adds to Weld, most notably, their creation of "box[es] of bark" adorned with porcupine quills (*253–56*), are anachronistic, for there is no evidence that these boxes were produced prior to the 1790s, when "Micmac families would camp near a white village to sell the goods the women made, such as baskets, quill boxes, and brooms" (L.F.S. Upton, qtd. in Parks, notes 49).

Like Richardson in *Tecumseh*, Howe also relies on Weld for his account of a Native dance. "In a sort of recitative," "every chief and warrior tells of his deeds in turn" "dwell[ing] particularly on the number of enemies he has killed ... making gestures ... and brandishing his weapons, as if actually engaged in performing the horrid operation," writes Weld of the "war dance"; "they all rise, and ... leaping about in the most frantic manner ... utter the most dreadful yells imaginable"

(2:292–94). "By degrees, the music's swelling strain / Sweeps through the Warriors' souls," echoes Howe; "Then, while the deeds of other days return ... ev'n the Dead, evoked by mem'ry's spell, / Burst into life, to fight where once they fell ... [W]ith frantic bounds they spring, / And rock and grove with shouts of triumph ring" (*294–306*). In addition to drawing upon Weld's work directly, Howe may have done so indirectly through Lambert, who relies heavily on his predecessor to describe the tents and dances of the "detachments of Micmacs ... and other small tribes ... [from] Nova Scotia, New Brunswick, and the south shore of the St. Lawrence" who annually visited Quebec (1:365). Howe's description of the "entrance" to a Micmac dwelling recalls Lambert's (1:371), as does his observation that at the height of their dance the Natives' "long dark hair / ... float[s] wildly on the ev'ning air" (*303–04*; Lambert has their "dishevelled locks ... [hanging] in wild disorder" [2:373]). As saturated in the four stages theory as Weld's "brief Account ... of the Indians," Lambert's chapter on the "Aborigines of North America" (2:353–85) also anticipates *Acadia* in its bitter-sweet recognition that for both Natives and Europeans "more misfortunes than blessings" attended the "discovery of America" (2:385; and see Weld 2:198–99).

Nowhere is *Acadia* more clearly imprinted with the four stages theory than in Howe's summary remarks about the state of the Native peoples of Nova Scotia prior to the arrival of John Cabot in 1497:

> For ages thus, the Micmac trod our soil,
> The chase his pastime, war his only toil,
> 'Till o'er the main, the adventurous Briton steer'd,
> And in the wild, his sylvan dwelling rear'd,
> With heart of steel, a thousand perils met,
> And won the land his children tread on yet.
>
> (*311–16*)

Not only does this passage imply that, as nomadic hunter-warriors, the Micmacs had little if any rights in the "soil": it also canvasses several legal principles – first discovery, consummation by possession, and conquest – under which Nova Scotia has become "our soil." As Haliburton states the case in his *Historical and Statistical Account*: "the discovery of Cabot, the formal possession taken by Sir Humphrey [Gilbert], and the actual residence of Sir John Gilbert [in Maine], are considered, by the English, as the foundations of the right and title of the crown of England, not only to the territory of Newfoundland, and the Fishery on its banks, but to the whole of its possessions in North America" (1:8, qtd. in Parks, notes 50). Haliburton's account in his *General Description* of the defeat of the Native peoples by English settlers in the Halifax area (47) is as pertinent here and in subsequent portions of *Acadia* as it was to *The Rising Village*, as is Murdoch's general discussion of the principles of discovery, possession, and conquest in his *Epitome* (2:55–56). Indeed, part of Murdoch's commentary "on the nature of the tenures of land in Nova Scotia" is worth quoting at some length since it has a bearing on Howe's account of both the Micmacs and the Acadians:

> the lands in the province are all either the property of the crown, or held by titles derived from it, the rights of the Acadian French settlers having been extinguished by the Provincial Act of 1759 ... which recites in its preamble, that this province ... always belonged of right to the crown of England, both by priority of discovery and ancient possession ... that the French king by the Treaty of Utrecht in 1713, had ceded to Queen Anne, the province and all rights therein ... [and] that many of the French by remaining in the province ... had become British subjects, but had refused to take the oath of allegiance ... committed treasons, rebellions, and murder by joining and aiding their countrymen and the savages in attacks on the English colonists, and had finally been removed from the province ... to save the colony from destruction.
>
> (2:76–77)

Sympathetic as parts of *Acadia* are to the Micmacs and the French, Howe leaves as little doubt as Haliburton and Murdoch as to the justice of British claims to Nova Scotia.

The first part of *Acadia* draws to a close with a typically sympathetic description of the Micmacs' first impressions of the English colonists and their subsequent feelings of dispossession and hostility. Probably drawing on an account of the arrival of the Dutch on the coast of New York which was attributed to "an intelligent Delaware Indian," Howe imagines a Micmac's response to the first sight of a European vessel. "Some believed it to be an uncommonly large fish or animal ... others ... a very big house floating on the sea," runs the version of the account printed in Buchanan's *Sketches*, but eventually all "concluded it to be a remarkably large house in which the Mannitto (the Great or Supreme Being) himself was present, and that he probably was coming to visit them (11–12; qtd. in Parks, notes 50–51). Howe attributes similar speculations to the Micmac, but concludes by emphasizing the disillusionment and hostility of the "lordly savage" at the Europeans' appropriation of his ancestral lands and their unknowing (or careless) desecration of his burial grounds:

> when the white man landed on the shore,
> His dream of Gods and Spirits soon was o'er;
> He saw them rear their dwellings on the sod
> Where his free fathers had for ages trod;

He saw them thoughtlessly remove the stones
His hands had gather'd o'er his parents' bones;
He saw them fell the trees which they had spared,
And war, eternal war, his soul declared.

(*333–40*)

There is judgement here as well as sympathy, for the final line of the
passage (and of the first part of the poem) alludes to Satan's resolve in
the first book of *Paradise Lost* to "wage by force of guile eternal war"
against God and Man (*1:121*). A later reference to the Micmacs' decision to use "force, not fraud" (*544*) against the English settlers combines with such terms as "howling crew" (*552*) and "demoniac strain"
(*660*) to confirm their alignment with Milton's fallen angels. When
insult is visited on an ignoble disposition the result will be violent in the
extreme.

A mixture of "historical retrospection" and "incidental meditation"
characterizes the beginning of the second part of *Acadia*. Turning away
from Nova Scotia for a few moments, Howe treats Britain as a fine example of the movement of all societies from rudeness to refinement. Today
the British Empire "Whose arch, like Heaven's, extends from clime to
clime" comprises "The hope – the guide – the glory of a world" (*350–
52*), but it was not always so. In a "darker age" when Rome, too, was
being overrun by violent and "lawless power," Britain was a "feeble land"
through which "each wand'ring horde / Of rude Barbarians roved"
(*342–45*). Credit for Britain's ascent of the ladder of progress goes by
Howe's reckoning to generations of past patriots whose bravery, eloquence, and intelligence broke the "fetters" of oppression and, like the
biblical "fire by night ... [and] cloud by day," guided their countrymen
through the wilderness to create "by ceaseless toil" the "glorious" edifice of the British Empire (*360–66*). "Shall we, then, disregard these
great lessons?" asks Howe after reciting the same patriotic lesson to the
Halifax Mechanics' Institute in 1834. "Shall the Muse of History teach
us this admirable philosophy in vain, or point unheeded to those bright
examples recorded by her pen? No – I trust not. Let us ... study them
with attention ... impress them upon the minds of our neighbours and
friends ... teach them to our children ... and seek from them consolation and encouragement, amidst the difficulties we may have to
encounter, in developing the resources of this young and growing
country" (16).

Since Howe's "Muse of History" has more than a nodding acquaintance with the four stages theory, it is predictable that when he turns
again to trace Nova Scotia's progress from rudeness to refinement he
sees first the "stout-hearted pioneers who "felled the forest trees with

sturdy stroke," who broke "The virgin soil, with gentle culture ... And Ceres lured to many a sylvan scene" (*385–88*). "Gone are the Patriarchs" of Acadia, he intones, but "Oh! could they now her smiling fields behold, / While in the breezes wave their crops of gold ... And Peace and Plenty crown the happy land" (*373, 379–82*). In these and ensuing lines, Howe draws upon Pope, Gray, Thomson and perhaps the Nova Scotian Goldsmith to produce a dignified yet realistic description of pioneer life. A comparison of Howe's "Log House" (*389*) with the same structure in *Talbot Road* reveals certain similarities ("Its roof with bark o'erspread – its humble door" [*391*]) and some regional differences ("Its seams by moss and sea weed well supplied" [*390*]), as well as an abundance of intimate and realistic details ("hissing green wood ... wooden cleats that from the walls extend" [*394, 399*]) reminiscent of Cowper, Crabbe, Campbell, and even the early Wordsworth. Nor does Howe's eye for domestic detail focus merely on the physical aspects of pioneer life. Directing his attention to the relationship among the settler, his wife, and their two children, he paints a vivid picture of the emotional life of a pioneer family: the "mother's pride" in "her firstborn, standing by her side, / Who waits the signal to his [father's] arms to spring"; the "Father's arm ... entwin[ing]" the "Mother's waist ... / While on their knees the fair-haired Boy reclines, / A prattling go-between"; and the "tears, uncall'd, that bedew the parents' eyes" at the sound of a ballad first heard "in Albion's isle" (*403–44*).

In the "waking trance" that follows the singing of this ballad, memory transports the settler and his wife "o'er the Atlantic's foam" to reexperience "the light and shade / Of early thought" and to relive the wrenching experience of emigration – to "feel the parting grasp of many a hand, / And see ... scenes they never shall behold again" (*445–74*). The note sounded in this portion of *Acadia* is that of such classics of emigrant plangency as Allan Ramsay's "Farewell to Lochaber" and Sir Walter Scott's "Mackrimmon's Lament," a note soon to be raised to skirling heights in McLachlan's *The Emigrant*. Nevertheless, Howe's descriptions of emigrant departure and nostalgia may have a particular source in the early chapters of *The Emigrant's Informant; or, a Guide to Upper Canada* (1834): "there is a peculiar something in a scene like this ... such light and shade ... and indiscribable emotions of hope and fear! ... the mental agonies of eternal separation! ... the faltering sound of – farewell for ever ... the last sad look at their deserted, and once happy cottage ... There is a melancholy in the retrospect of happy by-gone days ... [in] the land of our nativity ... – [t]he well-known fields and mountains, the glassy brook, the long-remembered oak, whose branches have so often sheltered us from noontide heat; the village bells, the ivy mantled tower of the long frequented distant church" (A Canadian Settler

18, 32–33). Intense as it is, however, the nostalgia experienced by Howe's emigrants is mitigated by the future embodied in the "gentle Boy" who sits in their lap. By the "verdant seat," "glassy streamlet," and "gallant oak" that they recall in England was "a crumbling castle, where decay / With silent tooth gnaw[ed] stone by stone away." In their new home in Nova Scotia, "Hope displays / The gifts prepared to gild their future days; / And thus they muse, and plan – now sad, now blest." That the settlers' "gentle Boy ... understands not how the shadowy past / O'er present bliss a sombre cloud may cast" may merely be due to his age, but it is also consistent with Howe's overall point that the patriotic feelings of Nova Scotia's native-born "children" are inevitably less divided than those of their emigrant parents.

Of course, a major purpose of the domestic scene in *Acadia* is to generate sympathy for the pioneer family and, by so doing, to intensify the effect on the reader of their brutal "Murder" by a "Hate"-filled band of Micmacs bent on "Revenge" (*511*). "Undoubtedly the most effectively written segment of the poem" (Parks, intro. xxiv), Howe's account of the Micmacs' clandestine assault on the "Log House" is also the most affective account of physical violence in early Canadian poetry. Like Priam and Hecuba defending their children at the fall of Troy, the settler and his wife kill several of their attackers before "*en masse*, the shrieking fiends leap in, / Till wounded, faint, o'erpowered, the Father falls / And hears the shout of triumph shake his walls" (*574–76*). Almost certainly the ensuing lines draw on the graphic description of the murder of a baby by "a wild untutored Huron" in *The Last of the Mohicans*: "he dashed the head of the infant against a rock, and cast its quivering remains to [its mother's] very feet. For an instant the mother stood ... looking wildly down at the unseemly object, which had so lately nestled in her bosom and smiled in her face" (J.F. Cooper 171–72):

> The wretched Mother from her babe is torn,
> Which on a red right hand aloft is borne,
> Then dashed to earth before its Parent's eyes,
> And, as its form, deform'd and quivering lies,
> Life from its fragile tenement is trod,
> And the bruised, senseless, and unsightly clod
> Is flung into the soft but bleeding breast
> To which so late in smiling peace 'twas press'd.
>
> (*577–84*)

"Nor does the boy escape" the cruelty which, according to the four stages theory, is as much a part of the Native disposition as vengefulness (Weld 2:203):

> the smouldering fire
> Is stirred, – and, as its feeble flames aspire,
> In wanton cruelty they thrust his hands
> Into the blaze, and on the reddening brands,
> Like Montezuma bid him seek repose
> As though his couch were but a perfumed rose.
> Sated with blood, at length the scalps they tear
> Ere life be yet extinct ...
>
> (*585–92*)

Almost as striking here as the cruelty of the Micmacs is the elaborate art-fulness of Howe's description. Where the reader might expect only hor-rified revulsion and moral indignation, there is also aesthetic curiosity, a tendency to see violence as beautiful as well as ugly. Howe's allusion to a statement by Montezuma when he is being similarly tortured by the Spaniards in Dryden's *The Indian Emperor* – "Think'st thou that I lie on beds of roses here" (qtd. in Parks, notes 53) – suggests a fascination with the aesthetics of cruelty.

In the lines that follow the massacre of the settlers Howe once again moves back and forth between the sad past and happy present of Aca-dia. Where once the "forest shade" (*513*) could erupt with Micmac vio-lence, now the woods harbour nothing "more unfriendly" than rabbits, squirrels, and birds which, though they lack the bright plumage of trop-ical species, "can sweeter strains impart / To charm the list'ning ear, or touch the heart" (*613–18*) – a neat and patriotic response to Weld's view that "the birds in America are much inferior to those in Europe in the melody of their notes, but ... superior in point of plumage" (2:195). This brief catalogue of Nova Scotia's less exotic fauna is followed by another "retrospective glance" at events that "checked improvement, kept repose at bay, / And frighten'd bright-eyed science far away" (*623–25*): the French-English conflicts in Acadia in the seventeenth and eigh-teenth centuries and the expulsion of the Acadians in the 1750s. The complex history of Port Royal (Annapolis Royal) is mentioned, as are the ignominious defeats of Madame La Tour in 1645 and the Duc d'An-ville in 1746, and the expulsion of the Acadians is recounted at length and with great sympathy (*668–732*). "Oh! for the Bard of Auburn's melting strain! ... To sing the horrors of that fatal day" (*673–75*), Howe exclaims before proceeding with as much help from *The Traveller* as *The Deserted Village* to imagine the homesickness of the "sons of Minas" after their exile from "Acadia's shore" (*677*). Clearly, Howe elaborates in detail upon the predicament of the exiled Acadians because their assumed feeling "that earth's wide breast / Contains but one dear spot where they would rest" (*687–88*) dovetails very well with his theme of the universal and powerful nature of patriotic love. Thus Howe moves effortlessly from his lengthy treatment of the Acadians to a fervent statement of his own affection for Acadia (*733–54*) and only then summarizes the retrospective portions of his poem (*755–70*). The fearful and stormy periods of Nova Scotia's history are well past, but their principal actors – the Micmacs, the Acadians, and the English settlers – share with the present inhabitants of the province the love of their country which, for Howe, was a prime motivating factor in human affairs.

Howe's celebration of present-day Nova Scotia as the product of a "friendly" and "happy union" (*Address* 5; *Acadia 744*) of peoples from England, Scotland, and Ireland (some – the Loyalists – by way of the United States) who have transcended their racial, political, and religious enmities confirms that, sympathetic though he was to the Micmacs and the Acadians, he did not view their supplantation and departure with great regret. Two relatively backward cultures have yielded to the advanced society that flourishes under "The flag of Britain":

> see, extending upon every side,
> Her Cottage Homes, Acadia's noblest pride;
> There honest Industry, by daily toil,
> Covers with fruits and flowers his native soil;
> And calm contentment, with an Angel's air,
> And humble hopes, and smiling joys, are there.
>
> (*803–08*)

Under British rule and through hard work, the inhabitants of Nova Scotia have achieved the colonial dream of independence and happiness. Where once there was an isolated "Camp" or "Log House" there are now numerous "Cottage Homes." Where once there were only wild plants there are now agricultural and domestic "fruits and flowers." Where once there were "scenes of hardship and ... strife" (*761*) there is now the peace upon which prosperity can be built.

To the question of whether agricultural development has "Defaced Acadia's wild and simple charms" Howe's answer is decisive: "Oh! no, together Art and Nature reign." Although "Labor's hand full many a scene has cleared ... Yet there are spots by Art still unprofaned / Where Nature reigns as ages since she reigned" (*810–18*). To support his claim that Nova Scotia is a diversified environment, Howe introduces "sweet Lochaber ... / ... the forest's gentle bride" – "A sparkling Diamond in an Emerald set," a pristine locale so secluded that "chaste Diana might [there] her beauties lave, / Nor fear to be observed," and, somewhat surprisingly, the object of a voyeuristic fantasy:

Now to the eye its glowing charms revealed,
Now, like a bashful Beauty, half concealed
Beneath the robe of spotless green she wears ...
. . . .
　Such is the scene, beneath Canaan's height,
Where Nature seems to shrink from human sight;
And shun the intruding step, and curious eye,
That seeks to know where her deep mysteries lie.
(819–46)

The full social and personal ramifications of this remarkable passage
are impossible to know with certainty. What does seem certain from the
references to hidden natural "mysteries" and the bathing goddess
Diana is that Howe knew both the pleasures and the dangers of surrep-
titiously observing the naked female body. (It was precisely for observing
Diana and her attendant bathing that the hunter Actaeon was changed
into a stag and devoured by his own hounds.) But, of course, Howe's
official purpose in describing Lochaber Lake is as clear in the poem as
it is in his dismayed letter to his wife in September 1833: "the forest's
gentle bride" is present in *Acadia* to indicate that co-existing with such
cultivated regions as the Annapolis Valley there are areas of Nova Scotia
that remain desirably innocent of human cultivation. In *Acadia*, as in
The Rising Village, the natural world has ceased to be the source of hardship and danger that it was to the early pioneers and has instead
become a supplement to agricultural land as a source of local pride and
local love.

In the tale of the "Fisher[man]" that occupies the remainder of *Acadia*, Howe celebrates the traits and values which he evidently regarded
as central to Nova Scotia life – cheerfulness, devotion to family, hardi-
ness, courage, industriousness, trust in God, and, of course, patriotic
love. An illustration of "the poor man's toil – the poor man's woes"
which all-too-often go unremarked by "The listless sons of wealth and
pride" (*921–22*), the fisherman's tale reveals the Christian democrat in
Howe as he recounts a near-fatal occurrence in the life of a "smil[ing],"
"hardy," and "reckless spirit" who "nightly braves" the "Ocean and ...
[its] storms" because "God has cast his bread upon the waves" (*853–70*).
But for an "earnest lingering look on high" that secures the pity of the
"omniscient Eye which looks o'er all, / And even notes the tiny spar-
row's fall" (*914–15*), the fisherman would have lost his life in a sudden
and violent storm whose literary ancestor is the "howling ... tempest"
that would have killed the "mariner" in Robert Montgomery's *The Omni-
presence of the Deity* (1828) but for his "consciousness of Preserving Providence," the "Eye that watches ... [the] Hand that saves" (13-18). By the

grace of God, the "free" and "hardy" boatman who typifies the "strength, the pride, and [the] sinews" of Acadia (*934–40*) – and, more specifically, the rural and fishing populations from which Howe drew much of his political support – returns unscathed to his anxious wife and children, one of whom is reading that classic of imperialistic self-reliance, *Robinson Crusoe* (*951–54*). Typical in another way is the fact that the fisherman's tale refers repeatedly to the process of seeing and being seen: God is figured as a Montgomeryesque "omniscient Eye"; the boatman's "cot o'erlooks the troubled tide" (946); the boatman "fondly stops to gaze" "Through the clear pane" before entering the cottage (*947*); and his wife "to the casement steals, / And tries to pierce, with enquiring eye, / The frightful doom that darkens earth and sky" (*956–58*). Nowhere more obviously than in the fisherman's tale are Acadia and her inhabitants subjected to a gaze that is male, invisible, omniscient, and tinged with voyeurism. In Howe's patriarchal panopticon the surveillance is constant and entire.

Acadia ends as it began with a celebration of a "still more precious charm" than the "Love" whose "soul-subduing power" permeates all levels of society from the "stately dome, or princely bower" to "The rude and lowly cabins of the poor" (*963–72*). Only "yesterday" the fisherman and his wife have received a letter from a son whose "ceaseless restlessness of soul" has caused him to "wander" for so long in "foreign lands" that they have long-since "deemed him dead" (977–90). As well as rendering the fisherman's wife speechless with happy memories of her "first-born on her breast," his "faint, first words," and "every smile he wore in boyhood days," the letter makes clear that the "long-lost Boy" (*999–1014*) still suffers from the highest love of all – the "amor patriae" which, like the "lengthening chain" (*4*) that draws the traveller home in Goldsmith's poem, binds him to his native Nova Scotia. "The letter told of much that he had viewed ... But still his spirit sighed for home again" (*1015–18*). With an eye perhaps on the loss of young people to greener pastures that plagued Nova Scotia during the decades of depression after the Napoleonic Wars, Howe concludes with an analysis of the abiding love of "Acadia's sons" for a homeland which, though harsher and less lush than some other places, possesses many endearing features:

> Though all that's fairest falls from Nature's hand,
> The exile pines to tread his native land;
> Her rocky mountains, and her wintry storms,
> Her fertile valleys, and her lovely forms,
> Crowd on the mind with dreams of mighty power,
> And cheer his heart in many a lonely hour.
> (*1025–30*)

"Has Nova Scotia received the power to attach her children to her bosom, and make them prouder and fonder of the bleak hills and sylvan vallies, than even of the fairer and more cultivated lands from which their parents came?" This was Howe's question to the Halifax Mechanics' Institute on 5 November 1834. At that time, he "pause[d] for no reply" but cited "the unerring law of nature" as his "answer" (*Address* 5). Whatever else it is or may be, *Acadia* is Howe's elaboration of that "unerring law of nature."

13 Standish O'Grady,
The Emigrant

Before we came to this decision [to emigrate], we ransacked all the booksellers' shops for every thing new and old, that had been published about America, in the shape of Histories, Recollections, Travels, Conversations, Emigrants' Guides, Letters to Friends, &c. &c. Indeed, we left no effort untried to obtain such information, as we thought might be depended upon.

Joseph Abbott, *Memoranda of a Settler in Lower Canada* 1.

The massive influx of emigrants to the Canadas in the 1820s, 1830s, and 1840s generated a large body of writing on emigration, including two early classics of Canadian prose: Catharine Parr Traill's *The Backwoods of Canada* (1836) and Susanna Moodie's *Roughing It in the Bush* (1852). At the heart of these and numerous less-accomplished and lesser-known works are opinions on the advantages and disadvantages of emigration to different parts of Canada for members of various social groups. Was Upper Canada a better destination for emigrants than Lower Canada? Was emigration more advantageous for agricultural workers or gentle folks, mechanics or paupers, families or single men and women? Most of the long poems on Canada written during the Georgian period touch on these and related issues. In *Quebec Hill*, for example, Mackay "summon[s] up a number of anti-Canadian spectres" (An Ex-Settler 29), and in *Talbot Road* Burwell sings the praises of Upper Canada for working-class emigrants. But the first long poem to concern itself principally with the issue of emigration to Canada is *The Emigrant* by Standish O'Grady (ca.1776–1846). Both in 1841, when it was "Printed and Published, for the Author, by John Lovell" of Montreal, and in 1842, when it was reissued without Lovell's signature, *The Emigrant* proclaimed itself to be the first of four cantos, the remainder of which were never published and probably not written. If Canto 1 of *The Emigrant* has sequels they must be two other long poems with the same title by John Newton (1846) and Alexander McLachlan (1861). It may be more than mere coincidence that McLachlan's *The Emigrant, and Other Poems* carries the same epigraph from Horace as O'Grady's poem: *"Coelum non animum mutant / Qui trans mare currunt"*: "they change their clime, not their mind, who rush across the sea" (325).

A native of Ireland who arrived at Quebec aboard the *Ocean* on 22 May 1836, O'Grady spent most of the rest of his life trying to farm near Sorel (William Henry) on the south shore of the St. Lawrence between Quebec and Montreal. A sometime student at Trinity College, Dublin, whose full name seems to have been Standish O'Grady Bennet, O'Grady apparently had aristocratic connections and was forced to emigrate when the stipend upon which he relied as a "lay impropriator" – a non-clerical beneficiary – of the Church of Ireland was drastically reduced by the combined Irish and British Parliament (Trehearne, intro. xvii–viii). "Disgusted with the government, and unable to exist at home," he writes in a note to *The Emigrant*, "I sailed for America, with a small competency ... My revenue amounted to £382 ... which is now owing to me these seven years" (71). If Standish O'Grady was indeed Standish O'Grady Bennet then he died in "poverty" in Toronto on 14 February 1846 "after a painful and protracted illness ... aged 70 years" (*British Colonist* [17 February 1846], qtd. in Trehearne, intro. xv).

A move from Sorel to Toronto in the early forties is certainly consistent with the views on emigration that O'Grady states crisply in his preface "to the Population of the Province of Canada": "let none imagine me an enemy to emigration; nothing, from my heart, do I desire more. This Lower Province, however, is not calculated to afford happiness to the European settler; the cold is excessive, and its winters are too long ... The Upper Province is by far a more desirable emporium for our redundant population; a corresponding scenery, a mutual intercourse and fellow-feeling for each other, will at all times render them more familiar, and less estranged, in a country so similar to their own" (*14–24*). The fact that here and elsewhere in *The Emigrant* O'Grady has his eye on audiences in both Britain and the Canadas only serves to emphasize the similarities between his poem and several of the emigrant guide books published in England, Scotland, and Ireland in the thirties. For example in *Emigration. The Advantages of Emigration to Canada*, a pair of lectures delivered and published in England in 1831, William Cattermole – an agent of the Canada Company – endorses the view of a Select Committee of the House of Commons that "voluntary emigration" is a viable solution to Britain's "redundant population," but urges agricultural emigrants especially to bypass Lower Canada, which is "too hot in summer, and too cold in winter," and head instead for the "milder" climate and more congenial surroundings of Upper Canada (139, 2–4). It is no more surprising that Strachan is quoted beside Malthus in Cattermole's "Extracts from the Reports of the Select Committee" (126–130) than it is that a quotation from Moore's "Ballad Stanzas" finds its way into the volume in a letter purporting to be from an emigrant happily settled in the Guelph area (203). Neither Strachan's local pride nor Moore's bucolic sentimentality should be excluded from the factors which drew the victims of poverty and famine from the British Isles to Upper Canada in such numbers that the population of the province increased by over fifty percent in the early thirties.

Coupled with the fact that O'Grady advertised *The Emigrant* as the first of four cantos (102), the seasonal emphasis of the poem points to Thomson's *The Seasons* as its principal poetic model. Like "Winter," Canto 1 of *The Emigrant* is a topographical and discursive poem that augments the poetical description of a landscape with "historical retrospection," "incidental meditation," social criticism, astronomical references, addresses to God, tributes to great men, and a Thomsonian tale of two lovers – Sylvia and Albert – who accompany the narrator from Ireland to Canada. *The Emigrant* even includes the equivalent of Thomson's Amanda ("Spring" *480 f.*; "Summer" *1401f.*): a "fair ... Nymph" named Maria (*722–81*) whom Brian Trehearne has tentatively identified with M. Ethelind Sawtell, a "poetess and neighbour of O'Grady in ... Sorel" (notes 149). Less indebted to Thomson's diction and phrasing than Cary, Mackay, and others, O'Grady nevertheless and predictably draws in at least two places (*885–94, 1108–25*) on the vignette of the "Swain" lost and frozen in a snow storm in "Winter" (*276–321*). When viewed in relation to *The Seasons*, Canto 1 of *The Emigrant* can be seen for what it surely was in O'Grady's projected four-part structure: the stark record of a wintry sojourn in Lower Canada that would be followed by a happier account of spring in the upper province. "I trust ... a finer prospect awaits me still," writes O'Grady in his preface; "this expanded and noble continent will no doubt furnish fit matter for the Muse. The diversity of the climate, the richness of the soil, the endearing qualities of a genial atmosphere, must ... furnish a just excitement to the Poetic mind, and arouse that energy correspondent with a richness of scenery, which the contemplative mind will studiously portray" (*7–13*). In its emphasis on natural scenery as the principal inspiration and subject of poetry, this statement is itself resonantly Thomsonian. It is also an indication that in the existing canto of *The Emigrant* O'Grady has sought studiously to portray a province remarkable for its monotonous climate, poor soil, and inhospitable social environment.

It is a sign of O'Grady's poetic and political conservatism, his urge to govern his uncongenial subject matter in a manner consistent with "nature's law and God's Providence" (Trehearne, intro. lxiii), that he cast his poem, not in Thomsonian blank verse, but in decasyllabic couplets reminiscent of Swift, Pope, Gray, Goldsmith, and the Thomas Campbell of *The Pleasures of Hope*. A xenophobic conservative in the "Burke tradition" (Trehearne, intro. xlvi), O'Grady is a champion of genuine liberty over tyranny but has no sympathy whatsoever for the opponents of just rule – "vaunting Yankees" (*1191*), Napoleon Boneparte ("The self-styled Autocrat of *fickle* France" [*1205*]), and, above all, the "vile," "glib-tongued Patriot Papineau" (*2156, 1374*). "I prize a just imperious sway, / Whose rights confirmed all subjects will obey" (*1194–95*), asserts O'Grady in a fulsome tribute to Sir John Colborne, the commander of the British forces in the Canadas who personally led his troops during the suppression of the rebellions of 1837–38 in Lower Canada. "Whilst suffering Britons chide" the moderate and reformist politics of Lord Gosford (who resigned as governor general on the eve of the rebellions) and Lord Durham (who worked towards conciliation in their aftermath), the poem concludes, "mighty Wolfe in Colborne still survives" (*2157–60*). That O'Grady's model of the "warrior statesmen" (*1175*) left Canada in October 1839 after briefly acting as governor general may explain the poet's bitterness at the absence of "some great personage to whom ... [to] address" *The Emigrant* (dedication *3–4*). In any event, it is consistent with O'Grady's admiration for conservative heroism that he was instrumental in restoring "peace and good order" during the Lachine Riots of March 1843 (*Montreal Transcript* [11 March 1843]; Trehearne, intro. xiv).

As well as participating in the debate about the merits of Upper and Lower Canada for various types of emigrants, O'Grady's poem draws heavily on several accounts of emigration to the Canadas that were published in the 1830s. Almost invariably the materials that find their way into *The Emigrant* from such accounts are those that emphasize the disadvantages of emigration, especially to Lower Canada. One example is the levies made by O'Grady on Joseph Pickering's *Inquiries of an Emigrant: Being the Narrative of an English Farmer, from the Year 1824 to 1834* (1831 f.), a work repeatedly recommended by the British *Farmer's Journal* and "much confided in by many Emigrants" (Inches 20). Soon after passing Cape Clear on the southern coast of Ireland, the vessel carrying

Pickering to North America would have been "capsized through the negligence of the mate" had not "the captain ... [come] instantly on deck" and, with the co-operation of the weather, "set all right again" (3). Some days after their "parting gaze on ... Cape Clear" (6), the passengers and crew of the *Ocean* also encounter a violent storm, but in this case (and in an early illustration of the fortitude required of emigrants) it is O'Grady who "spr[i]ng[s] aloft," "seize[s] the helm," and guides the vessel to safety (232–45). Both Pickering and O'Grady treat a storm at sea as a combination of the sublime and the capricious. "The grandest sight I have ever seen presented itself," enthuses the former: "the tremendous billows ... formed a thousand fantastical shapes, sometimes running up into high peaks or spires, then suddenly sinking into vast abysses; or two large waves meeting, rose into an immense ridge; or ... dashed their spray in all directions, as if in a rude frolicsome play, while the vessel rose up their mountain sides majestically, receiving now and then a salute from their gambols" (7). "*Waves* on *waves* in *monstrous mountains rise*," horripilates the latter; "All ocean heaves, high on their circling height / The playful waves reflect the moonbeam's light ... Each vivid flash [of lightning] ignites the awful gloom, / And murmuring waves forbode an awful doom" (246–56). To Pickering, O'Grady brings memories of Pope (*Essay on Criticism* 232: "*Alps* on *Alps* arise!") and Thomson ("Summer" 1700–03: "lambent lightnings ... by fearful murmuring crowds / Portentous deemed") to suggest that a storm at sea is a sublimely terrifying and "portentous" (257) sign of horrors yet to be encountered by the emigrants on the *Ocean*.

Given that O'Grady emigrated in 1836, it is quite likely that he read *The Emigrant's Informant, a Guide to Upper Canada* by A Canadian Settler, which was published simultaneously in 1834 in London, Edinburgh, and Dublin. Although addressed to various social groups throughout the British Isles, this exceptionally literary settlers' guide concentrates particularly on the social and political problems of Ireland and prudently recommends "voluntary exile" to "the upper province" to any Irishman who relishes the "prospect of bettering his condition" (7). The disadvantages to emigration set forth in *The Emigrant's Informant* are those chronicled with mordant gloom in *The Emigrant*: (1) "the perils and hardships that [the emigrant] must expect to undergo, and the difficulties that he has to meet ... "; (2) the "privations ... [of] the first two or three years"; and (3) "the breaking-up of long-established connections: the cutting at once [of] all those social ties of endearment, those silken threads of kindred love, and affection, and bidding farewell to the land of his nativity, and the scenes of his childhood. In a word to quit ... a pleasurable world, with all the alluring enchantments

of refined society, to seek a new home in the gloomy wilds of an immeasurable forest" (i–ii). It is a testament to the reach and affectivity of *An
Emigrant's Informant* that distinct echoes of this and other passages treating of the feelings of emigrants on leaving and recalling their native
land (17–19, 31–32, 131–33) can be heard not only in O'Grady's poem
but also in *Acadia* (*435–86*) and McLachlan's *Emigrant* (*1: 29–86*).

O'Grady's catalogue of severed relationships is an elaboration of A
Canadian Settler's:

> From peaceful homes and habitations spurned,
> From fond connections, aged parents mourned,
> From dear society, now friends no more,
> To cheer their wanderings on a distant shore,
> From all those tender ties on friendship wait,
> From links that bind and *fortify* a *state*,
> Behold proud Erin's sons promiscuous spread ...
>
> (*41–47*)

Where A Canadian Settler dwells at length on the "agonizing pangs of
eternal separation" from "dearest associates" and "once happy cottage[s]" (18), O'Grady goes a sentimental step further to depict the
death of an emigrant at sea among strangers. "No favouring friends, no
fond connexion nigh," the dying moments of "the sad wretch" are given
to reflections on "toils, and friends no more / ... [and] his native shore"
(*444–55*). As the body of the "unbefriended Soul" is unceremoniously
consigned to a "traceless grave," an echo of Gray's "Elegy" ("No Curfew
tolls for him") tugs yet further on the reader's heart strings. While
agreeing with A Canadian Settler that ultimately all emigrants have
"Providence" as their "guide" (*509*; see also *Paradise Lost 12:647*),
O'Grady treats departure from Britain, not as a "transient ... ordeal" in
a scheme "ordained ... for the wisest ends" (18–19, 32), but as a permanent condition of imminent death and continual disaster in which even
the best laid plans will come undone. "Be careful that all your provisions are all well packed in strong casks or boxes," advises A Canadian
Settler, "or with the rolling of the vessel, you will soon have them spoiled
... [A]nd do not make your packages very large" (24). "Here rolls a cask
among their shattered store ... Their well ranged stock in one sad hour
displaced," counters O'Grady, "Their liquid stores become a *watery
waste*, / Glass jars and packages no art can save / ... seem to dance alternate to the wave" (*191–95*).

Whereas nostalgia for Britain is also a poignant but transient emotion
in *An Emigrant's Informant* (as in the similarly optimistic *Acadia*), in *The
Emigrant* recollections of Ireland are a recurring feature of the narrative

and notes. Exiled from a very unhappy country in a thoroughly unpalatable one, O'Grady's memories of "the land of his nativity" are as ambivalent as they are continual. "Ah oh! 'tis sweet to think on Erin's soil, / Land lost to bliss and well requited toil" (*341–42*), he says in one place, and in another: "Sweet land! no hopes have I, then why recall / These past endearments ... / That link me captive to my native home?" (*1598–1601*). The "Remembrance" that "haunts" O'Grady's "solitude" (*1603*) is bitter as well as sweet, not only because it is directed towards a home and a country that are despised as well as loved, but also because it is at once a consequence of dislocation and an anodyne for discontinuity. By turns painful and pleasurable, remembrance enables O'Grady, like the transcendentally nostalgic Donald Ban in McLachlan's *Emigrant*, temporarily to overcome the disruptive, fracturing effect of emigration, to restore or recreate in fantasy and poetry an identity that would otherwise be lost. To quote O'Grady's own translation of his Horatian epigraph: "*What though you sail to different climes or strand, / You leave your heart upon its native land, / The mind still rests within its kindred sphere.*"

More engaging from a Canadian perspective than O'Grady's obsessive rehearsals of his Irish past is his depiction of Lower Canada as a subarctic realm of perpetual rather than temporary "perils ... hardships" and "privations" for even the most hardy emigrants from the British Isles. To prepare the way for his frosty assessment of the province, he indicates that, though the *Ocean* crossed the Atlantic in April and May (71), it arrived in Canada, not in spring, but in winter. After surviving two storms at sea, the emigrants on the vessel are eagerly anticipating arrival at "some prosperous shore" (*500*) when they are given a chilling hint of things to come in the form of a "wanderer from the northern sphere," an enormous and "castellated" iceberg (*468–87*) whose origins may lie less in personal experience than in the descriptions of ice "fields" and "floating masses of ice" in Thomas Pennant's *Arctic Zoology* ([1784] lxxxiv–vi, a source also for Pratt's iceberg in *The Titanic*) and in another principal foil for *The Emigrant*, George Heriot's *Travels through the Canadas* ([1807 f.] 32). "In fogs, and even in the gloom of night, they are discoverable at some distance, by the cold which they emit, and by their whiteness and effulgence," writes Heriot. "The air becomes cold as you approach the object, until at length the danger is manifest," adds O'Grady (73). After surviving this danger also, the *Ocean* nears the coast of Nova Scotia and the "crew ... crowd to view, / The land of promise, and explore the new" (*513–14*). What they see is worse than the "gloomy wilds of an immeasurable forest" described by a Canadian Settler. It is an "immeasurable" and "isolated land" of "Impenetrable woods" and "gloomy terror" whose forbidding aspect is compounded by "icebound cliffs" and "drifted snow" (*515–21*). By thus assimilating British North America to Greenland, Iceland, and other regions associated with extreme cold and barrenness, O'Grady prepares the way for the emigrants' perception of the banks of the St. Lawrence as a "pathless desert" and a "dreary waste" that "confounds" their remaining hopes and expectations (*522–29*). Much less the "garden of Eden" of some emigrant propaganda than a hellish extension of the "frozen Continent" (*Paradise Lost 2:587*) that lies to its north, O'Grady's Lower Canada is the graveyard of his emigrants' "long and fondly cherished fantasies" (Abbott 2).

Writing of the same landscapes, Heriot observes that, while "Canada presents few objects which can occupy the enquiries of the antiquarian" or the naturalist, the county abounds in lakes, rivers, and waterfalls that are "singularly sublime" and "inexhaustible in variety" (35). As the *Ocean* approaches Quebec, O'Grady draws conspicuously on Heriot's well-known description and illustrations of Montmorenci Falls to depict the "far famed water" as a sublime sight indeed, but also one whose "powerfully impelled ... torrent" (Heriot 76) is no match for the Lower Canadian winter: "thy cataract in vain / Pours forth ... on the ice bound plain, / Absorbing nature acts by strict control, / Arrests thy progress and ingulphs the whole" (*670–77*; and see Thomson, "Winter": "An icy gale ... in ... mid-career / Arrests the bickering stream" [*723–25*]). Where Heriot had been captivated by the "prismatic colours" in the "revolving sphere" of Montmorenci Falls (77), O'Grady sees "the Rainbow in its magic sphere" as a "Prismatic phantom" which is "As quickly wrought to universal shade" as it was "clad in majesty arrayed" (*680–93*). In effect, a natural wonder that impresses the spectator "with sentiments of grandeur and elevation" (Heriot 77) is treated by O'Grady as an analogue of the evanescent happiness of the emigrant. Notably absent from O'Grady's description are the carrioles which in Heriot's engraving of the "Fall of Montmorenci in Winter" speak of the "gratification and exercise" (74) to be had in Lower Canada when the rivers freeze over. Almost as critical as Weld of the French-Canadians' supposed "pride [in] a *cariole and bells*" (*1723*), O'Grady is impatient with the attempts of travel writers to make natural and social phenomena appealing and intriguing. "Let some Newton solve ... why ... though prominently placed / The moon's attraction is by far the least" (*127–30*), he huffs in response to Heriot's observation that, according to "the system of philosophy introduced by Sir Isaac Newton," the earth's tides are caused by "the combined attractive influence of the sun and moon, and the ... diurnal motion of the earth" (16). Niagara Falls appears in

The Emigrant only because they were the scene of the spectacular destruction of a rebel vessel, the *Caroline*, in 1837 (*1451–70*).

When he turns his attention to the Île d'Orléans, O'Grady once again undercuts the attractions of a famously "agreeable object" in Lower Canada (Heriot 87). Although still mantled in snow the "captivating Isle" is a "fertile land" which holds the promise of "summer smiles ... / Fruits, flowers, herbs," "lambent streams" (*694–706*), and other Edenic pleasures. But the fact that "love lies plaint" and the "shepherdesses weep" in the pastoral garden of O'Grady's fancy serves notice of dark thoughts that quickly surface with the revelation that the poet is the victim of two dispiriting blows: the faithlessness of the "Nymph" Maria and the death of his "best Dog" Rollo (*716–81*). "I fondly thought, but, ah! my hopes were vain, / To match the clime, love would not add its pain," he complains of the former catastrophe, and of the latter: "My bees have fled, my birds have pined away, / There Rollo rests, there flowerets decay" (*728–29, 758–59*). After recovering sufficiently to express the hope that the Île d'Orléans will one day rival "Ida's top or [the] fields of [Virgil's] Mantua" as a source of poetic inspiration (*782–96*), a forlorn O'Grady turns again to his chilling theme. "But, ah! alas! thy winters are too long!," he informs "fair Orleans"; "My joys are sped as passing summers smile, / They, like thy clime, seemed lovely for the while" (*810–11*). Some forty years earlier, Mackay had used the "fair, delightful isle" of Orleans to make a similar point: "Tho' gay the scene ... [when] view'd from far ... groundless hopes, and airy views deceive, / Ye know how chang'd your prospects still appear, / When you, like me, examine them more near" (*1:289–98*). In *The Emigrant*, as in *Quebec Hill*, attractive prospects in Lower Canada are usually bleak realities waiting to be recognized.

This pattern of disillusionment is repeated yet again when, following a lengthy digression on an obscure Irish poet name Edward Nagle, O'Grady focuses on the "inlet" below Quebec City, now with the help of Edward Allen Talbot's *Five Years' Residence in the Canadas* (1824). "Within [the] safe and ample bosom [of this basin] may be seen riding at anchor an immense number of ... trading vessels," observes Talbot, "but 'the forest of masts' ... dwindles ... into insignificance, in consequence of its contiguity to thicker and more towering woods" (1:38). "They almost seem a Forest of their own," agrees O'Grady, before turning from the ships below Quebec to the "towering woodlands" of the Canadian hinterland as a site of physical danger and financial disaster (*867–96*). By "shatter[ing]" a "well-wrought raft" of logs and sending lumbermen to graves as "unknown" as that of "the sad wretch" on the *Ocean*, a "reckless storm" on a Canadian lake or river can ruin the fortunes of a

British "merchant," reducing him to a "lonely Bankrupt" with "parted hopes" and darkened "prospects." Talbot turns from the "delightful ... scenery" around Quebec with the "utmost reluctance" (1:38), but O'Grady does so with grim relish, interrupting his description of the city and its harbour to comment on the "shattered fragments" of ice on the shore of the St. Lawrence (*896–912*; see Heriot 74) and on the "scanty, sad memento" (*920*) – the "pitiful tribute" (Talbot 1:49) – that marks the site of Wolfe's death on the Plains of Abraham (*913–20*). A later passage and note reveal that the memory of Brock has also been ill-served (*965*; 80). Evidently Canada is no less cruel to its military heroes than to its lumberjacks, merchants, and poets.

Differentiating himself from the other emigrants on the *Ocean*, who, on landing at Quebec, head for the "dangerous raft" or empty wilderness, O'Grady proclaims his desire "to find / Some peaceful spot, sequester'd from mankind" where he can enjoy contentment, supply "His wants," and "take from mighty providence his text" (*939–58*). But within moments of articulating this Thomsonian ideal of rural retirement, O'Grady characteristically advances the major barrier to its achievement in Lower Canada: political discontent and unrest in the wake of the Rebellions of 1837–38. Emigrants who have come to Canada to escape "political grievances" (Pickering vii) will find themselves sadly mistaken, for "e'en here ambition's sway / Proclaims a right the vanquished must obey" and "Revolting times uncertain prospects bring" (*959–63*). Only in the "wondrous space" of the west where "myriads" of Natives "rudely stray" are there societies governed by "natural law" and "Right reason" rather than "despot rule" and "a bill of rights" (*971–94*). "There might I rest, take thoughts from scenes sublime, / Nor fall the hapless victim of a clime" (*1004–05*) sighs O'Grady in a summary of his preference for Upper Canada that also serves as a prelude to his depiction of the existence of the Native peoples of Lower Canada as markedly less ideal both materially and philosophically than that of their counterparts in more southerly regions.

Apparently putting down his Talbot and picking up his Heriot, he first describes the crafts and trades of "the rude Indians at Loretto" (*1020–35*; Heriot 80–83) and then envisages their forays into the far north in search of moose, beaver, and other animals (*1036–51*). Guided by the fact that "certain trees in the forests [are] cloathed with moss towards the north ... [and] have a natural bend towards the south," states Heriot in one of his chapters on the "Manners and Customs of the American Indians," "the savage ... attains with unerring certainty the object of his march" (*447*). "Well versed by signs, the moss, the bending pine, / Or north or south they mark the unerring line" runs the equivalent passage in *The Emigrant* (*1042–43*). O'Grady's ensuing treatment of the practice of euthanasia by the Natives of the North (*1052–87*) is also indebted to Heriot (530–31, 535), as well as to Samuel Hearne's influential account in his *Journey ... to the Northern Ocean* (1795) of a sick woman left out of "necessity and [tribal] self-preservation" "to perish above-ground" on the barrens (131–32). Despite their natural piety and affectionate nature, O'Grady suggests, "hard necessity" (*1088*) forces the northern Natives to practice both passive and active euthanasia on those afflicted by incurable disease and "exhausted by old age" (Heriot 535). Clearly disapproving more of active than passive euthanasia (Trehearne, notes 157), O'Grady directs his most pointed condemnation, not at the brutal practices of the Native peoples, but at the "false pride" of the European culture whose craving for "far fetched luxuries" such as "fur" "tempt[s] with gold the savage heart to go, / Where life scarce warms to brave such scenes of woe" (*1088–97*).

Nowhere is O'Grady's argument against emigration to Lower Canada more pointed than in the passages that follow his account of the Native peoples. Two consecutive catalogues, the first a brief list of the charms of Britain's landscapes and the second a long roll of the horrors of the Lower Canadian winter, throw into stark relief the folly of leaving the frying pan for the freezer. To the "forsaken poor" for whom emigration is a harsh necessity, however, O'Grady offers detailed advice in a lengthy paragraph and a lengthier note (*1126–69*; 81–82): physical "*strength*" is the principal key to success in the Canadas (*1128–39*); Canadian egalitarianism will not sit well with "mistaken men" of "self prized consequence" (*1140–49*); and the French culture and "dreadful climate" of Lower Canada make it an uncongenial destination for British emigrants (*1150–69*). No doubt this advice stems in great measure from O'Grady's personal experience in Sorel and elsewhere, but it also echoes in substance and wording the advice contained in several emigrant guides of the thirties, most notably (and in addition to those already mentioned or quoted) William Hickey's *Hints on Emigration to Upper Canada; Especially Addressed to the Lower Classes in Great Britain and Ireland* (1831). Although "principally a compilation from other authors" such as Pickering, Hickey's book was widely touted as "the best manual on Emigration" (Inches 166–67; and see Buchan 10). Like *The Emigrant*, it emphasizes the advantages of "health ... strength ... able bodies, and willing hands" (6); like *The Emigrant* it canvasses the disadvantages of residing in a province where "the population [is] ... in a great degree, of French and other foreign origin" (13); and like *The Emigrant* it counts "excessive" cold and poor soil among the factors militating against the "more northerly" of the two Canadian provinces as a destination for emigrants (13). In entering the emigration debate on the side of Upper rather than Lower Canada, O'Grady was bound to make himself unpopular in the "*lower province*" (*1165*). Indeed it is tempting to see a rebuttal of O'Grady's position, perhaps even a pointed corrective to *The Emigrant*, in the *Memoranda of a Settler in Lower Canada* by "An Immigrant Farmer, of Twenty Years' Experience" (Joseph Abbott), which was published as a series in the *Quebec Mercury* between 18 January and 28 April 1842 and, later in the same year, issued in book form by Lovell and Gibson. Very much an immigrant rather than an emigrant, a happy resident rather than a miserable exile, Abbott shows contempt for instant experts on Lower Canada and traces to "the imagination and credulity of travellers" "the chief if not the only argument ever attempted ... against" Lower Canada, namely "the length and severity of our winters" (Abbott 21–22). *Memoranda of a Settler* "went through three editions in Canada and one in Britain," and, like Abbott's later novel *Philip Musgrave* (1846), "was used by the Canadian government as promotional literature ... to attract English immigrants to Canada" (Miller 4).

The climate remains the chief argument against Lower Canada in the latter part of *The Emigrant*, but by no means the only one. Increasingly "incoherent ... fragmented and disorderly" as the poem becomes after the poet's "debarkation at Quebec" (Trehearne, intro. xxxv), it nevertheless harps repeatedly in its desultory way on another of O'Grady's arguments against settling in Lower Canada: the prevalence in the province of social turmoil arising from "ambition's pride" and "zeal" (*1218, 1290*). Projecting a world-weary cosmopolitanism whose origins lie, at least in part, in *The Traveller* and *The Pleasures of Hope*, O'Grady proclaims "endless broil" a universal problem that cannot be avoided by migrating from one "Ill-fated spot" to another (*1751*). Thus the only effective means of coping with "life's alarms" is to "fix all ... hopes in heaven," to make the "mind [God's] kingdom," and to live according to His "holy Decalogue" (*1345, 1330, 1352, 1365, 1582*). To Burwell in *Talbot Road*, Ambition and Hope are motive forces in an emigrant's quest for a better life on earth and in heaven. To Howe in *Acadia* hope for the future enables an emigrant to cope with memories of the past. But in *The Emigrant* worldly "Ambition" is condemned as a "scourge [to] insatiate man" (*1211*) and "unassuming" Hope for the life to come is lauded as "the sole surviving refuge of mankind ... 'mid sepulchral gloom" (*1634–53*). O'Grady grants with the Burke of a *Philosophical Inquiry into the Origin of Our Ideas of the Sublime and Beautiful* that ambition may be praiseworthy when linked to such qualities as "virtue," "honour," and "dignity" (*1219–25*), but he is more inclined to see ambition's "dangerous plan" (*1210*) as the blueprint for social inequality, political unrest, and the destruction and death caused by the likes of Papineau (*1371–1470*). Only "*hope, reviving hope*" has the "benignant might" to "eclipse" the problems of a world that burns with ambition even as it fractures with cold (*1633–45*).

But not for long. As he focuses his frosty gaze yet again on his surroundings at Sorel, O'Grady sees a "barren waste," an "unprofitable strand," an "unproductive land" of "grasshoppers ... [and] toads" where the "frozen air on one bleak winter's night / Can metamorphose *dark brown hares to white*!" (*1679–83*; and see Pennant 94–96, Talbot 1:239–40, 258–62, 215, and George Henry 165). To the majority of earlier writers, the exotic inhabitants and sudden transformations to be observed in Canada were a source of wonder and delight. To O'Grady, they are a source of astonishment and disgust, with the emphasis decidedly on the latter. Where Cary saw "shining fire-flies" (*583*), O'Grady notices "vile mosquitoes ... / Whose stings could *blister a Rhinoceros*" (*1706–07*). Where Moore found colourful voyageurs, O'Grady describes an "Unlettered race" of liars, cowards, and traitors who "plot rebellion" and "talk, and smoke, and spit, and drink and sleep!" (*1718–41*). "The snow is six feet deep, so that we may be said to walk on our own heads," observes Arabella Fermor before proceeding to describe *both* the "undistinguished waste of snow" *and* the "exceedingly agreable ... whirl of the carrioles" (Brooke 101). Since his aim is to correct exaggeratedly positive accounts of Lower Canada (81), O'Grady offers neither a positive nor a balanced assessment of the province, but one which focuses on its unappealing features. Under his pen the deep snow that so amuses Arabella becomes the pretext for an angry disquisition on the rudimentary state of Lower Canada's roads and for a dismayed commentary on a bizarre effect of the Canadian winter:

> here the artist hath no means at hand,
> Whose sole *materials* are composed of *sand.*
> Thus roads are things, in this wild clime unknown,
> Where snow wrought highways must suffice for stone.
>
> In this vile spot, o'erhung with hoary tops
> Of lofty pines, which now the wild hare crops,
> Lay [an] abode, yet sadly sank below
> In subterraneous passages of snow.
>
> (*1857–64*)

The "abode" to which these last lines refer is a gruesomely parodic version of the idyllic "cottage" in Moore's "Ballad Stanzas." No "green elms," "voluptuous bee," tapping "woodpecker," and "gush of fountain" (124) surround O'Grady's "lonely ... cottage, dismal, cold and dank," but, rather, "stunted alders," "stagnant waters," "serpents, toads, and vile mosquitoes" (*1833–43*). Far from being associated with ideal love, "this drear abode" is the home of Sylvia, who, after ten years in Lower Canada, has lost her husband and her hopes. Care-worn, poorly dressed, burdened with seven children, and irreparably alienated from her home and family (*1891–2016*), Sylvia exemplifies the cruelty of life in Canada to "those of an higher order ... who can subsist themselves genteelly at home" (82). In a simulacrum of *The Emigrant* as a whole, Sylvia urges her brother Osmond, whom she has not seen since her "lonely exile from [her] princely dome," to recount to their father the sad tale of her "broken heart" and bad fortune (*1979, 1989–2014*). Promising to continue Sylvia's story in "canto 2d, 3d, and 4th" (102), O'Grady reinforces its message here by pointing to the destructive effects of the winter on even the indigenous flora and fauna of Lower Canada. In the "merciless blast" of a winter storm similar to those in Thomson's "Winter" (*117–201*), pine trees are laid low, "The Rook ... trembles ... and shudders" and "The sheltered squirrel from his attic height ... headlong falls ... His house a ruin, all its inmates cast / Outstretched to famish in the northern blast" (*2025–38*). And, while "the rook to other lands can fly" and "The desert still the squirrel may supply" (*2057–58*), Irish emigrants to Lower Canada will find themselves trapped in a province where the coldness of the people matches the coldness of the climate:

> O, my country! seek not, ask not, here,
> The sad lament, nor crave the stranger's tear;
> All fare alike, on scant subsistence fed,
> In vain we crave one morsel of their bread ...
> (*2063–66*)

Neither sympathy nor benevolence are to be expected where there are scarcely sufficient means to support human life.

After briefly modifying this view by referring specifically to the "bounteous" and "Benignant" Robert Harrower of Sorel as one of "some friends" whom he has "loved full well" in Lower Canada (*2067–84*), O'Grady draws Canto 1 of *The Emigrant* to a close by once again advising his countrymen either to emigrate to "happy climes where ... chilling want, and poverty [are] unknown" or to remain in Ireland where "faction's leaders," "Religion's chieftains," and "bounteous nobles" may yet find the "Wisdom ... and goodness [to] ... / Give labour recompence, and mend the law" (*2085–108*). Not for O'Grady is there a delighted appreciation of the season when "nature puts on her gayest attire" in Lower Canada (Weld 1:397):

> See now rude spring, his wished for visit pays,
> And teeming earth an hideous form displays;
> The ruptured rivers scarce their banks restrain,
> And fractured ice rolls headlong to the main;
> The swollen brooks extend their awful course,
> Dissolving snow supplies each trackless source ...
>   (*2109–14*)

Grudgingly conceding that the "chequered landscape ... adds to hope and promises repose," O'Grady briefly depicts the waterways of Lower Canada as a busy hive of happy "boatsmen ... [and] steaming engines" under the "control" of the province's shipping élite – "Wise, kind, beneficent" "Molson ... Tate and Torrance ... / A people's safeguard ... a public good," and, perhaps, a poet's potential patrons (*2115–24*). That O'Grady dedicated his volume "to Nobody, nobody having kindly offered himself as [a] patron on this vast portion of the globe" (dedication *6–8*) can be taken as evidence of the cool response to his flattering compliments by the captains of the Lower Canadian shipping industry.

Almost needless to say O'Grady's resurgence of optimism is short lived. No blue bird of happiness arrives with spring in Lower Canada: "here the rook his contrast visage brings, / Smooths his black plumes, and strokes his glittering wings" (*2125–26*). A catalogue of cacophonous and disgusting creatures drawn partly from Weld (1:194–97) and Talbot (1:259–70) reflect the revulsion and alienation of the emigrant:

> The chattering blackbird seeks the lonely glade,
> And tuneless birds flock murmuring to the shade,
> Discordant notes now rend the listening ear,
> As if to tell misfortune brought us here;
> ....
> The hissing serpent eager seeks his prize,
> Death in his grasp and terror in his eyes.
> The moss brown surface soon appears to view,
> Each poisonous herb assumes its different hue ...
>   (*2127–30, 2137–40*)

To this catalogue of natural horrors O'Grady appends a concluding litany of personal and political woes: "A Canadian stud horse with one miserable cow were all the remnants of [his] stock" that survived a "cruel winter" (102; *2145-46*); "Urged by Mackenzie and vile Papineau," "Rebellion rag[es], [and] ruthless is the foe" (*2155–56*); "Suffering Britons" disparage the "politics" and "pride" of recent governors general. In the circumstances, it is a cold comfort and a forlorn hope that "mighty Wolfe in Colborne still survives" (*2160*).

14 Charles Sangster,
The St. Lawrence and the Saguenay

Terrible and sublime, beyond the imagery of the most daring poet, are these cliffs; ... while they proclaim the omnipotent power of God, they, at the same time, whisper into the ear of man that he is but as the moth which flutters in the noontide air. And yet, is it not enough to fill the heart of man with holy pride and unbounded love, to remember that the soul within him shall have but commenced its existence, when all the mountains of the world shall have been consumed as a scroll?

Charles Lanman, *A Tour to the River Saguenay in Lower Canada*

In the late summer of 1853 Charles Sangster (1822–93), then a sub-editor of the *British Whig* in Kingston, Canada West, undertook a journey by steamboat down the St. Lawrence and up the Saguenay Rivers. The series of charming and effusive letters that he sent back to his newspaper during the trip leave no doubt that it provided the experiential basis for the long poem that gave its title to his first volume of poems, *The St. Lawrence and the Saguenay, and Other Poems*, published less than three years later in 1856. Both "Etchings by the Way" (as Sangster called his letters to the *British Whig*) and *The St. Lawrence and the Saguenay* participate in the touristic interest in Canadian water scenery that had one of its beginnings in Heriot's *Travels through the Canadas* (1807 f.), a work *Containing a Description of the Picturesque Scenery on Some of the Rivers and Lakes ... of those Provinces.* Evidence internal to Sangster's poem indicates that he consulted Heriot's *Travels* (671 n., 781–89 and 53–54), but relied much more heavily on a number of works of the late forties and early fifties that both fueled and capitalized upon the popularity of the St. Lawrence and the Saguenay as tourist regions. Prominent among these are Charles Lanman's *A Tour of the River Saguenay in Lower Canada* (1848) and the pamphlet that accompanied one of the showbusiness sensations of the time, William Burr's "Moving Panorama" or "Seven Mile Mirror" of the scenery from Niagara Falls to the upper reaches of the Saguenay, a series of enormous paintings with an extensive commentary that entertained hundreds of thousands of people in Boston, New York, and elsewhere between 1849 and ca.1851 (Arrington). It is no accident that *The St. Lawrence and the Saguenay, and Other Poems* was promoted by Sangster as a book "that ... will be in the hands of every tourist who visits, or may have visited, the beautiful scenery [it] so charmingly depicts" ("Opinions of the Press," *Hesperus, and Other Poems and Lyrics*). "The poem is manifestly designed as a companion, if not a guidebook, for the voyage to the Saguenay," wrote Daniel Wilson in 1858; "it will make an agreeable return to the tourist for the small space it claims in his baggage" (qtd. in Bentley, intro. lxiii–lix). Nor is it surprising that in the additional stanzas for the *St. Lawrence and the Saguenay* that Sangster published in the 1860s, as well as in several letters that he later wrote to W.D. Lighthall, he reveals his intention to expand the touristic aspects of the poem, a scheme that he finally abandoned in 1891 when circumstances prevented a repetition of his 1853 trip to the Saguenay (see Bentley, intro. xliv and appendix 133–47).

The genre and form that Sangster chose for his long poem are well suited to its touristic purposes. A member of the sub-species of topographical poetry that Ronald Arnold Aubin has identified as the "river poem" (225–41, 377–85), *The St. Lawrence and the Saguenay* uses the rivers of its title as a thread along which to string vignettes of "beautiful scenery" and passages of "historical retrospection" and "incidental meditation," categories that include a reminiscence about the pirate Bill Johnstone and his intrepid daughter Kate *(103–20)* and a speculation about the absence of an "atmosphere" on the moon *(326–43)*. In its use of the St. Lawrence River system as a unifying device, Sangster's poem coincidentally resembles *Abram's Plains*, but more likely derives from a convergence of Burr, Lanman, and the Wordsworth of the *River Duddon*, a sonnet-sequence that includes a reference to the "matted forests of Ontario's shore" (3:251). It was probably on the precedent of one of Byron's most touristic poems, *Childe Harold's Pilgrimage*, that Sangster cast *The St. Lawrence and the Saguenay* in Spenserian stanzas interspersed by a variety of song and hymn forms. As a medley of different forms, Sangster's poem also recalls works by Sir Walter Scott *(The Lady of the Lake)* and Philip James Bailey *(Festus)*, and in both form and content it shows traces of several other poems in Spenserian stanzas, including James Beattie's *The Minstrel,* Keats's "The Eve of St. Agnes," Shelley's *Adonais,* and *The Faerie Queen* itself.

The uses to which the Spenserian stanza is put in *The St. Lawrence and the Saguenay* are almost as diverse as its sources. At several points the stanza serves as the poetic equivalent of a picture frame: a matted container for the display of a picturesque scene. During his sight-seeing tour of 1853 Sangster was particularly inspired by Les Eboulements, an area on the north shore of the St. Lawrence below Quebec that had also impressed Heriot as "romantic," "luxuriant and novel" (52–55). "All the way from Murray Bay [Malbaie] to Eboulements the landscape is excellent, and as for variety – tis endless," Sangster told the readers of the *British Whig;*

I turned to take a last look – a last fond look – at the village on the hill ... I don't know why, except it be from its extreme beauty and its delightful site ... but this village, both on passing down the river and returning, had a charm for me that village never had before. But I was not the only one who loved to look at it; our American friends were in raptures with it, and one of them sketched it – lucky fellow! – a Lilliputian-looking village that one could almost hug for its intrinsic beauty – a something seemingly in miniature, creeping, from very coyness and innate modesty, close to the green bosom of the maternal old hill for protection, as if it were lately enticed into existence, half against its will, or brought hither from a fairy tale by one simple rubbing of some Aladdin's lamp – a little gem of a village, which, did you strike it with a stone, looks as if it might be shivered into fragments as it were a porcelain vase. So it seemed to me, that village of Eboulements.

(in Bentley, appendix 120–21)

In his note to the resulting stanza in *The St. Lawrence and the Saguenay* Sangster describes Les Eboulements as "a most delightful little village ... looking like a vision of Romance or Fairy-tale":

EBOULEMENTS sleeps serenely in the arms
Of the Maternal hill, upon whose breast
It lies, like a sweet, infant soul, whose charms
Fill some fond mother's bosom with that rest
Caused by the presence of a heavenly guest.
How coyly – close – it nestles! how retired,
Half conscious of its charms, and half oppress'd,
As with a blushing sense of being admired;
As modest as a gem, with gem-like beauty fired.

(*781–89* and *n.*)

Cloying as this is, it effectively combines the rectilinear form of the Spenserian stanza with visual analogies (the village as child and jewel) to create the poetic equivalent of a sketch or etching. In such picturesque tableaux – verbal renditions of "the most delightful pictures on the route" (*772 n.*) – *The St. Lawrence and the Saguenay* appears indebted to both the illustrations and the descriptions of Heriot and his successors.

Paul Fussel's astute perception that the Spenserian stanza is capable of reinforcing a shift from "noise to absolute silence" (749) points towards another effective use of the stanza in *The St. Lawrence and the Saguenay*. Especially when describing the sublime scenery of the upper Saguenay, Sangster uses the terminal alexandrine and centrifugal possibilities of the stanza to reflect the expansiveness of a landscape that draws his thoughts towards God:

> Over the darkening waters! on through scenes
> Whose unimaginable wildness fills
> The mind with joy insatiate, and weans
> The soul from earth, to Him whose Presence thrills
> All Beauty as all Truth. These iron Hills!
> In what profusion did He pile them here,
> Thick as the flowers that blossom where the rills
> Chant to the primal woods. Year after year
> In solitude eternal, rapt in contemplation drear ...
>   (*957–65*)

For a pre-Darwinian Christian like Sangster, nature's "profusion" is not extravagance for the purposes of survival and its forms are not manifestations of the gradual evolution of the cosmos; rather the external world is a constant reminder of God's power and generosity – the visible evidence of His all-pervasiveness and "Omnipotent Design" (*929*). Sangster's expression of his religious beliefs in this stanza becomes formalistically most interesting at the alexandrine, where the usual six feet of the line are extended to seven ("In Sólitúde etérnal, rápt in cóntempláton dréar") in a mimetic response to the enormous length of time being described, and where the impetus generated by the elision of 'they are' at the comma carries the reader centrifugally forward to the next stanza and the next, which are given over almost entirely to one long sentence treating of the immense past of the hills whose dreams of the "old years" and "long ages" the poet can only dimly imagine (*977–78*). Frye has commented on the capacity of the Spenserian stanza to arrest narrative and focus attention on "something else" ("The Road of Excess" 131), and in *The St. Lawrence and the Saguenay* this power is often effectively placed at the service of Sangster's big themes – God, the pre-history of the Canadian landscape, and (to quote the poem's final line) the unutterable depth and strength of "Human Love."

As instances of the weaknesses as well as the strengths of Sangster's poetic technique, two more stanzas may be briefly examined before the focus shifts to his theme of "Human Love." The mimetic enjambement between the two stanzas obviates the possibility of quoting them separately:

> Red walls of granite rise on either hand,
> Rugged and smooth; a proud young eagle soars
> Above the stately evergreens, that stand
> Like watchful sentinels on these God-built towers;
> And near yon beds of many-colored flowers
> Browse two majestic deer, and at their side
> A spotted fawn all innocently cowers;
> In the rank brushwood it attempts to hide,
> While the strong-antlered stag steps forth with lordly stride,
>
> And slakes his thirst, undaunted, at the stream.
> Isles of o'erwhelming beauty! surely here
> The wild enthusiast might live, and dream
> His life away. No Nymphic trains appear,
> To charm the pale Ideal Worshipper
> Of Beauty; nor Nereids from the deep below;
> Nor hideous Gnomes, to fill the breast with fear:
> But crystal streams through endless landscapes flow,
> And o'er the clustering Isles the softest breezes blow.
>
> (46–63)

Although the first of these two stanzas is by no means Sangster at his worst, it does contain a number of weaknesses that plague *The St. Lawrence and the Saguenay* as a whole: adjective-noun combinations that are dismayingly uninspired ("proud ... eagle," "stately evergreens," "many-colored flowers," "majestic deer"); adjectives and adverbs that are obviously present merely to fill out the metre ("a proud *young* eagle," "A spotted fawn *all* innocently cowers"); and rhymes that sacrifice perceptual accuracy and imaginative reason on the altar of poetic form (the "cowers" that follows "towers" and "flowers"). At many points in *The St. Lawrence and the Saguenay* such weaknesses bring the poem to the brink of parodying the tradition of nature poetry that it so obviously seeks to continue and ground in Canada, suggesting that all-too-often Sangster simply took words and phrases from the sort of poetry that he sought to emulate and reassembled them within the borders of his Spenserian stanzas. The loud echoes of Wordsworth's sonnet "Composed upon Westminster Bridge, September 3, 1802" later in the poem – "Beneath me, the vast city lay at rest; / Its heart throbbing gently" (*429–30*), and "Is there a soul so dead to Nature's charms, / That thrills not here in this divine retreat?" (*1164–65*) – further illustrate Sangster's often quite uncreative use of his poetic sources.

More impressive is the second of the two stanzas. Ranking them among "Sangster's best verses," A.J.M. Smith sees the success of these lines as residing in their resemblance "to the graceful neo-classicism of Pope's *Pastorals*" ("Our Poets" 82) or, it may be added, the *Essay on Criticism*, where *"Chrystal Streams with pleasing Murmurs creep"* (*352*). Yet the effect of the stanza's final couplet – "But crystal streams through endless landscapes flow, / And o'er the clustering Isles the softest breezes blow" – derives, not merely from its Popean elegance, but also from the words "endless" and "softest," where the suffixes of infinitude and superlativeness bespeak the poet's local pride and, in conjunction with other aspects of the lines (most notably, their trochaic rhythms and long or open vowels), invite the reader to contemplate the limitless expanses and freedom that are available in Canada to anyone who appreciates wild nature. Sangster's emphasis on the "Beauty" of the Thousand Islands in this and the surrounding stanzas was probably inspired by descriptions of the same area in John Howison's *Sketches of Upper Canada* (1821) and George Warburton's *Hochelaga; or, England in the New World* (1846), the latter being quoted in *Burr's Pictorial Voyage ...* (1850). "The scene reminded me of the beautiful description of the Happy Islands in ... [Joseph Addison's] Vision of Mirzah," enthuses Howison, "and I thought at the time, that if the Thousand Islands lay in the East, some chaste imagination would propose, that they should be made an asylum for suffering humanity" (32). "Now we are among the mazes of the 'Thousand Islands,'" gushes Warburton; "the eye does not weary to see, but the hand aches in ever writing the one word, beauty, wherever you steer over the great river – beauty, beauty still" (1:216–17, qtd. in Burr 20–21). No wonder that in the "Lyric of the Isles" which follows his stanzas on the Thousand Islands Sangster sees the area as home to "the Spirit of Beauty" (*64–93*).

True to his touristic sources and purposes, Sangster thus treats the St. Lawrence River system as a place of refuge and a source of entertainment – a treat for the eyes and souls of an urban population seeking physical and spiritual recreation. True to his poetic vocation and patriotic feelings, however, he also treats the Canadian landscape as a locale which, despite the absence of "Nymphic trains," "Nereids," and

"Gnomes," provides ample sources of inspiration and affection. To appreciate fully that this is so, it is necessary to recognize a further source of Sangster's second stanza on the Thousand Islands in Catharine Parr Trail's *The Backwoods of Canada* (1836), a work "too favourable" to Canada for James Inches (89) and, for this very reason, highly attractive to committed Canadians such as Sangster and Alexander McLachlan. "As to ghosts or spirits they appear totally banished from Canada," observes Traill a little sadly,

this is too matter-of-fact [a] country for such supernaturals to visit. Here there are no historical associations, no legendary tales of those that came before us ... We have neither fay nor fairy, ghost nor bogle, satyr nor wood-nymph; our forests disdain to shelter dryad or hamadryad. No naiad haunts the rushy margin of our lakes, or hallows with her presence our forest-rills ... I heard a friend exclaim ... 'It is the most unpoetical of lands; there is no scope for imagination ... no recollections of former deeds connected with the country ... ' This was the lamentation of a poet ... For myself, though I can easily enter into the feelings of the poet and the enthusiastic lover of the wild and wonderful of historic lore, I can yet make myself very happy and contented in this country. If its volume of history is yet blank, that of Nature is open, and eloquently marked by the finger of God; and from its pages I can extract a thousand sources of amusement and interest.

(153–54)

Sangster obviously concurred, but, as revealed by the numerous passages of historical retrospection in *The St. Lawrence and the Saguenay,* he found Canada less bereft than did Traill of "historical associations," "legendary tales," and "former deeds connected with the country." Moreover, the very blankness of the volume of Canadian history in places such as the Saguenay became another source of inspiration for Sangster – a *carte blanche* on which to liken a bluff to a "Magi," a "Prophet-Skald," or "the great Samson" (*997, 1062, 1187*). Whatever their differences, Traill and Sangster found ample scope for the imagination in Canada's human and natural history.

Nor was personal history neglected by the poet in whose work a British reviewer found "much of the spirit of Wordsworth," albeit with a tone more "religious [than] ... philosophical" ("Opinions of the Press," *Hesperus*). Lending emotional and spiritual intensity as well as an air of mystery to *The St. Lawrence and the Saguenay* is the narrator's relationship with the nameless "Maiden" (*10*) who accompanies him on his sightseeing tour. The fact that *The St. Lawrence and the Saguenay, and Other Poems* was printed and published in the spring and early summer of 1856, only months before Sangster's marriage on 16 September in

Kingston to Mary Kilborn, renders highly plausible the identification of the *monna innominata* of the volume's title poem with the poet's young bride-to-be. Among the other poems in the volume, there are two – "The Name of Mary" and "Mary's Twentieth Birthday" – which are almost certainly addresses to Mary Kilborn, whose inspiration may well lie behind Sangster's other meditations on "Human Love" in the years prior to her death of pneumonia in 1858. Taken together, these poems indicate that Sangster's view of love was profoundly conditioned by his Victorian Christianity and heavily coloured by his reading of such poets as Petrarch and Dante (both of whom are mentioned in "The Name of Mary"). Both the type of a spiritual love to be fulfilled in Heaven and an outlet for irrational passions to be avoided as sinful, "Human Love" had to be pure and "intellectual" (*10;* and see "Intellectual Love," qtd. in Bentley, intro. liii). In short, it had to be sanctified by holy matrimony and aligned with social good. Viewed in this context *The St. Lawrence and the Saguenay* is a record of Sangster's quest for a reconciliatory understanding of "Human Love," a journey towards the revelation of a "Truth" (*1208*) that would reconcile the sensual with the spiritual, the earthly with the heavenly.

The opening stanza of the poem introduces the theme of the narrator's love for the Maiden in a more complex way than might first appear:

> There is but one to whom my hopes are clinging,
> As clings the bee unto the morning flower,
> There is but one to whom my thoughts are winging
> Their dove-like passage through each silent hour:
> One who has made my heart her summer bower.
> Feeling and passion there forever bloom
> For her, who, by her love's mysterious power,
> Dispels the languor of my spirit's gloom,
> And lifts my dead heart up, like Lazarus from the tomb.
>
> (*1–9*)

As described here, Sangster's love is at once singular and self-centred: it is directed towards "one" woman who, he asserts (three times, and with no fewer than five uses of the word "my" [Latham 44]), constitutes the sole focus of his "hopes," "thoughts," "heart," "Feeling and passion." Both intellectual and passionate, the narrator's love for the Maiden is obsessive to the point of uxoriousness (the sin of Adam, of course, and also of "the great Samson"). It is also spiritually and emotionally renovating, lightening the narrator's melancholy spirit and gladdening his heart in a manner that he compares to the raising of Lazarus, an audacious reference that carries an evident and important double valancy: on the one hand, a negative – because blasphemous – suggestion that the Maiden's love is godlike in its "mysterious power" and, on the other hand, a positive – because reconciliatory – suggestion that the "mysterious power" of her love partakes of the miraculous, redemptive, and, indeed, "mysterious" love of God.

It is the power of love to regenerate and spiritualize, to inspire intimations of immortality and to counteract the effects of original sin, that provides the basis for the narrator's appeal to the Maiden in the second stanza to become the *inspiratrice* of his transcendental journey down the St. Lawrence and up the Saguenay (roughly equivalent here to "earth" and "heaven"):

> Maiden! from whose large, intellectual eyes,
> My soul first drank love's immortality,
> Plume my weak spirit for its chosen skies
> 'T would falter in its mission without thee.
> Conduct its flight; and if its musings be
> Oft'ner of earth than heaven, bear awhile
> With what is native to mortality:
> It dare not err exulting in thy smile:
> Look on it with thine eyes, and keep it free from guile.
>
> (*10–18*)

A recognition of the similarity of gesture between this stanza and the invocation of Urania in *Paradise Lost* (*1:1–26*) brings with it an awareness of the markedly un-Miltonic quality of the narrator's attitude to the Maiden at this point in the poem – his elevation of her to the status of an aid to transcendence and his implicit contrast of her purity and spirituality to the sinfulnesss and "mortality" of the rest of creation. Far more Dantean than Miltonic in its approach to both woman and the world, the stanza reveals the narrator's expectation (which is not radically modified until the final few stanzas of the poem) that, under the tutelage of the Maiden, he will eventually transcend earthly matters, but that, in the meantime, he will find himself concerned more often than not "With what is native to mortality." In the event this proves to be the case as the pair sails from Kingston through the Thousand Islands, and the narrator, as yet unchastened by the influence of the Maiden, chronicles the progress of their "love-fraught" boat along the "amorous current" and under a "passionate sun," noticing as he does so an erotic cornucopia of things "native to mortality": "The silver-sinewed arms of the proud Lake, / Love-wild, embrace each islet tenderly, / The zephyrs kiss the flowers when they wake / At morn ... " (*23–40*). A comparison of these lines with an anonymous poem quoted by Burr – "Hail Lake of Thousand Isles! / Which clustered lie within thy circling arms, / Their flower-strewn shores kissed by the silver tide!" (20) – indicates the extent to which Sangster has superimposed suggestions of human sexuality on his landscape and literary sources.

The "Spirit of Beauty" that presides over the Thousand Islands section of *The St. Lawrence and the Saguenay* may have its origins, not only in Burr, Warburton, and Howison, but also in the allegory concerning "the preference of grace to beauty" in *The Citizen of the World,* the work which, with the Bible, "constituted [Sangster's] library for many years" (qtd. in Pacey, *Ten Canadian Poets* 4). The *"region of beauty"* (a place of "pleasure without end") and the *"valley of the graces"* (a realm of "simplicity and nature") that comprise the "two landscapes" of Goldsmith's allegory (2:315) correspond to the St. Lawrence and the Saguenay in Sangster's poem, the former conveying the narrator and the Maiden, initially at least, through a region of sheer "pleasure" and picturesque beauty, and the latter conveying them ultimately towards spiritual revelation amid the "simplicity" of sublime nature. It may also be that the structure and movement of *The St. Lawrence and the Saguenay* were influenced by a second allegory in *The Citizen of the World:* a treatment of philosophical enquiry in which an "adventurer" under the guidance of various "angelic beings" attempts to travel from the *"valley of Ignorance"* to the *"Land of Certainty"* (2:158). Whatever his sources (and, almost needless to say, the Bible with its broad progression from the Old Testament to the New should not be disregarded as an influence on the structure of *The St. Lawrence and the Saguenay*), it is clear that Sangster, though he praises "Beauty" with considerable relish in his opening stanzas, can no more be content with mere "Beauty" than with *"ignorance"*; in fact he is quick to pair "Truth and Beauty" in Stanza 8 as the objects of "worship ... in [his] soul" (*95*) and, in the ensuing stanzas, to describe a distinctly Christian Book of Nature complete with "psalmy waves," "summer matins," and the "joyous carolling" and "choral hymn" of bird song, as well as to praise the "stars" in the "outspread scroll / Of heaven" as the guardians of his "Victor-Soul above Earth's prison bars" (*97–129*). Only when nature is allied to the supernatural can it be released from the stigma of "mortality."

Imbued with a natural theology that permits him to see through nature to nature's God, the narrator perceives a violent "Tempest" as a manifestation of Divine "Power," as a sublime experience that "fills [his] overburdened brain" with unsurpassable "joy" (*174–87*). In the same spirit he also elicits from the Maiden a "Hymn to the Lightning" that, in the manner of Isaac Watts, emphasizes the "insignific[ance] of Man" in relation to the "Immensity" of God and affirms the eternal life to come in the "After-Plan" (*216–19*). Here, very clearly, the Maiden is fulfilling her Beatricean role as a chastening guide in the narrator's quest for revelation. As he himself says after she has sung her "Hymn to the Lightning," "Thine eyes my grosser thoughts remove, / ... thy sweet voice doth give my spirit wings" (*223–24*). The conclusion of the storm is marked by the appearance of a "gorgeous rainbow" (*272*), a sign of God's favour which also presides over the coming of twilight and the movement of the boat beyond the alluring beauties of the Thousand Islands.

As they move into the St. Lawrence proper the lovers are smiled upon by "Hesper" (Hesperus, Venus), a planet associated here with both transformation and resurrection ("a chrysalis that has burst its tomb" [*286*]). Moreover they are bathed in "moon-beams" that seem to blend "earth and sky ... into one, / Even as [the lovers'] hearts' deep virtues ... unite, / Like meeting pilgrims at the set of sun" (*288–91*). Almost as strong in these lines as the sense of a unification of the heavenly and the earthly is the sense (particularly in the image of the pilgrims meeting at sunset) that a day and a human life contain analogous movements towards a meeting that is only fully and finally possible after death, and then only to those who have led a life dedicated to God. A comparison of "Mild Evening" with a Miltonically "pensive Vestal Nun" in the ensuing stanza continues this train of thought, as does the pairing in the same lines of "True Love" with "Virtue" (*293–98*). A "Twilight Hymn" reminiscent of John Keble's "Evening" then extends the analogy between nightfall and death into a collective thanksgiving for the "Promptings of Hope ... Joy ... Love" and "Peace" that come alike with "gentle-footed Twilight" and in "the calm Twilight of the Soul" (*310–25*). It is an index of the narrator's developing sense of the sanctity of all God's "wondrous works" (*308*) that the "Twilight Hymn" and the preceding stanzas are rich with echoes, not just of "Il Penseroso" and *The Christian Year,* but also of the Benedicite and Psalm 8 (*"God's glory magnified by his works"*).

Although the narrator's faith that "the threshold of life's close" is "the verge of heaven's goal" (*322–23*) enables him to face the coming night with equanimity, the descent of the rapids that constitutes the next phase of the journey down the St. Lawrence heralds his movement into a dark realm of personal experience in which he expresses a dread of failing to achieve unity with the Maiden. Not for the first or last time, the poem at this point raises large questions about the identity of the Maiden and the nature of the narrator's relationship with her. Is she a woman whom he has "worshipped" from afar with a "pure passion" since first encountering her in Montreal during his "Boyhood" (*454–55, 434*)? Or is she a more recent friend whom he fears will remain as distant from him as the Montreal girl (Snyder)? Whatever the case it is quite clear that the narrator wishes to be united with the Maiden ("How long / Will my lone spirit wander ... until it lives in thine?" he asks [*455–57*]) and, concomitantly, that he fears separation from her. To call this portion of *The St. Lawrence and the Saguenay* a journey through the dark night of the soul would be inflationary. Nevertheless it is evident that in the night section of his journey down the St. Lawrence the narrator's fear of separation from the Maiden takes up a central position in the poem, occasioning assertions of the strength of his affection for her (*458–60, 476–77*) and complaints about her failure to return his love (*461–72*). Allusions to two famous pairs of unhappy and ill-fated lovers – Hamlet and Ophelia (*527*) and Romeo and Juliet (*586*) – reinforce these themes, as do a bitter-sweet "Canzonet" affirming the durability of love (*461–76*) and a reference to Petrarch's separation from Laura during his years at Vaucluse (*494–97*).

The narrator's turbulent feelings are also reflected in his responses to the passing scenery of the St. Lawrence – his fear of separation from the Maiden in such lines as "Here stands a maiden cottage all alone, / There the low church extends its gleaming spire" (*488–89*) and his longing for unity with her in such images as the "bright spires reposing on [the] breast" of an old building in the Edenic village of "*Varennes*, on the south bank of the St. Lawrence" between Montreal and Quebec (Burr 30). As if to tease the narrator and assure him of her devotion, the Maiden responds to the request to "sing [him] one of [her] pleasing madrigals" (*530*) by telling in "The Whippoorwill" the story of a betrayal and reconciliation in love that indicates a certain sophistication and independence on her part in the realm of relations between the sexes. "Absent loves are all the fashion!" proclaims a jilted yet resilient Jeannie in the third stanza of a song that owes less to Weld than to the Edgar Allan Poe of "The Raven." But towards the end of "The Whippoorwill" the same Jeannie is described less flatteringly as "silly" and "little" when she unquestioningly forgives her lover's infidelity and holds "her mouth up like a flower, / That her bee might sip his fill" (577–80). Nevertheless, "The Whippoorwill" ends on a note of reconciliation and even exorcism as the "doleful" bird that gives the song its title ceases its "solitary ... cry" (*523*) and, in the stanza that follows, the narrator observes that "Th' inconstant moon has passed behind a cloud" (*586*).

This allaying of the fear of separation proves to be as temporary as the trope in which it is embodied implies. To be sure, several expressions and reflections of the narrator's hoped-for unity and felicity with the Maiden can be found in the ensuing stanzas, none more startling, perhaps, than his reference to the "One graceful column" that commemorates "WOLFE and MONTCALM" in Quebec (*604–10*) and none more affective than his empathetic account of the religious and domestic contentment that seems to characterize the "cheerful homes" of the habitants on the Île d'Orléans (*604–75*). "Kind, hospitable, contented, [the habitant] ... only desires to be allowed to do as his forefathers did before him," writes Burr; "on his saint's day, or on the Sabbath, he repairs to his village church clothed in the same style as his ancestors. During the summer he cultivates his land, and [in winter] ... accompanied by his happy family, [he] visits his neighbours" (29–30). "A courteous, gentle race, as ever blent / Religion and Simplicity," agrees Sangster; "The cheer / That greets the stranger who may wander here / Glows with the zeal of hospitality ... From the world's bitter strife the Habitant is free" (*651–57*). But as the moon begins to shine more brightly on the scene and the boat moves downriver from the Île d'Orléans towards, appropriately, "CAPE TORMENTE" (*709*), the narrator's fear of being parted from the Maiden reappears to find anguished expression in a "Parting Song" reminiscent of *The Bride of Abydos,* Byron's oriental tale of love destroyed by parental interference. An analogy in the opening stanza of this song – "Rivers meet and mix forever, / Why are we, love, doomed to sever?" (*667–88*) – suggests that, at this juncture at least, the two rivers of the poem's title are emblematic of the individual identities of the two lovers whose eternal union on earth and in heaven the narrator so earnestly desires. Although the precise nature of the "fiat" that could separate the lovers in not made clear in "Parting Song," the very thought that it might become a reality is utterly darkening and deeply disturbing to the narrator. "Not a star is shining o'er us; / ... the heav'n of love is clouded," he moans; "In my brain a fire is burning ... my nerves ... / Are re-strung to desp'rate madness!" (*696–97, 701–04*). "Parting Song" ends with the declaration that "our hearts shall not be broken!" (*708*) but, of course, it will take more than a mere assertion to pull the narrator back from the abyss into which his anguish has plunged him.

So it is that well beyond Cape Tormente, as the boat continues to move past such signs of sanctified human love as the "sacred" "Homestead" of a "faithful Habitant" (*716–18*), the seemingly manic narrator once again expresses his hopes and fears, now in a stanza composed of short, almost antiphonal statements:

Our spirits are as one. The morning, love,
Will part us. We have lived an age to-night.
Love is immortal. Hope is from above.
Sit nearer to me, for thine eyes are bright
With tears. There is a fairer land in sight.
Our love is sphered with truth. Eternity
Will crown that love, if we but love aright;
If Love be Truth, indeed. Soft-eyed one! we
Must seek beyond the veil what here can never be!
                                    (*799–807*)

Here again is Sangster's ideal of a personal love that, if aligned with right and identified with "Truth," will transcend the separations that are "native to mortality" in the "fairer land" of "Eternity." The fact that this stanza is introduced as the empathetic explanation of a "sigh" (*797*) from the Maiden whose "tears" are remarked at its centre seems to permit the inference that she does not, as yet, share the narrator's emerging (though still otherworldly) vision of eternal love. This conjectured doubt could be the occasion for the exemplary and Carlylean tale beginning two stanzas later of a nameless man (a representation, perhaps, of Sangster's own spiritual history?) whose Teufelsdröckhian loss and recovery of religious faith prompts observations about analogous movements from "Darkness" to "Light," "Error" to "Truth," "Evil" to "Good," sickness to "Health," and from "Life," through "Death," to revelation (*833–52*). That the presentation of these positive developments occurs at the point in the poem where night turns into day and the boat turns from the St. Lawrence into the Saguenay is one of many examples of Sangster's architectonic skill and allegorical intent – his use of temporal cycles, climatic phenomena, and Canadian geography to give shape and substance to his theme of "Human Love."

With the arrival of morning light comes a "Paean to the Dawn" that marks the beginning of what may be called the epithalamic movement of *The St. Lawrence and the Saguenay:* the poem's enactment of a wedding procession and a marriage service in the cathedral of northern nature. With references by way of *Paradise Lost* and *The Christian Year* to the prelapserian "Love, that at the primal waking / Of the Dawn in Eden's bowers, / Wandered through the Garden," the "Paean to the Dawn" calls upon the "Blessed light of early Morning" to illuminate what is dark in the narrator and the Maiden by filling them with "the love that comes from heaven, / With the hope that soars on high, / That [their] faults may all be shriven,/ As [the light's] splendors fill the sky" (*863–80*). To an extent Romantic in its consecration of human love (the Haidée episode of *Don Juan* comes particularly to mind), the "Paean to the Dawn" is also conventionally Christian in its association of ordinary light with divine light, as, too, is the ensuing typological interpretation of the "triumphant Sun" as a "Royal Witness" to the "existence of the Eternal One!" (*912–14*). Evidently the heavenly and the earthly, the human and the divine are moving increasingly towards harmony. Nowhere is this more evident than in the trope immediately following "Paean to the Dawn," an epithalamic likening of the "morn wait[ing] for the sun with a flushed cheek" "to a maid-wife waiting for her wedded lord" (*903–04*). It is a comparison that, in concert with "the songs of birds" accompanying the dawn (*905*), appropriately recalls the Song of Solomon. Little wonder that the narrator ascends the Saguenay in growing confidence that "No rocks can bar the way / Where Love and Hope lend wings to human clay" (*1071–72*) and in growing certainty that "When human hearts unite," the "trace / Of Eden that yet lingers in the heart" becomes manifest (*1080–82*). "In the first kiss of love," says Byron, "Some portion of paradise still is on earth, / And Eden revives" (93).

But despite the narrator's evidently secure conviction that God's "Presence thrills / All Beauty as all Truth" (*960–61*), one thing prevents his happiness from being complete: the Maiden has apparently not yet committed herself to him. "Oh! give me the love of your woman's heart" (*1086*) he asks in the poem's final interspersed "Song":

> Then the Sun of Hope
> Up Life's gleaming cope,
> The true Genius of Love would roll,
> And the dark Night no more
> Would obscure the shore
> Where beckons Love's mystic Soul.
>   (*1113–18*)

The effective absence of the Maiden from the narrative between "Paean to the Dawn" and the renovative "Song" that precedes the arrival of the boat at "CAPE ETERNITY" near the head of the Saguenay (*1120*) is explicable in terms of the epithalamic matrix of this portion of the poem. Arriving in the body of the church (the upper reaches of the Saguenay) as it were by separate ways, the bride and groom do not (re)encounter one another until they are at the chancel rail (Cape Eternity), where they plight their troth to each other in the sight of God and at a little remove from the altar (Trinity Rock) towards which they will later ascend with the priest. This may put the equivalencies between the Saguenay landscape and the marriage ceremony too boldly, but it does help to explain, not merely the virtual absence of the Maiden from the penultimate stage of the poem's epithalamic movement (*903–1085*), but also the definite sense that Sangster is investing Cape Eternity and Cape Trinity with ecclesiological significance when he describes the former as "a God / Holding communion with the distant cope" (*1121–22*) and the latter as an "anatomic form ... [with] triple crown / ... far above the earth's unrest" (*1206–07*).

The final test of any reading of *The St. Lawrence and the Saguenay* must lie in its success in explaining the events of the poem's conclusion – Stanzas 100–110 – set in the vicinity of Capes Eternity and Trinity. Preceding these climactic stanzas are several crisp statements that, to an extent, summarize the dilemmas experienced by the narrator from the outset. On the one hand these statements are about the Divine origin (and hence integrity) of all creation ("He ... who flushed the daisy built the world. / All things come perfect from His Master-hand" [*1137–38*]) and about the power of sublime nature to draw the mind of Man – the "supremest of the works He planned" – towards the Creator (*1137–43*). On the other hand the statements are about the insignificance of Man in relation to sublime nature ("How ... [puny] he seems, when thrown / In ... contrast to a work like this" [*1145–46*]) and about the ability of earthly pleasure to bring about the destruction of virtue ("unsuspecting Innocence, beguiled / By Pleasures ... that pierce the enamel of its dreams" [*1161–63*]). With his mind thus pulled by external nature towards God and by human nature towards sin, the narrator engages in Stanza 100 in a process of ratiocination akin to that of Adam at the Fall, but premised on the same Victorian dualism and natural theology that characterized the early stages of the poem:

> Love lures me evermore to Woman's arms,
> But here I kneel at Nature's hallowed feet!
> Love fills my being with a calm, replete,
> But regal Nature sets my spirit free
> With grateful praises to God's Mercy seat.
>
> (*1166–70*)

Very obviously the solution to the narrator's dilemma, the way out of the trap of either/or, lies in a reconciliation of the conflict in his mind between profane love – the "Love [that] lures [him] ... to Woman's arms" – and sacred love – the love of God through sublime "Nature." A *concordia discors* emerges when the narrator, by affirming a bond of human nature (literally "Nature" writ small), harmonizes attractions that now appear to him, not as opposite, but as related and comparable:

Yet nature binds me closer, love, to thee:
Ev'n as this dreamy Bay, in sweet felicity

Woos both the sun's light, and the cool shade
Of the umbrageous woods to its embrace.

(1171–74)

What enables the narrator ("this dreamy Bay") to love both God ("the sun's light") and "Woman" ("the cool shade") is the recognition that human "Love" when "pure [and] deep" is divinely inspired:

What deep imaginings of Peace pervade
[The Bay's] heavenly repose, as Nature's face
Peers down, in mild, unutterable grace,
Like a calm Student seeking Pearls of Thought
In some fair Beauty's mind, where he can trace
Through her warm slumber, how her soul is fraught
With pure deep Love, by heavenly inspiration taught.

(1175–81)

The "heavenly repose" of Trinity Bay, the "unutterable grace" of Nature (perhaps specifically Trinity Rock), and the "heavenly inspiration" of a "pure ... Love" – all these phrases speak of an interfusion of nature by grace, which, as the narrator now fully realizes, places in sanctified harmony the attraction towards God, "Nature," and "Woman" that he had earlier perceived as being in conflict.

With an achieved understanding in the cathedral of northern nature of the sanctity of a "Love" that is "pure," the narrator experiences a rush of verbal icons. As "Strong, eager thoughts come crowding to [his] eyes," he envisages Trinity Rock first as the "Monarch of the Bluffs" and then as "the great Samson of the Saguenay" *(1182–85)* – the Samson infused and strengthened, like the narrator himself, by God's grace. What follows now is a dumbfounding. Confessing that his "lips are mute," that he "cannot speak" his thoughts, the narrator – consistent with the strain of mystical thinking that sees silence as the most effective expression of awe – acknowledges that "'T were best [his thoughts] should not break / The silence, which itself is ecstacy / And Godlike Eloquence" *(1996–98)*. Yet for Sangster, as for the Carlyle of *Sartor Resartus*, silence is not an end but a means: it is "the element in which great things fashion themselves together; that at length they may emerge, full-formed and majestic, into the daylight of Life, which they are thence-forth to rule" (218). It is to this emergence, to the bringing

into life of a love that is all inclusive and multifaceted, that the final few
stanzas of *The St. Lawrence and the Saguenay* are given over.

After expressing the joyful completion of his quest for "Truth" in a
stanza devoted to Trinity Rock (and indebted, perhaps, to Moore's
description of Niagara Falls in "To the Lady Charlotte Rawdon"), the
narrator breaks his silence to deliver a central speech and major crux
of the poem:

> Let us return, love, for the goal is won.
> Here, by this Rock, 't is doomed that we must part,
> And part forever; for the glorious Sun
> Of Love, that quickeneth my earnest heart,
> Shines not for thee, alone.
>
> (*1209–13*)

The narrator's surprising assertion in these cryptic lines that he and the
Maiden must "part forever" seems to stem from a conviction on his part
that, since his "Love" has been expanded to include God and "Nature,"
it can no longer be directed – as it was at the beginning of the poem
("There is but one to whom my hopes are clinging") – exclusively
towards one person. Once the "glorious Sun" of a comprehensive
"Love" has shone for the narrator, he sees his earlier perceptions of his
"love," both the emotion and the beloved, as narrow and delusive, as a
mere "Dream" to be dispelled by the intense light of a new dawn:

> The Dream of Art
> That calms the happy Student's sweet repose,
> Is like our Dream of Love – the first swift dart
> Shot by young Phoebus from his chamber, goes
> Like lightning through his vision's blooming heart of rose.
>
> Already thou art gone, with one last look
> Of love from those exalted eyes of thine,
> That cheered me as we read from nature's book
> Together, and partook of the divine
> Ambrosial draught of love's celestial wine.
>
> (*1213–22*)

Here, as in much Victorian poetry and fiction (including *Sartor Resartus*), a love founded on youthful, romantic assumptions – "The sighing
of a certain varlet, / Werther" as Sangster calls it in "The Name of Mary"
(*The St. Lawrence and the Saguenay, and Other Poems* 123) – proves insufficient to survive and rule in "the daylight of Life." Once the chimera of

romantic love has evaporated it can be replaced by a love that is mature, serious, "earnest" (a word earlier applied to the narrator's "heart"), and eminently Victorian:

> Another earnest being at my side! –
> Not her whose Girlhood's dreamy love was mine;
> Not her whose heart Affliction's fire has tried;
> Not her of the Artistic soul, and stately pride ...
>
> (*1223–26*)

The first line of this passage can be taken to mean that another woman has appeared to take the place of the Maiden or, less jarringly, it can be read as referring to a transformation that has occurred either (or both) within the Maiden herself (she has become "Another ... being," a different person, through a spiritual conversion) or in the narrator's perception of her (he now sees her as "Another" like-minded "being" whose new found earnestness echoes his own). The implication of this reading is that the Maiden has, after all, shared the narrator's revelation at Cape Trinity and that, in their common outlook and new maturity, the two are now fully compatible with one another.

The bright ideal of love that is articulated and celebrated in the remaining stanzas of *The St. Lawrence and the Saguenay* is unmistakably Victorian in its emphasis on utility, action, faith, and the perfectibility of man:

> Loved-one! I hear
> The voice within syllabl'ing words that bind
> Our souls, and blend them for a nobler sphere
> Of usefulness and action – year by year
> Ascending in the scale of being, far
> Above the trifling mind's obscure career,
> And mounting to Perfection, like a star
> For whose triumphant flight heaven's crystalline gates unbar.
>
> (*1228–35*)

The "words" that the narrator hears spoken by the "voice within" may well be those of the marriage ceremony, a possibility that accords with the epithalamic aspect of this portion of *The St. Lawrence and the Saguenay.* If he could find the words to describe the strength and reach of his love, muses the narrator, then, like the woods in Spenser's *Epithalamion,* the "Silence" itself would echo him "vow for vow" (*1236–53*). The final stanza of the poem is a ringing endorsement of a love that is as passionate as it is mysterious:

All, all is thine, love, now: Each thought and hope
In the long future must be shared with thee.
Lean on my bosom; let my strong heart ope
Its founts of love, that the wild ecstacy
That quickens every pulse, and makes me free
As a God's wishes, may serenely move
Thy inmost being with the mystery
Of the new life that has just dawned, and prove
How unutterably deep and strong is Human Love.

(*1254–62*)

As Sangster doubtless knew, the phrase "new life" occurs in the bidding
prayer of the Anglican service of Holy Communion, which newly married couples are enjoined to receive either at or shortly after their marriage. It is to be found elsewhere in *The St. Lawrence and the Saguenay*
volume in "Love's Morning Lark" (the poem that follows "Mary's Twentieth Birthday") and may also lie behind the title of "Love's New Era," a
celebration of the joyful advent of a personal love (197–98, 215–16).
Such echoes within Sangster's first volume add credibility to the identification of the *monna innominata* of *The St. Lawrence and the Saguenay*
with Mary Kilborn. But the circumstantial evidence for this biographical connection, however convincing, should not obscure the literary
ancestry of Sangster's inspirational Maiden in figures such as the Beatrice of Dante's *Vita Nuova* (*The New Life*) and the Pilgrim of Byron's
Childe Harold, figures whose allegorical function and future dimension
ensure that they can never fully be "class'd / With forms which live and
suffer" (Byron 79).

By and large *The St. Lawrence and the Saguenay, and Other Poems* was
well received by reviewers in Canada, Britain, and the United States,
many of whom had special praise for the title poem of the volume. One
of the most astute and balanced assessments of *The St. Lawrence and the
Saguenay* is that of Thomas McQueen in the 11 December 1856 issue of
the *Weekly British Whig:* "Charles Sangster is a poet of a different order
[than Alexander McLachlan]. He has adopted far loftier models and
struck the Lyre on a much higher key. His whole soul seems steeped in
love and poesy, and finds utterance in expression generally eloquent,
bold and musical. He is thoroughly sentimental, teeming with ideas of
the sublime and the beautiful, which though somewhat diffuse at times,
bear evident marks of enthusiastic poetical conception. Mr. Sangster's
muse loves to revel in scenery, sentiment and simile – [s]he is essentially
etherial, and the common reader who attempts to follow her, will be in
some danger of getting wandered in the clouds. Still Mr. S[angster] is
a poet of no mean order, and his volume is far the most respectable con-

tribution of poetry that has yet been made to the infant literature of Canada." Because his sympathies lay with the Chartists and a "people's poet[ry]," McQueen saw very clearly that *The St. Lawrence and the Saguenay* is a work of high art aimed especially, if not exclusively, at a middle- and upper-class audience. "Neatly bound in Muslin, and uniform with the American Editions of the Poets" (*Weekly British Whig* [28 March 1856]), *The St. Lawrence and the Saguenay, and Other Poems* was designed for the libraries of its monied subscribers who, according to Sangster, included "the principal members of government, and the most eminent statesmen from both Houses of Parliament" (qtd. in Bentley, intro. xlix). Sangster's list of subscriptions indicates that of the thousand copies of his book that he had printed in New York, about 750 were quickly sold, a few to casual purchasers, but the bulk to some 350 subscribers (many of whom bought more than one book), first at seven shillings and sixpence and then at five shillings each. With *The St. Lawrence and the Saguenay, and Other Poems*, Canadian poetry takes its place in the well-to-do Victorian world of tourist excursions, sanctified affections, attractive furnishings, thoughtful gifts, and competitive prices.

15 William Kirby, *The U.E.*

In his introduction to the *Unpublished Correspondence* between William Kirby (1817–1906) and Alfred, Lord Tennyson, Lorne Pierce recognizes a curiously close connection between some important events of Kirby's times and the landmarks of his early life. The year in which Kirby left his native Yorkshire for the United States – 1832 – was also the year of the first Reform Bill and the death of Sir Walter Scott. "For the rest of his life," observes Pierce, "Kirby sought escape from encroaching reform." It was a quest that took him, after seven years in the United States, to Niagara-on-the-Lake where he was to become the "spokesman, interpreter, and bulwark of the Tory and Loyalist idea" (14,17). For his most extended poem – *The U.E.: A Tale of Upper Canada*, published at Niagara in 1859 – Kirby's principal model was *Marmion: A Tale of Flodden Field*, Scott's most successful poetic foray into the feudal world of the *Waverley Novels.* "Sir Walter Scott? Everywhere and always" (19) writes Pierce of Scott's influence on Kirby, whose own historical romance, *The Golden Dog* (1877), has been perceived as a retarding influence on the development of "anything native in Canadian romance" precisely because of its highly successful use of Scott (Klinck, "Literary Activity" 159).

The year in which Kirby arrived in Canada – 1839 – was the first year of peace after the Rebellions of 1837–38 and also the year of the Durham *Report,* a document which simultaneously advocated reform in the Canadas and sought "to perpetuate and strengthen the connexion between the Empire and the North American Colonies" (333). The traumatic events of 1837–38 furnish the climactic episodes of *The U.E.,* the final line of which is an imperialistic apostrophe to "England's proud Empire, One, for ever more." Nor can it be overlooked that according to its preface *The U.E.* was "written in ... 1846" (*1*), the year in which the Corn Laws were repealed and, as Kirby says in his *Annals of Niagara* (1896), Canada was "deprived ... of the preferential privileges she had enjoyed in Britain" (244; and see Berger 178). As the machinery that would produce Confederation ground forward, Kirby sought a foundation for the future in an idealized past, in a time when "obedience to the teachings of religion and to the law, and respect for the magistrates appointed by the king were marked features of the people who made Upper Canada one of the grandest members of the British Empire" (*Annals* 268). It is no more surprising that Kirby was presented to the Prince of Wales during the royal visit of 1860 than it is that this brief meeting with the future king made his "happiness ... complete" (Pierce, intro. to *Unpublished Correspondence* 22). This was the man who would preface his volume of *Canadian Idylls* (1884, 1894) with a passage from Tennyson expressing the hope that Queen Victoria would "rule us long, / And leave us rulers ... / As noble till the latest day!" (5).

The debt of *The U.E.* to *Marmion* is immediately apparent in the opening verse paragraphs of the Canadian poem. A definition of his own poetic enterprise in relation to that of Virgil, Kirby's introduction recalls Scott's famous introduction to Canto Third, where the poet counters William Erskine's suggestion that he emulate "those masters, o'er whose tomb / Immortal laurels ever bloom" by insisting on the integrity of his own "theme" and "measure" (6:123–35). The subjects of "heroic song" as classically conceived may be absent from Scotland, Scott concedes, but sufficient "poetic impulse" has nevertheless come to him from "mountain tower," "green hill," and "clear, blue heaven." Kirby agrees: "Let others far for foreign grandeurs roam, / Dearer to me the loveliness of home: / Our ocean-lakes ... / Our boundless woods ... / And cloudy Cataracts" (*7–12*). More classical in his orientation that Scott, Kirby invokes a traditional "Muse" at the end of his introduction, but one whose identity accords with the emphasis on place in *Marmion*:

> For me a wreath of modest cedar, still,
> May haply bloom on some Canadian hill.
> Then come my woodland Muse and fire my tongue,
> And let my lips the moving strain prolong,
> Till warm with life and radiant from above,
> My lay be worthy of my country's love.
>
>   (*29–34*)

As is apparent from these lines, Kirby chose not to emulate Scott's "untrimm'd" octosyllabic couplets, preferring instead the more conventionally conservative form of the decasyllabic couplet. A reference a few lines later to the "sweet bard, who sawest with mournful eye / 'The rural virtues from their Country fly'" (*1:13–14*) confirms that in formal matters at least Goldsmith was as much a "poetic mentor" to Kirby (Pierce, intro. to *Unpublished Correspondence* 18, 20) as he had been to Cary, Mackay, Bayley, and other conservative poets. In certain formalistic respects *The U.E.* resembles *Marmion*, however; the cantos of both poems are subdivided into numbered sections of uneven length, and both occasionally use alexandrines to emphasize a point or conclude a section.

In its overall structure *The U.E.* bears a striking resemblance to *Marmion*. By design a "Canadian Epic Poem" (*Annals* 85) rather than a mere "Romantic Tale" (Scott 6:5), *The U.E.* is divided into twelve cantos rather than *Marmion*'s six, but this is to a degree cosmetic, for the division of Kirby's poem by subject-matter is into three larger units: (1) the emigration of Walwyn and his two sons, Ethwald and Eric, from Yorkshire to the Niagara region sometime after the War of 1812 (Cantos 1–4); (2) their experience as settlers and their relationship with the old Loyalist Ranger John and his family prior to the Rebellions of 1837–38 (Cantos 5–8); and (3) the involvement of both families in the fighting in the Niagara area in 1837 and at the Battle of the Windmill near Prescott in 1838 (Cantos 9–12). Both *Marmion* and *The U.E.* begin with the departure and journey of a hero (Marmion from England to Scotland, Walwyn from England to Canada) and both end with a decisive battle (Flodden Field and the Battle of the Windmill). Of course an initial journey and a climactic battle also characterize the *Aeneid,* the poem to which Kirby's twelve-part structure primarily alludes. As Walwyn ascends the St. Lawrence, one of many epic similes likens him to Aeneas when he braved "crumbling streets and blood, and raging fire ... To found in other climes a happier Troy" (*2:205–08*). Allusions to the *Iliad* (*1:97*) and a heavy use of *Paradise Lost* in its final cantos deepen the epic resonances of *The U.E.* without enabling it to transcend its origins in Scott's "Romantic Tale." It is no accident that the name Constance is shared by the most engaging female character in *Marmion* and Ethwald's abidingly loyal fiancée in *The U.E.* Indeed Kirby's choice of Constance as the name of his heroine may be allusive as well as emblematic – a grateful nod to the poet and novelist whose vision of a vanished world of courageous patriarchs, contented yeomen, and graceful women so obviously lies in the background of *The U.E.*

Two other writers who obviously helped to shape the neo-Loyalist vision of *The U.E.* are Burke and Carlyle. Both are cited approvingly in Kirby's *Annals of Niagara,* and with quotations that reflect his particular preoccupations. "The age of chivalry is gone. That of sophisters, economists, and calculators has succeeded," wrote Burke in his *Reflections on the Revolution in France* (86), but in *Annals of Niagara* he is represented by an excerpt from the debate over the Constitutional Act of 1791 in which he advocates appointed rather than elected councils (92). "Like the Romans, and some few others," wrote Carlyle in *Past and Present,* "the ... Epic Poem [of Britain] is written on the Earth's surface: England her Mark!" (151), but in *Annals of Niagara* he is represented by some caustic remarks on the United States ("a wretched nation") and George Washington ("a monstrous bore [without] ambition ... religion ... or any good quality under the sun!" [37–38]). In Kirby the nostalgia for an honourable past and the repudiation of laissez-faire liberalism that are the hallmarks of British conservatism become a celebration of Loyalist Canada and a hatred of American democracy. On the title page of *The U.E.* are an epigraph and an engraving that typify Kirby's "Tory and Loyalist" values. The epigraph from *The Deserted Village* (*403–06*) lists the "rural virtues" – the components of a happy and cohesive community centred on God, country, and family – that according to Goldsmith emigrated from Britain with the enclosures: "Contented Toil ... hospitable Care ... kind connubial Tenderness ... Piety ... steady Loyalty and faithful Love." The engraving depicts the floral emblems of Great Britain and loyal America (roses, oak leaves, hollyhocks) enshrining a circular bee hive – that is, an interdependent community centred on a queen and diligently engaged in creating sustenance, fertility, and "sweetness" (Duffy 33). Time and again in the body of the poem, Kirby reinforces the analogy between Upper Canada and a beehive: when Walwyn and his sons arrive at Burlington Bay (Hamilton), they see "busy thousands ... / Like bees ... adding honey to their hive" (*3:193–94*); when they reach Niagara, their house is constructed "by the united help of ... neighbours" at a raising "bee" (*Annals* 68–69); and when American forces invade Upper Canada in 1837 they are likened to "a man ... / Who thrusts his hand for honey, in the hive, / Ere fire and smoke expel the stinging throng, / Who guard the treasure of their homes from wrong" (*11:331–34*). As peace loving as their apian counterparts (and fellow imports from Europe), the loyal settlers of Upper Canada are also, it transpires, fiercely protective of the home(s) that they have created through "Contented Toil ... and faithful Love."

During the Atlantic crossing, the heroic self-sacrifice of a sailor provides Walwyn with a pretext for regaling Ethwald with his pacifistic version of Kirby's neo-Loyalism:

> Our first great duty is to God alone;
> Our country next demands her sacred dues,
> And ne'er may son of mine her claim refuse.
> I cannot blame thee, if, some fatal day,
> Like him, should see thee give thy life away
> 'Tis what I taught thee, what I still commend ...
> . . . .
> [But] who, his honest calling worthily fills,
> Whom neither envy gnaws, nor avarice chills,
> Who uses riches as a trust from heaven;
> And fears not poverty if that be given;
> Who loves his country and obeys her laws,
> Honours his king and warms in Freedom's cause;
> That man no less adorns his native land
> Than he who for her draws the warrior's brand.
>   (*1:560–65, 569–76*)

A celebration of culture centred, not on the individual self, but on God, monarch, country, and family, *The U.E.* is also both implicitly and explicitly a critique of the utilitarian values of the "hard material age" heralded by the "Steamer" on which Walwyn and his sons travel from Montreal to Burlington Bay (*3:39–68*). As Carl Berger observes, a "rejection of individualism and industrialism pervade[s] everything that Kirby wrote," and the "Gigantic power of Steam" (*3:49*) is a product of an eighteenth-century "rationalism" that "distort[s] the order of creation" (179). For Kirby, as for other anti-modernists, "Science" is the "subtle serpent" in the garden that leaves life cold, joyless, and stripped of moral precepts. "The true Elysian plains" exist only in Heaven and a future age "As yet but dreamt of, by the mind / In secret converse with angelic kind" (*3:69–116*) – specifically, the mind of Emanuel Swedenborg, whose *Arcana Coelestia* Kirby apparently encountered in the Cincinatti school of Alexander Kinmont and thereafter cherished until "his dying day" (Pierce, intro. to *Unpublished Correspondence* 18; and see Silver 22–23 and Block 121). A "golden morn" to come will "Reveal the presence of the Lord of all," proclaim "Salvation and angelic life to man," and "unfold the leaves of Heaven's argentine gate." In the meantime, another anodyne for the iron age exists in the "golden morn" of Canada's Loyalists:

Religion was with them more deed than word;
To love their neighbour and to fear the Lord;
Honour their king and yield his high degree,
The loyal trust and homage of the free.
Their sober minds with healthful vigour blest,
The best of knowledge, how to live, possessed;
Unspoiled by sophistry, and clear and strong
Their plain good sense was never in the wrong;
While self-earned competence secured by these
Made daily industry a life of ease.

                                        (*5:335–44*)

It is a measure of Kirby's commitment to his Tory vision that when he purchased the *Niagara Mail* with money from his U.E.L. wife Eliza Magdalene Whitmore in 1850 he chose as a motto for the paper "Non mutat genu solum" – "The race [or stock] alone does not change." Later he took as his personal motto "The noblest motive is the public good" (Pierce, intro. to *Unpublished Correspondence* 20).

The conservatism that Kirby embodied in *The U.E.* has at least two Canadian antecedents with which he was probably familiar. The less obvious of these is Cary's *Abram's Plains,* a poem that treats of the Loyalists only in passing but continually propounds a conservative vision of Lower Canada. One passage especially in *The U.E.* ("And Dwarfish Esquimaux, with caution steal, / Their oily prey, and dress their nauseous meal" [*2:41–42*]) echoes *Abram's Plains* ("And Dwarfish *Esquimaux,* with small pig's eyes, / At cook'ry sick, raw seal and rank oil prize" [*164–65*]), and raises the possibility of a debt to Cary at other points in the poem – for example, in Kirby's account of the death of Wolfe (*2:153–68*), his reference to the tall-mast trade (*2:341–46*), and his description of Montreal as "Trade's potent Queen" (*2:370–82*). The more obvious and important Canadian source of Kirby's conservatism is the thought of Sir John Beverley Robinson, "the one time poet laureate of John Strachan's Grammar School at Cornwall" (Pierce, intro. to *Unpublished Correspondence* 20) to whom *The U.E.* is fulsomely dedicated by "HIS MUCH OBLIGED AND MOST OBEDIENT SERVANT." Six years before *The U.E.* was written Robinson published "a carefully articulated exposition of the well-respected principles of Burkean and Blackstonian conservatism" (Cook 93) in the form of *Canada and the Canada Bill,* the core ideas of which could serve as a summary of Kirby's beliefs: "immigration, the pyramidal society with its yeoman base, limited commerce, the imperial connection ... religion ... the fear of democracy, the elevation of honesty, diligence ... loyalty, and the admiration for a soci-

ety ultimately exuding 'refinement' and 'contentment'" (Cook 91, 93).
Kirby's links with Robinson and Cary align him with a Canadian conservative tradition that stretches back beyond Strachan and forward
through the likes of George Parkin and Stephen Leacock to George
Grant and his followers. By another of those curious coincidences
remarked by Pierce, Kirby's wife died on the same day as Sir John A.
Macdonald (intro. to *Annals* xvi).

"We glory in the gallant deeds of our fathers and dwell with delight
in the tales of Detroit and Lundy's Lane; it gives us a character among
nations, and inspires us with courage and energy to fulfil all our duties
vigorously as men and citizens" (Kirby, *Counter Manifesto* 14). So wrote
Kirby under the pseudonym "Britannicus" in response to the Manifesto
published by the Montreal Annexation Association in October 1849. In
the same pamphlet he castigates the annexationists for their "intense
selfishness" and compares neo-Loyalists such as himself to "the faithful
men of Israel," warning darkly that "the hereditary bitterness of U.E.
loyalty is surging up like a volcano – and the old tomahawk of the refugees, which has been preserved in our families, along with the fire-side
traditions of Oriskany and Wyoming, is taken from its hiding place"
(14). These are fighting words, and they suggest that *The U.E.* is also a
counter manifesto of sorts: a poetic attempt to fan the fires of Loyalism
against the proponents of annexation and reciprocity (the latter being
achieved in 1854 and persisting for a decade thereafter). "True poetry
is more than the truest prose," Kirby would write in *Annals of Niagara;*
"poetry is the chariot of truth, and its winged steeds ... bring light and
life into the thoughts and hearts of men, illumine history with a new
radiance and warm the emotions and inner chambers of the mind with
nobler feelings than we know of in the dull round of prosaic life" (70).
To illuminate the past and fire the reader with the "Tory and Loyalist
idea": this is the dual purpose of all Kirby's writing, not least *The U.E.* By
the lessons of history Canada's assimilation to the United States will be
prevented and her future within the British Empire assured.

In *Annals of Niagara* Kirby cites with approval a quotation likening the
time of the Loyalists to "'the days of Abraham'" (66) and at several
points in *The U.E.* he treats the representative founding fathers of
Upper Canada – Walwyn and Ranger John – as the Canadian equivalents of the great patriarchs of the Old Testament. As the narrative
opens, the "aged sire" Walwyn (*1:35*) looks back past the death of his
son Ethwald at the Battle of the Windmill (*1:47–60*) to his family's
"ancient homestead" on "the grassy banks of winding Swale" in Yorkshire (*1:137–38*). Widowed by his wife Hilda and impoverished by the
depression that followed the Napoleonic Wars, Walwyn had seen no

future in England for his "rising boys" and so had elected "For their dear sakes ... [to] leave [his] native shore" (*1:212, 227–28*). Because he had to leave his beloved Constance behind, the decision to emigrate was also "painful" for the sixteen-year old Ethwald, but the bitter pill was sweetened by Walwyn's conviction that in Canada the family is going to a place "Where freedom, peace, and plenty all combine, / And still rejoice 'neath England's rule benign" (*1:207–08*). To describe the departure and crossing of his proto-loyalists, Kirby draws principally on Pickering's *Inquiries of an Emigrant* (1831), which was published the year before his emigration from Yorkshire at about the age of sixteen. (As Riddell suggests, "Ethwald seems to have been drawn in part from Kirby himself" [*Kirby* 37].) To suit his own heroic and epical purposes, Kirby embellishes Pickering's account of the Atlantic crossing with the exemplary story of the self-sacrificing sailor (*1:485–554*) and invests the "old ocean" with suggestions of Scandinavian mythology ("Midgard's hoary serpent") derived, very likely, from the first volume of Benjamin Thorpe's *Northern Mythology* ([1851] 1:31, 49–50; *1:356–60*). Like their counterparts in *The Emigrant's Informant* and *Acadia* (and, according to *Annals of Niagara*, Kirby entertained Howe in 1853 [87]), Walwyn and his sons are torn by "conflicting passions" of "hope ... and fear" – "alternate" feelings which the concluding lines of Canto 1 warn the reader to respect because "'tis such as these, / That bear the seeds of Empire o'er the seas" and "In farthest lands, plant Britain's mighty name, / Spread her dominion, and exalt her fame!" (*1:591–604*).

Since Pickering landed in New York, he necessarily disqualified himself as a source for Kirby's account of the emigrants' journey up the St. Lawrence and along Lake Ontario to the Niagara region. With supplements from Cary and perhaps Sangster (Kirby's Cape Tourment is "The Titan of the lofty Capes" [*2:77*]), the principal prose sources for Canto 2 and Canto 3 of *The U.E.* are first Heriot and then Howison, the former for the area below Quebec City and the latter for the final stages of the journey. "After ... exhibiting a grateful variety throughout its course," observes Heriot, the Montmorenci River "is precipitated in an almost perpendicular fashion ... falling, where it touches the rock, in white clouds of rolling foam, and ... in numerous flakes like wool or cotton, which are gradually protracted in their descent, until they are received into the boiling, profound abyss, below" (76–77). "Oer precipices thrown, / A white cascade rolls like a curtain down," writes Kirby; "O'erhanging trees, half seen 'mid clouds of spray, / Spring from the rocks that wall the narrow way ... Deep in its rocky bed, the boiling mass / Of waters rushes through the narrow pass" (*2:117–24*). No O'Grady bent on downplaying the size and effect of Montmorenci Falls, Kirby agrees with Heriot that their "cloud[s] of vapour" (*2:113; 61,77*) are an impressive feature of a traveller or emigrant's first view of Quebec City (the equivalent in *The U.E.* of Marmion's first sight of Edinburgh in Scott's poem). Nor, later in the poem, does he contradict Howison's notion that in the Thousand Islands "Nature seems ... to have thrown sportively from her hand a profusion of masses" reminiscent of "the Happy Islands in the Vision of Mirzah" (32–33). "A thousand verdant spots on either beam / Glance like the happy isles of Mirza's dream, / And sportive Nature revels wild and free," he exclaims as the "rapid Steamer glides" towards Kingston (*3:1–6*). Kirby then contributes some fanciful touches of his own on the basis of Howison's speculation that the Thousand Islands will achieve a "fairy lovliness" when embellished by "art and architecture" (32). "Could it be / That nature formed this sweet epitome / For Oberon and all his elvish clan to colonize ... ?" he wonders, adding that here "The restless tribes of airy Fancy ... Upon their prancing steeds might urge the race, / Or backed on humming-birds the gad-fly chase" (*3:15–22*). Since Kirby was as familiar with Moore's Canadian poems as he was sympathetic to the Irishman's disillusionment with American culture (*Annals* 121–29), these last lines may also be indebted to the passage in "To the Lady Charlotte Rawdon" where the Puckish Indian Spirit "mount[s] ... the plume / Of [a] Wakon-Bird" and "chase[s]" a humming bird "Through his rosy realm of spring" (*Poetical Works* 127).

Appealing as they are, however, the natural sights of Canada are less engaging to Kirby than the evidences of "Man and his labours" (*2:54*). The most prominent of these is Quebec City, where the "cross-topped spires," "quays ... roofs," and "anchored fleets of commerce" create a "glorious sight" beneath the high centre of British Imperialism in Lower Canada: "proud Cape Diamond towers above them all ... Till on the loftiest point where birds scarce rise, / Old England's standard floats amid the skies" (*2:135–52*). After celebrating "gallant Wolfe" and "noble Montcalm" as heroes who died in "the consciousness of duty done" (*2:153–68*), Kirby praised the "hardy raftsmen from the upper floods" as "Bough pioneers who lead the sylvan war ... And scatter ... The seeds of cities, and the homes of men" (*2:225–30*), a militaristic conception of pioneering that anticipates the sentiments and activities of Max Gordon in *Malcolm's Katie*. Quebec City also affords Kirby the opportunity for brief but sympathetic vignettes of the French-Canadians and the Hurons. In accordance with a well-entrenched stereotype, the habitants are an "amiable people" because of their lack of ambition, their "contented mind," their "gentle manners," and their combination of piety and sociability (*2:231–52*). In contrast, the Hurons are "The last poor remnant of a race gone by"; "Heirs of a Continent," they have been forced off their "rightful soil" by the "force or guile" of "intruders" and reduced either to selling "venal trinkets" or to outright begging (*2:252–78*), an observation that seems less consonant with the state of the Native peoples in Quebec shortly after the War of 1812 than with their deteriorated condition in the late thirties when Kirby was given a tour of the city by John Neilson and others (Riddell, *Kirby* 7–8). Only marginally less attractive than Quebec for its combination of "Commerce" and religion, Montreal occasions dark thoughts of political "factions" and "civil discords" that, again, seem more apposite to Kirby's than Walwyn's time and indeed may indicate that this portion of the poem was written after the *Counter Manifesto to the Annexationists of Montreal*. Kirby's parting advice to "estranged" Montrealers is to "Think ... of the day" when French and English Canadians fought "side by side in woody Chateauguay ... and ... rolled invasion off [their] native plains" (*2:365–414*).

As Walwyn and his sons depart Montreal for the "fertile West" the scenery to come is likened to "some vast panorama's glorious show" (*2:417, 427*), a comparison which admits the possibility that Kirby at least knew of Burr's "Moving Panorama" of the scenery along the St. Lawrence River system. Be this as it may, the portion of the poem that follows the steamer's passage into the "upper land" is of considerable structural importance for its adumbration of things to come both geographically and historically. Not only do the language, laws, and place names of Upper Canada proclaim the province a congenial destination for British emigrants (*2:421–24*), but so too does the "Hospitality" of the "Glengarry ... Highland race" remarked by Howison (19–21; *2:487–514*). Even the "nobler oaks and spreading maples" of Upper Canada (*2:471*) – the former an emblem of England (*1:145*) and the latter a source of "liquid honey ... / Sweet as the cane that waves 'neath India's sun!" (*3:249–50*) – speak of British values and natural bounty. But there are also sights and signs that foreshadow darker things to come. At the "Indian settlement ... of St. Regis" (Heriot 123), the St. Lawrence River becomes "a mighty barrier" between "rival states" (*2:522*) and "On Prescott's soft declivities" – the site of the Battle of the Windmill – "the lithe / And flowing grass waves deep, ripe for the scythe" (*2:533–34*). Although the Swedenborgian "angels" who "guard" Ethwald and Eric spare the brothers a "prophetic" look into "The future horrors of this lovely scene" (*2:531–48*), Constance is less fortunate. As the brothers pass Prescott, and before her "holy watchers see her writhe in pain, / Divine the cause and stop delusion's reign," she is visited in a dream by "spirits" who allow her to glimpse the "battlefield" upon which Ethwald

will die "for his country ... in his bloom of years" (*2:549–78*). More blatantly than coincidence in a Dickens novel, this Swedenborgian interlude indicates the operation in human life of a "great design" (*10:512*)
that is not entirely inscrutable or ultimately cruel though it can be a
cause of destruction and distress.

Past the Thousand Islands on Lake Ontario, Kingston ("Our country's hope and trust, in danger's day" [*3:138*]), is given short shrift relative to Toronto ("the rightful Queen" among "rival cities of our land"
[*3:159–60*]), and both are bypassed for "Burlington's projected strand,
/ The ancient fastness of our Western land" (*3:201–10*). Here, Kirby
provides a lengthy description of the "rising city" of Hamilton, a busy
hive of "Fashion," "industry," and "trade" where "The Indian war-path
ran but yesterday / And fox and wolf their nightly discord made"
(*3:175–98*). Here, too, he compares John Harvey's decisive attack on an
invading American force at Stoney Creek in June 1813 to Leonides' courageous resistance to the invading Persians at Thermopylae in 480 BC
(*3:203–22*). Not far from this hallowed ground is "the detached place /
By Walwyn fixed to run his future race": a fertile, well-watered tract of
land forested, predictably, with "stately oaks" and "the rich maple"
(*3:233–80*). Initially the "Deep silence" of the forest engenders a
"strange and vacant fear," and then its daunting luxuriance provokes a
nostalgic yearning for "Swaledale's meadows" and the "oppressive
thought" that, at fifty, Walwyn is inadequate to the task of clearing his
land (*3:261–96*). But an "hour of prayer" dispels these misgivings and,
as if in answer to an entreaty, there suddenly appears from the forest
the "aged man, of stature large and strong," whose family and future are
destined to be intertwined with Walwyn's (*3:303–34*).

As intimated by his very apparel – "quilled mocassins," "a wampum
girdle," and "A simple suit of home-spun grey" (*3:339–41*) – Ranger
John is the most complex character in *The U.E.* Modeled in part on Kirby's father-in-law John Whitmore, a Loyalist who was adopted by "Delaware rebel Indians" following the murder of his family and survived to
die at "a great age" in 1853 (*Annals* 211–13), he also carries the name
of John Clement, a Loyalist "who took up a large tract of land in the
township [of Niagara]" after being "a most conspicuous and active
leader of the Northern Confederate Indians, an embodied force whose
services in scouting and hunting down the rebel bands of partizans and
Sons of Liberty were a striking feature of the [revolutionary] war." In
Kirby's words still, "Captain John Clement caught and destroyed a large
body of partizans under a noted rebel leader, Captain Bull. He acquired
the name of Ranger John, and as such is referred to in ... the U.E."
(*Annals* 85). Since the tale of the American Revolution that Ranger

John tells in Canto 4 also resembles the stories of two other Loyalists, Daniel and Jacob Servos, whose exploits Kirby chronicles in detail in *The United Empire Loyalists of Canada, Illustrated by Memorials of the Servos Family* (1884), it asks to "be taken as fairly representative of [the experience] of thousands of American Loyalists" (19). As Ranger John himself says at the conclusion of his narrative: "Such ... is my true tale of yore, / And that of many a dweller of this shore" (*4:445–46*).

At heart Ranger John's tale is an attempt to correct the Whig or Republican bias of most American interpretations of the events of 1776–83. "No unmilitary excesses were committed by the Loyalists or Indians" at the "alleged massacre of Wyoming" in 1778, asserts Kirby in *Annals of Niagara* (55). By depicting Joseph Brant as a monster in *Gertrude of Wyoming*, Campbell shows himself to be "a bitter Whig partizan" (56). Such men as "Lithe Servos" (*4:243*) and "Hawk-eyed Clement" (*4:247*), Sir William Johnson and Sir John Butler (of Butler's Rangers) were "brave and self-sacrificing" defenders of "the unity of the Empire" (*The United Empire Loyalists* 19). To judge by Ranger John's "true tale," they were also driven by the American rebels to acts of spectacular and – this is Kirby's contention – fully justified savagery. "By nature just ... kind, / ... frank ... truthful," and "noble" (*3:355–57*), Ranger John was launched on the downward journey to ignoble savagery when, as a Tory, he was "Marked out for vengeance by the rebel clan" (*4:56*). He reaches his nadir when, in a scene reminiscent of the massacre at Fort Michilimackinac, he kills the rebel Woodworth, scalps him, and, "mad with rage and hunger, [takes] ... bread / Stained with his blood and spitefully" eats it (*4:319–20, 335–36*). This Wacoustan descent to the lowest of the four stages of social development gains momentum with Ranger John's discovery of the bones of his murdered father, children, and wife Gertrude. "What could I do?," he asks, "my soul with madness raved";

> Revenge, revenge alone, my spirit craved.
> I donned the costume of the Indian race,
> And with the war-paint hideous stained my face.
> Then drew the hatchet and the scalping knife.
> And never, never, spared a rebel's life!
>
> (*4:169–76*)

Joining forces with "Oneida Joseph" and other Native chiefs, Ranger John is but one of many "white men, who to Indian arts, / United giant strength and steadfast hearts; / Whose butchered kindred ... cried for vengeance on the traitor race" (*4:235–38*). So immersed in savagery does Ranger John become that after exacting revenge on the murderer of his family he reenacts his triumph at a war dance, which, like Howe and Richardson, Kirby elaborates from Weld (*4:343–88;* 2:292–94). "Grief and revenge my childless bosom steeled," recalls Ranger John, "And as I told my tale, my trophy showed, / Neel Good! in thunder tones, burst from the approving crowd" (*4:352–54*). Ranger John's "Grief and ... childless bosom" attach whatever blame his behaviour merits to the rebels who murdered his family. To borrow a phrase applied to Le Gardeur in *The Golden Dog:* "he was more sinned against than sinning!" (620).

Like "the old tomahawk of the refugees" in Kirby's *Counter Manifesto,* Ranger John's Native accoutrements are a sign that the Loyalists have neither forgotten nor forgiven the sins of the American rebels and would, if necessary, rise again in defense of the British Empire. Ranger John affirms this at the conclusion of his tale: "if e'er my king / Command the trump of war anew to ring, / These aged hands would still his cause maintain, / And all they did before, would do again!" (*4:417–20*). Moreover, he asserts, the "loyal spirit of their hardy sires" lives on in the "brave sons and daughters" of the Loyalists (4:447–48). To this Walwyn adds a few cautionary words – "Woe to the State that lets domestic jars / Grow to a head and burst in factious wars" (4:459–60) – which also reflect more recent and current events in Canada. A "Type of the deed of Cain" (*4:465*), civil war is a continual danger on a continent whose culture has been shaped, in Kirby's analysis, by the bitter opposition between "monarchical and ...   republican tendencies" (*The United Empire Loyalists* 3). The wampum belt around Ranger John's waist is both an aid to memory (Weld 2:249–250) and a support for a tomahawk.

No sooner has a house been built for Walwyn and his sons than the shadow of Cain falls ominously across *The U.E.* A genial wrestling match among "robust swains" (*5:14*) leads to a conflict between Ethwald and "the youngest-born of Ranger John" by his second marriage, a "burly youth" named Hugh whose "rude," "vagrant," "selfish," "spiteful," greedy and, worst of all, disloyal nature make him an obvious candidate for American citizenship (*5:69–114*). "I hate my home, my country, kindred, all," Hugh informs a violently irate Ranger John; "To-morrow's sun will see me leave these woods, / For Southern lands ... Freed from your kingly rule, I there will roam / In golden paths undreamed of here at home" (*5:125, 150–158*). Oblivious like most Tories to any conflict between freedom and authority, Kirby depicts Hugh as the repository of the "causeless ire" (*5:66*) that initially manifests itself in filial rivalry and "filial rebellion" (Duffy 56), the far from harmless forerunners of fratricide, patricide, and – an inevitable corollary of Tory paternalism –

the justified execution of a rebellious son. Merely in material terms Hugh is also wrong, as becomes abundantly clear when, in a vain attempt to prevent him heading south, Ethwald visits Ranger John's homestead. An Upper Canada equivalent of the great Tory houses of the English literary tradition, Ranger John's "vast" and "spacious house of solid timbers" is the patriarchal centre of a "rural paradise" of picturesque and "profitable beauty" "where all things goodly gr[o]w for the use of man" (*Annals* 146; *5:248–90*). Providing evidence of refinement as well as "plenty" are the "snow-white" walls of the house, the "Parterres of flowers," that surround it, and the cushions that soften its "chairs of solid oaken wood." But this is not refinement at the cost of virtue: within Ranger John's "Plenteous, cleanly, warm Canadian home," his three "pure," "modest," and "graceful" daughters dutifully spin, cook, and weave in "robes of russet brown, / Whose neatness shame[s] the tinsel of the town" (*5:291–334*). Homemade curtains, a "well-kept rifle," "The family bible and the book of prayer" further reflect the "daily industry" and "simple truthfulness" of the household. As evident as Hugh's egregious error in this portion of *The U.E.* is the extent of Kirby's longing for the lost paradise of the Loyalists.

In the ensuing canto, Walwyn and his sons set about transforming another portion of the wilderness into a thriving homestead. Frequently Thomsonian in diction and imagery ("Now ... seven times yellow wreathed with corn in ear, / Had Libra, in her balance weighed the year" [*6:27–30*]), Canto 6 is structured on the seasonal rhythms that govern all agricultural life. After seven years Walwyn's "unremitting labours" have pushed back the "woody circle" of the forest to create a "spacious plain" on which "Fair meadows ... flocks, ... herds, and yellow harvests ... bless his labour and restore his fame" (*6:33–34*). Under the combined tutelage of their father and Ranger John, Eric and Ethwald have grown "to youth and robust manhood," the younger learning to earn the "leisure" of "sylvan sports" through "rural labour" and the older preparing to fetch "His lovely Constance" to a worthy homestead (*6:45–106*). Both boys are successful in their endeavours because "rural wisdom" and "long experience" – the ability to think and act in accordance with nature's rhythms and tokens – passes smoothly from wise patriarchs to receptive sons, thus ensuring the continuation through time of a social system that is symbiotically connected to the natural order. Some of the flora and fauna in Upper Canada may be strange to natives of Britain and the United States, but for the most part Canadian nature does not belie Walwyn's agricultural knowledge or Ranger John's "woodcraft." Wild turkeys are still stupid and easily trapped (*6:67–78*) and "watery rings" around the moon still hold the "promise

[of] rain" (*6:259–70*). As constant and predictable is human nature: men enjoy a cup of cider and a ribald joke with lunch (*6:177–86*); women enjoy practicing the arts of seduction at dances *(6:409–60)*; and poets enjoy creating "pretty stor[ies]" – in this case an Ovidian fable about the "divine origin" of maize (Mondamin) based, perhaps, on hints in Henry J. Schoolcraft's *Oneóta* ([1845] 82, 210) and material in James Athearn Jones's *Traditions of the North American Indians* ([1830] 1:149–72; *6:187–226;* and see Duffy 36). Loyalist values and, beneath them, a rural continuity that subsumes change: these are the foundations and bedrock of the "happy land" which Kirby sees stretching "From Labrador to Nootka's lonely Sound" while "Southern stars grow dim beneath [its] rising day" (*6:254–56*).

The England to which Ethwald returns to marry Constance in Canto 7 differs from Canada mainly in the depth and extent of its ancient customs and traditions. Several references to Scandinavian mythology near the beginning of this canto (*7:23–34;* see Thorpe 1:11–19, 82; and Taine 1:42–43) anticipate the journey into Britain's racial and folkloric past that begins when Ethwald arrives on the island once colonized by warriors from "Scania's rocky shore." True to their imperialistic heritage the "mighty" descendents of the Scandinavians now carry the "torch," "seeds," and "runes," of British civilization to distant "tribes of men" (*7:91–104*). Both the natural and the social environments of England are steeped in tradition. The "still enduring oaks of ancient days" under which Ethwald plighted his troth to Constance have "heard the bearded Druids' mystic lays" (*7:115–20*). When the couple's wedding day arrives, "Fresh garlands and green bays the house adorn / As antique custom ordered" (*7:180–81*). After the wedding, they "scatter ... mystic cake in fragments on the ground" – "An ancient rite that from their fathers came / When heathen offerings were devoid of blame, / And Freya ... Propitious smiled upon the vows of love" (*7:223–28;* see Thorpe 1:32–33, 196–97). The church in which the marriage takes place under the auspices of an "aged Pastor" is itself an "ancient house" hung with "banners and ... shields" which chivalrically recall the more recent history of the race of "free-born yeom[e]n" at the heart of the Empire (*7:191–220*).

Kirby's climactic celebration of the "Connubial love" of Ethwald and Constance as a "mystic marriage of the Good and True" (*7:237–78*) owes little to English folklore and tradition, however; typographically insistent on the allegorical significance of *"the Pair"* as a recreation of "the great Archetype of "MAN," the conclusion to Canto 7 derives almost everything but its versification from Swedenborg. "That the male and the female were created to be the very form of the marriage of good and truth" is a precept elaborated at great length, not only in the *Arcana Coelestia* (nn. 2508, 2618, 2728–29, 2739–41), but also in *Amor Conjugialis* (nn. 83–92, and *passim*). "MAN" (*homo* as opposed to *vir*) is a central concern of the *Heavenly Arcana* and *Conjugial Love*, and "*pairs*" – inwardly married couples who are received into heaven – are repeatedly discussed in the latter work. "The golden chain of true connubial love / Joins earth with heaven and both with God above," Kirby explains before returning Ethwald and Constance to Canada. "Its links electric with [God's] grace o'erflow / And bind forever, all they bound below" (*7:275–78*).

Towards the end of *Annals of Niagara*, Kirby suggests that the three species of oak found in Canada – "white, black, and red" (35, 268) – typify the country's three main racial groups. Nowhere in *The U.E.* is the oak used in this way, but as the Hurons of Canto 2, the Loyal Natives of Canto 4, and the corn legend of Canto 6 indicate, the poem does in places dwell sympathetically on peoples of other than European stock. Reflecting Kirby's "loath[ing] for slavery" (Pierce, intro. to *Unpublished Correspondence* 23), Canto 8 is given over almost entirely to the tale of an escaped slave called Mango who, despite his unrealistically florid diction (Riddell, *Kirby* 32) and unfortunately botanical name (actually a reference to slave–trading: 'mangonizing'), seems to be based on Johnson Molesby (or Moseby), a slave from Kentucky who sought refuge in Niagara early in 1837 and who later in the same year generated considerable public attention when the Black population of the town thwarted an attempt to return him to the United States (*Annals* 230–32; and see the *Niagara Reporter* [14 September 1837]). Molesby's "escape ... to the land of freedom" is embellished by Kirby with an incident apparently drawn from the life of the poet's father-in-law. Just as John Whitmore had passed up the opportunity to avenge himself on a Delaware chief during the War of 1812 (*Annals* 213), so Mango forgoes the chance to kill the slave trader who has "bought [his] wife" when an inner voice reminds him, not just of the sixth commandment ("Thou shalt not murder!"), but also of his kinship with the trader ("'Tis thy brother's blood!' ... His sire was mine in sin and shame" [*8:306–28*]). After overcoming this temptation to fratricide, Mango lies "Weak as an infant, till ... / The heavy dews f[a]ll" and then rises to follow "the polar star" to the "distant North ... Where equal laws and equal freedom, fall / Like dews of heaven, alike refreshing all" (*8:329–50*). Before dismissing this depiction of a black slave born again into freedom and equality in Upper Canada as a manipulative white lie, it should be observed that in the careful symmetry of *The U.E.* the tales of Mango (Canto 8) and Ranger John (Canto 4) are directly parallel. Differ though they do in importance in the poem, Mango and Ranger John are equally victims of American cruelty and tyranny.

In addition to being a representative Canadian Black, Mango is the means by which Ranger John and Walwyn hear news of an impending American invasion to support the Mackenzie Rebellion of 1837. "Say know you not / The secret Councils held in yonder spot?," asks Mango as he proceeds to explain that, before crossing from the United States, he had heard "A band of armed men" planning to "Combine ... with traitors" in Canada to ignite "Rebellion's sudden flame" (*8:385–86, 397–402*). Predictably "The master spirit of th[is] riot crew" (*11–6*) – the principal devil in Kirby's version of the "great consult" in the second book of *Paradise Lost* – is none other than Ranger John's rebellious son Hugh. Playing Moloch to Hugh's Satan is Rensselaer Van Rensselaer, the actual commander-in-chief of the rebel forces gathered at Navy Island in 1837. When Van Rensselaer "declare[s] for war" (*11:360*) after the defeat of the rebels in Toronto, he threatens to undermine Hugh's council of "wise delay, and ampler power, / A braver leader and a riper hour" (*11:321–22*), and – true to the Miltonic parallel – calls forth from him the "deeper guile" necessary to bend the "fierce natures" of his fellow "ruffians" to his "iron will" (*11:387–92*). Also present at Kirby's "secret Councils" are Miles Gustaf Von Shoultz, the commander of the rebel forces at the Battle of the Windmill, and a Judas among Judases named Roughwood whom Van Rensselaer sentences to death by drowning in Niagara Falls. Not present but angrily denounced in the midst of a catalogue of *patriote* defeats in Lower Canada is the "Arch-Traitor" Papineau "who began the strife" and then "Fled ... to save his abject life" (*11:417–18*). That Papineau shares Hugh's Satanic associations is a testament to the protean nature of rebellion: as both fictional toad and historical snake, evil has entered the Canadian garden.

Supporting Kirby's fictional Adams in their heroic struggle to save the Eden of Upper Canada are a host of militant Eves (*9:51–72*) and loyal archangels. Conspicuous among these luminaries are Sir Francis Bond Head (*9:43*), Sir William McNab (*11:366*), and James Fitz Gibbon, the officer who received the surrender of the American forces at Beaver Dam during the War of 1812. The actual adjutant general of Upper Canada in 1837, Fitz Gibbon is honoured by Kirby as "The friend of Brock" (*10:51*), a supremely "noble ... title" which, like numerous other references to the War of 1812 and a subsequent invocation of Brock's "martial spirit" (*10:317–28*), serves to indicate that the defense of Upper Canada in 1837–38 is to be viewed as a further manifestation of the Loyalist tradition. "The war of 1812 established forever the position of Canada as a member of the British Empire," asserts Kirby in

Annals of Niagara; "it taught us a lesson which will never be forgotten: that a loyal and determined people cannot be conquered" (207). In the War of 1812 a legacy of loss and defeat was augmented by a heritage of military victory and political confidence. Of course the living link in *The U.E.* between 1776, 1812, and 1837 is Ranger John, the implausibly sprightly incarnation of the Loyalist tradition. "A Chief and Captain" (*10:39–58*), he surprises a troop of Kentuckians in an ambush consisting of "watchful Iroquois" and "Lincoln's bold militia" (the First Lincoln Militia: participants in the assault on Fort Niagara in 1813). After the skirmish he proceeds to describe in graphic detail the carnage at Lundy's Lane (*10:89–142*). In his "girdle" he carries a "bright tomahawk" (*9:80*). Later he is dissuaded "with difficulty" (Duffy 36) from burying this "bright hatchet" in the "rebellious head" of his estranged son (*10:425–512*). *Non mutat genu solum.*

The fact that Ranger John's tomahawk is repeatedly described as "bright" and "glittering" (*9:91*) accords with Kirby's very Miltonic association of the Satanic Americans with night and darkness and the angelic Loyalists with light and fire. "Minions of night," Hugh and his "midnight crew" are bent on doing "deeds as black as hell's obscurest night" (*10:284; 9:232; 10:372*). In a "pall of blackness" they meet by an "infer. ¹ fire" in a "pit of darkness" (*10:272; 11:105, 21*). Across the river, the ι. embers of the First Lincoln Militia are "fiery riders" on "fiery steed[s]," and Ranger John's success against the Kentuckians gives him a "kindling eye" (*9:34, 39; 10:59*). When Ethwald joins a fight in which he knows he will meet his own death, his "features gleam" with "light supernal" and Constance assures him that his "bright example" will be a continuing inspiration to their son (*9:284, 296*). Very much like Eden prior to the Fall in *Paradise Lost,* Kirby's Upper Canada is poised between the demonic darkness of the United States and the divine light of the British Empire (in Swedenborg's terms the darkness [*tenebrae*] of falsity and the light [*lux*] of heaven, truth, and the like). The light that emanates from the fire in the American camp is thus a hellish and "fatuous" falsification of the true light (Swedenborg, *The Delights of Wisdom* 77, 233).

In Kirby's imperialistic adaptation of Milton's cosmology, the equivalent of Chaos can only lie in the river that runs between Upper Canada and the United States. Before Ranger John, Ethwald, and their companions cross the Niagara to observe the "great assembly" on Grand Island, they pause for a moment to observe a "wondrous vision":

Niagara's twin-born Cataracts descend
And eye and ear with their contention rend.

A spot of chaos, from Creation's day,
Left unsubdued to show the world alway,
What was the earth ere God's commandment ran,
That light should be, and order first began.
                                    (*10:157–62*)

Taking his cue from Howison's perception of Niagara Falls as "a magnificent amphitheatre of cataracts" (93), Kirby likens them to the "Olym-
pic Stadium" during the final round of a chariot race (*10:171–74*).
Probably by way of the footnotes in "To the Lady Charlotte Rawdon,"
he then borrows from Carver's *Travels* to invest the "mingling ... [and]
dividing" of the "transparent" and "dark" waters of the Canadian and
American Great Lakes at the Falls with allegorical significance:

There, waves that washed Superior's rocky strand
And rolled transparent o'er her silver sand,
So pure and limpid that they seemed to bear
The bark canoe afloat in very air,
Now lashed to madness, o'er the rapids ran
Yoked to the darker waves of Michigan;
St. Clair's shoal streams and Huron's haunted floods
That trembled round the Manitoulin woods,
And fretful Erie's waters, in dismay,
Sweep white with terror down the shelvy way.
                                    (*10:179–88*)

Confirmation of the political implications of these lines comes in the
next verse paragraph, where Goat Island is seen as the site of "an eternity of watery wars": "Here, face to face, the sundered torrents pour /
In rival cataracts ... / Mingle their sprays, and with their mighty war /
Shake earth's deep centre with eternal jar" (*10:189–200*). "Thus every
figure to a thinking mind / Shows something more," observes Kirby earlier in the poem, "And Gravity might sit with pondering glance, /
Extracting morals from the shifting dance" (*6:461–64*).

  With debts now to Heriot as well as Howison, Kirby looks into the
"dread abyss" below the Falls and sees the uneffable "horrors of [a]
watery hell":

  pent in craggy walls that gird the deep,
Imprisoned tempests howl, and madly sweep
The tortured floods, drifting from side to side
In furious vortices, that circling ride
Around the deep arena; or set free

From depths unfathomed, bursts a boiling sea
In showers of mist and spray, that leap and bound
Against the dripping rocks; while loud resound
Ten thousand thunders, that as one conspire
To strike the deepest note of Nature's lyre.

(*10:201–12*)

"Here terror seems to hold his habitation," writes Heriot; "the simulta-
neous report and smoke of a thousand cannon could scarcely equal
[the noise]" (171, 161). And Howison: "the water boils, mantles up, and
wreathes in a manner that proves its fearful depth and the confinement
it suffers" (89). Like Kirby's Loyalists, both travellers view the "stupendous scene" (*10:213;* Heriot 149) from the vantage point of Table Rock,
but with quite different results. To Heriot "the effect is awfully grand,
magnificent, and sublime. No object intervening between the spectator
and that profound abyss, he appears suspended in the atmosphere"
(160). To Howison the effect is more complex: after glimpsing the
"amphitheatre of cataracts," his view is curtailed by the spray "and the
... cataracts seem ... to encompass [him] on every side." Then "a host of
pyramidal clouds rose majestically ... and each, when it had ascended ...
displayed a beautiful rainbow, which in a few moments was gradually
transferred into the bosom of the cloud that immediately preceded it.
The spray of the Great Fall had extended itself through a wide space
directly over me, and, receiving the full influence of the sun, exhibited
a luminous and magnificent rainbow, which continued to over-arch
and irradiate the spot on which I stood" (93–94). "Oft-times," he concludes, "volumes of snow-white vapour ... envelop ... [the cliffs of Goat
Island] in the effulgence of Heaven, and, as it were, isolat[e] the terrestrial elysium which they encircle in the bosom of the clouds, lest its
delights should become common to the rest of the world" (104). For
both Heriot and Howison, as for Weld (to whom they are both
indebted), Niagara Falls is the catalyst for an "extatic" experience
(*10:219*) in which the world and the self yield temporarily to a consciousness far greater.

Adding Swedenborgian mysticism to Howison's Romantic enthusiasm, Kirby finally presents Niagara Falls as more than either a "spot of
chaos" or "Creation's wreck" (*10:218*). To those whose "vision [is]
clear," who can "read ... the mystic runes of flood and field," the Falls
reveal a "marvel":

Amid the droning thunder's outer din,
Sound tinkling harps and harmonies within,
And on his throne beneath the rainbows seen,
Th'eternal Manitou sits all serene

With robes unfluttered, and with look benign,
In great Niagara's holy inmost shrine;
While countless spirits with expanding wing
Float round his throne and ever upwards spring,
In vapoury robes that waving to and fro,
Seek the bright skies and leave the strife below.

(10:218–32)

These lines may derive partly from Moore's conception of Niagara Falls as a haunt of the Indian Spirit in "To the Lady Charlotte Rawdon" and they may also owe a debt to several passages in Jones's *Traditions of the North American Indians*, where large water falls are said to be the residence of the "God of the Waters" and other "unseen spirits" (1:239; 3:282–85; and see Howison 77). Whatever the sources of the lines, the spiritual significance of Niagara Falls is not lost on Ethwald who, acutely conscious of his own imminent death, quietistically drinks "the vision ... / Into his inmost soul" (*10:234–35*).

But Ethwald is not the first of the Canadian brothers in blood and loyalty to "leave the strife below." That distinction goes to the second of Ranger John's four sons, Herman, who receives a fatal wound from his brother Hugh while attempting to save Roughwood from the "dread abyss" of Niagara Falls. This truly, if accidentally, "fratricidal act" (*11:174*) occasions some of Kirby's finest poetry: two mournful stanzas culminating "In all the silent agony of [a father's] grief" (*11:237–310*) and an extended elegy for Ethwald which ends in a Swedenborgian prayer to the "Angelic ones" whose "fragrant odour of celestial balm" permeates Herman's death chamber to "Teach me like him to follow where you lead"(*11:237–310*). The lesson has not long to be learned, for in November 1838 "the swains of Gallic race ... / Relight the torch of civil war" (*12:11–12*) and the prophecy of Ethwald's death fulfils itself in the Battle of the Windmill. At the head of the rebel forces are Von Schoutz and, inevitably, Hugh, the "chosen leader" of the "outlaw hordes" (*12:29–30*). Among the "hardy yeomen from Ontario's strand" who once again take up arms "To serve their Queen and country" are Walwyn, Ranger John, and a loyal quadernity of their sons: Ethwald and Eric, Hendrick and Simcoe. On the pattern of Wolfe, both Hendrick and Ethwald die at the moment of the Loyalist victory, the latter with "His head reposing on his father's knee" (*12:220*) in a patriarchal version of the *Pietà* that recalls Benjamin West's painting of *The Death of General Wolfe*. Characteristically, Walwyn accepts his son's death as an act of God to which "Reason submits" (*12:288*). Just as characteristically, Ranger John sees the deaths of Hendrick and Ethwald as further cause for "vengeance" and, drawing a "tomahawk, already dyed / With

crimson stains," hands on to Eric the bloody emblem of "the old traditions of the ... race" that "time cannot efface" (*12:292–296; 12:74–75*).

Meanwhile, in the stone windmill that has served as a makeshift fort
for the rebels, Hugh has experienced and resisted the belated onset of
conscience typical of (melo)dramatic villains as diverse as Edmund in
King Lear and Alfred in *Malcolm's Katie:* "down! fell conscience! let thy
serpents twine / Round other breasts, in vain they gnaw in mine! ...
here at last I stand, / An open traitor to my land, / With scarce a wish
beyond the speedy gloom, / And hoped annihilation of the tomb"
(*12:141–48*). Hugh's resistance crumbles, however, when he is confronted by Ranger John with the fact that he is the murderer of his
brother Herman, the one person for whom he "still could feel a human
smart" (*12:140*). Kneeling below his father's upraised knife and begging for forgiveness, Hugh becomes a type of both Cain, the fraticidal
brother, and Isaac, the obedient son. But before the merciless Ranger
John can "recall" the "life [he] gave," "God's compassion" intervenes in
the form of "A treacherous shot from Hugh's retreating band" that
stretches the contrite rebel "bleeding on the sand" (*12:366, 388–90*).
Not only does God's sympathy clearly lie with Ranger John, but it prevents "the noble Patriarch" (preface *10*) from perpetrating an act of fili-
cide while also leaving uncompromised his reasons for doing so.
Hugh's final words – "Forgive me! and I'll take the stroke of death, /
And bless thee, Father! with my latest breath ... Forgive me now!"
(*12:379–80, 391*) – do nothing to sever the close association between
God the father and father the God throughout *The U.E.*

In the closing scenes of the poem, the Loyalist tradition is again
passed on when Ranger John hands his tomahawk to his only remaining
son Simcoe, whose very name, of course, remembers forward the first
governor general of Upper Canada and, in Kirby's eyes, "the father" of
the province (*Annals* 121). "Thanks my father! look!," exclaims the
delighted youth over "The fatal weapon,"

> In truer hand than mine it never lay,
> And I will keep it to my dying day,
> Make it my last bequest and on it trace
> Th' eternal tokens of our loyal race ...
> (*12:426–30*)

With this, father and son leap once more into the fray to loose the
"storm of vengeance" on the "outlaw bands." "Thus ended Prescott
fight ... And all was gladness, save where hearts still bleed, / And melting tears fell o'er the honoured dead" (*12:439–46*).

Of the two remaining verse paragraphs, the first describes Walwyn and Ranger John consoling each other with their "tender memories" and "loyal heritage" (*12:447–60*) and the second envisages a perpetual and Edenic continuation of the Loyalist line:

> Old John sits in his porch, and robins sing
> Amid the apple blossoms, while a ring
> Of children's children cluster round his knee,
> Filled with the spirit of the old U.E.,
> Learning to guard, like him, in days of yore
> England's proud Empire, One, for ever more.
> (*12:463–68*)

This is Kirby's reassuring answer to the question asked of men such as Ranger John at the close of the poem's preface: "Cui Pudor, et Justitae Soror, / Incorrupta Fides, nudaque Veritas; / Quando ullum invenient parem?": "When will Honour and Justice's sister, / Uncorrupted Faith, and naked Truth, / Find anyone equal to him?" (Horace, *Odes 1. 24:6–8*). "The virtual disappearance of the first-generation Loyalists, [Kirby] implies, does not affect the persistence of the ideology for which they fought" (Berger 93). Presumably the tomahawk is being safely kept nearby.

16 Alexander McLachlan,
The Emigrant

From the lone shieling of the misty island
  Mountains divide us, and the waste of seas –
Yet still the blood is strong, the heart is Highland,
  And we in dreams behold the Hebrides ...
              "The Canadian Boat-Song"

Published in 1861, exactly twenty years after O'Grady's poem of the same title, *The Emigrant* of Alexander McLachlan (1817–96) is also an unfinished work. "The principal poem in the book is an attempt to sketch the history of a backwoods settlement," writes McLachlan in his preface to *The Emigrant, and Other Poems;* "the first part is descriptive only of the manners and customs of the old pioneers of the forest. The concluding parts (which will shortly be published) will bring the history of the settlement down to the present day" (2–6). For reasons that will become apparent the concluding parts of *The Emigrant* were never published and probably not written. As it stands McLachlan's "history of a backwoods settlement" consists of an introduction and seven chapters – "Leaving Home," "The Journey," "The Arrival," "Cutting the First Tree," "The Log Cabin," "The Indian Battle," and "Donald Ban." Like O'Grady's Canto 1, McLachlan's "Part First" charts a physical and psychological journey from the Old World to the New, in this instance from Scotland to Upper Canada sometime after the War of 1812. No less nostalgic than O'Grady's poem, McLachlan's *Emigrant* is less personal and more historical in its retrospection. From a post-pioneering society infested with "public robbers," "cunning politicians," and other undesirable types (*7:311–18*), McLachlan looks back to the Scottish pioneers of Upper Canada as exemplars of "simple honest[y]" (*7:310*) who simultaneously created a new society in the Canadian forests and perpetuated a Highland culture of the sort glorified (and, in part, fabricated) by Robert Burns and Sir Walter Scott. Like Kirby, but from a communistic perspective, McLachlan credits the founding fathers of his province with personal virtues and communal values that are in need of preservation in pre-Confederation Canada.

As was the case with *The U.E.* one indication of Scott's influence on McLachlan is the presence in *The Emigrant* of a verse introduction. A combination of full and catalectic (or truncated) octosyllables, the "contrapuntal pattern" of the introduction to *The Emigrant* (Hughes, "McLachlan's Style" 3–4) appropriately evokes both Scott's depiction of the Highlands in *The Lay of the Last Minstrel* and Longfellow's treatment of the Great Lakes region in *The Song of Hiawatha* (which is also prefaced by a verse introduction). McLachlan's Canada West is a "Land of mighty lake and forest! / Where the winter's locks are hoarest; / Where the summer's leaf is greenest / And the winter's bite is keenest" (*1–4*). It is also a densely forested land "Where the crane her course is steering; / And the eagle is careering" (*19–20*). Similarly, Scott's "Caledonia! stern and wild" is a "Land of brown heath and shaggy wood, / Land of the mountain and the flood, / Land of my sires!" (5:174) and Longfellow's North American "mountains, moors, and fen-lands" are "the land ... / Where the heron, the Shuh-shuh-gah, / Feeds among the reeds and rushes" (255). It is as if McLachlan has combined aspects of the two poets to create a Scottish-North-American style, a poetic manner consonant with the "Anglo-American" character of Upper Canada (Gourlay 1:247) and suitable to both his Canadian landscape and his Scottish pioneers. Since the brief history of British settlement in Canada is his theme, McLachlan ignores Scott's emphasis on ancient history ("Caledonia! ... Land of my sires") and Longfellow's emphasis on Native mythology ("the heron, Shuh-shuh-gah") and concentrates instead on the natural features of an environment in the process of development, a Canada West in which "the gentle deer are bounding, / And the woodman's axe resounding" (*21–22*). Besides supporting Edward Hartley Dewart's contention that the "adaptation of ... metre to theme is a feature of ... McLachlan's poems" (13), the "contrapuntal pattern" of the introduction to *The Emigrant* prevents the verse from "settl[ing] into monotony" (Keith 30) and thus avoids the soporific effect of *The Song of Hiawatha*.

McLachlan's perception of Canada West as a place lacking in antiquity – a "land" without "story ... tradition, tale ... song ... bards ... sages ... [and] old heroes sweeping by, / In their warlike panoply" (*25–32*) – recalls the views of Sangster and Kirby, as does his conviction that sufficient poetic inspiration is to be found in his natural and human surroundings, "the cottage in the woods, / ... [and] the lonely solitudes" (*35–36*). "Why seek in a foreign land, / For the theme that's close at hand," he asks, "Human nature can be seen, / Here within the forest green" (*39–42*). As Kirby puts it (thinking of Scott's "poetic impulse" from "green hill and ... blue heaven" [6:131]): "Let others far for foreign grandeurs roam, / Dearer to me the loveliness of home: / Our ocean-lakes ... / Our boundless woods" (*7–11*). But perhaps the chief precedent for McLachlan's orientation towards the local is a passage in one of the principal prose sources of *The Emigrant*, a passage that also lies behind Sangster's comfortable acceptance of the absence of "Nymphic trains" and the like in Canada (*The St. Lawrence and the Saguenay 58–63*). Of course the passage in question is the one in *The Backwoods of Canada* where Traill remarks the lack of "ghosts ... spirits ... historical associations ... legendary tales ... [and] hoary ancient grandeur in the ... [Canadian] woods" and resolves to find "amusement and interest" in the natural world of "forest ... [and] lakes" (153–54). Unlike Sangster, McLachlan is not content to elaborate Traill's sentiments into a touristic paean to Canada's natural beauties. A Chartist sympathizer prior to his emigration from Scotland in 1840, "the people's poet" (as he was dubbed by the like-minded Thomas McQueen in "The Poets of Canada," in the *Weekly British Whig* [11 December 1856]) makes poetic inspiration both democratic and agrarian:

> Poetry is every where,
> In the common earth and air,
> In the pen, and in the stall,
> In the hyssop on the wall,
> In the wandering Arab's tent,
> In the backwoods settlement ...
> (*45–50*)

The word "common" here is politically charged, for it designates the "earth and air" not merely as ordinary and public but as equally available to all – a common wealth for the common people. On the basis of 1 Kings 4:33, the "hyssop" is a type of the lowly or humble. As the moveable shelter of a nomad, an "Arab's tent" suggests a paucity of material goods. To apprehend the poetry in such things – to put the "pen" at the service of the "pen" – requires sympathy: "Have we but the hearing ear," / [Poetry] is always whispering near / Have we but the heart to feel it, / All the world will reveal it" (*51–54*). The repetition of the collective pronoun "we" in these lines draws the reader into the commonality from and for which McLachlan purports to speak, often, it transpires, with a sprinkling of Scots diction that aligns him by association with Burns, a poet renowned for his celebration of the "democratic spirit" and his "reverential esteem for simple manhood, regardless of outward distinctions" (Dewart 12).

To the extent that it highlights this prominent aspect of McLachlan's work, Dewart's designation of him as "the Burns of Canada" rings true (11). But to the extent that it obscures McLachlan's selective approach to Burns and his considerable debts to other poets, the designation can and has been misleading. Between McLachlan and Burns there were affinities born of nationality, political orientation, and similar experiences, but hardly of temperament. Burns was a Georgian with a penchant for treating of the sensual life as well as the natural surroundings of the Scots. McLachlan was a provincial Victorian whose post-Romantic interest in the spiritual component of external nature was grafted on to a strong Presbyterian stem. Thus Burns's "gowans" (daisies) and "burnies" (streams) find their way into *The Emigrant* alongside his celebration of humble people and his condemnation of oppression, but his bawdiness and debauchery decidedly do not. Moreover McLachlan tends to restrict his borrowings from Burns to portions of *The Emigrant* that treat nostalgically of Scotland and to go elsewhere for models when dealing with other places, peoples, and themes. As the editors of *The Poetical Works of Alexander McLachlan* indicate when they list Shakespeare, Wordsworth, Coleridge, Shelley, Emerson, and Tennyson (among others) as poets and thinkers admired by McLachlan (26–28), Burns is merely a very prominent member of a chorus of writers who can frequently be heard singing together in the medley of songs and narratives that constitute *The Emigrant.*

Although entitled "Leaving Home" the first chapter of *The Emigrant* is set, not in Scotland, but in Canada. Echoing the scene in the introduction to *The Song of Hiawatha* where the reader is invited to contemplate the "stone walls grey with mosses, / ... by some neglected graveyard" (256), it begins with an invitation from the "very last" of the "old pioneers" to sit on a "stone, / With ... gray moss overgrown" and "talk about the past" (*1:1–4*). The burden of the Old Pioneer's discourse is the permanence of memory in face of the transitoriness and mutability of life. "Men," "meteors" and the "fifty years" since the foundation of the "backwoods settlement" have "Gone like shadows all away," he proclaims in preacher-like tones, but on this, the precise anniversary of his departure from Scotland, he can recall "Every circumstance" of his leave-taking, for "There are things in memory set, / Things we never can forget" (*1:11–28, 87–88*). So permanent and vivid are such memories that they provide emigrants like the Old Pioneer with a means of preserving continuity and, indeed, identity with the Old Country.

As in most accounts of the departure of emigrants from their native land, the Old Pioneer dwells especially on the sadness attendant upon leaving a beloved landscape, dear friends, and close family. The time of his departure – a "lovely morn in spring" (*1:43*) – is well chosen both for its historical accuracy (most emigrant vessels left Britain for North America in the spring) and for its symbolic appropriateness as a time of new light and new life. Soaring above the Old Pioneer as he prepares to leave the Cart valley in McLachlan's native Renfrewshire is a lark, a bird that might simply be an emblem of the emigrant's high hopes if it were not also a "Type of the wise who soar, but never roam, / True to the kindred points of heaven and home" (Wordsworth 2:141–42) and, thus, a comment on the dubious wisdom of his departure for the New World. All around him are flowers – the blue bell, the gowan, the cowslip, and the primrose – whose names are nearly synonymous with Britain and whose rootedness in their native soil provides another reminder of the sources of vitality from which the emigrant will soon be separated. One of the most resonant passages in the poem is the Old Pioneer's summary of his abiding affection for Scotland:

> For oh! there is a nameless tie,
> A strange mysterious sympathy
> Between us and material things
> Which into close communion brings
> Our spirits with the unseen power,
> Which looks from every tree and flower.
> (*1:59–64*)

This is not merely a rehearsal of Scott's analysis of patriotic love as a "secret power" and "unseen chain" in the introduction to the third canto of *Marmion* (6:129–31), but the statement of a Romantic pantheism that derives primarily from Wordsworth, Shelley, and Emerson. In McLachlan the spirit of place is a local manifestation of the world spirit.

After recalling past communions with the over-soul among Scotland's mountainous "realms sublime" (*1:69–86*), the Old Pioneer turns his attention to his "grandsire old and grey," a venerable patriarch whose advice, McLachlan's editors claim, "simply" repeats the "address" that the poet's maternal grandfather gave him at the time of his own emigration to Canada (*Poetical Works* 23). This may be largely true, but it does not preclude the possibility that McLachlan drew part of the inspiration for the grandsire's "bless[ing]" from another of the principal sources of *The Emigrant*, John Galt's *Lawrie Todd; or the Settlers in the Woods* (1830), an influential novel-cum-emigrant guide set in the United States but written, of course, by the enthusiastic promoter of colonial development and sometime director of the Canada Company who founded Guelph, Ontario, in 1827. Shortly after arriving in North America Galt's hero opens a small pocket Bible and, with his thoughts winging back to his Scottish home and "pious" father, he lights upon the words "'My son forget not my laws' ... and ... read[s] on to the end of the chapter – the 3rd of Proverbs." "Now, reader," says Todd, "if thou art a believer in a particular Providence ... take thy Bible and ... read that chapter, and say if it was a vain enthusiasm which made me ... look upon it as a divine instruction how to shape my course" (1:48). Apparently McLachlan took Todd's advice, for, beginning with his "O my son, / I'd have thee to remember" (*1:101–02*) much of the grandsire's blessing to the Old Pioneer derives in word and spirit from Proverbs 3 and similar biblical sources. "Trust in the Lord with all thine heart; and lean not unto thine own understanding," runs Proverbs 3:5. "Trust not in knowledge," says the grandsire, "But always ask the guidance of / The universal father" (*1:171–75*). Observations on the limitations of secular philosophy and the importance of things "not taught at college" (*1:163–78*) add Shakespearean and contemporary elements to the advice of the Polonius-like old patriarch. A repeated use of commercial metaphors such as "be sure and leave, / A margin for reverses" and "Something ... is withheld, / To bring the balance even" (*1:113–14, 133–34*) aligns the advice with the combination of material and spiritual reward promised by the Protestant work ethic and by Proverbs 3:9–10: "Honour the Lord with thy substance, and with the first fruits of all thine increase: So shall thy barns be filled with plenty." McLachlan's own political and religious beliefs, coupled with his expressed reservations about the "sincere" but "misdirected" teachings of his Presbyterian grandfather (*Poetical Works* 336–39), suggest that the grandsire's advice to the Old Pioneer is to be taken with a grain of salt. Nevertheless it is the kind of moral and practical advice that must have "shaped [the] course" of many Scottish immigrants to Canada. As Charles W. Dunn points out in *Highland Settler: a Portrait of the Scottish Gael in Nova Scotia*, a respect for "the proverb, or, to translate the Gaelic term literally, the 'old-word'," was a prominent part of the folk-culture that travelled from the Old to the New World (52).

The second chapter of the poem – "The Journey" – begins with a jaunty ballad that combines the folksy and the Coleridgean:

> In the good ship "Edward Thorn,"
> We were o'er the billows borne,
> A motley company were we,
> Sailing o'er that weary sea.
>
> *(2:1–4)*

Anyone seeking an autobiographical component to *The Emigrant* would find it in the fact that twice during the year in which McLachlan emigrated to Canada – 1840 – the ship *Edward Thorn* crossed to Quebec from Greenock on the Clyde River in Scotland. But with its "motley company" and "weary sea," the "'Edward Thorn'" of *The Emigrant* is more than the vessel in which the poet crossed the Atlantic: it is the "microcosm" of a new society (Hughes, "Completeness" 184) and, as several echoes of "The Rime of the Ancient Mariner" intimate, a vessel carrying its passengers towards momentous events in strange places. "Our ship was a type of the world," says Lawrie Todd of the emigrant vessel in Galt's novel (1:33), and perhaps this comment, coupled with the use of a quotation from Coleridge's poem during an ocean voyage in Galt's second novel of pioneer life, *Bogle Corbet; or, the Emigrant* ([1831] 1:285), helped to shape McLachlan's account of the Atlantic crossing in *The Emigrant.*

Despite the considerable differences of temperament, background, and occupation among its members, the group of emigrants on the "Edward Thorn" is a cohesive patriarchal "company" or "brotherhood" (Hughes, "Completeness" 181) with a common destination and purpose – "To form *a* [single] backwoods settlement" (*2:28*). An obvious source for this idea of a community of emigrants lies in the Canadian sections of *Bogle Corbet* where Galt focuses increasingly on his hero's relationship with a "society" of radical, working-class emigrants who, "on quitting Scotland, had agreed to live in a community" in Canada (and, as it happens, follow Corbet "by a ship from Greenock to Quebec" [3:32, 2:226]). McLachlan's "motley company" is more inclusive and international than Galt's society, however; as well as including a poet (and surrogate for McLachlan) called "Little Mac, the jocund singer" (*2:18*), it comprises a somewhat Falstaffian Englishman named "fighting Bill from Kent" (Hughes, "Completeness" 185; *2:21*) and various other cameo "portraits" of the kinds of "*conceited ... blustering,* and ... *hypocritical,* as well as ... wise ... persevering*" people who make up any community. "Hence," continues the reviewer in the 16 August 1861 issue of the *Globe*, "the reader not only finds in the poem beautiful descriptions of scenery, and just views of the hard toils of men in the wilderness, but, also, and not seldom striking descriptions of human passion and conduct, which affords scope for representing the ludicrous and mean, as well as the grand and pathetic, as they rise from the emotions of the heart." In addition to being more diverse than the "society" in *Bogle Corbet*, the "company" in *The Emigrant* is also more democratic and egalitarian. Unlike their literary ancestors, who place themselves under the near-feudal leadership of the squirarchical Corbet in order more efficiently to build their community in Canada, McLachlan's emigrants subordinate themselves to no such leader and, in this respect, represent a truer "brotherhood of man."

While the "Edward Thorn" makes its way across the Atlantic, the thoughts and activities of the emigrants turn on two main axes: the "deep distress" that has caused many of them "To seek a home beyond the wave" (*2:39,42*) and the abiding affection that they feel for their native Britain. These feelings find expression in two songs, the first a satirical ballad from another Englishman, "Tom, the politician" (*2:16*), and the second a farewell song to Scotland from "Little Mac, the jocund singer." Tom's song, "Old England is eaten by knaves" (*2:47–70*), is framed by expressions of affection for its author's "country and race" and suggests overpopulation ("too many spoons for the broth") as the reason for the emigration. To this Malthusian point it adds as further causes of England's woes the heartless and self-interested activities of the "squire," the "Justice," and the "Bishop," a catalogue of establishment types that smacks of Carlyle's social criticism, particularly in its characterization of the country land owner as a figure committed more to "preserving his game" than to considering the needs of the poor (see *Past and Present* and *Sartor Resartus* 94). Little Mac's song, "Farewell to Caledonia," is less morose than such classics of the genre as "Lochaber No More" and "MacCrimmon's Lament" because it combines sorrowful acceptance with happy memories, and couches its bitter-sweet theme in a form reminiscent of Tennyson's "Go not, happy day," one of the cheerier songs in *Maud* (and, not coincidentally, one of the few Tennyson poems with North American content):

How bright were my mornings,
  My evenings how calm,
I rose wi' the laverock,
  Lay down wi' the lamb;
Was blithe as the lintie

That sings on the tree,
And licht as the goudspink
   That lilts on the lee;
But tears, sighs and sorrow
   Are foolish and vain,
For the heart-light o' childhood
   Returns not again.

(*2:113–24*)

"Laverock" (skylark), "lintie" (linnet), and "goudspink" (goldfinch) –
all of these birds appear in poems by Burns, and all of them, like the
Scottish place names in the remainder of Little Mac's song (and in *The
Emigrant* as a whole), were obviously calculated by McLachlan to evoke
the Scotland of the heart, an earthly paradise of identity that has been
lost by the emigrants and is in the process of becoming what it probably
always was, more imaginary than real.

   Given that McLachlan himself was an emigrant who had made his
way in 1840 from Quebec to a bush farm in Canada West, the most striking thing about Chapter 3, "The Arrival," is the extent to which it
derives from written sources. Scarcely a line in his account of the emigrants' journey to the shores of Lake Ontario is not indebted to some
degree to one or more of *Lawrie Todd, Bogle Corbet, The Backwoods of Canada*, and, perhaps by way of Robert Gourlay's *Statistical Account of Upper
Canada* ([1822] 2:iii), that old standby for pre-Confederation poets,
Weld's *Travels*. As the emigrants near their destination they encounter
"Lovely birds of gorgeous dye" which are "Coloured like the setting sun,
/ But songless everyone; / No one like the linnet gray ... No one singing
like the thrush ... No one like the gentle lark" (*3:93–101*). Predictably,
McLachlan's catalogue of the colourful birds of Canada concludes with
"the whip-poor-will," a "stranger" that sounds to the emigrants like a
"cuckoo" (*3:114–15*). Far from following Traill to the defense of Canada's birds against Weld's charge that "the birds in America are much
inferior to those in Europe in the melody of their notes" (1:195),
McLachlan repeatedly emphasizes their songlessness. This difference is
instructive because it highlights the extent to which McLachlan is bent,
less on helping emigrants to accommodate themselves to a strange
world like Traill in *The Backwoods of Canada*, than on stressing the dis-
parities between the Old and the New Worlds and, through these, the
alienation and displacement experienced by the Scots in Canada.

   For a short time after their arrival in the "trackless solitudes" and
"interminable shade" of the Canadian wilderness, McLachlan's emigrants are conceived as carefree campers in the "greenwood shade" of

a new Arden (*1:6,8,29*). Behind them lie the "heartless strife," the Hogarthian vices, and the class structure of the city; before them, a pristine world of "Hope," "Freedom," and wildly picturesque beauty (*1:30–90*). Yet as "Pioneers of civilization, / Founders of a mighty nation," the emigrants are also violent intruders in the "forest free" (*1:3–4, 25*), a fact that becomes painfully evident when Bill from Kent spies a "lovely hind" that has "Suddenly ... / Started up and snuffed the wind." "Instantly bold Bill ... / Through its brain a bullet sen[ds]," and the sound of his rifle scatters the panicked herd, "the startled quail," and the "partridge ... with all her brood" in search of "a deeper solitude" (*3:119–34*). The slaughtered deer is then described in a highly empathetic manner:

> There the gentle thing lay dead,
> With a deep gash in its head,
> And its face and nostrils o'er
> Spattered with the reeking gore,
> There she lay, the lovely hind,
> She who could outstrip the wind,
> She the beauty of the wood,
> Slaughtered thus to be our food.
> (*3:135–42*)

As remarkable about this incident as its pathos is its double ideological valancy. On the one hand, the instantaneous shooting of a wild deer for food shows the freedom of the emigrants from the game-preserving squires and laws of Britain (see Strachan, *Visit* 181 and Cattermole 10); on the other, it reveals the emigrants as a destructive and disruptive presence in the Canadian wilderness.

It is not until well into Chapter 4 that the most positivistic of the emigrants, Orator John, offers a resolution to this conflict between the natural and human orders by rehearsing the classic, Providential justification of colonization:

> "Invaders of the ancient woods,
> These dark primeval solitudes,
> Where the prowling wolf and bear,
> Time unknown have made their lair,
> We are God-commissioned here,
> That howling wilderness to clear,
> Till with joy it overflows
> Blooms and blossoms like the rose!"
> (*4:89–96*)

The obvious source of the emigrants' commission is Genesis 1:28 ("And God ... said unto them ... replenish the earth, and subdue it; and have dominion over ... every living thing"), but it is also sanctioned by another biblical text that is frequently quoted in the literature of emigration: Isaiah 35:1 ("The wilderness and the solitary place shall be glad for them; and the desert shall rejoice, and blossom as the rose"). Figurative as Orator John's rose may be, it is the imported kin of the "eglantine" that will later adorn the emigrants' cabin and of the "swine," "sheep," and "cattle" that will later fill their barns (*5:24, 75–103*). Perhaps because of his pantheistic leanings, McLachlan was more sensitive than most colonial poets to the destruction of the natural order that came with the European settlement of Canada.

When Chapter 3 closes, the emigrants have not yet laid low the first tree of the "greenwood shade," let alone begun to recreate the social woes from which they are seeking refuge, but they have already killed one wild creature and driven others into the hinterlands. Little wonder that at the conclusion of "The Arrival" – at the end of a beginning which is also the beginning of an end – the Old Pioneer sounds a note of *ubi sunt* whose reverberations spread outwards past human companions dead and gone to a natural environment altered beyond recognition and with results that are, at best, mixed. That the emigrants "Hail ... with joy" their destination on the shore of Lake Ontario, not with dawn's new light, but with declining day (*3:144–45*) is but one of many suggestions in the chapter that the progress of European settlement in Canada can be viewed in a darker light than the one chosen by the Old Pioneer as he looks out on what was once a "secluded bay." "Then it was a lonely scene, / Where man's foot had never been," he recalls, but "Now it is a busy mart ... And I love to sit and trace, / Changes that have taken place; / Not a landmark does remain, / Not a feature seems the same ... And of all I'm left the last / Thus to chronicle the past" (*3:148–60*).

Where man's foot had never been? Almost unnoticed, this line removes the Native peoples from the area settled by the emigrants and quells any anxieties that the settlers or their descendants might have about their rights in land. As David Hume says in *An Enquiry Concerning the Principles of Morals,* "where a man bestows labor and industry upon any object which before belonged to nobody, as in cutting down and shaping a tree, in cultivating a field, etc., the alteration which he produces causes a relation between him and the object, and naturally engages us to annex it to him by the new relationship of property" (125–26 n.).

The event that provides the title and focus of McLachlan's fourth chapter, "Cutting the First Tree," comes from Galt's two novels of pioneer life. "The day being fixed for the ceremony of cutting down the first tree in the market-place-to-be of Judiville ... we were summoned to the ceremony at sunrise," begins the pertinent passage in *Lawrie Todd* (2:56–62); and that in *Bogle Corbet* reads: "after we had felled the first tree, I proceeded pretty much according to the plan in which Mr. Lawrie Todd ... did with Judeville" (3:37). Not as unimaginative in his imitation of Galt as Corbet is of Todd, McLachlan makes the ceremonial felling of the first tree an occasion for thought and debate about the implications and future of the new settlement on Lake Ontario. "'Twas a kind of sacrament; / Like to laying the foundation, / Of a city or a nation," says the Old Pioneer of the emigrants' preliminary assault on a "sturdy elm," "But the sturdy giant stood, / Let us strike him as we would" (*4:34–38*). To raise a human order the settlers must raze a natural one. Their heroism is that of a collective David doing battle with a sylvan Goliath. Where an individual settler "awkward at the axe" (*4:27*) would have faced almost unconquerable difficulties, a group can succeed with relative ease and speed. When they "gaze ... upon the sight" of the fallen elm "With a consciousness of might; / And ... cheer ... as when a foe / Or tyrant is laid low" (*4:81–84*), the settlers become aware for the first time of their power as a group to perform the acts of pioneer heroism that are necessary to lay the foundation of "a city or a nation."

Evidently understanding that both physically and metaphysically trees stood and fell near the centre of pioneer life in Canada, McLachlan makes the felling bee in *The Emigrant* the occasion for three philosophical and political speeches that are each connected in one way or another with the tree or with wood. Least constructive of these is the speech recited by Lazy Bill from where he lolls on an emblematically "rotten log" (*4:41–68*). Delivered in "doleful accents," it is the speech of a fatalist who has "groaned upon the loom" as a weaver (and like one of the Fates), and become convinced that ordinary people are powerless to influence such changes as may, or may not, occur in their lifetime. "We'll never fell that tree!" he concludes at precisely the moment when the tree refutes his fatalism by beginning to fall. Especially when they work energetically together, people are clearly far from powerless to effect changes in the external world and in their own lives.

Much more positive and constructive is the speech of Orator John, a rousing paean to "honest manly toil" that is delivered, appropriately (and in reference to political stump-oratory) from atop the "stump" of the fallen elm (*4:89–152*). Sternly Protestant in his emphasis on a Providential design that is fulfilled by "Perseverence," "determined will," and, above all, hard "Work," Orator John argues that man can be master of himself, his environment, and his destiny. Likening the fallen elm to "Caesar slain" by Brutus in the name of Republican Rome, he sees in its felling a heroic example of the kind of hard work and communal effort that, when combined with right reason and personal abstention, will lead to divine favour and its earthly evidences. "He who'd be a patriot now," he argues (echoing the cadences of Bunyan's "Who would true valour see"), "Sweat, not blood, must bathe his brow." If the emigrants add "industry ... temperance" and "common sense" to a toleration of "each other's success ... and weakness," then "God's blessing can be got ... And ... we'll hardly miss / Health and wealth and happiness" (*4:141–52*). Hughes has suggested that Orator John preaches a "doctrine of individual success" that aligns him with "early capitalism" and isolates him from the group in a "self-sufficient individualism" ("Completeness" 179), but surely this ignores the communal emphasis of a speech in which "we" and "us" appear nearly a dozen times. Orator John stresses individual effort certainly, but he also lauds the personal and social values necessary to prevent the work ethic from becoming selfish, cruel, and unrestrained.

The third and final speech in "Cutting the First Tree" is a utopian "parable" that McLachlan puts into the mouth of a "teacher" whose name, "doubting John," reflects a degree of uncertainty about the ability of the emigrants to create an ideal society in Canada. Quietly expounded over the fallen elm, Doubting John's "parable" concerns an agrarian society in the distant past that is communistic and non-commercial in its principles and operations (*4:159–224*). In contrast to the selfish, amoral, mannerless, competitive, money-grabbing, and essentially savage society that he sees in the contemporary world, Doubting John's "happy land" of "long ago" is a society without private property, currency, "lawgiver[s]," and social classes. "They had neither high nor low, / Rich nor poor; they did not know / Such distinctions ere could be, / Such was their simplicity" (*4:168–76*). To Doubting John, the felled elm is an emblem of a world fallen from grace into commerce, a world that the emigrants should strive to redeem by returning to the "proper way" of his "happy band." "I can see no reason why / We might not unite and try ... To redeem the world from gold," he argues;

> "Each for all, and all for each,
> Is the doctrine that I preach;
> Mind the fable of the wands,
> 'Tis a fact that always stands;
> Singly, we are poor and weak,
> But united, who can break."
> (*4: 215–24*)

The nub of Doubting John's doctrine – "Each for all, and all for each" – has resonances in Marx's *German Ideology* ("From each according to his abilities, to each according to his needs"), Dumas's *Three Musketeers* (*"All for one, one for all, that is our device"*), Shakespeare's *Rape of Lucrece* ("One for all, and all for one we gage"), and two of Aesop's fables ("The Four Oxen": "United we stand, divided we fall"; and "The Bundle of Sticks": "Union gives strength"). Indeed a perennial philosophy, it also has numerous echoes in the thoughts and schemes of a number of communistic thinkers of the eighteenth century who may have influenced McLachlan, most notably Thomas Spence and his followers in the Society of Spencean Philanthropists, who urged the adoption of a form of agrarian communism as a cure for modern social problems (see Hughes, "Poet Laureate").

But the principal source of Doubting John's climactic use of "the fable of the wands" is surely a speech given by Bogle Corbet to persuade some of his emigrants to stay in Canada rather than move to the United States. "Many of you ... must have heard the story of the old man and his sons with the bundle of sticks," says Corbet, " – apply it to your own case. If you separate ... you will soon find yourselves as weak as each of the several sticks when the bundle was loosened – but if you adhere to each other, your united strength will effect far more with less effort than your utmost separate endeavours" (3:33–34; and see Costain 32–36). As illuminating as the debt of *The Emigrant* to this speech and the surrounding incident in *Bogle Corbet* are McLachlan's departures from Galt – his pluralistic presentation of political and philosophical options to the emigrants (and to the reader) and his accompanying refusal to place his settlers in the position of following a leader whose power over them comes, as it does in Corbet's case, from money as well as merit. Yet Corbet's ideas and leadership do receive the reasoned assent of his recalcitrant emigrants and, moreover, the women in the group play a crucial part in their discussion and decision (3:35–36), an occurrence scarcely possible in a poem in which only one woman is named and none is characterized other than by marital status. Perhaps because McLachlan's aim was to expound in a literal way the brotherhood of man, *The Emigrant* manages to be in different places both patriarchal and egalitarian. But if women do not figure prominently in McLachlan's bundle of sticks they are a necessary presence in the man-made structure that gives its name to the ensuing chapter. What, after all, is the edifice that provides the title for that chapter – a log cabin – but a large bundle of sticks shaped so as to shelter a human family?

The most immediately striking thing about "The Log Cabin" is the substantial and complex form of the chapter's title poem (*5:1–36*).

Expanding into the margins and sectioning off the page like no other poem in *The Emigrant*, the four, eight-line stanzas describing the log cabin are as rectilinear and interlocked as the building that they describe. Mortised together, as it were, by an interstanzaic rhyme, they are written in a rhythm – a hushed and anapestic tetrameter – that recalls Moore's "Ballad Stanzas," the seminal poem about a "cottage" set in the woods of Upper Canada. Since Galt mentions it in *Bogle Corbet* (*3:4*), there can be no doubt that McLachlan knew of the "tradition" that Moore composed his poem under a tree on the north shore of Lake Ontario. Until near the end of the century, a tree known as "Moore's Oak," stood beside the road between Queenston Heights and Niagara Falls (Kirby, *Annals* 128; and see Bentley, "Historied Trees" 5–6). Less apparent than Moore's influence but nevertheless discernible in "The Log Cabin" is what Harold R. Shurtleff calls "the Log Cabin Myth" – the iconic association of log (as opposed to plank or rail) cabins with the virtues, ambitions, and heroism of (North) American pioneers that developed in the United States during and after William Henry Harrison's "log cabin campaign" for the presidency in 1840 (188–215).

Although McLachlan follows Moore in mentioning the peace and "solitude" to be found where "the foot of the wayfarer seldom comes [near]" (*5:2–3*), the emphasis of "The Log Cabin" does not lie with "Ballad Stanzas" on rural retirement and romantic love; rather, it falls on the mainly happy sounds and effects of British civilization in the wilderness. In Moore's poem the silence of the woods is broken only by the tapping of a woodpecker. In McLachlan's, "the ringing sound of ... [an] axe" draws a "roving ... savage" to the log cabin, where his "heart ... is tamed" by the warm welcome of children who, like their literary ancestors in Traill's "Story of an Indian" (*Backwoods* 217–19), once "gaze[d] in affright" at the Indian but now rush "to meet him with wild delight" (*5:10–18*). In "Ballad Stanzas" all the flora and fauna are indigenous and non-agricultural, but in "The Log Cabin" several wild species coexist with "eglantine" and "corn," imported and agricultural plants upon which "Hope" – the hope for future prosperity – gazes "with ... rapt uplifted air" (*5:23–25*). The "noisome glee" with which the children chase and scare ducklings and cranes in the final stanza of "The Log Cabin" echoes earlier and more violent disruptions of the natural order, but, on the whole, the poem treats the emigrants' presence in a region otherwise inhabited by nomadic hunters as a civilizing and fructifying influence. God's commission is on the way to being fulfilled.

In describing the seasonal activities of the settlers in the paragraphs that follow "The Log Cabin," McLachlan draws once again on Traill, Weld, and Galt. "Just at the commencement of ... November ... we experienced three or four warm hazy days," runs part of the description of Indian summer in *The Backwoods of Canada*; "the sun looked red through the misty atmosphere, tinging the fantastic clouds that hung in smoky volumes, with saffron and pale crimson light" (127). "The heavens were swathed in smoke [i.e., mist]," run the equivalent lines in *The Emigrant,* and "The sun a hazy circle drew, / And his bloody eye looked through" (*5:64–66*). When winter comes, it brings terrifying packs of wolves with eyes "like fire-flies" (*5:94*) and "many merry meetings" around a "roaring fire" – "Social gatherings, [and] kindly greetings" (*5:105–06*) of the sort described by Weld in his account of the long winters in Lower Canada. But whereas Weld's French-Canadians "beguile the time" with "music, dancing, and card-playing" (1:391), McLachlan's less effervescent British settlers sing songs and tell stories, as do their fictional counterparts on "rainy, do-nothing days" in *Lawrie Todd.* "On these occasions, they were wont to assemble in the large shed to tell stories and sing songs for a pastime," observes Galt's hero, adding in his usual self-congratulatory way: "it was to me they were indebted for the suggestion, that every one should tell a story either of himself or some adventure that had taken place within his own knowledge" (1:202).

In *The Emigrant* a parallel importance accrues to McLachlan's surrogate, Little Mac, who, instead of telling a personal story like Todd, sings two songs arising out of the shared, Canadian experiences of the settlers. The first of these picks up the romantic component of Moore's "Ballad Stanzas" that was largely omitted from "The Log Cabin" and adds to it an egalitarian dimension and a Tennysonian cadence:

> But give me the cabin,
>   Tho' far, far apart;
> I'll make it love's dwelling –
>   The home of the heart.
> With some one to love me –
>   Joy's roses to wreathe;
> With no one above me,
>   And no one beneath.
>   (*5:139–46*)

Following this somewhat bathetic performance, Little Mac's enthusiastic audience requests the song of the "jolly hunter ... Who ... Wooed and won the Indian Maid" (*5:151–74*). This turns out to be a frontier version of Marlowe's "The Passionate Shepherd to His Love," with additions from a variety of other sources, including the Song of Solomon, Wordsworth's "Lucy" poems and perhaps Keats's *Endymion.* "O come my love! O come with me! ... My pretty bounding fawn!" exclaims the Jolly Hunter, "I'll deck thy hair with jewels rare – / Thy neck with rich brocade ... Then come, my love, O come with me ... Sweet flow'ret of the shade, / And of my bower thou'lt lady be – / My lovely Indian Maid!" Fanciful pastiche though it is, the Jolly Hunter's song carries forward from the previous song the idea that love can eliminate social and, here, racial barriers, if only by assimilating attractive "Indian Maid[s]" into a wealthier and more sophisticated European society.

When the time comes for the "elder ones" to contribute to the *ceilidh*, the focus of the entertainment shifts to the past, to stories of "the days when they were young" in Britain and to "ballad rhymes – / Histories of other times; / Of manners past away, / Living in the minstrel's lay" (*5:177, 181–85*). Probably drawing the bulk of his knowledge of "balladical lore" (*8:20*) from Thomas Percy's *Reliques of Ancient English Poetry* and John Gilchrist's *Collection of Scottish Ballads, Tales, and Songs, Ancient and Modern*, McLachlan gives to "old Aunty Jane" a composite of traditional ballad motifs drawn primarily from "Little Musgrave" and "The Gypsy Laddie." Typical of the tamer Victorian imitations of old ballads, "The Ballad of the Gypsy King" (*5:201–60*) mutes suggestions of sexual impropriety in its sources but (and perhaps in compensation?) retains a modicum of graphic violence. Whereas in "The Gypsy Laddie" a lady deserts her husband for a gypsy, in "The Ballad of the Gypsy King," she merely leaves home for her father, Lord Sempill (another element of *The Emigrant* drawn from McLachlan's native Renfrewshire: see Playfair 3:569–77). As in "Little Musgrave," the errant lady is gorily killed in "The Ballad of the Gypsy King" but by mistake rather than by design, and without the sadistic violence of the original (Percy 213). No Morris or Swinburne bent on confronting his Victorian audience with the extremes of sex and violence, love and death, McLachlan offers up the "mournful tones" of "The Ballad of the Gypsy King" as an emotional experience of the sort that in simpler and less artificial days made "tears ... fall like rain" (*5:197*) and may still so affect those who, as stated in the introduction to *The Emigrant*, "Have ... but the heart to feel it."

The anecdote upon which McLachlan's sixth chapter, "The Indian Battle," is partly based – Traill's "Story of an Indian" – purportedly took place in about 1816 when "a feeling of dread still existed in the minds of ... British settlers towards the Indians, from the remembrance of atrocities committed during the war of independence" (217). At that time a widow and her children were terrified by the "sudden appearance of an Indian in [their] log-hut" but, like their descendants in "The Log Cabin," quickly overcame their fear and befriended the Chippewa hunter. After causing similar panic ("Oh! to think I came here / To be roasted like a deer" screams Lazy Bill [*6:23–24*]), the Native peoples in McLachlan's highly contrived story soon show their intent to do violence to each other rather than the settlers, who, on discovering this, set off to witness a "duel" between a Huron and a Mohawk Chief with all the "delight" of Romans going to watch gladiators fight to the death in the Coliseum. Despite their various differences, the unstated point of both stories is the same: the Native peoples may at one time have been a threat to European settlers in North America, but they have long since ceased to be so. At the end of the very garbled version of their history in Ontario that constitutes McLachlan's "Indian Battle," the defeated Hurons (and, for all intents and purposes, the victorious Mohawks) disappear into the forest and are "seen and heard no more" (*6:90*). To judge by the amiable "savage" of "The Log Cabin" and the hospitable "Peter, the Chief" in *The Backwoods of Canada*, the few Natives who remained in the area north of Lake Ontario were a throroughly "tamed" and "childish" source of entertainment for women and children (Traill 288).

One indication of McLachlan's indifference to the Native peoples is the lack of veracity in his treatment of their history: the defeat of the Hurons by the Iroquois Confederacy occurred in 1659, not "shortly after" the arrival of the Scottish emigrants in Upper Canada (*6:2*). Another is his treatment of their chiefs in entirely literary and stereotypical terms. "Eagle," the Mohawk chief, is animalistic both in name and nature ("Agile as a stag was he," "Sudden as the panther ... Or the deadly rattle-snake" [*6:115, 165–68*]), and only the lack of a mellifluous and polysyllabic name differentiates him from the Megissogwon of Longfellow's "Hiawatha and the Pearl-Feather," another tall, dark, and well-armed warrior of European fears and fantasies (276–79). "Hemlock," the Huron Chief, is "A model savage dark and dun, / A devil if there e'er was one," who wears the equivalent of a melodramatic villain's black moustache or hat: a "raven's plume" that matches the "savage gloom" of his "eye" (*6:127–32*). Both are prepared to fight to the death for reasons that are never revealed because in the primitive and one-dimensional world created for them by McLachlan there are no real reasons to speak of, no complex motivations and ideas, only intense feelings such as "Hate" and instinctual reactions like those of the rattle-snake (*6:107*).

This is, of course, a world far different from the one inhabited by the settlers, and clearly one purpose of "The Indian Battle" is, as Hughes intimates ("Completeness" 184–86), to emphasize the peaceful, constructive, and *complex* heroism of the pioneers by contrasting it to the violent, destructive, and *simple* heroism of peoples at an earlier and "savage" stage of social development. As they initially and, it transpires, unnecessarily gather together "muskets ... pitchforks ... a dirk" and "axe[s]" to do battle under "*old soldier* Hugh ... In his *old* commanding mood" (*6:52–55, 47, 50;* emphasis added), the settlers are temporarily throw-backs to times and places in which the locale of heroic deeds was the field of battle rather than the field of agriculture. From the perspective that sees pioneer heroism as the true heroism, they are "mock-heroic" duffers (Hughes, "Completeness" 184) whose resolve "to do or die" (*6:65*) echoes absurdly the famous final line – "Forward, let us do or die" – of Burns's "Bannockburn" (3:50–52; and see also Tennyson's "Charge of the Light Brigade"). No wonder that what they witness in the "duel" between Eagle and Hemlock is a hand-to-hand combat reminiscent, not only of Hiawatha's fight with Megissogwon, but also of the violent heroism of medieval British knights and ancient Greek and Roman warriors. It is no more fortuitous that the gladiatorial Eagle and Hemlock are described as "lordly" and "herculean" (*6:112, 123*) than it is that their "duel" recalls the joust to the death between Richard of Musgrave and William of Deloraine in *The Lay of the Last Minstrel* (5:139–70). As the bellicose Lord Sempill of "The Ballad of the Gypsy King" confirms, the true heroes of *The Emigrant* are no more aristocratic than they are classical or military. They are the common people whose field of action is agricultural life and whose weapons are axes and pitchforks used for their proper purposes of clearing and farming land.

Almost as admirable as the pioneers in *The Emigrant* are the poem's custodians and creators of art, one of whom gives his name to the poem's final chapter. A Gael who is both versed and celebrated in "balladic lore," Donald Ban is the emigrant equivalent of the "infirm," "old," and "gray" "last ... Bard" of *The Lay of the Last Minstrel*, a figure who similarly ends his days in a "lonely bower; / A simple hut" (5:9, 205). Driven from Scotland with his family during the so-called Highland clearances – the depopulation of the Highlands by aristocratic landowners to make room for hunting and livestock (Prebble, Bumstead) – Donald Ban lost his wife and three sons soon after arriving in Lower Canada (*7:113–30*). "Heartless [and] homeless," he eventually found "at least a kind of home" in the emigrant settlement some twenty years after its foundation (*7:131–34*). In the ensuing years he became a familiar figure in the backwoods as, bardically blind, accompanied by his dog Fleetwood, and dressed in Highland regalia, "he wandered far and wide" playing the bagpipes for dances and recounting his "strange" adventures (*7:135–90*). His death in the company of his "faithful hound" (*7:231*) and the Old Pioneer is handled with a sentimentality that is abhorrent to the modern sensibility, but to anyone with the "heart to feel," it is a moving and appropriate climax to the first part of *The Emigrant*. As the reviewer for the *Globe* said in 1861: "the character of the Highland piper is ... beautiful in its parts; but the death scene is peculiarly tender."

Donald Ban's eviction from his home in the Highlands associates him with a man who may have been known personally to McLachlan: Donald McLeod, the author of the seminal document on the Highland clearances, a series of letters first published in book form in Scotland in 1841 as a *History of the Destitution of Sutherlandshire* and several times reprinted as Donald McLeod's *Gloomy Memories in the Highlands of Scotland*. The second of these reprintings was in Toronto in 1857, after McLeod had moved to Canada in the 1850s and settled in Woodstock, near enough to Toronto and McLachlan's home in Erin to make acquaintance with the poet a distinct possibility. In any case McLachlan certainly knew McLeod's book (see *The Emigrant, and Other Poems* 143) and, just as certainly, used it as a basis for his description of the Highland clearances in Chapter 8. Indeed, the emphasis placed by McLachlan on the burning of the "old roof-tree" (main beam) of Donald Ban's house and the felling of a "tall, lofty pine" nearby "to feed the wasting flame" (*7:63–70*) acquires its full significance only in the light of McLeod's account of the special horrors of the 1814 clearances in Sutherlandshire (the home, incidentally, of McLachlan's maternal grandmother): "the houses ... were timbered chiefly with bog fir, which ... by immemorial usage ... was considered the property of the tenant on whose lands it was found. In former removals the tenants had been allowed to carry away the timber to erect houses on their new allotments, but now a more summary mode was adopted, by setting fire to the houses! ... Timber, furniture, and every other article that could not be instantly removed, was consumed by fire, or otherwise utterly destroyed" (8–9). When he exonerates Donald Ban of all blame for his bitter condemnation of the perpetrators of the Highland clearances (*7:72–82*) McLachlan may have been thinking specifically of McLeod and his *Gloomy Memories*.

A somewhat pathetic composite of literary and actual characters though he may be, Donald Ban is yet in his own right a memorable and sympathetic character of some depth. At the heart of his characterization are two overwhelming and understandable emotions: nostalgia for his native Highlands and regret at having been forced to leave them for Canada. The two songs given to Donald Ban express these feelings of nostalgia and regret while also allowing him to transcend the Canada that he cannot in any case see in a sort of ecstasy brought on by an apostrophic evocation of the highland landscape and the hypnotic repetition of Scottish place names. "These plains are rich laden as summer's deep sigh," he concedes in the incantory opening stanza of his first song, "But give me the bare cliffs that tower to the sky ... Benledi! Benlomond! Benawe! Benvenue! / Old monarchs, forever enthroned in the blue" (*7:93–98*). Both the Old Pioneer and Donald Ban himself comment on the transcendental power of his nostalgic and regretful songs and music. "He'd ... play, / 'Till his heart was far away ... Wafted to the hills again," says the former, and the latter: "often I croon o'er some auld Scottish strain[s], / Till I'm roving in the hills of my country again" (*7:85–88, 107–08*). As in his "auld Scottish strain[s]," so in his sleep Donald Ban overcomes his alienation from Scotland, for as he says in his second song, "in my dreams / I see the blue peaks of the lone cliffs of Jura, / And wander again by her wild dashing streams" (*7:196–98*). "Yet still the blood is strong, the heart is Highland, / And we in dreams behold the Hebrides."

In his death, as in his life, Donald Ban illustrates the conservative truth of the epigraph of *The Emigrant, and Other Poems*, a line from Horace's *Epistles 1.27* that translates as "they change their clime, not their mind, who rush across the sea." Though "old, and blind, and maim, / ... [Donald Ban's] heart is still the same" (*7:219–20*) and, as he approaches death, his mind returns to Scotland. "Hush! the hills are calling on me, / Their great spirit is upon me," he exclaims, "Listen! that is old Ben More ... See! a gleam of light is shed, / Afar from Bennevis' head" (*7:255–60*). At the moment of his death, he speaks as if returning to Scotland with his lost wife and children, "Never, never more to roam, / From our 'native Highland home'" (*7:281–82*). From a Christian perspective this can only be a delusion, but it has a logic born of Donald Ban's character and probably should be taken seriously in view of McLachlan's spiritualistic leanings. The Old Pioneer's final assessment of Donald Ban's "soul" confirms the truth of McLachlan's epigraph: the man may be removed from Scotland, but not Scotland from the man:

> O! thy soul was like thy land,
> Stern and gloomy, great and grand,
> Yet each yawning gulf between,
> Had its nooks of sweetest green:
> Little flowers surpassing fair,
> Flowers that bloom no other where
> Little natives of the rock,
> Smiling midst the thunder shock;
> Then the rainbow gleams of glory,

Hanging from the chasms hoary,
Dearer for each savage sound,
And the desolation round.
(*7:295–306*)

Not inappropriately, this passage echoes Scott's description of the "naked cliffs," "loveliest green," and tenacious "wild flower[s]" of his beloved Scotland in the introduction to Canto Third of *Marmion* (6:132). The effect is one of identity between Donald Ban and his native Highlands, an identity temporarily severed but ultimately restored. The essence of the Highlands is moveable but not changeable. *Coelum non animum mutant qui trans mare curunt* (epigraph).

The final verse paragraph of *The Emigrant* brings the poem to an anticlimactic and provisional conclusion. "Much remains to be told" of the history of the "backwoods settlement," and "With to-morrow," the Old Pioneer promises, "we'll not fail, / To resume our humble tale" (*7:307, 323–24*). In the meantime, the listener and reader are offered an unpleasant glimpse of the corruption of the settlement from the outside by a poisonous flood of undesirable types whose principles and practices overwhelm the "simple honest ways" of the original pioneers – "quacks on spoil intent ... public robbers, / Speculators ... land jobbers ... [bad] teachers ... bogus ... preachers ... herb physicians, / And ... cunning politicians" (*7:310–18*). What most if not all of these villains have in common is a greedy and lazy self-interest that seeks to get more than it gives, to achieve wealth and status without the hard work, moral integrity, and communal responsibility that lie at the heart of McLachlan's co-operative and Presbyterian vision of Canada. Like the incompetent schoolmaster in *The Rising Village*, the "smooth-coated men" in *Malcolm's Katie* (*2:230*), and the treacherous suitors in both of these poems, they are the darkening edge of a nightmare which, if left uncontrolled, will destroy the bright dream of a fresh start and a new society in North America. It would seem that here, as in the deer-slaying incident and at the tonally ambivalent conclusion of "The Arrival," McLachlan's aim was to question the facile belief in social progress that characterized much mid-nineteenth-century thinking and writing about Canada. Indeed, the celebratory preamble to the first article in the first issue of the *Anglo-American Magazine* (July 1852) – a "brief résumé" of Toronto's development "which is equivalent to the statement of the aims of *The Rising Village*" (Rashley 25) – could have provided him with the foil as well as the programme for parts of *The Emigrant:*

dwelling in a city, whose every stone and brick has been placed in its present position, under the eye of many who remember the locality as the site of primeval woods, the region of swamp – of some who have seen the lonely wigwam of the Mississauga give place to the log-house of the earlier settler, and this in turn disappear, to be replaced by the substantial and elegant structures of modern art – we feel that we are justified in yielding to the pardonable, if vain desire, of telling the wondrous metamorphosis of forty years. It is meet that we should rejoice over the triumph of civilization, the onward progress of our race ... In no spot within British territory could we find aggregated in so striking a manner, the evidences of this startling change; in none should we trace so strongly marked the imprint of national migration; in few discover such ripened fruits of successful colonization.

("Cities" 1)

In *The Emigrant*, the "fruits" have "ripened," but they have also been spoiled.

Why, then, did McLachlan not complete *The Emigrant* as promised? Perhaps his heart was not in the project of chronicling the demise of the "simple honest ways" of his early emigrants. Perhaps time did not permit him to complete his ambitious project. Or perhaps both of these suggestions are correct, and in a very specific way, for in 1862 – within a year of the publication of *The Emigrant, and Other Poems* – McLachlan was appointed through the good offices of his friend Thomas D'Arcy McGee "an emigration agent for the province of Canada in Scotland" (Edwards, "McLachlan" 662). As well as occupying McLachlan's time with a trip to Scotland and lectures to potential emigrants, this appointment may have scotched the plan to up-date *The Emigrant* with accounts of "quacks ... public robbers, / Speculators" and the rest. To say the least, it would have been unseemly for an emigration agent to publish a long poem describing the venality and phoniness rampant in the sort of place he was promoting in his lectures as a destination and, indeed, describing in the same realistic but positive terms that characterize the central chapters of the first part of *The Emigrant*. By hard work and "steady perseverence," McLachlan told the Paisley Emigration Society in 1862, many poor emigrants from Scotland had done more than create for themselves a good life in Canada; they had become "true heroes." The cold of the Canadian winter is "very keen," he informed the same group, but "the winter ... is welcomed ... as the most enjoyable of all the seasons of the year for out-door recreations, and visits, and reunions, and festivities of all descriptions" (qtd. in Edwards, "McLachlan" 663). It is as difficult to doubt that *The Emigrant* helped to secure McLachlan his job as an emigration agent in Scotland as it is to doubt that, if he read sections of it aloud to groups like the Paisley Emigration Society, one section left unread was his concluding promise to chronicle the ascent of verminous characters and dishonest practices in his typical "backwoods settlement."

"He is now before us," reads a note in the "New and Important Books" column of the *Globe* on 17 August 1861, "let us heartily recognize him as one who does honour not only to the land of his birth, but also the country of his adoption." Published in Toronto by Rollo and Adam, a firm of "booksellers and importers" that specialized in books by and about Scotland, *The Emigrant, and Other Poems* was the last emanation until his *Poems and Songs* of 1874 of a Scottish-Canadian poetic identity that McLachlan had been constructing since the early 1850s. It was an identity that brought him many rewards. On a tour of Scotland after the publication of *Poems and Songs,* he was given sets of Shakespeare and Scott by subscribers in the town of his birth. At a banquet in his honour in 1890 he was given a gift of $2,100 by members of the Scottish-Canadian and American communities. After he died in 1896 members of the same community set to work raising a "modest monument" by his grave in Orangeville, Ontario. "Today a plaque in the Orangeville Public Library commemorates [him] as 'The Robbie Burns of Canada'" (Edwards, "McLachlan" 663). If there is justice in the world of spirits, McLachlan's soul rests in the mid-Atlantic somewhere between the Hebrides and Nova Scotia.

17 Isabella Valancy Crawford, *Malcolm's Katie*

Little is known about the life of Isabella Valancy Crawford (ca.1850–87) and less about the genesis of *Malcolm's Katie: A Love Story*. Born in Dublin, Ireland, in about 1850, Crawford came to Canada West in the late 1850s and spent the next twenty years or so living in Paisley, Lakefield, and Peterborough before moving to Toronto in about 1876. These movements were dictated by the activities of her spendthrift and probably dishonest father, a physician of dubious qualifications and competence, whose death in 1875 left his wife and family in severely straightened circumstances (Martin; Farmiloe). Already by this time the author of several poems published in the Toronto *Mail* (Margo Dunn), Crawford may have moved to the city with her mother in the hope of expanding her literary earnings and reputation. Certainly she was quick to begin exploiting the opportunities of residing in the commercial and cultural capital of Canada West. On 20 June 1876 she joined the Toronto Mechanics' Institute, the home of an extensive library, and by 1879 her poems were beginning to appear regularly in the *Toronto Evening Telegram* (Farmiloe 50–51). On the evidence of the surviving manuscripts and the prose sources of *Malcolm's Katie*, the poem was largely written between 1876 and its appearance in 1884 in *Old Spookses' Pass, Malcolm's Katie, and Other Poems,* the book upon which Crawford's poetic reputation rested until the posthumous publication of her *Collected Poems* in 1905.

"A book superior to the average milk-and-water run of colonial productions" (Harrison 202), *Old Spookses' Pass, Malcolm's Katie, and Other*

Poems was published in Toronto at Crawford's (and possibly her mother's) expense. Although well noticed in the *Globe,* the *Telegram,* and other Toronto publications, and more-or-less favourably reviewed by a number of prestigious British periodicals, the volume was a commercial disaster: "1,000 copies of [it] were printed for the author, but the book practically fell dead from the press, not more, perhaps, than fifty copies being actually sold" at "50 cents a copy" (Donald Bain, qtd. in Hale 113; *Globe* [3 June 1884]). Probably in an attempt to cut her losses and secure a readership, Crawford re-issued the unsold copies of *Old Spookses' Pass, Malcolm's Katie, and Other Poems* in 1886 with a fresh cover, a new title page, and some laudatory "press notices of the volume from various Canadian and English newspapers and other publications" (Hale 113–14). Evidently the scheme was not entirely successful because some eleven years after Crawford's premature death from heart disease on 12 February 1887 "a considerable store of unsold copies of what may be called 'the author's edition' [of *Old Spookses' Pass, Malcolm's Katie, and Other Poems*] ... was found ... rebound ... [and] put on the market by William Briggs," the Toronto publisher who would later produce her *Collected Poems* (Hale 114). "In her death," wrote Susie Frances Harrison, "Canada has lost one of her most original, powerful, and inspired singers, albeit unknown to the general public of the Dominion, and I very much fear to the literary few among us who sometimes give a passing thought to Canadian literature." Among the admirable qualities that Harrison finds in Crawford's "best work, notably 'Malcolm's Katie,'" are "scholarship," an "intimate knowledge of Nature," "a positive riot of imagery," "a wonderful command over various trying forms of verse," and the "deep spiritual strain ... that proclaim[s] the thinker as well as the versifier" (202).

As its subtitle – *A Love Story* – intimates, the narrative line of *Malcolm's Katie* is uncomplicated and melodramatic. A young pioneer, Max Gordon, plights his troth to Katie, the beautiful and diminutive daughter of a prosperous farmer, Malcolm Graem (whose name recalls that of a young highlander in *The Lady of the Lake*). While Max is away in the West establishing his worth by clearing a farm for his future wife, Katie is wooed by Alfred, a materialistic villain who rescues Malcolm's sole heir from drowning and then, Iago-like, attempts to convince each of the lovers in turn that the other has been unfaithful. Less resistant to Alfred's calumnies than Katie, Max is about to take his axe to the villain when Providence intervenes in the form of a falling tree. Left for dead under the "pointed" and "piercing branches" of this tree (*5:213–19*), Max returns to Malcolm's farm just in time to rescue Katie from a second drowning, this time in the arms of a thwarted and suicidal Alfred.

The poem ends with Max and Katie happily installed in their western home with her father and a child named Alfred "as the seal of pardon set / Upon the heart of one who sinn'd and woke / To sorrow for his sins" (*7:8–10*). In the dialogue among Malcolm, his daughter, and his son-in-law in the poem's final lines, Max reckons Katie superior to Eve and Katie credits Max with having a greater "soul" than Adam. As they amiably debate whether the "woods and wilds" of their new home equal or surpass the "sward ... [and] bowers" of Eden, Max and Katie seem set to live happily ever after.

Dismissed by many modernist critics as "a preposterously romantic love story on a Tennysonian model in which a wildly creaking plot delivers true love safe and triumphant" (Daniells 408; and see Pacey, *Creative Writing* 70 and Dudek 123), *Malcolm's Katie* has been viewed less harshly by writers sympathetic to the mythopoeic elements evident in its conclusion and elsewhere. From the perspective of James Reaney and others, the poem enacts a conflict and reconciliation of the forces of innocence and experience, a struggle between good and evil, light and darkness, summer and winter in which, as Catherine Ross argues, Max plays solar hero to Katie's vegetation goddess. (Thus the "pointed" and "piercing branches" of the tree that falls on Max become the equivalent of the tusks of the boar that killed Adonis in a classical version of the myth.) In an extension of these mythopoeic readings, Max and Malcolm have been seen as Herculean heroes, massively strong men whose roles are consistent, not only with the classical view of Hercules as "almost the ideal embodiment of the Greek settler" (C.M. Bowra, qtd. in Galinsky 20), but also with the nineteenth-century view of him as a representation of the sun whose "marriage to Hebe, the goddess of youth, whom he espoused after he had ended his labours, denotes the renewal of the year at the end of each solar resolution" (Lemprière, *Bibliotheca Classica,* qtd. in Bentley, intro. to *Malcolm's Katie* xliv). (Thus the "lion-throated roar" of the first tree felled by Max makes this event the equivalent of Hercules' first labour, the slaying of the Nemean lion [*2:148–65*].) Further light has been shed on the poem by a variety of feminist readings that have raised complex questions about the status of Crawford's heroine – Malcolm's "chiefest treasure" (*3:216*) and Max's "little Katie" (*7:27*) – in the predominantly male culture that surrounds her (Thomas; Bentley, intro. xiv–xxviii; Mary Joy MacDonald; Wanda Campbell, *"Bildungsgedicht"* 88–114; Relke). "In the trellis'd porch" of "The home of Max" is Katie a confined woman who has lost her independence of action and thought? Max is "twist[ing]" her "hair / About his naked arm" and her final words are "if I knew my mind!" (*7:3–4, 16–17, 40*). Or is she a wise matriarch with an ecological vision of her surroundings?

"Bounteous mothers they," she says of the "wild woods and plains ... Beck'ning pale starvelings with their fresh, green hands" (*7:31–33*). Could she be both a confined woman *and* a wise matriarch? No matter how these and similar questions are answered, it is clear that *Malcolm's Katie* is very much more than the *Love Story* that it superficially appears to be.

In praising Crawford's "scholarship" and noting the presence in her work of "little, if any, direct Canadian inspiration" (203), Harrison suggests that, like its pre-Confederation predecessors, *Malcolm's Katie* relies heavily on written sources. True to expectations these are of two kinds: the long poems of a selection of British and, in this case, American and Canadian writers, and one or more prose accounts of the relevant physical and social landscapes. In the former category the principal debts of *Malcolm's Katie* are to the long poems of Tennyson. A domestic idyll in the tradition of such works as *Enoch Arden* and *The Gardener's Daughter,* Crawford's poem follows several of its prototypes in focusing on the relationship between a widowed father and an only child. A blank verse narrative with interspersed songs like *The Princess,* it also draws extensively on the imagery of *In Memoriam* and *Maud,* particularly when comparing the attributes and affections of its hero and heroine to "jewels and flowers" (Waterston 73). Max's comparison of Katie to a "perfect rose" echoes the same phrase in the "Epilogue" to *In Memoriam* (*34*), for example, and his "daffodil apocalypse" (Reaney 276) – his sustaining vision of "Love" as "one great daffodil ... on which do lie / The sun, the moon, the stars" (*2:184–90*) – loudly echoes a famous passage near the beginning of *Maud:* "the planet of Love is on high, / Beginning to faint in the light that she loves / On a bed of daffodil sky" (*1:857–59*). That "[water] lilies and ... crocuses" also figure in *Malcolm's Katie* is scarcely surprising since these are two more flowers that "fall within the Tennysonian range of favoured images" (Waterston 73).

A marginally less pervasive presence in the poem than Tennyson is Longfellow. To "signal ... the passage of time" while Max is away from Katie (Waterson 75) and to associate his destructive and creative activities with the cycles of nature, Crawford draws extensively on "The Four Winds" section of *The Song of Hiawatha* as well as on the "Vocabulary" that the poet appended to his "Indian Edda" (Longfellow 615–17). Crawford's "South Wind" and "Moon of Falling Leaves" (September) are taken from Longfellow, as are such locutions as "Ugh!" and "Esa! esa! shame upon you" (*2:1, 61–62, 10, 108*); so, too, is the inspiration for her bantering exchanges between the seasons and her energetic depiction of the seasonal cycle. Perhaps Crawford hoped that Longfellow's signature on parts of *Malcolm's Katie* would endear the poem to the American audience towards whom she directed her fictional prose (Farmiloe v). Be this as it may Crawford's chosen medium of blank verse ensures that the "thumping trochees" of *The Song of Hiawatha* (Waterston 75) register even less in *Malcolm's Katie* than they did in *The Emigrant*. A juxtaposition of Longfellow's description of the South-Wind (Shawondasee) with Crawford's description of summer reveals some remarkable parallels and differences:

> From his [Shawondasee's] pipe the smoke ascending
> Filled the sky with haze and vapor,
> Filled the air with dreamy softness,
> Gave a twinkle to the water,
> Touched the rugged hills with smoothness,
> Brought the tender Indian Summer
> To the melancholy North-land
> In the dreary Moon of Snow-shoes.
>
> (Longfellow 260)

> "She [the Summer] will turn again and come to meet me,
> "With the ghosts of all the slain flowers,
> "In a blue mist round her shining tresses,
> "In a blue smoke in her naked forests –
> "She will linger, kissing all the branches;
> "She will linger, touching all the places,
> "Bare and naked, with her golden fingers,
> "Saying, 'Sleep, and dream of me, my children;
> "Dream of me, the mystic Indian Summer."
>
> (*2:118–26*)

The Crawford passage recalls Longfellow's in its diction, trochaic rhythms, syntactical repetition, and, above all, personification of the seasons; but with its "*ghosts* of slain flowers," "*mystic* Indian summer," and slower pace, it also exhibits the "spiritual strain" admired by Harrison. Moreover Crawford's blank verse is richer in adjectives and adverbs than Longfellow's trochaic tetrameter can be and, correspondingly, more languorously sensual – indeed, sexual. As a Victorian woman Crawford was obliged to write indirectly about sexuality (Poovey 42), but write about it she did in the Amerindian portions of *Malcolm's Katie* and in Max's floral descriptions of Katie (*1:27–34; 3:175–97*). In such lines as "She will linger, kissing all the branches; / She will linger, touching all the places, / Bare and naked, with her golden fingers" a poetic tradition dominated by male writers is refracted through a female sensibility and directed towards areas never before illuminated in a long poem on Canada. No doubt the impetus for this refraction came from Crawford herself, but the echoes of Elizabeth Barrett Browning, Christina Rossetti, and others that have been detected in *Malcolm's Katie* (Wanda Campbell, "Crawford"; Bentley, intro. xxiv and notes, 62, 69–70) suggest that her forays into male literary territory were supported by the examples of other nineteenth-century women writers.

The Canadian poets whose presence can be detected in *Malcolm's Katie* are Kirby and McLachlan. In Crawford's poem, as in *The U.E.*, the cycle of the seasons with which the destructive and creative activities of the settlers are synchronized begins with "Indian Summer" (*The U.E. 6:1–26*), and in both poems military metaphors are extensively used to describe the process of beating back the forest to make room for a "circle" of "yellow corn" (*The U.E. 2:227–30; 5:40; 6:30–44; Malcolm's Katie 1:81–115*). In both poems the brush fires of the settlers brighten the night and their dark smoke blackens the day (*The U.E. 6:39–40, Malcolm's Katie 2:174–81*), and in both wise patriarchs impart agricultural wisdom to receptive children (*The U.E. 6:119–44; Malcolm's Katie 3:36–42*). Most striking of all is the similar way in which Kirby and Crawford render their respective villain's crisis of conscience. "But down! fell conscience! let thy serpents twine / Round other breasts, in vain they gnaw at mine!" exclaims Hugh before admitting that he has "scarce a wish beyond the speedy gloom / And hoped annihilation of the tomb" (*12:141–48*). "Down, Pity! ... Get thee hence ... For thou dost bear upon they downy breast / Remorse, shap'd like a serpent," exclaims Alfred, and he, too, longs for the oblivion of "great Nothingness" (*4:235–59; 5:140–67; 6:88–113*).

Common sources or shared conventions may explain some or all of the parallels between *Malcolm's Katie* and *The U.E.*, but the similarities between Hugh and Alfred are nevertheless useful for throwing into relief several important differences between the two villains and the poems they inhabit. At no point in *The U.E.* does Kirby give the reader cause to admire Hugh, but in several places in *Malcolm's Katie* Crawford endows Alfred with physical and intellectual attributes that make him powerfully attractive. Gifted with "the fair, clear face, / And stalwart form that most women love" (*3:57–58*), he impresses Malcolm with his knowledge of "the ways / Of men and things" (*3:70–71*) and dazzles the reader with his analysis of the rise and fall of civilizations (*4:57–136*). An eloquent and consistent exponent of the materialistic philosophy that "give[s] to Chance, blind Chance, ... / The glory of [God's] work" (Cowper, *The Task 5:865–66; Malcolm's Katie 3:145; 4:76, 243–244*), he offers a critique of Max's conception of himself as a nation-builder that undermines the Providential foundations, not just of pioneer endeavour, but of human existence. "My axe and I – we do immortal tasks – / We build up nations," asserts Max, to which Alfred replies: "Nations are not immortal! ... Naught is immortal save immortal – Death" (*4:55–58, 136*). And when he envisages Katie drowning in his arms, Alfred is given some of the most memorable lines in the poem: "O you shall slumber soundly, tho' the white, / Wild waters pluck the crocus of your hair, / And scaly spies stare with round, lightless eyes / At your small face laid on my stony breast" (*6:108–11*). So memorable is Alfred as a thinker and a talker that his subversive ideas outlive his change of heart and bring to the poem as a whole an element of philosophical debate and uncertainty. Of all the villains in early long poems on Canada Alfred is the one who most suggests a sympathy for the devil's party on the part of his creator.

The similarities between *Malcolm's Katie* and McLachlan's *Emigrant* also throw into relief some important differences between Crawford's poem and its precursors. The "lean weaver" and the "pallid clerk" of Max's settlement who look "No[t] backward" to their sedentary professions but "forward" to agricultural prosperity certainly recall McLachlan and, behind him, Galt (Zezulka 237; *Bogle Corbet* 1:37). So does the prominence given to Max's cutting of his first tree. It could be Orator John rather than Max who "leap[s] on / The vast, prone trunk" of the tree and proclaims that "Above [its] ashes [he] will build [his] house – / No slave beneath its pillars, but – a king" (*2:161–64*). But Crawford's emphasis on the ownership of land ("mine and thine!", "*Mine own!* [*1:108; 2:229*]) and on the complex feeling that this engenders ("joyous anguish" [*2:227*]) is scarcely consonant with the communism of *The Emigrant*. Nor is the cutting of the first tree in *Malcolm's Katie* a communal act: on the contrary, and despite the presence at his side of a "half-breed lad" (the equivalent of Hercules' helper Iolaus), Max works "alone," felling trees and raising a house for himself and his future family (*2:165–66*). A hero in the (North) American mould of the self-reliant and self-made man, his slaying of the "King of Desolation" is a preliminary triumph of individual effort over social hierarchy. "All men may have the same / That owns an axe! an' has a strong right arm!" read the final lines of the last poem in *Old Spookses' Pass, Malcolm's Katie, and Other Poems* (224), and, as Allan Smith has shown, this statement accords well with the view "frequently articulated" in the late nineteenth century that "the farmer was the creator of the nation's wealth, the builder of his own world, and a natural aristocrat unrivalled by those whose position was owing solely to lineage and descent" (192–93 n.). The social ideal advanced by *Malcolm's Katie* is not the bonded community of McLachlan's "backwoods settlement" but the pyramidal family with a self-made man at its apex. That Crawford both advances and interrogates the ideal of the man with the axe as a nation builder should not be surprising since as a woman and a writer she was doubly excluded from participating in the myth.

To be a worthy occupant of the apex, Max must make himself not just financially but also spiritually: he must undergo a process of internal as well as external self-construction. When introduced in Part 1 of the poem he is a boy on the verge of manhood with all the aggressive confidence and gnawing insecurity of that age-group; he doubts the strength of Katie's love for him, but teases and condescends to her nevertheless; he admires Malcolm's achievements, but derides and scoffs at them; and – though he already owns "some dim, dusky woods / In a far land" (*1:114–15*) – his arms are merely "indifferent strong" because as yet untried by prolonged and purposeful labour. "Are you content?" Katie asks him, and his answer – "Yes – crescent wise – but not to round full moon" (*1:47–48*) – speaks of physical and spiritual growth to come through the first of several echoes of *Hamlet*: "Nature crescent does not grow alone / In thews and bulk, but as the temple waxes / The inward service of the mind and soul / Grows wide withal" (*1.3.11–14*). By the end of Part 2 a still "boy-like" Max has already achieved a measure of physical and spiritual maturity: his "thews" (muscles, but also, in a wider sense, mental and moral qualities) are "practised," and he is now described as "social-soul'd" (*2:240*). Clearly his ascent of the pyramid has been well begun.

Augmenting hard work as an agent of Max's *Bildung* are various degrees of suffering, from his pangs of longing for Katie, through the agonies of doubt caused by Alfred, to the near-fatal wounds inflicted by the falling tree. "With the constant yearning of his heart / Towards little Katie ... / His young soul grew and shew'd a virile front, / Full-muscled and large statur'd, like his flesh (*2:170–73*). With his acceptance of Alfred's lies about Katie, her "image" falls "Doubt-wounded ... in his heart / And [can] not rise to pluck the sharp spear out" (*4:192–93*). With the tree pinning "him to the earth," he is "Wounded and torn" and "bleeds and moans!" (*5:218, 226, 243*). A choric passage at the beginning of Part 6 glosses the sufferings of both Max and Katie in terms reminiscent of *In Memoriam*, where "Sorrow" is a bitter-sweet "Priestess" and "bosom-friend" (*3:1–3; 59:1–3*):

> *Who curseth Sorrow knows her not at all.*
> *Dark matrix she, from which the human soul*
> *Has its last birth; whence, with its misty thews,*
> *Close-knitted in her blackness, issues out,*
> *Strong for immortal toil ...*
>
> (*6:1–5*)

Sorrow, this profoundly Victorian passage concludes, is the *"Helper of the Universe, / ... – [an] instrument / Close clasp'd within the great Creative Hand!" (6:16–19).* "Deep, unspeakable suffering," writes George Eliot in *Adam Bede*, "may well be called a baptism, a regeneration, the initiation into a new state" (412). So it is that when Max has rescued Katie from drowning in Alfred's arms she sees "within his eyes a larger soul / Than [the] light spirit that before she knew" (*6:132–33*). As Max readies himself for the final, Christlike act of heroism that will put "man's triumph in his eyes" – the rescue of Alfred from the "white riot of waters" – Katie "cast[s] herself from his large arms upon / The mosses at his feet, and hid[es] her face ... lest the terror in her shining eyes ... prevent his soul [from] / Work[ing] out its greatness" (*6:125–61*). Here is a man worthy of the apex of the pyramid.

It is scarcely surprising that most of the male-authored prose works upon which Crawford relied as a scholar of farm life in the East and pioneer life in the West contain glimpses or vignettes of self-made men. Prominent among these are two books – W.F. Butler's *The Great Lone Land* (1872 f.) and J.C. Hamilton's *The Prairie Province* (1876) – which provided much of the detail in *Malcolm's Katie* about the "far land" surrounding Max's homestead (*1:115*). "The effect of sunset over these oceans of verdure is very beautiful," observes Butler in one of his famous purple patches; "a thousand hues spread themselves upon the grassy plains; a thousand tints of gold are cast along the heavens, and the two oceans of the sky and of the earth intermingle in one great blaze of glory at the very gates of the setting sun. But to speak of sunsets now is only to anticipate. Here at the Red River we are only at the threshold of the sunset, its true home yet lies many days' journey to the west; there ... the long shadows of the vast herds of bison trails slowly over the immense plains, huge and dark against the golden west; there ... the red man still sees in the glory of the setting sun the realization of his dream of heaven" (95). And a little later: "the sun resting on the rim of the prairie cast over the vast expanse of grass a flood of light ... The whole western sky was full of wild-looking thunder clouds, through which the rays of sunlight shot upward in great trembling shafts of glory" (101). As certainly as Butler's "oceans of verdure" lie behind Crawford's elaborate treatment the "wide prairies [as] deep-struggling seas" (*2:16*), his descriptions of prairie sunsets combine with elements from Tennyson and elsewhere to produce the following:

Who journey'd where the prairies made a pause,
Saw burnish'd ramparts flaming in the sun,
With beacon fires, tall on their rustling walls.
And when the vast, horn'd herds at sunset drew

Their sullen masses into one black cloud,
Rolling thund'rous o'er the quick pulsating plain,
They seem'd to sweep between two fierce red suns
Which, hunter-wise, shot at their glaring balls
Keen shafts, with scarlet feathers and gold barbs.
                                        (*2:68–76*)

No mere versifier of Butler, Crawford has transformed passages from *The Great Lone Land* into poetry that is "vivid, energetic, imaginative, [and] intellectual." To adapt another of A.J.M. Smith's comments on Crawford's best poems: it is as if "the very spirit of the [prairies] ... has passed into the imagery and rhythm of the verse" ("Our Poets" 83).

As much indebted to *The Great Lone Land* as Crawford, Hamilton also employs the "prairie ... sea" metaphor, but shows himself more interested than Butler in the mining and construction operations that he encountered during his journey by water from Ontario to Manitoba. As he travels towards "the western end of Lake Superior," he remarks in quick succession the "crushing mills" of "a great American Company," the "quartz and other mineral-bearing rocks ... that are found throughout ... [the] region," the "extensive lumber works" and "pile[s] ... of steel rails, ready for the track of the Canadian Pacific Railway" at Port Arthur, and the plans underway to increase access to Manitoba by "steamer" (3–10). In *Malcolm's Katie*, it is "smooth-coated men, with eager eyes," who

    talk ... of steamers on the cliff-bound lakes;
    And iron tracks across the prairie lands;
    And mills to crush the quartz of wealthy hills;
    And mills to saw the great, wide-arm'd trees;
    And mills to grind the singing stream of grain ...
                                        (*2:230–35*)

The reservations about these post-pioneering activities that are conveyed by the characterization of the developers as "smooth-coated" and by the personification of the "great ... trees" as "wide-arm'd" exists in tension with the "singing ... of [the] grain" and the dynamic rhythm of the passage as a whole. Apparently Crawford shared the ambivalence of Carlyle and other Victorian thinkers about "the Age of Machinery" that was simultaneously waging "war with rude Nature" in its quest for "spoils" and providing food, clothing, housing and occupations for many segments of mankind. It will be the task of "Political Economists," continues Carlyle in "Signs of the Times" (1829), to ponder "how wealth has more and more increased, and at the same time gathered itself more and more into masses, strangely altering old relations, and increasing the distance between the rich and the poor" (*Essays* 196). Nor are such misgivings inconsistent with the social ideal of the heart of *Malcolm's Katie*, for the successful small farmer – the yeoman – that Max works hard to become occupies a middle ground between poverty and monopoly or, in his own terms, brutalized "serfs" and imperialistic "Commerce" (*1:81–104;* and see Gagan 315). Crawford was no "Political Economist" but she well knew that making "war with rude Nature" to create a farm and to amass a fortune are two separate, but not necessarily unrelated, things. That is why the sounds of axes and machines are heard together in the slightly elegiac final lines that follow the passage based on Hamilton: "And with such busy clamour mingled still / The throbbing music of the bold, bright axe" (*2:236–37*). It is also why Malcolm's great wealth is regarded with suspicion by Max (*1:60–67*) and why Max's own modest home is associated with "the music of the axe" (*7:1*). By such means Crawford positions her yeoman ideal in relation to the spectrum of western development that was admired and advocated by Hamilton and others like him.

While *The Great Lone Land* and *The Prairie Province* must have been useful to Crawford mainly as sources of information about regions that she probably never visited, the two books may have contributed to other aspects of *Malcolm's Katie*. Both Butler and Hamilton allude repeatedly to Longfellow, the former in relation to the role of the birch-bark canoe in the seasonal activities of the Ojibway of Manitoba (145–46) and the latter in relation to "Lake Superior, the ... Gitche-Gumee of ... 'Hiawatha'" (3). Both envisage the West as a land of "rich[es]" and "Plenty" that is destined to be the "future home of millions yet unborn" (Butler 9, 230; Hamilton 96, 21). In *The Great Lone Land* Butler finds northern Minnesota already populated by a "portion of the 'down-trodden millions' who 'starve in the garrets of Europe'" (90) and in *Malcolm's Katie* Max is followed to the land of "Plenty" by "panting, human waves / Upheav'd by throbs of angry poverty, / And driven by keen blasts of hunger, from / Their native strands" (*1:208, 219, 201–04*). In *The Prairie Province* Hamilton concludes his chapter on the Red River with a poem that envisages the "Northern Plain" as "The home of thousands blest and free / From despot's rod, from priestcraft's snare" (33) and, as already remarked, Katie sees the "woods and plains" of the West as a welcoming home to "pale starvellings" and "fleers from the waves of want" (*7:31–38*). Of course the conception of the American and Canadian mid-West as "a poor man's paradise" (E. Hepple Hall 81) was ubiquitous in the 1870s and 1880s, but the evidence suggests that *The Great*

Lone Land and *The Prairie Provinces* were two of the channels through which the idea found its way to Crawford.

A third and equally important prose source for the pioneering portions of *Malcolm's Katie* is J. Sheridan Hogan's *Canada. An Essay: To Which Was Awarded the First Prize by the Paris Exhibition Committee of Canada* (1855). For the most part a general survey of its subject, Hogan's essay contains two sections – "The Early Settler of Upper Canada" and "The Farmer of Upper Canada, as Distinguished from the Early Settler" – that are more anecdotal, evocative, and poetically useable. Set in the "valley of the Grand River," the first of these seems to have provided Crawford with a basis for the pioneering experiences and attitudes of both Malcolm and Max. At the outset Hogan's settler is not even "possessed of oxen" to pull a plough, but he sustains himself among "tall pine trees, girdled and blackened by fires" and "stumps whose very roots interlace" with "great hopes of a large farm and rich corn fields" (25–27). "There is, happily, a poetry in every man's nature," writes Hogan, "and there is no scene in life, how cheerless so ever it may seem, where that poetry may not spring up." Thus the "lonely" settler's clearing is "a source of bright and cheering dreams" and his few "blades of corn ... [are] associated by him with large stacks and full granaries; and the very thought nerve[s] his arm" with the promise of independence and prosperity (25). By Max's account, Malcolm faced similar hardships with similar dreams: "He and his brother Reuben ... / Yok'd themselves, side by side, to the new plough," dragging it through "knotted sod" and "tortuous lanes of blacken'd, smoking stumps" in the knowledge they "OWN'D the rugged soil" and would eventually achieve "wealth and pow'r / And honest ease and fair esteem of men" (*1:71–88*). Max's own motivating dream is more modest than his future father-in-law's:

> "four walls, perhaps a lowly roof;
> "Kine in a peaceful posture; modest fields;
> "A man and woman standing hand in hand
> "In hale old age, who, looking o'er the land,
> "Say: 'Thank the Lord, it all is mine and thine!'"
>
> (*1:104–08*)

The allusion to *Paradise Lost* ("hand in hand") and the superadded rhymes ("hand ... land," "mine ... thine") indicate the presence here of a high ideal and a harmonious order. Later Max will transcend his world of "shanties" and "blacken'd stumps" (*1:210–11*) with his "daffodil apocalypse" and his dream of a house with "snowy walls, deep porches, and the gleam / Of Katie's garments flitting through the rooms" (*1:247–53*). When Hogan visited the Grand River valley several years after his first encounter with the early settler, he found a prosperous farm surrounding a "two story frame house, painted white" (26). On "enquiring of the man 'who was the owner of the property ...?'" he receives the reply: "'It is mine, sir ... I settled on it nine years ago, and have, thank God, had tolerable success'" (26).

In Hogan's "The Farmer of Upper Canada, as Distinguished from the Early Settler" lies a probable model for Malcolm, a man given to sitting in his "great farm house" and "Look[ing] out upon his riches" – his golden "corn-field[s]," his "peak-roofed barns," his flocks of sheep and herds of cattle and, most of all, his only daughter (*1:60–66; 3:1–9*). "He has plenty, and he enjoys it," writes Hogan of the Upper Canadian farmer; "plenty reigns in his granary, plenty is exhibited in his farm yard, plenty gleams from his cornfields, and plenty smiles in the faces of his children" (31), a statement also echoed in Crawford's comment that the "lean weaver" looks forward to seeing "the rose of Plenty in the cheeks / Of [his] wife and children" (*2:229–30*). After Max's awed but critical catalogue of Malcolm's achievements, which include the "voice in Council and in Church" of a "man of standing" (Galbraith 43–56), Katie insists that her father has "work'd for all" that he has accomplished (*1:68*). Although Hogan's analysis is hardly original, the terms of his assertion that "continuous labour, and the exercise of judgement and intelligence" are the qualities that "convert ... the labourer into the lord" (31) in Upper Canada raise strong echoes in *Malcolm's Katie*. Laziness is a guarantee of failure in a pioneer society, he observes, but any man "who is willing ... as the Yankees quaintly observe, 'to march forward to the music of his own axe,' may be certain of plenty" (31–32). "A pioneer of the forest, or an adventurous speculator, sets himself down, and says ... 'here shall be a city.' If his judgement be good, and the country around his imaginary 'Thebes or Athens' be inviting, the waves of population which perpetually flow westward ... verify his dream" (39). "I promise thee all joyous things, / That furnish forth the life of kings," sings Max's operatic axe; "For ev'ry silver ringing blow, / Cities and palaces shall grow! ... When rust hath gnaw'd me deep and red, / A nation strong shall lift his head" (*4:41–48*). Perhaps Crawford had Hogan's westering "waves of population" in mind when she envisaged migrants "spread about the earth" as "troubl'd, groaning waves" coming to rest in "valley[s]" irradiated by "sun-ey'd Plenty" (*2:192–208;* see also Burrows 7).

Just as Max and Malcolm are on one level representative pioneer and post-pioneer types, so also are the two other principal characters in the poem. "Reputed wealthy; with ... azure eyes / And Saxon-gilded locks" (*3:56–57*), Alfred is an "ornamental settler" (*A Year in Manitoba* 96) or a "feather-bed farmer" – an immigrant "accustomed to a life of idleness, luxury and ease" (Trow 60). As lazy as he is loquacious Alfred seeks wealth without labour. While Max works hard to prepare a homestead for Katie, he lounges about with his "pipe and [a] book" (*3:217–18*) on Malcolm's farm, scheming to acquire the old man's property through marriage to his only daughter. As Alfred says in a soliloquy that draws him by its very form towards Edmund, Iago, Satan and other calumniators, the passion that drives him is the love, "not of Katie's face, / But of her father's riches!" (*3:131–32*). Predictably his only purpose in going out west is to disillusion and deceive Max into believing that Katie has been unfaithful to him.

The social type represented by Katie is the refined child of a generation that, by dint of its pioneering work, has "necessarily but a bony hand and a rough visage" (Hogan 29). In Hogan's analysis, refinement occurs in the backwoods with the arrival during the post-pioneering period of educated families who impart "taste and manners" to their "rude" neighbours, thus teaching "manly but ill-tutored success ... to enjoy its gains" (30). The result is that the wives and daughters of prosperous farmers, and, indeed, the farmers themselves, have the same taste in clothes as "you see in the cities" (27), or, as Crawford states it, "such as win their wealth most aptly take / Smooth, urban ways and blend them with their own; / And Katie's dainty raiment was as fine / As the smooth, silken petals of the rose" (*3:24–27*). As further evidence of the combination of wealth and taste in the Graem household, Crawford cites "the prim-cut modern sills" of the "stone" house, its "Velvet and sheer" lawn, and the "light feet ... nimble mind and voice" of its young chatelaine (*3:20–26*).

But Katie's initiation into the "city's ways" is the result of "city schools" rather than refined neighbours. When Max left for the West, she was a well-read sixteen-year old with the self-confidence to challenge his pronouncements, not just about her father, but also about herself. To Max's flattering and sensual description of her as a "budding" rose with an as yet unrecognized "core [of] ... crimson and ... perfume sweet," she replies "O, words ... only words! / You build them up that I may push them down," and then proceeds to elaborate the comparison into a metaphysical conceit in which Max's heart is the "soil" in which she has chosen to plant the flower of her love:

> "I have made
> "Your heart my garden. If I am a bud

"And only feel unfoldment feebly stir
"Within my leaves, wait patiently; some June,
"I'll blush a full-blown rose, and queen it, dear,
"In your lov'd garden. Tho' I be a bud,
"My roots strike deep, and torn from that dear soil
"Would shriek like mandrakes – those witch things I read
"Of in your quaint old books."

$(1:39–47)$

This passage is redolent with echoes of the literature of love from the Song of Solomon and *Romeo and Juliet* to *In Memoriam* and *Maud*, but at its centre is a characterization of Katie as the knowledgeable "queen" of a "garden" that is strikingly reminiscent of John Ruskin's (in)famous discussion of female education and potential in "Of Queens' Gardens" (1871 f.). An invitation to "consider ... what special portion or kind of ... royal authority, arising out of noble education, may rightly be possessed by women; and how far they ... are called to a true queenly power, – not in their household merely, but over all within their sphere," Ruskin's lecture repeatedly likens women to delicate plants and animals: a girl "grows as a flower does," and "flowers only flourish rightly in the garden of someone who loves them"; a girl is a "fawn" who should be let loose in a library of good books as into a nurturing field; and in the climactic conclusion of the lecture, after several quotations from *Maud*, a girl is a "vine" whose "tendrils" are to be guided and whose "tender grapes" are to be protected (103, 118, 120). It is surely no coincidence that in Part 3 of *Malcolm's Katie* Katie is compared to a "healthy, lovely vine" upon which hang both the "blossoms" of her city education and the "fruit" of her agricultural knowledge *(3:30–31)*. Katie now has "her sceptre in her hand," comments Crawford, "And wield[s] it right queenly here and there" *(3:32–33)*.

It is easy to see why "Of Queens' Gardens" has caused controversy among feminist critics (Millet 88–108; Auerbach 58–61). On the one hand, it argues for innate sexual differences and roles: "the man's power is active; defensive. He is eminently the doer, the creator, the discoverer, the defender ... But the woman's power is for rule ... for sweet ordering, arrangement, and decision. She sees the qualities of things, their claims, and their places. Her great function is Praise ... She must be enduringly, incorrupting good; instinctively, infallibly wise – wise, not for self-development, but for self-renunciation: wise, not that she may set herself above her husband, but that she may never fail from his side" (91, 93). On the other hand, it implies that gender roles and spheres are not immutable: no firm line exists between the sheltered, feminine realm of the "home" and "garden" and the "open world" in which men encounter "peril and trial," for "wherever the true wife comes ... home is always around her ... and for a noble woman it stretches far round her ... shedding its quiet light ... for those who else were homeless" (91–92). Wise self-renunciation leading to expansive beneficence: unpalatable as it may be to many modern readers, this is the goal that shapes female education and development in "Of Queens' Gardens" and *Malcolm's Katie*.

Perhaps from the moment that she accepts Max's ring in the opening lines of the poem, and certainly from the time that she bids his axe "God speed" with "pray'rful palms close seal'd" (*1:136*), Katie allows her actions and thoughts to be subordinated to the rules that governed the roles and spheres of the sexes in middle-class Victorian society. Making no attempt to accompany Max she accedes to the "gendered process" of pioneering that begins "for men with a solitary experiment in distant lands [and] for women with a long interlude between two worlds ... wait[ing] word that it is safe to follow" (Parr 529). While Max is actively engaged in creating a homestead, Katie will secure her father's approval of their marriage. "I'll kiss him and keep still – that way is sure," she tells Max, to which he replies in a symmetrical affirmation of their asymmetrical roles "God speed the kiss" (*1:133–35*). When next seen in Part 3 Katie has expanded her appointed sphere as far as patriarchy permits and necessity requires. An active propagator of flowers and vines, she has created a "gay garden [that] foam[s]" about "the walls, / ... rush[s] / Up the stone walls – and br[eaks] on the peak'd roof" of her father's house (*3:29–31*) – a garden which surmounts but cannot transcend the patriarchal edifice that supports it. The only child of a farmer and a widower, she has also been required to wield her queenly "sceptre," not just "In dairy, store-room, kitchen – ev'ry spot / Where women's ways [are] needed on the place" – but also in several traditionally masculine spheres (Ward 36):

> [For] Malcolm took her through his mighty fields,
> And taught her lore about the change of crops;
> And how to see a handsome furrow plough'd;
> And how to choose the cattle for the mart;
> And how to know a fair day's work when done;
> And where to plant young orchards; for he said,
> "God sent a lassie, but I need a son –
> "Bethankit for His mercies all the same."
>
> (*3:34–43*)

Not without regret Malcolm has allowed the queen's realm to extend into the king's domain. He has also created an ideal helpmate for Max: in Ruskin's terms, an unequivocally feminine woman who has acquired the power "for rule ... for sweet ordering, arrangement, and decision." It is almost as if Malcolm has followed the advice in "Of Queens' Gardens" to "fill and temper [a girl's] mind with ... such knowledge ... as may enable her to understand, and even aid, the work of men" (96).

As she continues to grow in knowledge and in influence, Katie demonstrates several of the qualities – tact, patience, and self-control – that grow in the same flowerbed as the Ruskinian wisdom of "self-renunciation." When Malcolm hankers after a son, she thinks of Max as a "filial surrogate" (Robert Alan Burns 17), but "all in silence" (*3:47*). When Alfred proposes to her, she says "him 'Nay,' / In all the maiden, speechless, gentle ways / A woman has" (*3:89–90*). When Malcolm and Alfred ask her to sing to them, she obliges with the song of the "Forget-me-not" (*5:25–67*). Only once – and with dire and, perhaps, punitive consequences – does Katie swerve from the straight-and-narrow path to self-renunciation. Sometime after refusing Alfred's proposal, she is drawn by a "yearning for the ice-pale blooms" of water-lilies to a bay "close pack'd with groaning logs" destined for her father's logging mills (*3:154–65*). That this is a masculine domain fraught with moral and ethical danger for a young woman is indicated by several things, not least the demonic, phallic, and commercial associations of Malcolm's logs, each of which is a "monster" "stamp'd with the potent 'G.'" and 'M.' / ... [that] much he lov'd to see upon his goods" (*3:203, 223, 166–67;* and see Rowan 266–67). As unwary of the dangers surrounding her as Laura when she enters the goblin market in Christina Rossetti's poem, Katie makes "bare the lilies of her feet" and sings the sexually charged "lily-song that Max had made ... always meaning [her]" (*3:171–97*). Then, as if urged on in her quest for "lily-love" by such lines as "Thou dost desire / With all thy trembling heart of sinless fire, / But to be fill'd / With dew distill'd," she indulges in an act of dionysiac impetuosity. "With bright eyes of laughter, and wild hair," she leaps "from log to log" towards the "white smiles" of some "silver lilies" near an island and has almost reached her goal when her weight on "the last great log of all" causes it to rise up "like a column brac'd" and, in falling, to pull all but her "upflung hand" beneath the "angry grind" of "vast logs roll'd together" (*3:175–212*). But for the enlightened self-interest of Alfred, Katie would not have survived the appalling consequence of her essentially innocent and ignorant flurry of self-indulgence.

Nor do the consequences of her acts quite cease with her rescue, for she is now vulnerably indebted to a man who will not scruple to use her "gratitude" to achieve his materialistic ends (*3:257–64*). What enables Katie to say Alfred "'Nay' at last, in words / Of ... true-sounding silver" is the fact that she has devoted herself entirely to her future husband: her "mind [is] like the plain, broad shield / Of a table di'mond, nor [has] a score of sides; / And in its shield, so precious and so plain, / [Is] cut, thro' all its clear depths – Max's name" (*3:265–68*). Like Catherine in *Wuthering Heights* when she declares "I *am* Heathcliff – he's always, always in my mind ... as my own being" (70; and see Gilbert and Gubar 248–308), Katie has given over her very identity to the man she loves. With her diamond-like strength and clarity thus permeated by Max's presence, Katie is more than impervious to Alfred's wooing and lies; she is "incorruptibly good ... [and] infallibly wise ... for self-renunciation." Little wonder that when Max returns in the nick of time to rescue her from the river and reveals in his "glance and words" his desire to do the same for Alfred, Katie unquestioningly subordinates her feelings and fears to his wishes and destiny. "Do as you will, my Max," she urges, "I would not keep / You back with one light-falling finger-tip" (*6:134–36*). While Max once again exercises his power as a "doer," Katie "sees the qualities of things, their claims, and their places," a task in which she is assisted by an inner "voice" – the voice of internalized patriarchy – informing her of the Christlike quality of Max's heroism: "If he should perish, 'twill be as a God, / For he would die to save his enemy" (*6:148–49*). The parallelism of the "My Max, O God" with which Katie registers the successful outcome of Max's ordeal risks blasphemy to confirm his high place in her estimation.

That Max is so eminently worthy explains the flattering terms in which Katie fulfils Ruskin's "great function ... [of] Praise." "Adam had not Max's soul ... And these wild woods and plains are fairer far / Than Eden's self" because the agricultural lands of the West are not "that old garden where the fiery sword is set," but what Ruskin calls the "sweeter garden" (120): the garden created by Christ for the willing and the needy. As well as being consonant with her very high estimation of Max, Katie's closing vision of the western "woods and plains" as "bounteous mothers" welcoming the poor and the starving suggests that she has achieved the expansive beneficence promised by wise self-renunciation. Inhabiting both a narrow sphere and an "open world," she is a "true wife" and a "noble woman" whose "home is always around her ... shedding its quiet light ... for those who else were homeless." Of course the expanded "home" and "garden" to which Ruskin refers is Britain, but his eloquent concern with the "power" of women, "not in their households merely, but over all within their sphere" is presented through biblical references and landscapes that resonate easily with pioneer and post-pioneer life in Canada. "Among the hills and happy greenwood of this land of yours ... and in your cities, shall the stones cry out against you, that they are the only pillows where the Son of Man can lay His Head?" (121). Ruskin's concluding exhortation to his female readers could refer to Canada as well as to England. So, too, (and almost uncannily) could his epigraph, a version of the same verse of Isaiah's prophecy of Christ's kingdom ("The wilderness ... shall ... blossom as the rose") that Orator John cites in his justification of the colonization of Upper Canada: "Be thou glad, oh thirsting desert; let the desert be made cheerful, and bloom as the lily; and the barren places of Jordan shall run wild with wood" (74; Isaiah 35:1). It is far from inconceivable that there is a trace of this passage in the "wild woods and plains" of Katie's final vision of the West.

A final question to be addressed is that of the location of Max's homestead. No place name is given in the poem, possibly because Crawford wished to appeal to the widest possible audience in Canada, Britain, and the United States. Indeed, a reader coming to *Malcolm's Katie* by way of *Old Spookses' Pass,* a poem in the manner of the American dialect poets John Hay and Bret Harte, could be forgiven for thinking that the poem is set south of the border, an impression sustained by Longfellow's presence in the volume. Nor do the flora, fauna, or geographical formations mentioned in *Malcolm's Katie* provide a definitive means of telling whether it is set in Canada or the United States. Most of Crawford's prose sources, however, point to a Canadian location for Max's homestead, either in far western Ontario, the Keywatin district between Ontario and the Northwest Territories, or, most likely of all, Manitoba. Certainly readers in Toronto and surrounding areas in 1884 would have connected the poem to the enthusiasm for Manitoba that had been generated in previous decades by the Canadian expansionist movement (Owram). In the late seventies and early eighties "Manitoba fever" (Morton, *Kingdom* 361) reached something of a peak with the publication of thousands of books, pamphlets, reports, and articles, including such classics of expansionism as Acton Burrows' *North-Western Canada, its Climate, Soil and Productions* (1880), George Bryce's *Manitoba: its Infancy, Growth, and Position* (1882), and John Macoun's *Manitoba and the Great North-West: the Field for Investment; the Home of the Emigrant* (1882). To the extent that they were touched by this intense interest in the settlement of Manitoba, Crawford's original readers would have recognized the "half-breed lad, / With tough, lithe sinews and deep Indian eyes, / Lit with a Gallic sparkle" (*2:165–67*) who works beside Max as a Métis, and perhaps understood his friendliness as a sign that the resistance to Canadian expansion that had led to the Red River Rebellion of

1869–70 was a thing of the past (see O'Leary 114). They would have read Crawford's assertion that Max builds his homestead where the "warrior stag" has "never ... Seen ... the plume or bow / Of the red hunter" (*2:80–90*) as poetic testimony that the Northwest was, indeed, as many expansionists claimed, largely empty of Native peoples (Horetzky 3). And in Katie's statement that the "woods and plains" of the West "mellow the earth" with "their ashes ... / That she may yield her increase willingly" (*7:34–35*), they would have heard a version of the theory that the great fertility and "dark color" of the prairie soil in Manitoba was "in part due to the gradual accumulation of the charred grasses left by prairie fires" (George M. Dawson, qtd. in Macoun 36; and see Burrows 13, 59). They might even have nodded their heads knowingly at Max's departure from Ontario in late summer, for fall was regarded by most authorities as the ideal time to start a homestead in Manitoba (E. Hepple Hall 77 n.; Burrows 79).

But if the pathetic sales of *Old Spookses' Pass, Malcolm's Katie, and Other Poems* are anything to go by, there were few readers of Crawford's poem either in 1884 or 1886. One reason for this may have been the dramatic cooling of interest in migration to Manitoba that occurred in 1883 with the collapse of the province's economic boom. "Practically every indicator of the economy in the West showed marked improvement in the years surrounding 1880," writes Doug Owram in *Promise of Eden: the Canadian Expansionist Movement and the Idea of the West, 1856–1900.* "Land sales, homesteads, and pre-emptions rose from 132,918 acres in 1876 to over a million acres by 1879 and an astonishing 2,699,145 acres by 1882 ... In 1883, [however,] 1,831,982 acres of land were alienated, down over 800,000 acres from the year before. Thereafter things got worse instead of better. In 1884 this figure dropped to 1,110,512 acres and in the troubled year of 1885, 481,814 acres" (168–71). These figures do not tell the entire story, of course, for there are many poems besides *Malcolm's Katie* in Crawford's book, but they do point to unfortunate economic timing as one of the factors which "Denied in life ... [the] fame" that should certainly have come to the one woman writer in nineteenth-century Canada whose literary reputation now rests primarily on her poetry (Stewart 81–82).

18 Archibald Lampman,
The Story of an Affinity

Archibald Lampman (1861–99) probably began working on *The Story of an Affinity* in late October or early November 1892 (Early, "Chronology" 83, 87 n. 15), but he did not refer to the poem by its title until a letter of 25 April 1894. "I am going to send you in a little while my 'Story of an Affinity,' which is a small novel in blank verse," he told Edward William Thomson at that time. "If it does not gain the suffrages of the wise, I shall take it that I must stop doing that kind of work. It is going to be the *test*" (*Annotated Correspondence* 120). Although a card accompanying the manuscript of the poem in the Library of Parliament, Ottawa, confirms that it was completed in "April 1894," *The Story of an Affinity* was not published in Lampman's lifetime. This may suggest that the poem did not meet with Thomson's valued endorsement or that, even if it did, it was too long for publication in a periodical such as the *Atlantic Monthly* or for inclusion in the two collections of poetry that succeeded *Among the Millet* (1888) in the last decade of Lampman's life, *Lyrics of the Earth* (1895–96) and *Alcyone* (1899). Both of these possibilities are supported by Duncan Campbell Scott's decision to print only a shortened version of *The Story of an Affinity* in the posthumous *Poems of Archibald Lampman* (1900). Not until 1986 in the Canadian Poetry Press Series was the most accomplished and engaging, albeit, in places, programmatic, long poem of Canada's finest nineteenth-century poet published in its entirety.

Before turning to *The Story of an Affinity* in his letter of 25 April 1894, Lampman responds to some comments from Thomson about an earlier, and, as yet, unpublished, long poem entitled "Lisa": "the Keats at the beginning was very natural, for I could not write anything at that time with[out] writing Keats. I am only just now getting quite clear of the spell of that marvellous person; and it has taken me ten years to do it. Keats has always had such a fascination for me and has so permeated my mental outfit that I have an idea that he has found a sort of faint reincarnation in me. I should not write the poem that way, if I were writing it now – but then I should not be writing it at all" (*Annotated Correspondence* 119). Despite the echoes of Keats that can be heard at several points in *The Story of an Affinity*, not least in the "richest harvests" and "mellow juices" of its opening lines (*1:9–10*), the poem as a whole confirms Lampman's conviction that by 1894 he was "getting ... clear of the spell of that marvellous person."

Much more prominent than Keats among the poetic sources of Lampman's "novelette in verse" (*Annotated Correspondence* 103) are Wordsworth and Tennyson – the Wordsworth of "Michael," *The Prelude*, and *The Excursion* ("The Ruined Cottage") and the Tennyson of *The Lover's Tale*, *The Princess*, and the domestic idylls (*Dora, Enoch Arden, The Miller's Daughter*, and *The Gardener's Daughter*). The name of the heroine in *The Story of an Affinity* – Margaret Hawthorne – recalls that of the woman in "The Ruined Cottage," the excerpt from the first book of *The Excursion* that Arnold entitles simply "Margaret" in his influential selection of *The Poems of William Wordsworth* (1879 f.). The enormous strength of Lampman's hero – Richard Stahlberg ("Steelmountain") – recalls that of Eustace in *The Gardener's Daughter*, a man "So muscular ... [and] broad of breast" that "he might have sat for Hercules" (7–8). A Wordsworthian locution ("Now it chanced" [1:157]) and a Tennysonian onomatopoeia ("soft murmuring sound" [1:180]) accompany Richard to a momentous meeting with Margaret that recalls both the "spots of time" in *The Prelude* and the initial encounters of the lovers in *The Miller's Daughter* and *The Gardener's Daughter*. Like Wordsworth in *The Prelude* Richard Stahlberg moves from the country to the "great city" (1:36) to further his education, and, like the heroines of several of Tennyson's domestic idylls, Margaret Hawthorne is an only daughter (and, in time, the only daughter of a widower). Even the staid form of Lampman's poem – long verse paragraphs of blank verse – recalls the major narrative poems of Tennyson, Wordsworth, and behind them, Milton. Indeed, as intimated by such lines as "So through the humming garden and between / The shadowy ranks of vines they took their way" (1:503–04), *Paradise Lost* looms as large as any poem in Lampman's treatment of love, education, and suffering as paths to a paradise regained.

Since some of Lampman's poems are included with excerpts from *Malcolm's Katie* in W.D. Lighthall's *Songs of the Great Dominion* (1889) and J.E. Wetherell's *Later Canadian Poems* (1893; and see *Annotated Correspon-*

dence 82–87) it is quite possible that he knew Crawford's poem as a whole and that it helped to shape the constellation of Herculean hero, motherless daughter, educational growth, and Edenic vision in *The Story of an Affinity*. No verbal echoes sustain this possibility, however, and in any case the similarities between the two poems are perhaps less important that their differences. Most remarkable of these are the activities and settings of their heroes, for while Max Gordon is a pioneer who develops physically and spiritually on the Manitoba(?) frontier, Richard Stahlberg is a scholar whose development from farm boy to college lecturer takes place in a metropolitan centre. Behind this divergence lay the growing recognition in the economically depressed and increasingly industrialized Ontario of the late eighties and early nineties that pioneering and farming were no longer reliable or expanding avenues to prosperity. What was required in a complex society was a broad yet specialized training of the sort possessed by the men in William Cochrane's *Canadian Album ... or, Success by Example, in Religion, Patriotism, Business, Law, Medicine, Education and Agriculture* (1891). Settlerheroes would return to Canadian writing with the renewal of western expansion around and after the turn of the century, but in the meantime numerous "fictional heroes ... displayed a marked appetite for study and eventually became successful doctors or lawyers" (Allan Smith 195) – or, it may be added, successful "lecturer[s] in ... famous college hall[s]" (*2:658*). *The Story of an Affinity* is an internalized Herculean narrative in which the mind is the sole frontier to be expanded and built up.

That this is so helps to explain the near absence of prose accounts of Canadian landscapes and related subjects in the background of the poem. Only in setting the scene for the introduction of Richard, Margaret, and their families does Lampman appear to draw on a prose account of the same subject: Louise Murray's chapter on "The Niagara District" in *Picturesque Canada; the Country as it Was and Is* (1882). In the fall of 1893, a few months before he wrote "a large quantity" of *The Story of an Affinity*, Lampman paid a nostalgic visit to "St. Catharines in the Niagara District – the land of [his] forefathers" – and "enjoyed wandering about again among [his] uncle's grapes ... [and] pick[ing] the last of the early peaches off the trees" (*Annotated Correspondence* 94). Perhaps it was at this time that he read Murray's essay on the "peninsula jutting out between lakes Erie and Ontario" where "the beauty of the ... peach orchards, when the trees are bending down beneath the weight of their lovely globes of pink and white and gold-tinted fruit, recalls the fabled gardens of the Hesperides" (392). Perhaps it was after reading this description that Lampman resolved to set his poem "Between the overlapping of two seas / Ontario and Erie," in "a land / Rich with wide fields and sloped with trellised vine[,] / The blossoming garden of the northern world" (Notebook 10). Perhaps it was Murray's resonantly *fin-de-siècle* description of the transition from the lovely "blossoms" and "delicate green" of spring to the "ripe fruit" and "beauteous blight" of autumn in the "richly-cultivated country" near St. Catharines (371) that prompted Lampman to give a similar emphasis and movement to the opening verse paragraph of the poem as it appears in the fair copy of April 1894. By this time, however, the opening lines of the poem have been divested of their geographical specificity ("Ontario and Erie" have become "two seas"), and whatever they contain of Murray's description has been augmented by details that are likely to have been observed by Lampman himself in the fall of 1893: "the peach / Puffs up its yellow juices till it cracks / Splitting the stone ... / The robins storm the vine-yard, and the wasp / Punctures the swollen grapes and drains and drains" (*1:9–13*). Laden with suggestions of natural excess and predac-ity, the initial setting of *The Story of an Affinity* is less an outer than an inner landscape, less the Niagara District than a *paysage moralisé* that gives a prelusive hint of the ripe and rotten psychological state of the poem's hero.

When Richard appears on the scene after a paragraph of introduc-tion to the Stahlberg and Hawthorne families, he is presented as a young man of great physical "stature and strength" but dismayingly lim-ited intelligence and education. "Vast-shouldered with a broad and mighty head ... He tower[s] above his fellows like a king, / A king whom slow magic ha[s] dethroned," for his mind, though once the seat of "a strange intelligence," has taken on "A sullen and impenetrable sloth" (*1:68–72, 59–62*). Worse, within his Herculean body there lurks "an inly smouldering fire" whose energy can be uncontrolled, capricious and amoral:

> There was a fitful and ungoverned force
> In his huge frame, a lawless energy
> That yielded to no guidance, but stormed out
> In passionate whim, and were it good or evil
> Wrought each in desperate and titanic measure.
>
> (*1:79–84*)

Although this "fitful giant" is capable of "Labouring as no other three could labour / In all the friendly farms" (*1:97, 99–100*), he is equally capable, when the "mood" takes him, of impulsively abandoning farm work and, instead, engaging in such unproductive and self-indulgent activities as solitary "wandering," raucous socializing, and "tremendous feats of strength" (*1:102–25*). On one occasion (when, significantly for a Herculean hero, he is blind to the "Hebe-loveliness of leaf / And flower" [*1:164–65*]), the sights and sounds of external nature that he does perceive "touch ... his spirit with a passionate thrill" and awaken in him "A single gleam of wild intelligence" (*1:190–96*). But this Wordsworthian moment of awakening finds expression only in "the sheer strength of ... [a] violent deed," a travesty of a labour of Hercules: tearing "a young birch-tree ... root, stem, and branches, from the earth," he hurls it "Into the centre of [a] wind-waved field" (*1:197–208*). Here is Herculean strength that must be directed by an ethical and constructive purpose if it is not to issue forth in acts of greater destruction and turpitude.

The direction that is necessary to Richard comes through his motivating encounter with Margaret Hawthorne, a figure who can be taken in one sense as representing his "good genius." "As he comes up from the open meadows of youth," writes Lampman in his essay on "Happiness" (1896), "every man" is met by a female representation of "the radical gift through which he is intended by nature to be operative and fruitful among men. If he yields to her, she will ... become his guide" and "he will journey by upward and difficult paths" until he reaches "high tablelands, from which he will survey the world and mankind, and perceive that even the cloudiest tracts, are over-arched by the interminable blue, and dreamed upon by inexhaustible sunshine. This is the road of happiness" (*Selected Prose* 105). Very obviously a version of the classical theme of "The Choice of Hercules" (Xenophon, *Memorabilia* 2:10; Shaftesbury, *Characteristicks* 3:370–71), the opening paragraphs of the "Happiness" essay supplement Hercules' traditional choice between an austere woman representative of heroic virtue (man's "good genius") and an alluring woman representative of hedonistic pleasure ("every man's desire") with a third alternative: a "portal ... broad and obvious and unattended" where "no goddess stands ... for it is an entrance abhorred and shunned by all the immortals[:] ... the way of the commonplace, the path of routine" (*Selected Prose* 105–06). Little does he know it, but as he makes his way with "gentler tread / And brow less imminent and less disturbed" (*1:219–20*) from the "wind-waved field" towards the "orchard" where Margaret lies asleep (*1:221–65*), Richard is about to embark with her help on the "upward and difficult path" to happiness.

In addition to being an allegorical representation of Richard's "good genius," Margaret is a character of some depth who has to make a number of difficult choices of her own in the course of the poem. Educated by her father for "A larger future than the farm could give[:] ... another life / In the great city" (*1:34–36*), she had

> built a dream
> Of her own future, full of noble aims,
> Traced out in many an ardour of bright thought,
> A dream of onward and heroic toil,
> Of growth and mind-enlargement for herself,
> And generous labour for the common good.
> (*1:284–89*)

In "a sheer / Reversal of his former mind," however, Margaret's father has decided that he wants her at home with him, a decision that she has protested bitterly but finally accepted, resolving to "Rebuild ... in ... lowlier shape / The ruined fabric of her hope" (*1:275–96*). Henceforth she will combine household tasks with "study ... the loved companionship / Of books," "A loving friendship with all ... creatures that inhabit earth and stream," and an attempt to be "A help, a refreshment, and a grace / To all about her" (*1:297–309*). This is an admirably dutiful and intelligent response to circumstances, and it might very well allow Margaret "To tread / The circuit of her house-kept days content" (*1:296–97*), but it nevertheless runs the risk of becoming in time "the way of the commonplace, the path of routine." That it never quite does so is no small tribute to a "spirit" and a "dream" that will be sorely tried again before the poem is over.

As Richard approaches his Sleeping Beauty where she lies dreaming of "golden purposes" on an "old ... rustic seat" (*1:311–17*), knowledge of his violent tendencies combines with comments on her physical charms to produce apprehensions of an impending rape. Although not allayed by intimations of Satan's approaches to Eve in *Paradise Lost,* such apprehensions prove short-lived, for the effect on Richard of the neo-Platonic fusion of beauty ("rounded grace"), wisdom ("bright thought"), and goodness ("spiritual loveliness") now represented by Margaret is nothing short of visionary: the mere sight of her makes him instantaneously comprehend the shortcomings of his life as it now is and prompts him to contemplate for himself "A life bred in a loftier air, and steeped / In pleasures of a daintier sense, distilled / From studious research and fine experience" (*1:378–81*). Dante's first encounter with Beatrice in the *Vita Nuova* is scarcely more affective and renovating. "A vision, rare and beautiful to him / As any by ... Saint [John] of Patmos seen / Ha[s] slid beneath the cloud-bands of his soul, / And flooded all with one enchanted gleam" (*1:335–38*) – "gleam," of course, being a resonantly Tennysonian word for mystical illumination. As the "guide and symbol" (*2:189*) of his desire to conquer his own "ignorance" and "wretched[ness]," Richard borrows from Margaret the "little book" that she was reading before she fell asleep (*1:370–71, 385*). A motive emblem like the similarly unnamed volume in William Morris's *The Pilgrims of Hope*, Richard's guide book is the equivalent of Hercules' club and Max's axe in Lampman's tale of a Herculean hero's achievement of inner governance through the cultivation of his mental and social faculties. As if to emphasize the parallel and continuity between external and internal settlement, Lampman interrupts the dialogue that occurs after Margaret awakens with a reminiscence of pioneering times when the "founder" of the Hawthorne "homestead" "first / Made his axe echo in these wilds, and hewed / A circle in the frowning woods, and joined / Trunk upon trunk to house his little ones" (*1:471–72*).

No one familiar with "Heat," "Among the Timothy," and other Lampman lyrics of illumination will be surprised to learn that, like Richard's irradiating encounter with Margaret, the next stage of his journey towards enlightenment takes place at noon when the heat and light of the sun are at their most intense (Bentley, "Watchful Dreams"). Earlier, in the "warmth and shadowy sweetness" of the orchard, the "stroke of noonday" had found Richard gazing raptly at Margaret as "the noonday glow / Scatter[ed] with golden points her restful hair" (*1:324, 350, 353–54*). Later, as Richard walks home after a "midday meal" at the Hawthorne homestead (*1:490*), a "perfect noon with not a single cloud ... sh[ines] down / On the meadows and the heat-drowsèd fields" (*1:589–91*). By turns "wading among timothy, waist high," passing fences overgrown with "coneflower" ("That symbol of the blazing heart of June"), and hearing "the oven-bird / Assault the brooding fervour of the hour / With its increasing and accentuate note" (*1:595–610*), Richard once more partakes of what Wordsworth calls the "Influence of Natural Objects," this time with constructive rather than destructive results:

> These things although indeed he marked them not
> Distinctly, yet upon his spirit breathed
> A gentle influence, and the quieted will
> Shaped gradually the tumult of his thoughts
> Into an ordered counsel, bringing forth
> A single stream of purpose large and clear.
>
> (*1:613–18*)

With a plan and a direction in mind, Richard begins to feel more like a "man" than a "brute" (*1:653–54*), and soon resolves to "make a new beginning of [his] life" by expanding his "power to think and learn" in "the great city, where the minds of men are busiest, and most alive" (*1:695, 698–99*). Although Old Stahlberg initially opposes his son's plan, fearing like Wordsworth's Michael the "evils and temptations" of the "treacherous city," he eventually gives Richard his "consent" (*1:717–18, 731*), and, with this, the first part of *The Story of an Affinity* moves towards its happy and hopeful conclusion.

Unfortunately Scott's editing of Part 2 of the poem – particularly his omission of two lengthy passages, the first treating of Richard's initiation into "merciful work" in the slums by Charlotte Ambray (*2:373–450*) and the second his acquisition of the social graces through contact with three "Fine ladies of an exquisite way of life" (*2:564–648*) – obscured for many years the overall shape of Lampman's agenda for the humanizing education of his Herculean hero. When these passages are considered there emerges a distinctively Arnoldian pattern to Richard's programme of studies. Nor is this entirely unexpected since Lampman regarded Arnold (whom he heard lecture in Ottawa in February 1884) as a consummate philosopher-poet to whom "the whole range of life, time, and eternity, the mysteries and beauties of existence and its deepest spiritual problems are continually present" (*At the Mermaid Inn* 97). It has even been suggested that Lampman "tried to model his own activities" as poet, essayist, and public lecturer on "the great English man of letters" (Gnarowski, intro. to *Selected Poetry* 27). "Culture ... properly described ... [has] its origin in the love of perfection," declares Arnold in *Culture and Anarchy* (1869 f.); "it is a *study of perfection*. It moves by the force, not merely or primarily of the scientific passion for pure knowledge, but also of the moral and social passion for doing good" (5:91). Like religion, culture "places human perfection ... in the growth and predominance of our humanity proper, as distinguished from our animality," and it teaches us to conceive "human perfection" as "a harmonious expansion of *all* the powers which make the beauty and worth of human nature" (5:94). Elsewhere, for example in "A Speech at Eton" reprinted in *Irish Essays and Others* (1882), Arnold is more specific in identifying the four "powers" or "lines" that are developed in man's "general instinct for expansion" as "the lines of conduct, of intellect and knowledge, of beauty, of social life and manners" (9:26–27; and see 9:142; 8:287 and 372). As Richard concentrates successively on "enlarging studies" (*2:136–372*; "intellect and knowledge"), "merciful work" (*2:373–450*; "conduct"), the "Beauty" of nature and literature (*2:452–563*; "beauty") and, finally, the "smoothe grace and glamour ... of speech" (*2:564–648*; "social life and manners"), he engages in an Arnoldian "*study of perfection*" that takes him from the darkness and disorder of "a nature not finely tempered" towards the "*sweetness and light*" which famously characterize the fully cultured and well-balanced human being in *Culture and Anarchy* (5:99; and see Connell 157–202).

This is not to say that other forces did not help to shape Richard's humanizing curriculum. Wanda Campbell has discerned convincing parallels between Richard's laborious ascent of the "mount of knowledge" (*2:158*) and the educational model set out by Milton in his tract *On Education* and in the concluding books of *Paradise Lost* ("*Bildungsgedicht*" 128–33), and it is certainly likely that Lampman's inclusion of experience in "workshops and ... haunts of skill / Where men [are] busy at various crafts" (*2:232–34*) in his hero's education reflects the views, not only of Milton, but also of Ruskin, Morris, and others on the dignity and value of skilled labour. It is also likely that Lampman's educational agenda derives in part from his own experiences as a pupil (and outstanding classics scholar) at Trinity College School, Port Hope, as a student at Trinity College, Toronto, and, briefly, as a high school teacher in Orangeville (Connor 30–64). In its very breadth and diversity, Richard's education reflects the "broadening of the curriculum" in Ontario's schools that took place in the last three decades of the nineteenth-century (Wilson, Stamp, and Audet 323). The very fact that Richard studies astronomy, geology, botany, and zoology (*2:452–75*) reflects the influence of such works as Herbert Spencer's *Education: Intellectual, Moral, and Physical* (1861 f.) and Thomas Huxley's *Science and Education* (1894 f.) in expanding the earlier English-Canadian "programme of English, mathematics, and classics" to include the sciences (Wilson, Stamp, and Audet 294–96, 323).

Yet many of the specific details of Richard's "enlarging studies," both inside and outside the classroom, support the view that, at base, Lampman's educational agenda is a reflection of Arnold's argument in *Culture and Anarchy* and elsewhere that education should involve the study of "all the voices of human experience ... of art, science, poetry, philosophy [and] history, as well as of religion" (5:93). Arnold's presence is especially apparent when in his ascent towards "the desirèd light" (*2:172*) Richard arrives at the "golden fire" of English literature:

> He lived in Shakespeare's venturous world, and passed
> That eloquent multitude of living shapes,
> Lovely or terrible; and Milton's line
> Bore him upon its volume vast and stern
> In august cadences to the sheer height
> Of earthly vision; Wordsworth, Keats and Gray,
> The spell of Coleridge in his magic mood,
> And Shelley's wild daedalian web of song,

Opened his soul to every mystery
And heavenly likeness of the things of earth.
                    (*2:546–56*)

Like the omission from this catalogue of Byron, the admiration at its conclusion for Coleridge and Shelley accords less with Arnold's views of these poets (see *Collected Prose* 9:217–37 and 11:305–27) than with Lampman's opinion of them as expressed in his essays on "The Revolt of Islam," "The Poetry of Byron," "Poetic Interpretation," and "Style" (*Selected Prose* 11–16 and 87–91). The references to Shakespeare, Milton, Wordsworth, Keats, and Gray, however, point cumulatively to Arnold's formative influence on Lampman's conception of the central corpus of English poetry. Both Shakespeare and Milton were continually important to Arnold ("Milton's line" was for him, as evidently for Lampman, a model of the grand style), and, of course, Wordsworth, Keats, and Gray are the subjects of three of Arnold's finest and most influential later essays (*Collected Prose* 9:36–55, 189–204, 205–16). Indeed it would probably be no exaggeration to say that, as much as Wordsworth's poems themselves, Arnold's estimate of him as the "most considerable" English poet after Shakespeare and Milton was responsible for the Wordsworthian presence in *The Story of an Affinity*.

In the course of his education Richard is assisted by a number of characters, two of whom demand special attention. The first of these is the social worker who introduces him to "human service" in "the grim city's" "haunt[s] of vice and agony" (*2:416–21*). A "fair" woman in both the ethical and aesthetic meanings of the word (*1:401*), Charlotte Ambray is a manifestation of Lampman's growing awareness in the 1890s of the changes being brought about in the social position of women by such interrelated developments as the New Woman and the women's suffrage movement. Only months before he began *The Story of an Affinity*, Lampman wrote strongly in favour of women's rights and independence in his *At the Mermaid Inn* column in the Toronto *Globe*. "The sentimentalist of the old school ... pictures to himself with disgust and dread the 'masculine' woman of the future," he told the *Globe*'s readers on 9 April 1892, "but [t]he rest of us need have no fear ... Give [women] perfect independence, place them upon an exactly even footing with men in all the activities and the responsibilities of life, and the result for good will be attained which is almost beyond the power of imagination to picture." With "the moral and intellectual emancipation of women" there will not be a decrease in "the grace and beauty which we think to be [their] chiefest charm"; "rather there will be added to these a power, a beneficence, a dignity which are only the exception now" (47–48). When he wrote this, Lampman had already envisaged the "goodlier ... stature" and strength of the "tall fair women" of his Morrissian utopia, "The Land of Pallas," as the embodiment of the social advances achieved by their foremothers (*Poems* 202, 205). Although the exemplary Charlotte Ambray participates in the Victorian stereotype of the angelically selfless and "queenly" woman (*1:399*), her first name – a feminine version of Charles, which means manly – associates her with the "'masculine' woman of the future," as do her physical and intellectual qualities. "Tall," "firm," "massy brow[ed]," and "grandly made," she possesses a "restless beauty and [a] wilful strength" that is "Self-conscious, bold, and uncontrollably free" (*2:377, 396–97, 427–28*). Beautiful, charming, and emotionally complex, she is not the focus of romantic love (in fact, her marital status is never mentioned), but an educative "companion" whose "noble friendship" teaches Richard "more / Than all his contact with life's outer forms" (*2:423, 449–50*). A "delicious presence" and "An inexhaustible source of changing lights," she is linked even through her surname – a contraction of ambrosia and ray – with the "*sweetness and light*" towards which Richard is travelling.

The second figure who demands special attention is the poet who guides Richard on the final two stages of his journey: his reading of the masters of English poetry and his assimilation to refined society in the company of the poem's equivalent of the three graces. Because he is an anonymous yet individualized character, the "slight, and somewhat tall" "young man ... With thin clear cheeks, bright eyes and lofty brow" (*2:500–01*) who plays Virgil to Richard's Dante both encourages and frustrates identification. Could he be a representation of Keats, or of Lampman himself, or a "faint reincarnation" of both? A third possibility is Arnold, particulary since he is conspicuously absent from the Arnoldian list of English writers whom Richard studies after meeting the poet. But what is to be made of the fact that the poet introduces himself to Richard when he is leaning "across a broken fence" listening to "The murmurs of a shallow reedy pool" – the prelude to the "soft Pandean voices" which accompany their "close communion" as they walk back towards the city together (*2:494–540*)? Could this indicate that Lampman thought of the relationship between the two men as analogous to his own relationship with Charles G.D. Roberts? By Lampman's own admission, his reading of Roberts's *Orion, and Other Poems* (1880) while a student at Toronto was an Archimedean point in his poetic development, and, as Sandra Djwa has shown, his association of frogs with Pan in "The Favorites of Pan" and other works reveals the seminal influence of Roberts's "The Pipes of Pan" (132). "Everything was transfigured for me beyond description," Lampman said of the May morning after he "read ... and re-read ... *Orion*" – "bathed in an old-world radiance of beauty [by] ... those divine verses, as they seemed to me, with their Tennyson-like richness and strange, earth-loving, Greekish flavour. I have never forgotten that morning, and its influence has always remained with me" ("Two Canadian Poets" 410). Very likely, Roberts's work in general and "The Pipes of Pan" in particular were one of the channels through which Lampman absorbed the notion, present also in Wordsworth and Arnold (not to mention Bliss Carman [see Bentley, "Carman and Mind Cure"]), that periodic forays into the natural world have therapeutic value for people living amid "the heedless throngs and traffic of ... cities (Roberts, *Poems* 27). "I confess that my design for instance in writing 'Among the Timothy' was not in the first place to describe a landscape," Lampman told Hamlin Garland in 1889, "but to describe the effect of a few hours spent among the summer fields on a mind in a troubled and despondent condition" (qtd. in James Doyle 42). Central to Lampman's canon, as to the *Vagabondia* volumes of Carman and Richard Hovey (1894 f.), is a therapeutic rhythm of excursion to nature and return to the city that the poems enact in order that – to quote "April" in *Among the Millet* – "we toil, brothers, without distress / In calm-eyed peace and godlike blamelessness" (*Poems* 6). So it is that Richard flees "the city's wearying roar" to "Cool ... his hot brain amid the blossoming fields / Or salve ... his spirit in the peaceful woods," and after he and the poet have talked "far / Into the April evening" they "plunge ... again into the city's roar" (*2:480–82, 517–18, 538*). Having communed with nature and with each other in a period of "wise idleness" (Oxley 56), both will be better able to cope with what Arnold in "The Scholar Gypsy" calls the "strange disease of modern life, / With its sick hurry, its divided aims, / Its heads o'ertax'd, [and] its palsied hearts" (*Poetical Works* 279).

To an extent Richard himself has become a scholar gypsy by the time his education is complete. Intellectually replete with "sciences, ... old philosophies, / And all the harvest of the modern light" (*2:651–53*), he still experiences his "old desire of wandering, the delight of solitude, and hunger for the wilds" (*2:476–77*), but now with the "balance and regulation of mind" which constitutes the goal of an Arnoldian education (*Prose Works* 9:91). As he thinks back to the "old wildness of his darkened youth," Richard recognizes that this was not a "meaningless power" but an irrational version of the "sympathy of Earth, the blind desire of Beauty" that he now experiences in a "more restrained, less desperate" way because it is "illumined by the conscious mind" (*2:489–93*). This is a "finely tempered nature ... in which the characters of beauty and intelligence are both present, which unites ... *sweetness and light*" (5:99), and, to be consistent with Arnold's views, it must be directed beyond the individual to the social sphere. "Perfection, as culture conceives it, is not possible while the individual remains isolated," runs a key passage in *Culture and Anarchy;* "the individual is required [by culture] ... to carry others along with him in his march towards perfection, to be continually doing all he can to enlarge and increase the volume of the human stream sweeping thitherward" (5:94). Just as Richard is assisted in his journey by various teachers, so he, in turn, becomes a "teacher" and a "lecturer" (*2:656–58*) and, in the third and final part of the poem, returns like "the wise Odysseus," to his Penelope and his Ithaca (*2:279–80;* and see Early, "Lampman's Love Poetry" 129–30). In Lampman's thought, as in Arnold's, culture and happiness are imperfect unless they are shared.

While Richard has been growing "through triumphant toil / And steadfast will, and prospering fortunes ... / To his soul's spreading stature" (*3:1–3*), Margaret has been enveloped in "A mist of melancholy industry" by "the monotonous round / Of duties and ... petty cares" that compose her day-to-day life (*3:14, 8–9*). All but dispossessed of her "dream of onward and heroic toil" she has nevertheless retained enough "grace," "beauty," and "amplitude of thought" (*3:97, 98, 48*) to attract a suitor whose name – John Vantassel – associates him with the Sleepy Hollow of Washington Irving's *Sketch Book* (1820 f.). Not without a great deal of soul-searching, Margaret has accepted Vantassel's proposal, knowing that, though she does not reciprocate his love, he is a decent man who will offer her at least a modest expansion of her restricted compass – "The same long round of plain activities, / Performed upon a larger field" with someone whom she likes, admires, and trusts (*3:195–200*). "Less slender" and "pale" than she was when Richard left ten years earlier, Margaret has been matured and enhanced by time and compromise: "graver of eye," "mellower" of voice, and "firmlier" of "figure," she has now achieved "perfect womanhood / With charm and influence gracious and supreme" (*13:252–66*).

When Richard and Margaret first meet again his actions and her responses suggest that for her their relationship will be restrictive and regressive. "Taking both her hands between his two," Richard speaks her name "And Margaret's eyes f[a]ll, stricken and abashed, / And her cheeks redden ... but her helpless hands / Remain in [his] having no power to move" (*3:276–80*). What follows is an epiphany of affection in which a Margaret "robbed ... of control" senses intuitively, emotionally, and passionately (but *not* rationally) that Richard has "gone beyond her, and [stands] now / Her spiritual master, large, and armed with power" (*3:283, 294–95*). Initial appearances to the contrary, however, this is to be a relationship founded on more than female submission to male "power." As indicated by the allusion to Goethe's "Elective Affinities" (*Die Wahlverwandtshaften*) in Lampman's title and confirmed by Margaret's recognition of Richard as "her spirit's answering type" (*3:306*), they have been drawn together by a mysterious spiritual sympathy which, on the analogy of a chemical reaction, makes their effect upon one another reciprocally responsive and transformative. "All my life / Is linked with Margaret's," Richard later explains to Vantassel; "I draw from her / All that I am, and all I hope to be! ... There is a bond between us, sacred and inherent; / She too has felt it ... and turns to me / With the one love that cannot be gainsaid" (*3:666–72*). Both because of the mutuality generated by this "bond" and because of his achieved "*sweetness and light*" Richard moves quickly during his first meeting with Margaret to allow her to re-gain her composure and equality:

> for a moment *like a girl* she stood
> Flushed and tongue-tied, but Richard marking this
> *Released her hands,* and *turning to her side*
> Went forward *with her* up the quiet walk;
> And *both* regaining in a moment's space
> *Command of thought and speech,* their tongues were loosed ...
> (*3:308–13;* emphasis added)

Not only does the action of walking side by side "up the quiet walk" suggest a mutual movement towards perfection, but it anticipates the similar procession that occurs in the final lines of the poem and the wedding ceremony which, more likely than not, will formalize the couple's affinity.

It is a measure of the importance Lampman attached to female choice, particularly as regards marriage, that a large proportion of what remains of *The Story of an Affinity* is given over to tracing Margaret's response to the dilemma that she now faces over her two suitors. First in a "broad porch" and then by an "open window" (*3:342, 384*) – two locations suggestive of the laying "open" once again of her "old dreamed of path" (*3:361*) – Margaret wrestles with her own Lampmanian version of "The Choice of Hercules." On the one hand lies "the way of the commonplace, the path of routine" with Vantassel, on the other "upward ... paths" of "general rightness ... gratified individuality," and "happiness" with Richard (*Selected Prose* 105). Bound to the former by duty and the latter by love, she refuses each one, becoming, in the process, so "white and pale" (*3:460, 495*) that her affinities seem to lie less with the living than with the dead. Indeed, when she ascends the "narrow stair" to her "room" and, sinking beside her bed, "l[ays] her head between her hands and we[eps]" (*3:499–501*), her location and actions recall those of Dante Gabriel Rossetti's Blessed Damozel as she waits in Heaven for her tardy lover (*Works* 5). Driven past independent thought and action by her double-bind, Margaret verges finally on complete passivity while, unbeknownst to her, Richard is deciding her "destiny" for her in a final test of his "finely tempered nature": the "govern[ing]" of an angry and irrational Vantassel, first with reasoned explanations delivered in a "gentle voice" and then, when that fails, with the careful deployment of his Herculean strength (*3:606–90*). Momentous as its outcome may be for Margaret, this male confrontation does not obliterate her freedom of choice, however, for, before Richard returns with the news that Vantassel has released her from her commitment to him, she has decided and stated that she will accept neither of her two suitors. Much less reassuring in its implications for female independence is Margaret's sense that, having made this decision, she must merely "follow with obedient feet / The beck of destiny" and passively accept "the next / And final stroke of some impersonal fate" (*3:701–15*). The possibility is even raised that she considers taking her own life. What else is to be made of "The final sad memorial of her strife, / A letter, soiled and blotted with her tears" that she has left on "her bed / In the dark farm-house" (*3:704–07*)? To whom is the "sad memorial" addressed? Is it a farewell letter or a suicide note? It is as impossible to give unequivocal answers to these questions as it is to say finally whether Margaret is a dependent or an independent woman. She is both, and could hardly be otherwise, given the ideas of spiritual affinity and cultural interdependence upon which *The Story of an Affinity* is founded.

Yet even in the poem's obligatory happy ending the tension in Margaret between dependence and independence remains. In lines that recall her first meeting with Richard after his return, her eyes "G[i]ve themselves utterly to his" in "one look / Of silent full surrenderment" (*3:730–31*). Then, in a gesture that affirms their mutuality if not their equality, "They t[ake] *each other's hands*" (emphasis added) and, like bride and groom, walk

> Up the cool path between the orchard trees,
> Wrapt in such thoughts as only they can know,
> Whose hearts through tears and effort have attained
> The portals of the perfect fields of life,
> And thence, half-dazzled by the glow, perceive
> The endless road before them, clear and free.
>
> (*3:737–43*)

That the path is "cool" and the future bright may be taken as a final indication of the temperance and enlightenment attained by a Herculean hero whose passions were once as hot as his mind was dark. Where once there were decaying fruit and voracious animals there is now a composed and peaceful landscape through which a hierarchically organized and mutually supportive couple are processing towards "such happiness as can be commonly attained by man" (*Selected Prose 105*).

Less than five years after he completed *The Story of an Affinity* Lampman was dead at the age of thirty-eight, killed by a combination of acute pneumonia and a chronically weak heart. If he had lived a few months longer he would have seen Canada enter the twentieth century that was supposed to belong to her. If he had lived a few years longer he would have witnessed the deaths of Queen Victoria and Edward VII, the sinking of the *Titanic,* and the First World War. As it was he died with most of his hopes and dreams for his country and the human race intact. In its intense idealism, as in its Romantic and Victorian literary models, *The Story of an Affinity* stands near the end of an era.

Envoi

"I have been endeavouring to think up some plan for a strictly Canadian poem, local in its incident and spirit, but cosmopolitan in form and manner," Lampman informed J.E. Collins in the summer of 1884; "it is a hard thing to get at. I have been dreaming, however, of locating some simple story in the Niagara district, among the old farmsteads – something in accordance with the quiet toilsome life there – maybe dated forty or fifty years back in rougher times – making it sober and realistic, so to speak, in the metre of [Longfellow's] *Evangeline* but more like [Goethe's] *Hermann and Dorothea*, or, nearer still, to the translations from a Swedish poet, [Johan Ludwig] Runeberg, who wrote lovely things about the peasants of Finland. I think I shall endeavour to carry this idea out" (qtd. in Connor 78). Besides anticipating *The Story of an Affinity* by several years, these remarks throw into relief many of the shared characteristics of early long poems on Canada. Each of the components of Lampman's plan casts light, not just on individual long poems, but also on the poetic continuity to which they belong.

A strictly Canadian poem, local in its incident and spirit. With his initial statement, Lampman firmly locates his projected poem in Canada and unwittingly aligns it with a patriotic continuity that stretches back more than a century to *Abram's Plains*. A combination of Canadian content and local affection cannot be taken as a definition of Canadian poetry, but it does help to explain why Cary and Goldsmith have been assimilated more closely to the Canadian canon than Mackay or O'Grady, and why the Canadian poems of Moore were so well received by Sangster, McLachlan, and others. In a developing and insecure culture, special welcome will always be extended to poets who address the local scene with affection and the local audience with respect. Whether motivated by affection and respect or dislike and disdain, however, any poem that focuses with care on the particulars of place, on "local incident and spirit," will always exercise a certain appeal, not least to those living in the same place at a later time. Such are the poems – and the assumptions – upon which this study is based.

But is there a Canadian "spirit," and, if so, can it be captured or reflected in a poem? To an extent the history of poetry written in and about Canada from Kelsey to the present has been a series of responses to these questions. Part of Cary's answer is to evoke the bright and "mimic fires" of an enchanting local insect. Bayley offers religious and political conservatism as a defining characteristic of Canada. Longmore focuses on a "transplanted" custom whose cacophony accords with the raucousness of the Lower Canadian landscape. Howe endows his beloved Acadia with the erotic charms of a semi-clad woman. McLachlan interweaves the associations of literary forms to position Canada West between Scott's Caledonia and Longfellow's Great Lakes. And Lampman himself courts the *genius loci* of Ontario by carefully recording its rural sights and sounds at different times of the day and year. In contrast, Mackay and O'Grady treat the spirit of place as malevolent and destructive. "Dread diseases ... hover o'er the plains" of Upper Canada during the summer in *Quebec Hill* and for the remainder of the year "Stern Winter rules" in Lower Canada, concealing the "sleeping earth" beneath his "hoary robe" and binding "the swelling wave" in "frozen fetters" (*1:87–88; 2:25–28, 43–44*). O'Grady's *Emigrant* is a relentless catalogue of the foul creatures, grim conditions, and poor treatment to be encountered by Irishmen in Canada's "northern sphere" *(2098)*.

A major reason for the concentration on the attractions and horrors of the country's landscape and seasons in early long poems on Canada was the conviction that climate and scenery have a formative effect on individual and national character. "In the physical universe ... what is most exalted, is most influential on the best minds," wrote E.L. Magoon in *The Home Book of the Picturesque* (1852); "national intellect receives a prevailing tone from the peculiar scenery that most abounds ... In old Greece, the lovely climate had just vicissitudes enough to impress a happy variety on the experience and coinage of the mind ... But England, and the kindred regions of Germany, have in their less favoured climates a depth of gloom which is known to characterize the northern spirit, in which external nature is admirably harmonious with the intellectual structure, by its influence thereupon eliciting the noblest efforts" (4, 34). "As is the scenery, so are national works of art," asserts Magoon as he explains the American preference for "romantic beauty" as a function of the "mists, clouds, woods, darkening tempests, and weeping rain" of the American climate (34–35). Predictably Mackay and O'Grady are convinced that, far from being productive of "noble ... effort," the grand scenery and extreme climate of Canada are ineffectual or, worse, debasing. On the contrary, argues Strachan, "Here simple nature noble ... thoughts inspires / And views of grandeur banish low desires" ("Verses ... 1802" *127–28*). In the same positive spirit as Strachan, Cary, Bayley, and Sangster stress the ennobling effect of Niagara Falls and the Saguenay fjord and Cary, Burwell, and Howe allude to the health-giving properties of the Canadian winter. In Upper Canada at least, thought O'Grady, the "diversity of climate" and the "richness of scenery" would impart the "excitement" and "energy" necessary for the production of poetry (preface *9–13*).

It is Lampman, however, who most explicitly describes the implications of the Canadian environment for national character and "national works of art." "We know that climatic and scenic conditions have much to do with the moulding of national character," he told the Ottawa Literary and Scientific Society in February 1891. "In the climate of this country we have the pitiless severity of the climate of Sweden, with the sunshine and the sky of the north of Italy, a combination not found in the same degree anywhere else in the world. The northern winters of Europe are seasons of terror and gloom; our winters are seasons of glittering splendour and incomparable richness of colour. At the same time we have the utmost diversity of scenery, a country exhibiting every variety of beauty and grandeur. A Canadian race, we imagine, might combine the energy, the seriousness, the perseverance of the Scandinavians with something of the gayety, the elasticity, the quickness of spirit of the south. If these qualities could be united in a literature, the result would indeed be novel and wonderful" ("Two Canadian Poets" 408). If Magoon's essay in *The Home Book of the Picturesque* is one source of these remarks, Washington Irving's essay on "The Catskill Mountains" in the same volume is another: "if ... changes from hot to cold ... [annoy us occasionally], they give us the brilliant sunshine of the south of Europe with the fresh verdure of the north ... Our seasons are all poetical; the phenomena of our heavens are full of sublimity and beauty. Winter with us has none of its poetical gloom ... [I]t has ... long intervals of cloudless sunshine, when the snow-clad earth gives redoubled brightness to the day" (74–75; and qtd. in Copleston 91–92). Derivative though they may be, Lampman's remarks to the Ottawa Literary and Scientific Society are typical of a mode of thinking about the Canadian climate, character, and culture that gained momentum in the pre-

Confederation period and, with the assistance of such works as R.G. Haliburton's *The Men of the North and Their Place in History* (1869), became a staple ingredient of the environmental nationalism of the new Dominion (Berger 53, 128–33). A belief in the interdependence of people and their environment is a persistent (and not entirely dated) assumption of early long poems on Canada and the emerging culture of which they are a part.

An aspect of the concern of Canada's early poets with "local ... incident and spirit" is the historical and commemorative component of many long poems. *Abram's Plains* celebrates Wolfe's decisive victory thirty years after the event. *Talbot Road* pays tribute to the "dauntless spirit" of Brock *(374)*. *Tecumseh* is a verbal monument to another hero of the War of 1812. *The U.E.* retells the events of the American Revolution and the Rebellions of 1837–38 as a means of sustaining the "Tory and Loyalist idea." For Cary, Burwell, Richardson, Kirby and others, the military leaders of 1775–83, 1812–14, and 1837–38 were the patriarchal creators and preservers of British North America. For poets who were inclined to temper or replace military with agricultural heroism, the founding fathers of the country were its early settlers: Colonel Thomas Talbot, Orator John, Malcolm Graem, and the unnamed pioneers of "Verses ... 1802," *Talbot Road, The Rising Village,* and *Acadia* who cleared the land and, when necessary, defended it – or died defending it – from the Native peoples. For poets with an eye on non-agricultural industries (and, perhaps, financial or political support from these quarters), the fur-trader (Cary), the merchant (Bayley), the fisherman (Howe), and the ship-owner (O'Grady) were also worthy of praise. In *Abram's Plains* even the cooks and tavern-keepers of Montreal and Quebec receive their due in passages which are so "local ... in incident and spirit" that they define their audience as residents and visitors to Lower Canada. No less than Goldsmith's depiction of Nova Scotia's pioneers or Kirby's celebration of Upper Canada's Loyalists, Cary's extravagent praise of Dillon's "culinary art," Horton's "soupes and jellies," and Le Moine's *"ragouts" (168–70)* cater to a community's desire to see itself reflected, honoured, advised, and teased in accomplished and enduring works of art.

The more mindful Canada's early poets were of the American Revolution, the War of 1812, the Rebellions of 1837–38, and the American treatment of Blacks and Native peoples, the more likely they were to imbue the Canadian "spirit" with an anti-American tincture. Thus *Abram's Plains* and "Verses ... 1802" are mildly anti-American, *Canada* and *The Huron Chief* more aggressively so, and *Tecumseh* and *The U.E.* virulent in their condemnation of American behaviour and attitudes. In

Kirby's poem especially the United States is portrayed as the selfish, materialistic, and godless antithesis of all that is good. Defined partly in contrast to demonic America, Canada emerges from Kirby's unique amalgam of Swedenborg, agrarian idealism, Scandinavian mythology, and neo-Loyalism as a conservative and spiritual community of the north – a "Forest Land" *(4:444)* in which the anti-American and pro-British heritage of the Loyalists provides the cornerstone of an "honoured Country" within a "proud Empire" *(6:245; 12:468)*. Such sentiments are understandable in a poem begun in the year of the repeal of the Corn Laws, but when *The U.E.* was published in 1859, after several years of reciprocity with the United States, they must have seemed delusively quaint to many Canadians. *The St. Lawrence and the Saguenay* makes no anti-American gestures but, rather, presents a body of materials with which middle-class tourists from both Canada and the United States could easily identify themselves: paradisial islands, cosy domestic scenes, uplifting bluffs, a devoted lover, and a coy "Maiden." As indicated by the nameless, and, therefore, not exclusively Canadian locales of *Malcolm's Katie* and *The Story of an Affinity,* the desire to cater to audiences on both sides of an increasingly undefended border did not diminish with Confederation. The Canadian spirit had become a commodity in the United States as well as Canada.

But cosmopolitan in form and manner. As this study has continually sought to demonstrate, early long poems on Canada occur at the inter-section of Canadian subject-matter and a variety of imported forms and genres, from the heroic couplet and the verse epistle to blank verse and the domestic idyll. Although several poets, most notably Cary and Lampman, gave explicit expression to their thoughts on the suitability of different types of verse to the matter at hand, none seems to have entertained the possibility of working outside the "cosmopolitan ... form and manner" of the day. Inevitably, the results have depended on the ability and desire of individual poets to modify their chosen model. Lampman's "song is not the mere echo of high poetic culture, he has a genuine note of his own" (Nicholas Flood Davin, qtd. in Koester 103), but many poems from pre- and post-Confederation Canada are what the reviewer of George A. Mackenzie's *Malcolm* in the 7 April 1887 issue of the *Week* calls "a somewhat faint echo of the song of greater bards, sometimes ... a mere weaving together of phrases culled from earlier writings" (306). When read with care and sympathy in relation to their models, most early long poems on Canada, including *The Story of an Affinity,* can be seen to fall between these extremes and to partake of both. *The St. Lawrence and the Saguenay,* for example, is in many places more than a "mere echo of high poetic culture," but in others it does read like a "weaving together" of elements drawn from Byron, Shelley, Wordsworth, and elsewhere. Behind the meeting of the Canadian and the cosmopolitan lies an urge to articulation and emulation that has yielded poetry of considerable accomplishment and, on occasion, delightful incongruity and dismaying bathos. In one couplet of *Abram's Plains* there is a "bleak northern gale" and the "balmy breeze" of a Thomsonian "Zephyrus" *(9–10)* and, of course, in *Acadia* there is that "gay Moose" which "in jocund gambol springs, / Cropping the foliage Nature round him flings" *(175–76)*.

It is scarcely surprising that readers coming to Canada's early poetry with high modern or "post-Romantic assumptions relating to artistic originality" and innovation have tended to dismiss the poets examined here as merely inept, derivative, and immature (Vincent vi; and see Bentley, *The Gay] Grey Moose* 262–63). Nor is it surprising that such readers have failed to discern the properties that make a canonical ensemble of early long poems on Canada. Where, they have asked, are the Canadian Wordsworth and the Canadian Whitman? Where are the original voices rather than the echoes, the radical innovators rather than the deferential imitators? The quest for such paragons is futile and frustrating for two reasons. First, eighteenth- and nineteenth-century English-Canadian culture persistently strove, not to supplant or transgress the British tradition, but to transplant and adapt it. An affirmation of cultural continuity amid new beginnings lies near the heart of poems as diverse as Strachan's "Verses ... 1802" and McLachlan's *Emigrant. Canada* is a celebration of British values and *The Rising Village* is a supplement to *The Deserted Village*. Secondly the continuity of early long poems on Canada does not reside, as readers accustomed to the British and American poetic traditions might well expect, in the truculent responses of later Canadian poets to earlier ones. Rather it consists of a respectful emulation of mainly British models coupled with responses to written materials of a sort still regarded by many critics as unworthy of serious attention: the non-fictional prose of Jonathan Carver, Isaac Weld, Joseph Pickering, Catharine Parr Traill, Charles Lanman, Sheridan Hogan, and a host of other explorers, travellers, settlers, and commentators. If Canada's early long poems are tapestries, as implied by the reviewer in the *Week,* they are tapestries woven of threads drawn, not just from their cosmopolitan poetic models, but also from prose sources closer to home. As has been seen, they do occasionally include materials taken from earlier poems on Canada: the presence of *Abram's Plains* in *The U.E.* is a case in point, as is the presence of Moore's "Ballad Stanzas" in "The Log Cabin" of McLachlan's *Emigrant.* But such examples are the exceptions to the general rule that the weft and warp of early long poems on Canada are their "cosmopolitan" poetic models and "local" prose sources.

Some simple story [located] in the Niagara district, among the old farmsteads – something in accordance with the quiet toilsome life there – maybe dated forty or fifty years back in rougher times. While *The Story of an Affinity* is not "dated forty or fifty years back," it confirms its kinship with early settler poems by alluding briefly to the "rougher times" of the pioneers. The Stahlberg and Hawthorne farms are the fruit of a lifetime or more of the "quiet toilsome life" that is chronicled in much greater detail (and often with Herculean associations and Lockean implications) in *Talbot Road, The Rising Village, Acadia, The U.E.,* and elsewhere. So, too, are the social and educational opportunities afforded to Margaret Hawthorne and Richard Stahlberg. The elegance and refinement of Katie Graem in *Malcolm's Katie* is a happy product of her father's and uncle's immense labours and the lax education and careless play of the young people in *The Rising Village* is a dispiriting insult to the "patient firmness and industrious toil" of previous generations *(103)*. Perhaps because it is a period of time that allows the post-pioneering generation to realize the benefits of their parents' and grandparents' "toilsome life," "forty or fifty years" is the favoured retrospective reach of Canadian settlement poems. In *The Rising Village,* "Not fifty Summers yet have blessed [Acadia's] clime" *(499)* and in McLachlan's *Emigrant* "Fifty years have passed away, / Fifty years this very day" since the Old Pioneer left Scotland *(1:29–30)*. When the children of Mariposa look at the headstones in the old Anglican cemetery, they find that "some of them are ever so old – forty or fifty years back" (Leacock 58).

The economic and architectural progression from the log hut of the pioneer to the "white-washed" house of the successful farmer is long-since complete in *The Story of an Affinity* (*1:465*). Like Malcolm Graem, Ranger John, and the panoptic farmer whom Burwell envisages in his "stately mansion" when he "summon[s] dark futurity to light" *(615, 546)*, the Stahlbergs and the Hawthornes have achieved the comfortable and independent life that constitutes the goal of pioneer hope, ambition, and dream. Not stressed but still evident in *The Story of an Affinity* are several of the emblems of pioneer progress and achievement: fields of golden corn, well-established orchards, barns filled with livestock, and what Kirby calls "Plenteous, cleanly, warm Canadian home[s]" *(5:320)*. To achieve such sufficiency and comfort is right and proper in a land of opportunity, provided always that success is achieved by honest work and accompanied by social responsibility. "Ye great, ye rich, by heart this lesson learn, / Nor, in pride of pow'r, the wretched spurn," cautions Cary *(532–33)*, and his advice is repeated in different ways by many other poets from the Colonial period. That this is so attests to the participation of early Canadian poetry in the ethical values and didactic tradition of Christianity. *The Huron Chief* celebrates the natural virtues of the Native peoples. Heterodox religious beliefs are present in *The U.E.* and McLachlan's *Emigrant.* But not until the Arnoldian shift from religion to culture that is reflected in *The Story of an Affinity* does a long poem on Canada distance itself radically from the Christian tradition to offer the therapy of nature and poetry as a cure for the psychological and spiritual diseases of modern, urban, society.

Whether Christian, Rousseauian, heterodox, or Arnoldian, however, early long poems on Canada agree in their moral insistence on the subordination of the individual to the communal. From Cary (and even Kelsey) to Lampman, the individual is deficient unless part of a group. In *The U.E.* American individualism destroys those whom it seduces and threatens the very existence of Canada. A prominent component of the villainy, not only of Hugh and his satanic co-conspirators, but also of Albert in *The Rising Village* and Alfred in *Malcolm's Katie* is their elevation of individual desire over communal responsibility. Near the core of *Tecumseh* is a military ethos that places great value on comradeship. One of the many faults that O'Grady finds with Lower Canada is a lack of fellow-feeling. In the final lines of *Acadia* the hardy fisherman and his loving family joyfully anticipate the return of their son. At the climax of Doubting John's speech in McLachlan's *Emigrant* "the fable of the wands" *(4:221)* is offered as a metaphor for a successful community in Canada. And at the conclusion of *The U.E.* Kirby places the "spirit" of Canada's founding fathers at the service of "England's proud Empire, One, for ever more" *(12:466–68).* Between the patriarchal family and the British Empire lies the space within which the "imagined community" (Anderson) of Canada gradually took shape, and not without the encouragement and assistance of its imaginative writers. "See what an empire is here," proclaims Sam Slick, "surely the best in climate, soil, mineral, and other productions in the world, and peopled by such a race as no country under the sun can produce. Here, Sir, are the bundle of sticks; all they want is to be well united" (T.C. Haliburton, qtd. in Morris 56).

A by-product of the insistence on community and the respect for the past in early Canadian poetry is a tolerance of individual eccentricities and cultural differences in so far as they pose no threat to a collectivity based on traditional British values. Partly because of the difficulty of creating rounded characters in poetry, most of the personae in early long poems on Canada are types: the Loyalist, the voyageur, the habitant, the settler, the bourgeois gentilhomme, the Highlander, the escaped slave, the successful farmer, the refined daughter, the New Woman, the Indian ... Whether they are viewed as ignoble or noble savages largely determines whether the Native peoples stand below or above the social space covered by this catalogue. Cary looks down on the Hurons at Lorette and Kidd looks up to the Huron chief. More ambivalently Richardson gives Tecumseh the elevation of an epic hero and the associations of Milton's Satan. In a couple of notable instances, however, Native peoples and their descendants stand almost beside Canadians of European origin. Reflecting the Christian view that "every individual" of every race is "a child of Adam, a brother, a person of the same feelings and of the same natural powers with ourselves, though differently modified by peculiar circumstances and habits" (Strachan, *Opinions* 28), Bayley sees beyond superficial appearances to the "form superior and reason great" of his typically "wild Indian" *(69–72).* Reflecting the assimilationist and reconciliatory views that were becoming widely accepted in the late nineteenth century, Crawford interfuses Max Gordon's pioneering activities with materials drawn from Native mythology and provides him with a "half-breed lad" as a helper *(2:165).* Below, above, beside, half-inside: the depiction of the Natives and Métis in early long poems on Canada indicates some of the limits of the hierarchical and Eurocentric culture that John Porter once described as a "vertical mosaic."

Sober and realistic, so to speak. Lampman illustrates this final point by referring in ascending order to works by Longfellow, Goethe, and Runenberg, a Swedish poet whom Edmund Gosse characterizes as "the great Finnish realist" and praises for a "rich severity of style" reminiscent of *Evangeline* and *Hermann and Dorothea* (133, 107, 105, 108). Apparently, the "cosmopolitan ... form and manner" that Lampman originally had in mind for *The Story of an Affinity* was hexameter – the metre of the *Iliad*, the *Odyssey*, the *Aeneid*. This is consistent with the urge to high seriousness, if not always to epic, that marks long poems on Canada well into the Victorian period. *Abram's Plains* begins with a delayed verb reminiscent of the opening of Dryden's translation of the *Aeneid; Tecumseh* contains several epic devices; *The U.E.* is epical in structure. But by the 1860s – as witness the "chapters" of McLachlan's *Emigrant* – the epic ambition was being replaced by the novelistic desire to tell a story, preferably one containing at least some of the sentimental elements valued by mid-Victorian audiences. With its tearful departure and even more tearful death scene, McLachlan's poem fulfils these expectations, as to an extent does Crawford's. Despite Lampman's description of it as "a small novel in blank verse," *The Story of an Affinity* does not, however, and for an obvious reason: by the 1890s sentimental romance was well on its way to being displaced by genteel realism as the dominant mode of Canadian fiction. In its combination of romantic and realistic elements, with the balance tipped slightly towards the latter, Lampman's poem is a product of the period in Canada that would soon yield Sara Jeannette Duncan's *The Imperialist* (1904) and Stephen Leacock's *Sunshine Sketches of a Little Town* (1912).

As a description and a celebration of a part of Canada and its people, *The Story of an Affinity* is also consonant with the continuity of the long poem that had its tentative beginnings almost exactly two centuries before Lampman started giving Thomson sporadic bulletins on the progress of his "novelette in verse." Of course numerous changes occurred in the two intervening centuries, many as the result of the growing European presence in Canada and not all of them good. In the book that he received as a "Gift ... in the year of our Lord 1693" Kelsey applied the word "Buffillo" to the North American bison for the first time in written English. In his *At the Mermaid Inn* column on 24 June 1893 Lampman recorded "the buffalo practically extinct and the wild pigeon rapidly becoming so" (339). At the end of the eighteenth century the most sublime sight in Canada was Niagara Falls, but by the end of the nineteenth this natural wonder was being joined by other fearfully sublime sights: "legions of grimed [railway] cars and ranks / Of sooty walls, and ... the reeking depths / Of ringing foundries, and the flaring gleams / Of smoke-veiled forges" (*The Story of an Affinity* 2:29–32). Different they certainly were, and in countless ways, but Kelsey, Lampman, and most of the poets writing about Canada in the centuries between them surely shared, not only Cary's respect for "descriptive poetry," but also his desire "to vary, harmonize, soften and add the necessary graces to description to make it palatable to a judicious and poetical reader" (preface 7–11). The results of this desire inevitably vary in their success and appeal, but all offer insights of enduring interest to any reader "judicious and poetical" enough to care about Canada as it was and is.

Works Cited

To avoid needless repetition and prolixity, most items in newspapers have been identified at the point of citation only. Items that have been filmed by the Canadian Institute for Historical Microreproductions are followed by the CIHM fiche number in square brackets.

Abbott, Joseph. *Memoranda of a Settler in Lower Canada; or, the Emigrant to North America*. Montreal: Lovell and Gibson for the Author, 1842. [21859]

Adams, Levi. *Jean Baptiste: a Poetic Olio, in II Cantos*. 1825. Reprint, ed. Carl F. Klinck. Early Canadian Poetry Series. Ottawa: The Golden Dog Press, 1978.

Adams, Percy G. *Travel Literature and the Evolution of the Novel*. Lexington: University of Kentucky Press, 1983.

Aikin, J. *An Essay on the Application of Natural History to Poetry*. 1777. Reprint, New York: Garland, 1970.

Anburey, Thomas. *Travels through the Interior Parts of America. In a Series of Letters*. London: William Lane, 1789. [39152]

Anderson, Benedict. *Imagined Communities: Reflections on the Origin and Spread of Nationalism*. London: Verso and NLB, 1983.

Aristotle. *The Art of Rhetoric*. Trans. John H. Freese. New York: Loeb, 1926.

Arnold, Matthew. *The Complete Prose Works*. Ed. R.H. Super. 11 vols. Ann Arbor: University of Michigan Press, 1960–77.

——. *Poetical Works*. London: Macmillan, 1890.

Arrington, Joseph Earl. "William Burr's Moving Panorama of the Great Lakes, the Niagara, St. Lawrence and Saguenay Rivers." *Ontario History* 51 (1959): 141–62.

Atwood, Margaret. *The Journals of Susanna Moodie*. Toronto: Oxford University Press, 1970.

Aubin, R.A. *Topographical Poetry in XVIII-Century England*. New York: Modern Language Association of America, 1936.

Auerbach, Nina. *Woman and the Demon: the Life of a Victorian Myth*. Cambridge: Harvard University Press, 1982.

Axon, Ernest. *The Bayley Family of Manchester and Hope*. Manchester: Manchester Press, 1890.

Baker, Ray Palmer. *A History of English-Canadian Literature to the Confederation*. Cambridge, Mass.: Harvard University Press, 1920.

Bartram, John. *Observations on the Inhabitants, Climate, Soil, Rivers, Productions, Animals, and Other Matters Worthy of Notice. Made ... in His Travels from Pennsylvania to Onondago, Oswego and the Lake Ontario in Canada. To Which Is Annex'd, a Curious Account of the Cataracts at Niagara by Mr. Peter Kalm, a Swedish Gentlemen Who Travelled There*. London: J. Whiston and B. White, 1751. [11915]

Bayley, Cornwall. *Canada. A Descriptive Poem. Written at Quebec, 1805*. 1806. Reprint, ed. D.M.R. Bentley. London: Canadian Poetry Press, 1990.

Beasley, David R. *The Canadian Don Quixote: the Life and Works of Major John Richardson, Canada's First Novelist*. Erin, Ont.: The Porcupine's Quill, 1977.

Beck, J. Murray. "Joseph Howe." *Dictionary of Canadian Biography* 10: 362–70.

Bentley, D.M.R. "Breaking the 'Cake of Custom': the Atlantic Crossing as a Rubicon for Female Emigrants to Canada?" In *Re(Dis)covering Our Foremothers: Nineteenth-Century Canadian Women Writers*, ed. Lorraine McMullen. Re-Appraisals: Canadian Writers, 15. Ottawa: University of Ottawa Press, 1990. 91–122.

———. "Carman and Mind Cure." In *Bliss Carman: A Reappraisal*, ed. Gerald Lynch. Re-Appraisals: Canadian Writers, 16. Ottawa: University of Ottawa Press, 1990. 85–110.

———. "Concepts of Native Peoples and Property Rights in Early Canadian Poetry." *Recherches sémiotiques / Semiotic Inquiry* 12 (1992): 29–51.

———. "An Early 'Specimen of Canadian Poetry.'" *Canadian Poetry: Studies, Documents, Reviews* 26 (1990): 70–74.

———. *The Gay]Grey Moose: Essays on the Ecologies and Mythologies of Canadian Poetry, 1690–1990*. Ottawa: University of Ottawa Press, 1992.

———. "Historied Trees." *Canadian Poetry: Studies, Documents, Reviews* 34 (1994): 1-19.

———. Introduction and Editorial Notes to *Abram's Plains* by Thomas Cary. London: Canadian Poetry Press, 1986. xi–xlviii, 27–43.

———. Introduction and Editorial Notes to *Canada* by Cornwall Bayley. London: Canadian Poetry Press, 1990. xi–liii, 27–81.

———. Introduction and Editorial Notes to *The Charivari* by George Longmore. London: Canadian Poetry Press, 1991. xi–li, 69–131.

———. Introduction, Editorial Notes, and Appendix to *The Emigrant* by Alexander McLachlan. London: Canadian Poetry Press, 1991. xi–lxii, 65–108, 109–144.

———. Introduction, Editorial Notes, Appendices to *The Huron Chief* by Adam Kidd. London: Canadian Poetry Press, 1987. xi–xliii, 61–106, 107–132.

———. Introduction, Editorial Notes, and Appendices to *Malcolm's Katie* by Isabella Valancy Crawford. London: Canadian Poetry Press, 1987. xi–lxi, 39–74, 75–101.

———. Introduction and Editorial Notes to *Quebec Hill* by J. Mackay. London: Canadian Poetry Press, 1988. xi–xlvii, 29–63.

———. Introduction, Explanatory Notes, and Appendices to *The St. Lawrence and the Saguenay* by Charles Sangster. London: Canadian Poetry Press, 1990. xi–lxi, 45–94, 95–147.

———. Introduction to *Talbot Road* by Adam Hood Burwell. London: Canadian Poetry Press, 1991. xi–xlviii.

———. "Isaac Weld and the Continuity of Canadian Poetry." In *Biography and Autobiography: Essays on Irish and Canadian History and Literature*, ed. James Noonan. Ottawa: Carleton University Press, 1993. 223–36.

———. "Monumentalités." *Canadian Poetry: Studies, Documents, Reviews* 32 (1993): 1–16.

———. "Oliver Goldsmith and *The Rising Village.*" *Studies in Canadian Literature* 15.1 (1990): 21–61.

———. "Savage, Degenerate, and Dispossessed: Some Sociological, Anthropological, and Legal Backgrounds to the Depiction of Native Peoples in Early Long Poems on Canada." *Canadian Literature* 124–25 (1990): 76–90. Also in *Native Writers and Canadian Writing*, ed. W.H. New. Vancouver: University of British Columbia Press, 1990. 76–90.

———. "'Set Forth as Plainly May Appear': the Verse Journal of Henry Kelsey." *Ariel* 21.4 (1990): 9–30.

———. "Watchful Dreams and Sweet Unrest: an Essay on the Vision of Archibald Lampman," Parts 1 and 2. *Studies in Canadian Literature* 6.2 (1981): 188–210 and *SCL* 7 (1982): 5–26.

Berger, Carl. *The Sense of Power: Studies in the Ideas of Canadian Imperialism, 1867–1914.* Toronto: University of Toronto Press, 1970.

Bermingham, Anne. *Landscape and Ideology: the English Rustic Tradition, 1740–1860.* Berkeley: University of California Press, 1986.

Black, Robert Merrill. "Stablished in the Faith: the Church of England in Upper Canada, 1780–1867." In *By Grace Co-Workers: Building the Anglican Diocese of Toronto, 1780–1789*, ed. Alan L. Hayes. Toronto: Anglican Book Centre, 1989. 21–41.

Blackstone, Sir William. *Commentaries on the Laws of England.* 15th ed. 2 vols. London: A. Strachan, 1809.

Block, Marguerite Beck. *The New Church in the New World: a Study of Swedenborgianism in America.* New York: Henry Holt, 1932.

Brerewood, Edward. *Enquiries Touching the Diversity of Languages and Religions, through the Chief Parts of the World.* London: John Norton, 1635.

Bristol, Michael. *Carnival and Theatre: Plebeian Culture and the Structure of Authority.* New York: Methuen, 1985.

Brontë, Emily. *Wuthering Heights.* 1847. Reprint, Boston: Houghton Mifflin, 1956.

Brooke, Francis. *The History of Emily Montague.* 1769. Reprint, ed. Mary Jane Edwards. Ottawa: Carleton University Press, 1985.

Brunger, Alan G. "Thomas Talbot." *Dictionary of Canadian Biography* 8: 857–61.

Bryce, George. *Manitoba: its Infancy, Growth and Present Position.* London: S. Low, Marston, Searle and Rivington, 1882. [30042]

Buchan, William F. *Remarks on Emigration: More Particularly Applicable to the Eastern Townships, Lower Canada.* 2nd ed. Devonport: Soper and Richards; London: Baldwin and Cradock, [1831]. [21858]

Buchanan, James. *Sketches of the History, Manners, and Customs of the North American Indians.* London: Black, Young, and Young, 1825. [28448]

Bumstead, J.M. *The People's Clearance: Highland Emigration to British North America, 1770–1815.* Edinburgh: Edinburgh University Press, 1982.

Burke, Edmund. *Philosophical Enquiry into the Origin of Our Ideas of the Sublime and the Beautiful.* 1756. Reprint, New York: Garland, 1971.

——. *Reflections on the Revolution in France.* 1790. Reprint, ed. Thomas H.D. Mahoney. Indianapolis: Liberal Arts Press, 1955.

Burns, Robert. *The Poetical Works.* 3 vols. London: Bell and Daldy, 1839.

Burns, Robert Alan. "Crawford and Gounod: Ambiguity and Irony in *Malcolm's Katie.*" *Canadian Poetry: Studies, Documents, Reviews* 15 (1984): 1–30.

Burr, William. *Descriptive and Historical View of Burr's Moving Mirror of the Lakes, the Niagara, St. Lawrence, and Saguenay Rivers, Embracing the Entire Range of Border Scenery of the United States and Canadian Shores, from Lake Erie to the Atlantic.* Boston: Dutton and Wentworth, 1850. [43092]

Burrows, Acton. *North-Western Canada, Its Climate, Soil and Productions with a Sketch of Its Natural Features and Social Condition.* Winnipeg: n.p., 1880. [30068]

Burwell, Adam Hood. *The Poems.* Ed. Carl F. Klinck. Western Ontario History Nuggets 30. London: Lawson Memorial Library, University of Western Ontario, 1963.

——. *Talbot Road: a Poem.* 1818. Reprint, ed. Michael Williams, with intro. by D.M.R. Bentley. London: Canadian Poetry Press, 1991.

Butler, W.F. *The Great Lone Land: a Narrative of Travel and Adventure in the North-West of America.* 1872. 8th ed. Reprint, London: Sampson Low, Marston, Searle, and Rivington, 1878. [30041]

Byron, Lord. *The Complete Poetical Works of Lord Byron.* Ed. Paul E. More. Boston: Houghton Mifflin, 1905.

Campbell, Thomas. *The Complete Poetical Works.* 1907. Ed. J. Logie Robertson. Reprint, New York: Haskell House, 1968.

Campbell, Wanda. "The *Bildungsgedicht* as Garden in Nineteenth- and Twenti-eth-Century Canadian Long Poems." Ph.D. diss., University of Western Ontario, 1991.

Campbell, William Wilfred. *The Scotsman in Canada.* 2 vols. Toronto: Musson, n.d.

Canadian Settler, Late of Portsea, Hants. *The Emigrant's Informant; or, a Guide to Upper Canada: Containing Reasons for Emigration, Who Should Emigrate, Neces-saries for Outfit, and Charges of Voyage, Travelling Expenses, Manners of the Amer-icans; Qualities and Capabilities of the Soil, Price Current of the Country for 1833.* London: G. Cowie; Edinburgh: Stirling and Kenny; Dublin: John Cumming, 1834. [21477]

Careless, J.M.S. "The 1850's." In *Colonists and Canadians,* ed. J.M.S. Careless. Toronto: Macmillan, 1971. 226–48.

——. Introduction to *The Defended Border: Upper Canada and the War of 1812.* Ed. M. Zaslow. Toronto: Macmillan, 1964. 1–8.

——. "'Limited Identities' in Canada." *Canadian Historical Review* 50 (1969): 1–10.

Carlyle, Thomas. *Critical and Miscellaneous Essays.* 1840. Reprint, Philadelphia: A. Hart, Late Carey and Hart, 1850.

——. *Past and Present.* 1843. Reprint, London: Dent, 1966.

——. *Sartor Resartus.* 1833. Reprint, ed. Charles Frederick Harold. New York: Odyssey, 1937.

Carman, Bliss. *Sappho: One Hundred Lyrics.* 1903. Reprint, London: Chatto and Windus, 1930.

Carver, Jonathan. *Travels through the Interior Parts of North America in the Years 1766, 1767, and 1768.* 1778. 3rd ed. 1781. Reprint, Minneapolis: Ross and Haines, 1956.

Cary, Thomas. *Abram's Plains: a Poem.* 1789. Reprint, ed. D.M.R. Bentley. Lon-don: Canadian Poetry Press, 1986.

Casselman, Alexander Clark. Introduction *Richardson's War of 1812; with Notes and Life of the Author.* Toronto: Historical Publishing Company, 1902.

Cattermole, William. *Emigration. The Advantages of Emigration to Canada.* Lon-don: Simpkin and Marshall, 1831. [32464]

Charlevoix, P[ierre] de. *Journal of a Voyage to North-America. Undertaken by Order of the French King. Containing the Geographical Description and History of Canada. Together with an Account of the Customs, Characters, Religion, Manners and Tradi-tions of the Original Inhabitants. In a Series of Letters to the Duchess of Lesdiguieres.* 2 vols. London: R. and J. Dodsley, 1761. [32770]

Charters, Statutes, Orders in Council & c. Relating to the Hudson's Bay Company. Lon-don: Hudson's Bay Company, 1931.

Chisholme, David. Review of *The Charivari,* by George Longmore. *The Canadian Review and Literary and Historical Journal* 1 (July 1824): 183–201.

Christy, Miller. Introduction to *The Voyages of Captain Luke Foxe and Captain Thomas James of Bristol, in Search of the North-West Passage, in 1631–32.* Works Issued by the Hakluyt Society, No. 88. 2 vols. London: Hakluyt Society, 1894. 1: i–l. [11869]

"The Cities of Canada: Toronto." *Anglo-American Magazine* 1 (July 1852): 1–4.

Cochrane, William. *The Canadian Album. Men of Canada; or, Success by Example, in Religion, Patriotism, Business, Law, Medicine, Education and Agriculture* .... 3 vols. Brantford, Ont.: Bradley, Garretson, 1891.

Cohen, Ralph. *The Unfolding of the Seasons.* Baltimore: John Hopkins, 1970.

Coke, Sir Edward. *The Third Part of the Institutes of the Laws of England: Concerning High Treason, and Other Pleas of the Crown, and Criminal Cases.* 4th ed. London: A. Crooke et al., 1669.

Colden, Cadwallader. *History of the Five Indian Nations of Canada, Which Are Dependent on the Province of New-York in America, and Are the Barrier Between the English and French in That Part of the World.* London: Printed for T. Osborne, 1747. [33241]

Collins, William. *The Poems of Thomas Gray, William Collins, Oliver Goldsmith.* Ed. Roger Lonsdale. London: Longmans, Green, 1969.

Connell, W.F. *The Educational Thought and Influence of Matthew Arnold.* International Library of Sociology and Social Reconstruction. London: Routledge and Kegan Paul, 1950.

Connor, Carl Y. *Archibald Lampman: Canadian Poet of Nature.* New York and Montreal: Louis Carrier, 1929.

Cook, Terry. "John Beverley Robinson and the Conservative Blueprint for the Upper Canadian Community." *Ontario History* 64 (1972): 79–94.

Cooper, Anthony Ashley, Earl of Shaftesbury. *Characteristicks.* 1714. Reprint, 3 vols. London: n.p., 1733.

Cooper, James Fenimore. *The Last of the Mohicans.* 1826. Reprint, London: Collins, 1953.

Copleston, Mrs. Edward. *Canada: Why We Live in It, and Why We Like It.* London: Parker, Son, and Bourn, 1861. [48475]

Costain, Keith. "Sticks and Bundle: *Lawrie Todd* and *Bogle Corbet:* Galt's Portraits of Two Nations." *British Journal of Canadian Studies* 7.1 (1992): 26–38.

Cowper, William. *The Poetical Works of William Cowper.* Ed. H.S. Milford. 4th ed. London: Oxford University Press, 1950.

Craig, G.M. "John Strachan." *Dictionary of Canadian Biography* 9: 751–66.

Crawford, Isabella Valancy. *The Collected Poems.* Ed. J.W. Garvin. Toronto: Briggs, 1905.

———. *Malcolm's Katie: a Love Story.* Ed. D.M.R. Bentley. London: Canadian Poetry Press, 1987.

———. *Old Spookses' Pass, Malcolm's Katie, and Other Poems.* Toronto: James Bain and Son, 1884.

Creighton, Donald. *The Empire of the St. Lawrence.* 1937. Reprint, Toronto: Macmillan, 1956.

Crèvecoeur, St. John. *Letters from an American Farmer.* 1782. Reprint, London: Chatto and Windus; New York: Duffield, 1908.

Cullen, Michael. "A Scholarly Edition of George Longmore's *The Charivari; or Canadian Poetics.*" M.A. diss., University of Western Ontario, 1989.

Curtius, Ernst Robert. *European Literature and the Latin Middle Ages.* Trans. Willard R. Trask. Bollingen Series, No. 36. New York: Pantheon, 1953.

Daniells, Roy. "Crawford, Carman, and D.C. Scott." *Literary History of Canada.* Ed. Carl F. Klinck. 1965. Reprint, Toronto: University of Toronto Press, 1973. 406–21.

Davidson, Donald. *Inquiries into Truth and Interpretation.* Oxford: Clarendon, 1984.

Davies, Barrie, ed. *At the Mermaid Inn: Wilfred Campbell, Archibald Lampman, Duncan Campbell Scott, in the Globe 1892–93.* Literature of Canada: Poetry and Prose in Reprint. Toronto: University of Toronto Press, 1979.

Davies, K.G. "Henry Kelsey." *Dictionary of Canadian Biography* 2: 307–15.

Daymond, Douglas and Leslie Monkman. Introduction, Editorial Notes, and Appendices to *Tecumseh* by John Richardson. London: Canadian Poetry Press, 1992. xi–xlviii, 73–182, 183–86.

——, eds. *Towards a Canadian Literature: Essays, Editorials and Manifestos.* 2 vols. Ottawa: Tecumseh, 1984.

Denham, John. *The Poetical Works.* Ed. Theodore Howard Banks. 2nd ed. Reprint, Hamden, Conn.: Archan Books, 1969.

Dent, John Charles. *The Story of the Upper Canadian Rebellion; Largely Derived from Original Sources and Documents.* 2 vols. Toronto: C.B. Robinson, 1985.

Dewart, E.H. "Introductory Essay." In *The Poetical Works of Alexander McLachlan.* 1900. Reprint, ed. E. Margaret Fulton. Literature of Canada: Poetry and Prose in Reprint. Toronto: University of Toronto Press, 1974. 9–15.

Dixon, W. MacNeile, and H.J.C. Grierson, eds. *The English Parnassus: an Anthology Chiefly of Longer Poems.* 1909. Reprint, Oxford: Clarendon, 1961.

Djwa, Sandra. "Lampman's Fleeting Vision." In *Colony and Confederation: Early Canadian Poets and Their Background,* ed. George Woodcock. Vancouver: University of British Columbia Press, 1974. 124–41.

Doige, Thomas. *An Alphabetical List of Merchants, Traders, and Housekeepers, Residing in Montreal.* Montreal: James Lane, 1819. [36464]

Dowse, Thomas. *Manitoba and the Northwest Territories. The Real New Northwest.* Rev. ed. St. Paul, Minnesota: n.p. [1879]. [26087]

Doyle, James. "Archibald Lampman and Hamlin Garland." *Canadian Poetry: Studies, Documents, Reviews* 16 (1985): 38–46.

Dudek, Louis. "Crawford's Achievement." In *The Crawford Symposium,* ed. Frank M. Tierney. Re-Appraisals: Canadian Writers. Ottawa: University of Ottawa Press, 1979: 123–25.

Duffy, Dennis. *Gardens, Covenants, Exiles: Loyalism in the Literature of Upper Canada/Ontario.* Toronto: University of Toronto Press, 1982.

Duncan, Sara Jeannette. *The Imperialist.* 1904. Reprint, ed. Thomas E. Tausky. Ottawa: Tecumseh, 1988.

Dunn, Charles W. *Highland Settler: a Portrait of the Scottish Gael in Nova Scotia.* Toronto: University of Toronto Press, 1973.

Dunn, Margo. "A Preliminary Checklist of the Writings of Isabella Valancy Crawford." In *The Crawford Symposium,* ed. Frank M. Tierney. Re-Appraisals: Canadian Writers. Ottawa: University of Ottawa Press, 1979. 141–55.

Durham, the Earl of. *Report on the Affairs of British North America.* 3 vols. Ed. Sir C.P. Lucas. Oxford: Clarendon, 1912.

Early, L.R. "A Chronology of Lampman's Poems." *Canadian Poetry: Studies, Documents, Reviews* 14 (1984): 75–87.

———. "Lampman's Love Poetry." *Essays on Canadian Writing* 27 (1983–84): 116–49.

Edwards, Mary Jane. "Adam Kidd." *Dictionary of Canadian Biography* 6: 375–77.

———. "Alexander McLachlan." *Dictionary of Canadian Biography* 12: 660–64.

Eldridge, Herbert G. "Anacreon Moore and America." *PMLA* 83 (1968): 54–62.

Eliot, George. *Adam Bede.* 1859. Reprint, London and Edinburgh: W. and R. Chambers, [1925].

Ex-Settler. *Canada in the Years 1832, 1833, and 1834.* Dublin: Philip Dixon Hardy; London: Richard Groombridge, 1835. [21476]

Fabricant, Carole. "Binding and Dressing Nature's Loose Tresses: the Ideology of Augustan Landscape Design." *In Studies in Eighteenth-Century Culture,* ed. Roseann Runte. Madison: University of Wisconsin Press, 1979. 8: 109–35.

Fairchild, Hoxie Neale. *The Noble Savage: a Study in Romantic Naturalism.* New York: Columbia University Press, 1928.

Farmiloe, Dorothy. *Isabella Valancy Crawford: the Life and Legends.* Ottawa: Tecumseh, 1983.

Fingard, Judith. *The Anglican Design in Loyalist Nova Scotia, 1783–1816.* London: SPCK, 1972.

Flint, David. *John Strachan: Pastor and Politician.* Toronto: Oxford University Press, 1971.

Foster, John Wilson. "A Redefinition of Topographical Poetry." *Journal of English and Germanic Philology* 69 (1970): 394–406.

"Frost." *Encyclopedia Britannica.* 1771.

Frye, Northrop. *Anatomy of Criticism: Four Essays.* Princeton: Princeton University Press, 1957.

———. "The Road of Excess." In *Contexts of Canadian Criticism: a Collection of Critical Essays,* ed. Eli Mandel. 1971. Reprint, Toronto: University of Toronto Press, 1977. 125–39.

Fussell, Paul. *Poetic Meter and Poetic Form.* Rev. ed. 1965. New York: Random House, 1973.

Gagan, David. "Land, Population, and Social Change: the 'Critical Years' in Rural Canada West." *Canadian Historical Review* 69 (1978): 293–318.

Galbraith, John Kenneth. *The Scotch.* 1964. Reprint, Baltimore: Penguin, 1966.

Galinsky, G. Karl. *The Herakles Theme: the Adaptations of the Hero in Literature from Homer to the Twentieth Century.* Oxford: Basil Blackwell, 1972.

Galt, John. *Bogle Corbet; or, the Emigrants.* 3 vols. London: Henry Colburn and R. Bentley, [1831]. [42427]

——. *Lawrie Todd; or, the Settlers in the Woods.* 3 vols. London: Colburn and Bentley, 1830. [44268]

Garland, Martha McMackin. *Cambridge before Darwin: the Ideal of a Liberal Education, 1800–1860.* Cambridge: Cambridge University Press, 1980.

Gauvin, Daniel. "Thomas Cary." *Dictionary of Canadian Biography* 6: 123–24.

Geertz, Clifford. *The Interpretation of Cultures: Selected Essays.* New York: Basic Books, 1973.

Gilbert, Sandra M. and Susan Gubar. *The Madwoman in the Attic: the Woman Writer and the Nineteenth-Century Literary Imagination.* New Haven: Yale University Press, 1979.

Gilchrist, John. *Collection of Scottish Ballads, Tales, and Songs, Ancient and Modern.* 2 vols. Leith: Gilchrist and Heriot, 1814.

Gingell-Beckmann. "Joseph Howe's *Acadia:* Document of a Divided Sensibility." *Canadian Poetry: Studies, Documents, Reviews* 10 (1982): 18–31.

Glickman, Susan. "Canadian Prospects: *Abram's Plains* in Context." *University of Toronto Quarterly* 59 (1990): 498–515.

Gnarowski, Michael. Introduction and Notes to *The Rising Village* by Oliver Goldsmith. Montreal: Delta, 1969, ix–xii, *passim.*

——. Introduction to *Selected Poetry of Archibald Lampman,* ed. M. Gnarowski. Ottawa: Tecumseh, 1990. 1–36.

——. ed. *Three Early Poems from Lower Canada.* Montreal: Lawrence Lande Foundation, 1969.

Goldsmith, Oliver. *The Collected Works of Oliver Goldsmith.* Ed. Arthur Friedman. 5 vols. Oxford: Clarendon, 1966.

——. *History of Man and Quadrupeds; with Numerous Original Notes, &c. &c.* 1774. Reprint, 2 vols. London: Smith, Elder, and Co. and T. Tegg and Son, 1838.

Goldsmith, Oliver. *Autobiography of Oliver Goldsmith: a Chapter in Canada's Literary History.* 2nd ed. Ed. Wilfred Myatt. Hauntsport, N.S.: Lancelot, 1985.

——. *The Rising Village.* Ed. Michael Gnarowski. Montreal: Delta, 1968.

——. *The Rising Village.* Ed. Gerald Lynch. London: Canadian Poetry Press, 1989.

Goltz, Herbert C.W. "Tecumseh." *Dictionary of Canadian Biography* 5: 795–801.

Gosse, Edmund W. *Studies in the Literature of Northern Europe.* London: Kegan Paul, 1879.

Gourlay, Robert. *Statistical Account of Upper Canada. Compiled with a View to a Grand System of Emigration.* London: Simpkins, Marshall, 1822. [35936]

Gowans, Alan. *Building Canada: an Architectural History of Canadian Life.* Toronto: Oxford University Press, 1966.

Grant, George M. *Ocean to Ocean: Sanford Fleming's Expedition through Canada in 1872.* Toronto: James Campbell and Son; London: Sampson, Low, Marston, Low and Searle, 1873. [29013]

Grant, John Webster. *A Profusion of Spires: Religion in Nineteenth-Century Ontario.* The Ontario Historical Studies Series. Toronto: University of Toronto Press, 1988.

Gray, Thomas. *The Poems of Thomas Gray, William Collins, Oliver Goldsmith.* Ed. Roger Lonsdale. London: Longmans, Green, 1969.

Green, David. "Land, Population, and Social Change: the 'Critical Years' in Rural Canada West." *Canadian Historical Review* 59 (1978): 293–318.

Greenblatt, Stephen. *Marvelous Possessions: the Wonder of the New World.* Chicago: University of Chicago Press, 1991.

Gross, Conrad. "Coureurs-de-bois, Voyageurs, and Trappers: the Fur Trade and the Emergence of an Ignored Canadian Literary Tradition." *Canadian Literature* 127 (1990): 76–91.

Guerin v. The Queen [1984] 2 SCR 335–95.

Hale, Katherine. *Isabella Valancy Crawford.* Makers of Canadian Literature. Toronto: Ryerson, [1923].

Haliburton, R.G. *The Men of the North and Their Place in History: a Lecture Delivered before the Montreal Literary Club, March 31st, 1869.* Montreal: J. Lovell, 1869. [23595]

Haliburton, Thomas Chandler. *A General Description of Nova Scotia.* 2nd ed. Halifax: Royal Acadian School, 1825. [61044]

——. *An Historical and Statistical Account of Nova Scotia.* Halifax: Joseph Howe, 1829. [35689]

Hall, Basil. *Travels in North America in the Years 1827 and 1828.* 3 vols. Edinburgh: Cadell; London: Simpkin and Marshall, 1829.

Hall, E. Hepple. *Lands of Plenty. British North America for Health, Sport, and Profit. A Book for All Travellers and Settlers.* London: W.H. Allen; Toronto: James Campbell and Son, 1879. [05336]

Hall, Francis. *Travels in Canada and the United States in 1816 and 1817.* London: Longman, Hurst, Rees, Orme and Brown, 1818. [35674]

Hamilton, J.C. *The Prairie Province; Sketches of Travel from Lake Ontario to Lake Winnipeg, and an Account of the Geographical Position, Climate, Civil Insititutions, Inhabitants, Productions and Resources of the Red River Valley ....* Toronto: Belford Brothers, 1876. [30290]

Harrison, Susie Frances ["Seranus"]. "Isabella Valancy Crawford." *The Week* (14 February 1887): 202–03.

——. *Pine, Rose, and Fleur de Lis.* Toronto: Hart, 1891. [05387]

Hartman, Geoffrey H. *The Fate of Reading and Other Essays.* Chicago: Phoenix Books, 1975.

Hearne, Samuel. *A Journey from Prince of Wales's Fort in Hudson's Bay to the Northern Ocean, 1769, 1770, 1771, 1772.* 1795. Reprint, ed. Richard G. Glover. Toronto: Macmillan, 1958.

Heintzman, Ralph. "The Spirit of Confederation: Professor Creighton, Biculturalism and the Use of History." *Canadian Historical Review* 52 (1971): 245–75.

Henry, George. *The Emigrant's Guide, or Canada as It Is.* Quebec: William Gray, n.d. [35678]

Heriot, George. *Travels through the Canadas, Containing a Description of the Picturesque Scenery on Some of the Rivers and Lakes; with an Account of the Productions, Commerce, and Inhabitants of those Provinces. To Which Is Subjoined a Comparative View of the Manners and Customs of Several of the Indian Nations of North and South America.* 1807. Reprint, Edmonton: M.G. Hurtig, 1971.

Herodotus. *The History of Herodotus.* Trans. G.C. Macauley. 2 vols. London: Macmillan, 1914.

Hickey, William ["Martin Doyle"]. *Hints on Emigration to Upper Canada; Especially Addressed to the Lower Classes in Great Britain and Ireland.* Dublin: William Curry, Jun.; London: Hurst, Chance; Edinburgh: Oliver and Boyd, 1831. [34771]

Hogan, J. Sheridan. *Canada. An Essay: to Which Was Awarded the First Prize by the Paris Exhibition Committee of Canada.* Montreal: John Lovell, 1855. [12981]

Hollander, John. *Vision and Resonance: Two Senses of Poetic Form.* 2nd ed. New Haven: Yale University Press, 1985.

[Hollingsworth, S.]. *Nova Scotia: with a Brief Account of Canada, and the British Islands on the Coast of North America.* 2nd ed. Edinburgh: William Creech, 1787. [35778]

Horace. *The Odes and Epodes.* Trans. C.E. Bennett. Loeb Classical Library. Cambridge, Mass.: Harvard University Press, 1960.

——. *Satires, Epistles and Ars Poetica.* 1926. Trans. H. Rushton Fairclough. Loeb Classical Library. Reprint, Cambridge, Mass.: Harvard University Press; London: William Heinemann, 1961.

Horetzky, Charles. *The North-West of Canada: Being a Brief Sketch of the North-Western Regions, and a Treatise on the Future Resources of the Country.* Ottawa: Printed at the Office of A.S. Woodburn, 1873. [23833]

Howe, Joseph. *Acadia.* Ed. M.G. Parks. London: Canadian Poetry Press, 1989.

——. *An Address Delivered before the Halifax Mechanics' Institute, On the 5th November, 1834.* Halifax, N.S.: Published by Request of the Institute, 1834. [45235]

——. *An Opening Address, Delivered at the First Meeting of the Halifax Mechanics' Institute, on Wednesday, January 11, 1832.* Halifax, N.S.: P.J. Holland, at the Acadian Recorder Office, 1832. [21391]

——. *Poems and Essays.* 1874. Reprint, intro. M.G. Parks. Literature of Canada: Poetry and Prose in Reprint. Toronto: University of Toronto Press, 1973.

——. *Western and Eastern Rambles: Travel Sketches of Nova Scotia.* Ed. M.G. Parks. Toronto: University of Toronto Press, 1973.

Howison, John. *Sketches of Upper Canada, Domestic, Local, and Characteristic: to Which Are Added, Practical Details for the Information of Emigrants of Every Class; and Some Recollections of the United States of America.* Edinburgh: Oliver and Boyd; London: G. and W.B. Whittaker, 1821. [35723]

Huddlestone, Lee Eldridge. *Origins of the American Indians: European Concepts, 1492–1729.* Latin American Monographs, No. 11; Institute of Latin American Studies. Austin: University of Texas Press, 1967.

Hughes, Kenneth J. "The Completeness of McLachlan's 'The Emigrant'." *English Studies in Canada* 1 (1975): 172–87.

——. "McLachlan's Style." *Journal of Canadian Poetry* 1 (1978): 1–4.

——. "Oliver Goldsmith's 'The Rising Village'." *Canadian Poetry: Studies, Documents, Reviews* 1 (1977): 27–43.

——. "Poet Laureate of Labour." *Canadian Dimension* 11.3 (1976): 33–40.

Hume, David. *An Inquiry Concerning the Principles of Morals.* 1751. Reprint, ed. Charles W. Handel. Indianapolis: Liberal Arts Press, 1957.

Huxley, Thomas H. *Science and Education: Essays.* 1894. Reprint, New York: D. Appleton, 1898.

Inches, James. *Letters on Emigration to Canada: Addressed to the Very Rev. Principal Baird.* 2nd ed. Perth: Printed for the Author by C.G. Sidney, 1836. [21570]

Irving, Washington. "The Catskill Mountains." In *The Home Book of the Picturesque; or American Scenery, Art, and Literature,* 1852. Reprint, intro. Motley F. Deakin. Gainesville, Fl.: Scholars' Facsimiles and Reprints, 1967. 71–78.

——. *The Sketch Book of Geoffrey Crayon, Gent.* 1820. Reprint, London: Bell and Daldy, 1865.

Jaenan, C.J. *Friend and Foe: Aspects of French-Amerindian Cultural Contact in the Sixteenth and Seventeenth Centuries.* Toronto: McClelland and Stewart, 1976.

James, Thomas. *The Strange and Dangerous Voyage of Captain Thomas James.* 1663. Reprint, ed. W.A. Kenyon. Toronto: Royal Ontario Museum, 1975.

Johnson, Samuel. "Denham." In *Lives of the English Poets,* ed. George Birbeck Hill. 1905. Reprint, 3 vols. New York: Octagon, 1967. 1:70–83.

Jones, James Athearn. *Traditions of the North American Indians: Being a Second and Revised Edition of "Tales of an Indian Camp."* 3 vols. London: Henry Colburn and Richard Bentley, 1830. [39341]

Jonson, Ben. *The Complete Poetry.* Ed. William B. Hunter Jr. The Stuart Editions. New York: New York University Press, 1963.

Jordan, Hoover H. *Bolt Upright: the Life of Thomas Moore.* Romantic Reassessment; Salzburg Studies in English Literature. 2 vols. Salzburg: Institut für Englische Sprache und Literatur, 1975.

Kalm, Peter. *Travels into North America; Containing Its Natural History, and a Circumstantial Account of Its Plantations and Agriculture in General, with the Civil, Ecclesiastical and Commercial State of the Country, the Manners of the Inhabitants, and Several Curious and Important Remarks on Various Subjects.* Trans. John Reinhold Foster. 2nd ed. 3 vols. London: T. Lowndes, 1772. [35950]

Kamboureli, Smaro. *On the Edge of Genre: the Contemporary Canadian Long Poem.* Theory/Culture. Toronto: University of Toronto Press, 1991.

Keble, John. *The Christian Year; Thoughts in Verse for the Sundays and Holydays throughout the Year.* 2 vols. Oxford: J. Parker, 1827.

Keith, W.J. *Canadian Literature in English.* Longman Literature in English Series. London and New York: Longman, 1985.

Kelsey, Henry. *The Kelsey Papers.* Ed. Arthur G. Doughty and Chester Martin. Ottawa: Public Archives of Canada and the Public Record Office of Ireland, 1929.

Kennedy, George A. *Classical Rhetoric and Its Christian and Secular Tradition from Ancient to Modern Times.* Chapel Hill: University of North Carolina Press, 1980.

Kenney, James F. "The Career of Henry Kelsey." *Proceedings and Transactions of the Royal Society of Canada.* 3rd. ser., vol. 28.2 (1929): 37–71.

Kenyon, Walter. *Arctic Argonauts.* Waterloo: Penumbra, 1990.

Kidd, Adam. *The Huron Chief.* Ed. D.M.R. Bentley. London: Canadian Poetry Press, 1987.

——. *The Huron Chief, and Other Poems.* Montreal: Printed at the Office of the *Herald* and *New Gazette,* 1830. [32893]

Kirby, William. *Annals of Niagara.* Welland, Ont.: Tribune Presses, 1896. [09996]

——. *Canadian Idylls.* 2nd ed. Welland, Ont.: n.p., 1894. [12926]

——. ["Britannicus"]. *Counter Manifesto to the Annexationists of Montreal.* Niagara: James A. Davidson at the Office of the *Niagara Mail,* 1849. [45329]

——. *The Golden Dog (Le Chien D'Or): a Romance of the Days of Louis Quinze in Quebec.* 1877. Authorized Ed. Montreal: Montreal News, 1897. [29280]

——. *The U.E.: a Tale of Upper Canada.* Niagara: Printed at the *Mail* Office, 1859. [36153]

——. *The United Empire Loyalists of Canada, Illustrated by Memorials of the Servos Family.* Toronto: William Briggs, 1884. [07946]

Klein, Melanie. *Love, Guilt, and Reparation and Other Works, 1921–1945.* New York: Doubleday, 1977.

Klinck, Carl F. "Adam Kidd: an Early Canadian Poet." *Queen's Quarterly* 65 (1958): 495–506.

——. "*The Charivari* and Levi Adams." *Dalhousie Review* 40 (1960): 34–42.

——. "Early Creative Literature of Western Ontario." *Ontario History* 45 (1953): 155–163.

——. "Literary Activity in Canada East and West, 1841–1880." *Literary History of Canada.* 1965. Ed. Carl F. Klinck. Reprint, Toronto: University of Toronto Press, 1973. 145–62.

——. "Literary Activity in the Canadas, 1812–1814." *Literary History of Canada.* Ed. Carl F. Klinck. 1965. Reprint, Toronto: University of Toronto Press, 1973. 125–44.

Koester, C.B. *Mr. Davin: a Biography of Nicholas Flood Davin.* Saskatoon: Western Producer Prairie Books, 1980.

Lambert, John. *Travels through Canada, and the United States of North America, in the Years 1806, 1807, and 1808.* 3rd ed. 2 vols. London: Baldwin, Cradock, and Joy, 1816. [49388]

Lampman, Archibald. Notebook 10. National Archives, Ottawa.

——. *The Poems.* Ed. Duncan Campbell Scott. Toronto: George M. Morang, 1900. [06952]

——. "The Poetry of Byron." Ed. D.M.R. Bentley. *Queen's Quarterly* 83 (1976): 623–32.

——. *Selected Prose.* Ed. Barrie Davies. Ottawa: Tecumseh, 1975.

——. "The Story of an Affinity." MS PS 8473 A56 S8. Library of Parliament, Ottawa.

——. *The Story of an Affinity.* Ed. D.M.R. Bentley. London: Canadian Poetry Press, 1986.

——. "Two Poets: a Lecture." Ed. E.K. Brown. *University of Toronto Quarterly* 13 (1944): 406–23.

——. "Style." Ed. Sue Mothersill. *Canadian Poetry: Studies, Documents, Reviews* 7 (1980): 56–72.

Latham, David. "Charles Sangster." In *Profiles in Canadian Literature,* ed. Jeffrey M. Heath. Toronto: Dundurn, 1986. 5:41–48.

——. "Two Canadian Poets: a Lecture." *University of Toronto Quarterly* 13 (1944): 406–23.

Leacock, Stephen. *Sunshine Sketches of a Little Town.* 1912. Reprint, New Canadian Library 15. Toronto: McClelland and Stewart, 1970.

Lefebvre, Jacques and Edouard Desjardins. "Le Docteur George Selby, Médicin de L'Hôtel Dieu de 1807 à 1829, et sa famille." *L'Union Médicale du Canada* 100 (1971): 1592–94.

LeGoff, T.J.A. "The Agricultural Crisis in Lower Canada, 1802–1812: a Review of the Controversy." *Canadian Historical Review* 55 (1974): 1–31.

Lemoine, J.M. *Picturesque Quebec: a Sequel to Quebec Past and Present.* Montreal: Dawson Brothers, 1882. [08554]

Lessard, Renald. "George Selby." *Dictionary of Canadian Biography* 6: 699–700.

Lighthall, William Douw. *Songs of the Great Dominion: Voices from the Forests and Waters, the Settlements and Cities of Canada.* London: Walter Scott, 1889. [24303]

Livesay, Dorothy. "The Documentary Poem: a Canadian Genre." In *Contexts of Canadian Criticism: a Collection of Critical Essays,* ed. Eli Mandel. 1971. Reprint, Toronto: University of Toronto Press, 1977. 267–81.

Locke, John. *An Essay Concerning Human Understanding.* 1689. Reprint, ed. Alexander Campbell Fraser. New York: Dover, 1959.

——. *Two Treatises of Government.* 1690. Reprint, ed. Thomas I. Cook. New York: Hafner, 1965.

Longfellow, Henry Wadsworth. *The Poetical Works.* London: Griffith, Farran, Okeden, and Welsh, 1882.

Longmore, George. *The Charivari; or, Canadian Poetics: a Tale After the Manner of Beppo.* 1824. Reprint, ed. D.M.R. Bentley. London: Canadian Poetry Press, 1991.

——. *Tales of Chivalry and Romance.* Edinburgh: James Robertson; London: Baldwin Cradock and Joy, 1826.

——. *Tecumthe, a Poetical Tale. In Three Cantos.* Ed. Mary Lu MacDonald. London: Canadian Poetry Press, 1993.

Lopez, Barry. *Arctic Dreams: Imagination and Desire in a Northern Landscape.* New York: Charles Scribner's Sons, 1986.

Lynch, Gerald. Introduction and Editorial Notes to *The Rising Village* by Oliver Goldsmith. London: Canadian Poetry Press, 1989. xi–xxx, 41–57.

McCulloch, Thomas. *The Mephibosheth Stepsure Letters.* Ed. Gwendolyn Davies. Centre for Editing Early Canadian Text Series 7. Ottawa: Carleton University Press, 1990.

McDonald, John. *Narrative of a Voyage to Quebec, and Journey from Thence to New Lanark in Upper Canada.* 2nd. ed. Glasglow: William Lang, 1822. [21116]

MacDonald, Mary Joy. "Inglorious Battles: People and Power in Crawford's *Malcolm's Katie.*" *Canadian Poetry: Studies, Documents, Reviews* 23 (1988): 31–46.

MacDonald, Mary Lu. "Further Light on a Life: George Longmore in Cape Colony." *Canadian Poetry: Studies, Documents, Reviews* 24 (1989): 62–77.

——. "George Longmore: a New Literary Ancestor." *Dalhousie Review* 59 (1979): 265–85.

——. Introduction to *The Charivari, or Canadian Poetics* by George Longmore. Ottawa: The Golden Dog Press, 1977. 3–10.

——. *Literature and Society in the Canadas 1817–1850.* Lewiston, Queenston, Lampeter: The Mellen Press, 1992.

——. "'New' Poems of Adam Hood Burwell." *Canadian Poetry: Studies, Documents, Reviews* 18 (1986): 99–117.

——. "Some Notes on the Montreal Literary Scene in the Mid-1820's." *Canadian Poetry: Studies, Documents, Reviews* 5 (1979): 29–40.

McInnis, Edgar. *Canada: a Political and Social History.* New York: Holt, 1959.

Mackay, J. *Quebec Hill; or, Canadian Scenery. A Poem. In Two Parts.* 1797. Reprint, ed. D.M.R. Bentley. London: Canadian Poetry Press, 1988.

Mackenzie, Alexander. *Voyages from Montreal on the River St. Laurence. through the Continent of North America to the Frozen and Pacific Oceans in the Years 1789 and 1793, with a Preliminary Account of the Rise, Progress, and Present State of the Fur Trade of That Country.* 1801. Reprint, Edmonton: M.G. Hurtig, 1971. [33950]

McLachlan, Alexander. *The Emigrant.* Ed. D.M.R. Bentley. London: Canadian Poetry Press, 1991.

———. *The Emigrant, and Other Poems.* Toronto: Rollo and Adam, 1861. [46136]

———. *Poems and Songs.* Toronto: Hunter, Rose, 1874. [09585]

———. *The Poetical Works.* 1900. Ed. E. Margaret Fulton. Literature of Canada: Poetry and Prose in Reprint. Toronto: University of Toronto Press, 1974.

MacLaren, I.S. "The Influence of Eighteenth-Century British Landscape Aesthetics on Narrative and Pictorial Responses to the British North American North and West 1769–1872." Ph.D. diss., University of Western Ontario, 1983.

———. "The Pastoral and the Wilderness in Early Canada." *Landscape Research Group Ltd.* 14.1 (1989): 15–19.

MacLean, R.A. "John Young." *Dictionary of Canadian Biography* 7: 930–35.

McLeod, Donald. *Gloomy Memories in the Highlands of Scotland: Versus Mrs. Harriet Beecher Stowe's Sunny Memories in (England) a Foreign Land: or a Faithful Picture of the Extirpation of the Celtic Race from the Highlands of Scotland.* 1841. Reprint, Toronto: Thompson, 1857.

McNaught, Kenneth. *The Pelican History of Canada.* 1969. Rev. ed. Harmondsworth: Penguin, 1973.

MacNutt, W.S. *The Atlantic Provinces: the Emergence of Colonial Society, 1712–1857.* The Canadian Centenary Series. Toronto: McClelland and Stewart, 1965.

Macoun, John. *Manitoba and the Great North-West: the Field for Investment; the Home of the Emigrant, Being a Full and Complete History of the Country.* Guelph, Ont.: World Publishing, 1882. [30333]

Macpherson, James. *The Poems of Ossian.* 1765. Reprint, 3 vols. London: James Miller, John Murray, John Harding, 1805.

Magoon, E.L. "Scenery and Mind." In *The Home Book of the Picturesque: or American Scenery, Art, and Literature,* 1852. Reprint, intro. Motley F. Deakin. Gainesville, Fl.: Scholars' Facsimiles and Reprints, 1967. 1–48.

Martin, Mary F. "The Short Life of Isabella Valancy Crawford." *Dalhousie Review* 52 (1972): 391–400.

Marx, Leo. *The Machine in the Garden: Technology and the Pastoral Ideal in America.* London: Oxford University Press, 1967.

Massicotte, E.-Z. "Le Charivari au Canada." *Bulletin des recherches historiques* 32 (1926): 712–25.

———. "Les Mutations d'un coin de rue." *Bulletin des recherches historiques* 45 (1939): 271.

Meek, Ronald L. *Social Science and the Ignoble Savage.* Cambridge Studies in the History and Theory of Politics. Cambridge: Cambridge University Press, 1976.

Millar, John. *The Origin of the Distinction of Ranks: or, an Inquiry into the Circumstances That Give Rise to Influence and Authority, in the Different Members of Society.* 1771. 4th ed. London: Longman, 1806.

Miller, Carman. "Joseph Abbott." *Dictionary of Canadian Biography* 9: 3–4.

Millet, Kate. *Sexual Politics*. Garden City, NY: Doubleday, 1970.

Mills, David. *The Idea of Loyalty in Upper Canada, 1784–1850*. Kingston and Montreal: McGill-Queen's University Press, 1988.

Milton, John. *Complete Poems and Major Prose*. Ed. Merritt Y. Hughes. New York: Odyssey, 1957.

Monière, Denis. *Ideologie in Quebec: the Historical Development*. Trans. Richard Howard. Toronto: University of Toronto Press, 1981.

Monkman, Leslie. *A Native Heritage: Images of the Indian in English-Canadian Literature*. Toronto: University of Toronto Press, 1981.

Montgomery, James. *The Poetical Works*. 3 vols. London: Longman, Rees, Orme, Brown, Green, and Longman, 1836.

Montgomery, Robert. *The Poetical Works*. London: Chapman and Hall, 1854.

Moodie, Susanna. 1853. *Life in the Clearings*. Reprint, ed. R.L. McDougall. Toronto: Macmillan, 1959.

——. *Roughing It in the Bush; or, Life in Canada*. 1852. Reprint, ed. Carl Ballstadt. Ottawa: Carleton University Press, 1988.

Moore, Thomas. *Epistles, Odes, and Other Poems*. London: James Carpenter, 1806.

——. *Letters*. Ed. Wilfred S. Dowdon. 2 vols. Oxford: Clarendon, 1964.

——. *Poetical Works*. Ed. A. D. Godley. London: Humphrey Milford, Oxford University Press, 1915.

——. *The Poetical Works of the Late Thomas Little, Esq*. 1801. Reprint, Oxford: Woodstock Books, 1990.

Moorsom, W. *Letters from Nova Scotia; Comprising Sketches of a Young Country*. London: Henry Colburn and Richard Bentley, 1830. [38019]

Morris, Alexander. *Nova Britannia; or, British North America, Its Extent and Future*. Montreal: John Lovell, 1858. [38245]

Morse, Jedidiah. *American Geography; or, a View of the Present Situation of the United States of America: Containing Astronomical Geography, Geographical Definitions, Discovery, and General Description ... With a Particular Description of Kentucky, the Western Territory, and Vermont ... to Which Is Added, an Abridgement of the Geography of the British, Spanish, French and Dutch Dominions in America and the West Indies of Europe, Asia and Africa*. London: Stockdale, 1792.

Morton, W.L. *The Kingdom of Canada: a General History from Earlier Times*. 2nd ed. Toronto: McClelland and Stewart, 1969.

——. "The Relevance of Canadian History." In *Contexts of Canadian Criticism: a Collection of Critical Essays*, ed. Eli Mandel. 1971. Reprint, Toronto: University of Toronto Press, 1977. 48–70.

Murdoch, Beamish. *Epitome of the Laws of Nova Scotia*. 4 vols. Halifax, N.S.: Joseph Howe, 1832–33. [59436]

Murray, Louise. "The Niagara District." In *Picturesque Canada; the Country as it Was and Is*, ed. George Monro Grant. 3 vols. Toronto: Belden Bros., 1882. 1:343–98. [07691]

Neilson, John. Day and account books. MG 24; B1, vols. 81 and 90. National Archives, Ottawa.

Newton, John. *The Emigrant, and Other Pieces.* Hamilton: J. Robertson, 1846.

O'Grady, Standish. *The Emigrant.* Ed. Brian Trehearne. London: Canadian Poetry Press, 1989.

O'Leary, Peter. *Travels and Experiences in Canada, the Red River Territory and the United States.* London: John B. Day, [1877]. [30423]

Oliver, Andrew, Late of Montreal. *A View of Lower Canada; Interspersed with Canadian Tales and Anecdotes, and Interesting Information to Intending Emigrants.* Edinburgh: R. Menzies ... for the Author, 1821. [39149]

Ouellet, Fernand. "Toussaint Pothier et la problème des classes sociales (1829)." *Bulletin des recherches historiques* 61 (1955): 147–59.

Owram, Doug. *Promise of Eden: the Canadian Expansionist Movement and the Idea of the West, 1856–1900.* Toronto: University of Toronto Press, 1980.

Oxley, J. MacDonald. "Busy People." *Man, a Canadian Home Magazine* 1.2 (1885): 55–57.

Pacey, Desmond. *Creative Writing in Canada: a Short History of English Canadian Literature.* 2nd ed. Toronto: McGraw-Hill Ryerson, 1961.

——. *Ten Canadian Poets: a Group of Biographical and Critical Essays.* Toronto: Ryerson, 1958.

Palmer, Bryan D. "Charivaris and Whitecapping in Nineteenth-Century North America." *Labour / Le travailleur* 3 (1978): 5–62.

Parker, John. Introduction to *The Journals of Jonathan Carver and Related Documents, 1766–1770,* ed. J. Parker. St. Paul: Minnesota Historical Society Press, 1976.

Parks, M.G. Introduction, Editorial Notes, and Appendix to *Acadia,* by Joseph Howe. London: Canadian Poetry Press, 1989. ix–xl, 33–60, 61–64.

Parr, Joy. "The Skilled Emigrant and Her Kin: Gender, Culture, and Labour Recruitment." *Canadian Historical Review* 68 (1987): 529–51.

Peile, John. *Biographical Register of Christ's College, 1505–1905, and of the Earlier Foundation, God's House, 1448–1505.* 2 vols. Cambridge, 1913.

Pennant, Thomas. *Arctic Zoology.* London: Henry Hughes, 1784. [40367]

Percy, Thomas. *Reliques of Ancient English Poetry: Consisting of Old Heroic Ballads, Songs, and Other Pieces, of Our Earlier Poets, Together with Some Few of Later Date, and a Copious Glossary.* 1765. 4th ed. London: Henry G. Bohn, 1847.

Pickering, Joseph. *Inquiries of an Emigrant: Being the Narrative of an English Farmer, from the Year 1824 to 1830; During Which Period He Traversed the United States of America, and the British Province of Canada, with a View to Settle as an Emigrant.* 1831. New ed., London: Effingham Wilson, 1831. [39836]

Pierce, Lorne. Introduction to *Alfred, Lord Tennyson and William Kirby: Unpublished Correspondence to Which Are Added Some Letters from Hallam, Lord Tennyson.* Toronto: Macmillan, 1929. 14–31.

——. Introduction to *Annals of Niagara*, by William Kirby. Toronto: Macmillan, 1927. ix–xviii.

Pinkerton, John. *Modern Geography*. New ed. 3 vols. London: T. Cadell and W. Davies, Longman, Hurst, Rees and Orme, 1807. [39423]

Playfair, William. *British Family Antiquity; Illustrative of the Origin and Progress of the Rank, Honours, and Personal Merit, of the Nobility of the United Kingdom*. 2 vols. London: Thomas Reynolds, 1809.

A Plea for the Early Development of Our Resources. Winnipeg, Man.: Kenny and Luxton, Free Press Printing House, 1873. [23831]

Poovey, Mary. *The Proper Lady and the Woman Writer: Ideology as Style in the Works of Mary Wollstonecraft, Mary Shelley, and Jane Austen*. Chicago: University of Chicage Press, 1984.

Pope, Alexander. *The Poems*. Ed. John Butt. London: Methuen, 1963.

Porter, John. *The Vertical Mosaic: an Analysis of Social Class and Power in Canada*. Toronto: University of Toronto Press, 1965.

Pothier, Philippe. "Toussaint Pothier." *Dictionary of Canadian Biography* 7: 702–04.

Pound, Ezra. *The Letters of Ezra Pound, 1907–1941*. Ed. D.D. Paige. New York: Harcourt, Brace and World, 1950.

Prebble, John. *The Highland Clearances*. London: Secker and Warburg, 1963.

Priestley, Joseph. *Hartley's Theory of the Human Mind, on the Principle of the Association of Ideas; with Essays Relating to the Subject*. 1775. 2nd ed. London: J. Johnson, 1790.

——. *Lectures on History, and General Policy, to Which Is Prefixed an Essay on a Course of Liberal Education for Civil and Active Life. New ed. with Numerous Enlargements: Comprising a Lecture on "The Constitution of the United States" from the Author's American Ed., and Additional Notes, by J.T. Rutt*. London: Thomas Tegg, 1826.

Pugin, A. Welby. *An Apology for the Revival of Christian Architecture in England*. London: John Weale, 1843.

Pye, Henry James. *The Progress of Refinement. A Poem. In Three Parts*. Oxford: Clarendon, 1783.

Rashley, R.E. *Poetry in Canada: the First Three Steps*. 1958. Reprint, Ottawa: Tecumseh, 1979.

Ray, Arthur J. and Donald B. Freeman. *'Give Us Good Measure': an Economic Analysis of Relations between the Indians and the Hudson's Bay Company before 1763*. Toronto: University of Toronto Press, 1978.

Reaney, James. "Isabella Valancy Crawford." In *Our Living Tradition*, Second and Third Series, ed. Robert L. McDougall. Toronto: University of Toronto Press, 1959, 268–86.

Reid, Dennis. *A Concise History of Canadian Painting*. 1973. 2nd ed. Toronto: Oxford University Press, 1988.

Relke, Diana M.A. "The Ecological Vision of Isabella Valancy Crawford: a Reading of 'Malcolm's Katie.'" *Ariel* 22.3 (1991): 51–71.

Rempel, John I. *Building with Wood and Other Aspects of Nineteenth-Century Building in Ontario.* Toronto: University of Toronto Press, 1967.

Reports of Tenant Farmers' Delegates on the Dominion of Canada as a Field for Settlement. 2nd ed. Canada: Department of Agriculture, 1880. [35538]

Repton, Humphry. *The Landscape Gardening and Landscape Architecture.* Ed. J.C. Loudon. London: Printed for the Editor, 1840.

Richards, I.A. *Principles of Literary Criticism.* London: Kegan, Paul, Trench, Trubner, 1924.

Richardson, John. *Tecumseh; or, the Warrior of the West: a Poem, in Four Cantos, with Notes.* 1828. Reprint, intro. by William F.E. Morley. Ottawa: The Golden Dog Press, 1978.

——. *Tecumseh, a Poem in Four Cantos.* 1842. Reprint, ed. Douglas Daymond and Leslie Monkman. London: Canadian Poetry Press, 1992.

——. *Wacousta, or, the Prophecy; a Tale of the Canadas.* 1832. Reprint, ed. Douglas Cronk. Ottawa: Carleton University Press, 1987.

——. *War of 1812.* 1842. Reprint, with Notes and Life of Author, ed. Alexander Clark Casselman. Toronto: Historical Publishing Co., 1902.

——. *War of 1812. First Series. Containing a Full and Detailed Narrative of the Operations of the Right Division, of the Canadian Army.* Brockville: n.p., 1842. [32818]

Riddell, William Renwick. *John Richardson.* Makers of Canadian Literature. Toronto: Ryerson, 1923.

——. *William Kirby.* Makers of Canadian Literature. Toronto: Ryerson, 1923.

Roberts, Charles G.D. *The Collected Letters.* Ed. Laurel Boone. Fredericton: Goose Lane Editions, 1989.

——. *A History of Canada.* Boston; New York: Lamson, Wolffe, 1897.

——. *Poems.* New Complete Ed. Toronto: Copp, Clark, 1907.

Roberts, David. "William Grant." *Dictionary of Canadian Biography* 5: 367–76.

Robertson, William. *The History of America.* 1777. 9th ed. 3 vols. London: A. Strachan, 1800. [40631]

Robinson, John Beverley. *Canada and the Canada Bill: Being an Examination of the Proposed Measure for the Future Government of Canada; with an Introductory Chapter, Containing Some General Views Respecting the British Provinces of North America.* London: J. Hatchard and Son, 1840. [21776]

Robson, Joseph. *An Account of Six Years Residence in Hudson's Bay, from 1733 to 1736 and 1744 to 1747.* 1752. Reprint, New York: Johnson Reprint, 1965.

Roe, Gilbert. *The North American Bison: a Critical Study of the Species in Its Wild State.* 2nd ed. Toronto: University of Toronto Press, 1970.

Rosenmeyer, Thomas G. *The Green Cabinet: Theocritus and the European Pastoral Lyric.* Berkeley: University of California Press, 1969.

Ross, Catherine. "Dark Matrix: a Study of Isabella Valancy Crawford." Ph.D. diss., University of Western Ontario, 1975.

Rossetti, Dante Gabriel. *The Works.* Ed. William Michael Rossetti. London: Ellis, 1911.

Rotstein, Abraham. *The Precarious Homestead: Essays on Economics, Technology and Nationalism.* Toronto: New Press, 1973.

Rowan, John J. *The Emigrant and Sportsman in Canada. Some Experiences of an Old Country Settler. With Sketches of Canadian Life, Sporting Adventures, and Observations of the Forests and Fauna.* London: Edward Sanford, 1876. [12695]

Ruddel, Dave T. *Quebec City, 1765–1832: the Evolution of a Colonial Town.* Ottawa: Canadian Museum of Civilization, 1987.

Ruskin, John. *Sesame and Lilies. Three Lectures.* 1871. 3rd ed. Orpington, Kent: George Allen, 1876.

Said, Edward. *Orientalism.* 1978. Reprint, New York: Vintage, 1979.

Saint John, Henry, Viscount Bolingbroke. *Letters on the Spirit of Patriotism: On the Patriot King: and On the State of Parties, at the Accession of King George the First.* London: A. Millar, 1749.

Sangster, Charles. *Hesperus, and Other Poems and Lyrics.* Montreal: J. Lovell; Kingston, Ont.: J. Creighton, 1860. [41940]

——. *The St. Lawrence and the Saguenay.* Ed. D.M.R. Bentley. London: Canadian Poetry Press, 1990.

——. *The St. Lawrence and the Saguenay, and Other Poems.* Kingston: John Creighton and John Duff; New York: Miller, Orton, and Mulligan, 1856. [40351]

Saunders, Robert E. "Sir John Berverley Robinson." *Dictionary of Canadian Biography* 9: 668–79.

Saunders, R.E. "The Emergence of the Coureur de bois as a Social Type." *Canadian Historical Association Report of the Annual Meeting Held at Montreal May 25–26, 1939 with Historical Papers.* Toronto: University of Toronto Press, 1939. 22–33.

Schama, Simon. "The Many Deaths of General Wolfe." *Granta* 32 (1990): 13–56.

Schoolcraft, Henry Rowe. *Narrative Journal of Travels through the NorthWestern Regions of the United States: Extending from Detroit through the Great Chain of American Lakes to the Sources of the Mississippi River, Performed as a Member of the Expedition Under Governor Cass in the Year 1820.* Albany, N.Y.: E. and E. Hosford, 1821.

——. *Onéota, or Characteristics of the Red Race of America. From Original Notes and Manuscripts.* New York and London: Wiley and Putnam, 1845. [40434]

Scott, F.R. and A.J.M. Smith. Introduction to *The Blasted Pine: an Anthology of Satire, Invective, and Disrespectful Verse, Chiefly by Canadian Writers,* ed. Scott and Smith. Toronto: Macmillan, 1957. xv–xix.

Scott, Sir Walter. *The Poetical Works.* 11 vols. Edinburgh: Cadell, 1830.

Séguin, Maurice. *La 'Nation candienne' et l'agriculture (1760–1850).* Trois Rivières: Boréal Express, 1970.

Shakespeare, William. *The Complete Works.* Ed. G.B. Harrison. New York: Harcourt, Brace, and World, 1948.

Shurtleff, Harold R. *The Log Cabin Myth: a Study of the Early Dwellings of the English Colonists in North America.* Ed. Samuel Eliot Morison. Cambridge, Mass.: Harvard University Press, 1939.

Silver, Ednah C. *Sketches of the New Churches in America.* Boston: Massachusetts New Church Union, 1920.

Sinclair, David. Introduction to *Nineteenth-Century Narrative Poems*, ed. David Sinclair. New Canadian Library 8. Toronto: McClelland and Stewart, 1972. vi–xiii.

Sioui, Georges E. (Atsistahonra). "Nicholas Vincent." *Dictionary of Canadian Biography* 7: 889–90.

Smith, A.J.M. "'Our Poets': a Sketch of Canadian Poetry in the Nineteenth Century." *University of Toronto Quarterly* 12 (1942–43): 75–94.

Smith, Allan. "Metaphor and Nationality in North America." *Canadian Historical Review* 11 (1970): 247–75.

——. "The Myth of the Self-made Man in English Canada, 1850–1914." *Canadian Historical Review* 59 (1978): 189–219.

Smith, Goldwin. *Canada and the Canadian Question.* 1891. Reprint, Toronto: University of Toronto Press, 1971.

Snyder, J.R. "The Conflict of Ideal and Human Love in Charles Sangster's 'The St. Lawrence and the Saguenay'." *Canadian Literature* 134 (1992): 186–91.

Spencer, Herbert. *Education: Intellectual, Moral, and Physical.* New York: D. Appleton, 1861.

Spenser, Edmund. *The Poetical Works.* London: Oxford University Press, 1916.

Stamer, W. *The Gentleman Emigrant: His Daily Life, Sports, and Pastimes in Canada, Australia, and the United States.* 2 vols. London: Tinsley Brothers, 1874. [27728]

Steiner, George. *Real Presences.* Chicago: University of Chicago Press, 1989.

Stewart, A.C. "The Poetical Review: a Brief Notice of Canadian Poets and Poetry." Ed. D.M.R. Bentley. *Canadian Poetry: Studies, Documents, Reviews* 1 (1977): 66–88.

Stillingfleet, Edward. *Origines Sacrae: or, a Rational Account of the Grounds of Christian Faith, as to the Truth and Divine Authority of the Scriptures, and the Matter Therein Contained.* London: Henry Mortlock, 1662.

Stirling, A.M.W. *Coke of Norfolk and His Friends. The Life of Thomas William Coke, First Earl of Leicester of Holkham, Containing an Account of His Ancestry, Surroundings, Public Services and Private Friendships and Including Many Unpublished Letters from Noted Men of His Day, English and American, by A.M.W. Stirling. with 22 Illustrations from Contemporary Portraits, Prints, etc.* New ed. London: J. Lane, 1912.

Stouck, David. "The Wardell Family and the Origins of Loyalism." *Canadian Historical Review* 68 (1987): 63–82.

Strachan, John. *Documents and Opinions.* Ed. J.L.H. Henderson. The Carleton Library 44. Toronto: McClelland and Stewart, 1969.

——. "Poetry." Notebook. John Strachan Papers. F983, MU2907. Archives of Ontario, Toronto.

——. "Verses ... 1802." Ed. D.M.R. Bentley and Wanda Campbell. *Canadian Poetry: Studies, Documents, Reviews* 32 (1993): 82–93.

——. *A Visit to the Province of Upper Canada in 1819.* Aberdeen: James Strachan, 1820. [63384]

Strickland, Samuel. *Twenty Seven Years in Canada West: or, The Experience of an Early Settler.* 1852. 2 vols. 2nd ed. 1853. Reprint, Edmonton: Hurtig, 1970.

Swedenborg, Emanuel. *Arcana Coelestia.* 10 vols. New York: American Swedenborg Printing and Publishing Society, 1857.

——. *The Delights of Wisdom Pertaining to Conjugial Love.* Trans. Samuel M. Warren. New York: Swedenborg Foundation, 1856.

Swift, Jonathan. *The Complete Poems.* Ed. Pat Rodgers. New Haven: Yale University Press, 1983.

Taine, Adolphe Hippolyte. *History of English Literature.* Trans. Henry Van Laun. 1871. Rev. ed. 3 vols. New York and London: Co-operative Publication Society, 1900.

Talbot, Edward Allen. *Five Years' Residence in the Canadas: Including a Tour through Part of the United States of America, in the Year 1823.* London: Longman, Hurst, Rees, Orme, Brown, and Green, 1824. [40913]

Talman, James and Ruth. "A Note on the Authorship of 'Canada, A Descriptive Poem', Quebec, 1806." *Canadian Notes and Queries* 20 (1977): 12–13.

Tehariolina, Marguerite Vincent. *La Nationne Huronne: son histoire, sa culture, son éspirit.* Québec: éditions du Pélican, 1984.

Tennyson, Alfred Lord and William Kirby. *Unpublished Correspondence to Which are Added Some Letters from Hallam, Lord Tennyson.* Ed. Lorne Pierce. Toronto: Macmillan, 1929.

Thomas, Clara. "Crawford's Achievement." In *The Crawford Symposium,* ed. Frank M. Tierney. Re-Appraisals: Canadian Writers. Ottawa: University of Ottawa Press, 1979. 131–36.

Thompson, E.P. *The Making of the English Working Class.* London: Victor Gollancz, 1963.

Thomson, James. *The Seasons.* Ed. James Sambrook. Oxford: Clarendon, 1981.

Thorpe, Benjamin. *Northern Mythology, Compromising the Principal Popular Traditions and Superstitions of Scandinavia, North Germany, and the Netherlands.* 3 vols. London: n.p., 1851.

Tooke, Andrew. *The Pantheon: Representing, the Fabulous Histories of the Heathen Gods, and the Other Most Illustrious Heroes of Antiquity in a Short, Plain, and Familiar Method, By the Way of Dialogue.* New ed. Edinburgh: William Greece, 1808.

Traill, Catharine Parr. *The Backwoods of Canada.* London: Charles Knight, 1836. [41930]

Trehearne, Brian. Introduction, Editorial Notes, and Appendix to *The Emigrant* by Standish O'Grady. London: Canadian Poetry Press, 1989. xi–lxxii, 105–189, 191.

Trigger, Bruce G. *The Children of Aataentsic: a History of the Huron People to 1660.* 2 vols. Montreal: McGill-Queen's University Press, 1976.

——. *Natives and Newcomers: Canada's "Heroic Age" Reconsidered.* 1985. Reprint, Kingston and Montreal: McGill-Queen's University Press; Manchester: Manchester University Press, 1987.

Trimpi, Wesley. *Ben Jonson's Poems: a Study in the Plain Style.* Stanford: Stanford University Press, 1962.

Trow, James. *A Trip to Manitoba.* Quebec: S. Marcotte, 1875. [24030]

Tudor, William. *Letters on the Eastern States.* 1820. 2nd ed. Boston: Wells and Lily, 1821.

Underhill, F.H. *The Image of Confederation.* Toronto: C.B.C. Publications, 1964.

Upton, L.F.S. *Micmacs and Colonists: Indian-White Relations in the Maritimes, 1713–1867.* Vancouver: University of British Columbia Press, 1979.

Vincent, Thomas B. Introduction. *Eighteenth-Century Canadian Poetry: an Anthology.* Kingston: Loyal Colonies Press, 1980. v–ix.

Warburton, George. *Hochelaga; or, England in the New World.* Ed. Eliot Warburton. 2 vols. New York: Wiley and Putnam, 1846. [27922]

Ward, Peter. "Courtship and Social Space in Nineteenth-Century English Canada." *Canadian Historical Review* 68 (1987): 35–62.

Ware, Tracy. "George Longmore." *Canadian Writers Before 1890.* Vol. 99 of *Dictionary of Literary Biography*, ed. W.H. New. Detroit: Bruccoli Clark Layman, 1990. 214–16.

——. "George Longmore's *The Charivari:* a Poem 'After the Manner of *Beppo.*" *Canadian Poetry: Studies, Documents, Reviews* 10 (1982): 1–17.

Warkentin, Germaine. "'The Boy Henry Kelsey': Generic Disjunction in Henry Kelsey's Verse Journal." In *Literary Genres / Les Genres Littéraires*, ed. I.S. MacLaren and C. Potvin. Research Institute for Comparative Literature, University of Alberta. Edmonton, 1991: 99–114.

Waterston, Elizabeth. "Crawford, Tennyson, and the Domestic Idyll." In *The Crawford Symposium*, ed. Frank M. Tierney. Re-Appraisals: Canadian Writers. Ottawa: University of Ottawa Press, 1979. 61–77.

——. *The Travellers: Canada to 1900: an Annotated Bibliography of Works Published in English Prose from 1577.* Guelph: University of Guelph, 1989.

Weld, Isaac. *Travels through the States of North America, and the Provinces of Upper and Lower Canada, during the Years 1795, 1796, and 1797.* 1799. 2 vols. 4th ed. 1807. Reprint, New York: Johnson Reprint, 1968.

Whillans, James M. *First in the West: the Story of Henry Kelsey, Discoverer of Canadian Prairies.* Edmonton: Applied Art Products, 1955.

Wilcocke, Samuel Hull. Review (Parts 1 and 2) of George Longmore, *The Charivari. The Scribbler* 5 (13 May 1824): 141–46 and *Scribbler* 5 (10 June 1824): 164–72.

Wilson, J. Donald, Robert W. Stamp and Louis-Philippe Audet, ed. *Canadian Education: a History.* Scarborough, Ont.: Prentice-Hall of Canada, 1970.

Wise, S.F. *God's Peculiar Peoples: Essays on Political Culture in Nineteenth-Century Canada.* Ed. A.B. McKillop and Paul Romney. Carleton Library Series 173. Ottawa: Carleton University Press, 1993.

Wordsworth, William. *The Poetical Works.* Ed. E. de Selincourt and Helen Derbyshire. 2nd ed. 5 vols. Oxford: Oxford University Press, 1952.

Wyatt, Geo. H. *Dominion of Canada. Manitoba, the Canadian North-West and Ontario.* Toronto: n.p., 1880. [36975]

A Year in Manitoba. Being the Experience of a Retired Officer in Settling His Sons. With Illustrations, Observations on the Country, and Suggestions for Settlers Generally. London and Edinburgh: W. and R. Chambers, 1882. [29003]

Xenophon. *Memorabilia.* Oxford: Clarendon, 1890.

Young, John. *The Letters of Agricola on the Principle of Vegetation and Tillage, Written for Nova Scotia, and Published First in the Acadian Recorder.* Halifax: Holland, 1822. [42538]

Zezulka, J.M. "The Pastoral Vision in Nineteenth-Century Canada." *Dalhousie Review* 57 (1977): 224–41.

Index

Louis XV, 72

Louis XVI, 72

Lovell, John, 6, 189, 199

Lovell and Gibson (printers), 199

Loyalism (Loyalists, Loyalist attitudes), 4–5, 32, 74–75, 77–78, 122, 170–71, 184, 225, 228–31, 235–38, 239, 242, 246–47, 311, 312, 315

Lundy's Lane, Battle of (1814), 231, 242

Lunn, William, 126

Lynch, Gerald, 110, 112, 114, 117, 120

Lyric: 4, 117. See also Poetics

Macoun, John, 290, 291

Magoon, E.L., 309–10

Mail (Toronto), 272

Mair, Charles, 1

Malcolm's Katie: see Crawford

Malthus, Thomas Robert, 190, 255

Mantinea, Battle of (362 BC), 72

Marathon, Battle of (490 BC), 72

Marchand, Leslie, 132

Marischal College, Aberdeen, 70

Marlowe, Christopher, 262–63

Marshall, John, Chief Justice, 111–12

Martin, Mary F., 272

Marx, Karl, 261

Massicotte, E-Z, 131

Mathias, Thomas James, 70

Medley poem, 205–06, 275. See also Poetics

Meek, Ronald L., 7, 31–32

Mercantilism: see Economics

Métis, 11, 278, 290–91, 316

Miasma theory of disease, 43, 98–99

Michilimackinac, massacre at Fort, 144, 236

Micmacs, 7, 110–11, 171, 175–80, 182–83, 184

Millar, John, 121–22

Miller, Carman, 199

Millet, Kate, 286

Mills, David, 74

Milton, John, 44, 45, 47, 51, 55, 56, 62–63, 78, 97–98, 110, 114, 121, 137, 148–49, 152, 164–66, 180, 193, 195, 212, 214, 217, 227, 241–43, 283, 293, 297, 300–01, 316

Mind cure, 303

Mingo, 163

Modernism (modern literature, attitudes), 11, 229, 266, 274, 281, 303

Mohawks, 264–66

Mohicans, 167. See also James Fenimore Cooper

Moira, Francis, Earl of, 85–86, 89

Molesby (or Moseby), Johnson, 240–41

Molson, John, and sons, 202

Mondelet, Dominique, 84

Monière, Denis, 8

Monkman, Leslie, 5, 7, 39, 101, 139, 140, 144, 148

Montcalm, Louis Joseph de, 8, 140, 216, 233

Montesquieu, Baron de la Brède et de, 44

Montezuma, 183

Montgomery, James, 172, 174

Montgomery, Robert, 185

Montreal Gazette, 126, 136, 138, 155, 156

Montreal Herald, 125, 131, 155

Montreal Transcript, 191

Moodie, Susanna, 81, 98, 188

Moore, Thomas, ix, 4, 8, 53, 61, 80–92, 156, 158, 160, 174, 190, 200, 201,

221, 233, 243, 245, 262–63, 308, 313

Moorsom, Captain W., 108, 176

Moraviantown, Battle of, 7, 139, 143, 148

Morris, Alexander, 10, 315

Morris, William, 264, 298, 300, 302

Morse, Jedidiah, 87

Morton, W.L., 9, 290

Mountain, Archdeacon George Jehoshaphat, 154, 155, 156, 158, 159

Mountain, Jacob, Bishop of Quebec, 40, 154, 155, 156, 158, 159

Murdoch, Beamish, 176, 179

Murray, Louise, 294–95

Mythology (myths, mythological figures), classical: Venus, 36, 239; Mars, 36; Atlantis, 86; Flora, 97, 120–22, 174; Hercules, 101, 103, 274, 278, 295–306, 314; Hebe, 274, 276; Cyclops, 156; Diana, 184–85; Odysseus (Ulysses), 90, 304; Penelope, 304; Adonis, 274. Hesperides, 294–95; Scandinavian: 210; Midgard, 232; Freya, 239. Native: 46, 117, 239, 249; Solar, 274; Sleeping Beauty, 297. See also entries under the Bible and Native people(s)

McAuley, John, 79

McCulloch, Thomas ("Mephibosheth Stepsure"), 119

Macdonald, Sir John A., 231

MacDonald, Mary Joy, 274

MacDonald, Mary Lu, 32, 124, 126, 138

McGee, Thomas D'Arcy, 270